SOME
DO
CARE

*Contemporary Lives of
Moral Commitment*

ANNE COLBY
WILLIAM DAMON

The Free Press
A Division of Macmillan, Inc.
866 Third Avenue, New York, N.Y. 10022

Maxwell Macmillan Canada, Inc.
1200 Eglinton Avenue East
Suite 200
Don Mills, Ontario M3C 3N1

Macmillan, Inc. is part of the Maxwell Communication
Group of Companies.

First Free Press Paperback Edition 1994

Printed in the United States of America

printing number

1 2 3 4 5 6 7 8 9 10

Selected quotations from *Outside the Magic Circle: The Autobiography of Virginia Foster Durr* (currently published by The University of Alabama Press, Tuscaloosa, Alabama) are used in Chapter 5 with permission of Virginia F. Durr.

Selected quotations from the Charleszetta Waddles interview, *Black Women Oral History Project,* Schlesinger Library, Radcliffe College (published by K.G. Saur, Inc., Stamford, Connecticut) are used in Chapter 8 with permission of the Schlesinger Library.

The photograph of Charleszetta Waddles on page 201 was taken by Judith Sedwick and is part of the "Women of Courage" photo exhibit assembled under the auspices of Radcliffe College.

Library of Congress Cataloging–in–Publication Data

Colby, Anne.
    Some do care : contemporary lives of moral commitment/Anne
Colby, William Damon.
      p. cm.
    Includes bibliographical references and index.
    ISBN 0–02–906356–6
     1.Voluntarism—United States—Case studies. 2. Helping behavior—
Case studies.   3. United States—Moral conditions.   4.Volunteers—
United States—Biography.   I. Damon,William.
II. Title.
HN90.V64C62   1992
302'.14—dc20   92–15178
                                        CIP

To our much loved
FAMILY AND FRIENDS
who supported and inspired us
during this work,
and to the memories of
LOUIS MEYERS AND MALCOLM YOUNG COLBY, JR.

CONTENTS

PREFACE

We conceived the idea for this project back in the mid-1980s while at a small conference organized by the Social Science Research Council. This was early in the Gorbachev era, some years before the fall of communism, and tensions were running high between the superpowers. The specter of tyranny and the dangers of nuclear conflict continued to haunt the public mind. Also in the news of the day, disease and hunger in Africa were destroying millions of families with numbing regularity. Around the world social scientists were looking for ways to address these threats to humanity. At the same time, the Social Science Research Council had developed a special interest in giftedness and creativity. Someone then decided to join the two sets of concerns in one meeting. The first question behind the SSRC conference was whether there was such a thing as *moral* giftedness. The second was whether moral giftedness, if such a thing indeed existed, might be enlarged and brought to bear on the pressing evils in the world.

For Anne Colby and me, these questions crystallized some concerns each of us had been struggling with in our own work. By then we had both been studying moral development for well over a decade, although we had been working separately and with different methods, theories, and populations. Anne had worked with Lawrence Kohlberg on longitudinal studies of moral judgment from childhood through early adulthood. I had focused on children and adolescents and had been more interested in moral action as it plays out in real social situations than in reflective moral judgment. In addition, I had reservations about Kohlberg's global stages and preferred a more context-sensitive approach. Still, despite our different approaches, Anne and I had found a number of professional and personal things to communicate about and had been married for some time.

The questions about "moral giftedness" struck both of us as linked to a constellation of important and unsolved concerns. We recognized the outstanding societal contributions of great moral leaders such as Mahatma Gandhi, Andrei Sakharov, and Mother Teresa. We believed that these people had developed an exceptional capacity for moral action. Although neither Anne nor I were convinced that this capacity should be called a "gift," in the sense of a native endowment, we did believe that their lives represented epitomes of human moral excellence. Understanding how people acquire such excellence could open a pathway toward moral progress, both for individuals and for society. The problem was that Anne and I could find little in our own theories, or in social science generally, to help us gain such understanding.

With an initial supportive boost from the SSRC committee (David Feldman was the chair, Lonnie Sherrod the program officer, and Helen Haste, Howard Gardner, and Howard Gruber among the active members), Anne and I started our first research collaboration. We spent two years in search of unambiguous criteria for identifying living people who demonstrate moral excellence—people whom we came to call "moral exemplars." We were aided in this process by some wise theologians, philosophers, and moral scholars from a wide range of doctrinal backgrounds. When we were satisfied with our criteria, we identified a number of living Americans who fit. At this point, the Altruistic Spirit program of the Institute of Noetic Sciences (Tom Hurley was the program officer) provided us with support to interview as many of these extraordinary people—our exemplars—as would agree to participate in our study. Over the next four years, Anne and I filled our schedules with some of the most memorable meetings of our lives.

When we began the study, we had little premonition of the delights and surprises in store for us. We were well aware that traditional psychological methods would be insufficient for capturing the remarkable life stories about which we would hear. So it was without hesitation that we brought some unconventional assumptions and procedures to our venture. We considered the exemplars to be "coinvestigators" in our exploration of their lives, and not "subjects" of an experimental manipulation or psychometric test. We took their own beliefs as our primary data source, and we negotiated with them our interpretations of the meaning of their life events.

Beginning with new premises and asking new kinds of questions, we did indeed expect different sorts of answers. But even our most seasoned intuitions left us unprepared for the answers we finally received. There was nothing in our knowledge of moral development literature that enabled us to anticipate the exemplars' impervious sense of certainty, their disclaimers of courage, their positive attitudes toward hardship and challenge, their receptivity toward new ideas and goals, their lifelong capacity for growth through social influence, or the powerful role of faith and spirituality in their lives. We were also surprised by the extent of common developmental patterns among their extremely varied lives. Despite the individuality of each exemplar, there were startling parallels in how they had acquired and sustained their moral commitments. The developmental pattern of goals and strategies looked very much the same from exemplar to exemplar.

Nor were the delights limited to the scholarly realm. Unexpectedly, we soon became more personally engaged and affected than one would expect in the course of a scholarly study. Time and again, we came back from our interview sessions with an exhilarating feeling of inspiration. The object of our intellectual interest—examples of compelling moral commitment—was directly touching our own lives. Not only were we observing moral influence, but we were experiencing it as well. Our sense of scientific revelation began to merge with a more personal one. Together the two combined to arouse in us a feeling of wonder, extravagant though this word may seem in social science discourse, and the feeling endures to this day.

I recall flying back to Boston from the bleak hills of Juarez, Mexico, where Suzie Valadez spends her days handing out sandwiches and building medical clinics for families that forage in the nearby garbage dump. Suzie is not the sort of person that you find in the ivory towers of a modern university. She dropped out of school in the tenth grade, had four children, and became a fervent born-again Christian. When she saw a vision of tattered children carrying a banner that read "Cuidad Juarez," Suzie decided on the spot to change her life. She packed her meager belongings and her children and within a few weeks had moved to El Paso, Texas. From that south Texas base, Suzie has spent the last twenty-eight years ministering to impoverished Mexicans. Often she herself has been penniless. But she has always been resourceful. Through stubborn determination and untutored organizational skills, Suzie has founded a mission, collected enough money to build two medical centers, subsidized schools, and fed vast numbers of poor (three thousand a day by one count). She has mobilized high-level government officials, businesses, and foundations, as well as troops of ordinary men, women, and young people who follow her example and make the daily trek over the Rio Grande.

While flying across the country on the return trip, my mind kept returning to images of Suzie, filled with amazement at what she has been able to accomplish. The simple *effectiveness* of this unpretentious woman is both humbling and inspiring. And her presence is magnetic. When she hands out sandwiches to ''her'' Mexican children or leads them in prayer, she is radiant, not to mention tireless. At sixty-six, she bounces from meeting to meeting in a twelve-hour day with the vigor of a teenager.

How are we to understand this? What accounts for the qualities of dedication, effectiveness, and charismatic radiance that distinguish moral leaders such as Suzie? What accounts for tirelessness in the face of daunting problems such as entrenched poverty? What accounts for joy in the face of misery and suffering?

I am reminded of some comments that Bishop Desmond Tutu made on a recent visit to Brown University.[1] Bishop Tutu was speaking of Mother Teresa, clearly a living moral exemplar for this man who has himself stood as a moral exemplar for so many others. Bishop Tutu said that one of the things that most astonished him about Mother Teresa was her capacity to give and receive joy while holding a hopelessly ill infant. How could she bear the anguish of so many confrontations with sickness and death? The answer, he said, was simple: Mother Teresa was filled with gratitude for the opportunity to fulfill her own human and spiritual potential.

Among the twenty-three exemplars we came to know, Anne and I witnessed many versions of a similar sensibility. It is not so much that they overcome their fears, doubts, or resentments over the risks and hardships in their lives; it is more that they treasure the chance to take them on. The exemplars create for themselves a world of certainty rather than doubt, a perspective of faith rather than despair. Despite the frustrations and disappointments that inevitably await those who try to make the world a better place, the exemplars consider themselves fortunate to be in a position to try. They are indeed, we believe, deeply fortunate to have developed such a powerfully life-affirming perspective. How did they come by such a perspective? How do they maintain and enhance it through all the travails they take on?

Clearly it has nothing to do with being in a powerful or privileged position, with having access to material resources, or even with having educational advantages in the traditional sense. What, then, explains it? Is it early family influence? Religious faith? The companionship of other dedicated and principled people? Do moral exemplars have sudden awakenings or watershed experiences of some kind? Have they been affected by books or sermons, perhaps? Are we encountering a deep-seated personality disposition? Or is it, after all, some special moral gift, paralleling the kinds of talent that mark great dancers or poets?

If these questions reflect our curiosity, they also reflect our joy in encountering a hopeful feature of our national scene. There has been a great deal of cynicism and pessimism in American life over the past decade. We may read about some good deeds in the newspaper, but the brief coverage portraying acts of charity and principle always seems drowned out by a lead story on a bloody drug war or the latest billionaire's corruption trial. We are assailed by media images of greed, corruption, crime, and violence. At such times it may seem that we are losing the special part of our national identity that represents the best of our history. One wonders whether our indigenous moral leaders are becoming extinct.

The exemplars of this book answer any such doubts. Suzie Valadez; Virginia Durr, Cabell Brand, Mother Waddles, Jack Coleman, and the rest may not all be national celebrities, but they play a prominent and influential role in American life. And they are not alone. One of this study's many delights was the ease with which we were able to find genuine moral leaders throughout our society. Every time we explored one lead, several others turned up. We identified many more people who were worthy of study than we could ever dream of meeting firsthand.

Anne and I do not presume to have come away from this project with a definitive "explanation" or "analysis" of moral leadership. This is too complex—and too human—a phenomenon to be captured finally in any single account. But we are confident that we have gained some insight. It is insight about the nature of human commitment to morality; and it is insight of a sort that was unavailable to us before we interviewed our exemplars. We have written this book to impart this insight and to draw out its implications for how we live our lives and raise our children.

W. D.
Providence, Rhode Island
January 1992

CHAPTER 1

Mysteries of Moral Commitment

In human nature, generous impulses are occasional or reversible. They are spent in childhood, in dreams, in extremities, and they are often weak or soured in old age. They form amiable interludes like tearful sentiments in a ruffian, or they are pleasant self-deceptive hypocrisies acted out, like civility to strangers, because such is in society the path of least resistance. Strain the situation, however, dig a little beneath the surface, and you will find a ferocious, persistent, profoundly selfish man.

—*George Santayana*

I believe in aristocracy—if that is the right word, and if a democrat may use it. Not an aristocracy of power, based on rank and influence, but an aristocracy of the sensitive, the considerate, and the plucky. Its members are to be found in all nations and classes, and all through the ages, and there is an understanding between them when they meet. They represent the true human tradition, the one permanent victory of our queer race over cruelty and chaos. Thousands of them perish in obscurity, a few are great names. They are sensitive for others as well as for themselves, they are considerate without being fussy, their pluck is not swankiness but the power to endure, and they can take a joke.

—*E. M. Forster*

What I do is as simple and as common as the laughter of a child.

—*Mother Teresa*

There is much in human nature to be doubtful about. For long, bleak stretches of history, goodness has seemed endangered and hard to find. In the very best of times, morality may still remain a questionable presence in human affairs. Many conclude that morality is a sentimental illusion, a high-minded rationalization, a transparent display of human hypocrisy: perhaps a figment of afterthought without any tangible impact of its own. Moral commitment, by this light, is no more than an indirect exercise in self-interest—or worse, a craftily disguised version of personal ambition. Even for those with less cynical views, moral commitment may seem uncertain and undependable when the chips are down.

Yet despite its elusiveness, morality does indeed touch the daily lives of everyone. Not only do we guide our behavior by it, but we also come to count on its many gifts, however unpredictable they may be. It is a bit like the anonymous benefactors who bless some fortunate families and groups. We may know little about the benefactors' origins, identities, or whereabouts. We may deny their existence. Yet from time to time, often at the most critical junctures, their contributions save the day.

In the bleakest of historical epochs, there are people who step forward with noble purposes and inspiring acts. Good faith and virtue shine through their deeds; the sincerity of their intentions resists suspicion. Sometimes such people galvanize the world's attention, gathering a large following. They provide examples for the many others who are seeking ways to express their own benevolent impulses. Other times, these moral leaders work in relative isolation, emerging from obscurity only at critical moments when an urgent need is sensed. Over the centuries, good people such as these have provided repeated proof that moral commitment is an undeniable fact, a mainstay of human existence and progress.

Human goodness, in fact, is both persistent and fragile. It appears when we least expect it, under conditions that are little understood and difficult to create. It can arise in settings that seem devoid of anything but sheer evil, deep within a totalitarian society, in a forlorn prison or concentration camp. It can vanish in the midst of fortune and happy companionship.

Perhaps this is why goodness still brings an air of surprise whenever it asserts or reasserts itself. Although goodness is as much a part of human history as destruction and bloodshed, there is often a sense of wonder when it prevails. We readily recognize it, yet we do not quite trust its strength or genuineness.

This is why an assertion of moral commitment—the sight of Mother Teresa nursing a dying child, the image of vulnerable individ-

2

uals standing up against tyranny—often brings with it a sense of wonder and surprise. And perhaps this is an indication of how little we understand true moral commitment, how mysterious it seems at its core.

Part of the mystery may be the apparent contradiction embedded in any moral commitment, which, by nature, is directed toward goals that are not primarily self-serving. Only in a highly ''enlightened'' sense may a moral commitment be said to benefit one's personal welfare. If self-promotion is really all one has in mind, there usually are more direct and effective ways to pursue it than through moral service to others.

Selfless goals are only a small part of the mystery. The essence goes more deeply into the timeless, universal, yet still elusive notion of character—an oddly old-fashioned word that implies personal integrity in word and deed. Personal integrity goes beyond selfless goals. In itself, a goal, no matter how noble or altruistic, can neither lend integrity nor constitute character; there must also be a moral manner of pursuing the goal. Personal integrity requires constant attention to the means as well as the ends of one's actions. It requires standards of honesty and decency in the methods that one uses, even when one's goals—noble or otherwise—seem in jeopardy. This is what makes integrity so difficult, so rare, and so noteworthy. This is what separates common good intentions from acts of unquestionable goodness, sustained sometimes over decades of a person's life.

Examples of sustained moral commitment are especially striking and inspiring, for they are rooted in character and personal integrity. Such examples are extraordinary. Still, and fortunately for all of us, they are hardly unknown. In fact, they are familiar to everyone. From time to time in every community, there are people who take on moral commitments that dominate their entire lives. They dedicate all their resources to fulfilling these commitments, pursuing them with great energy and effect. These people provide inspiring examples for others, multiplying their own effectiveness by attracting waves of followers.

How is it that some people are drawn over and over again to acts that serve others rather than only themselves? How do certain people muster the courage to stick by their principles when under enormous pressure to abandon them? How can such people maintain their integrity in the face of endless temptations to compromise it?

Like many, we are interested in these questions because they go to the heart of our hopes for human life. But we have more particular interests as well. As developmental psychologists, we are curious about how character is acquired, how it grows, and how it may foster sustained moral commitment. We wish to know how personal integrity may be maintained over years of trial and temptation.

Our interest extends from the most minimal presence of morality in human life to the highest reaches of exceptional moral commitment. We consider the entire spectrum to be mysterious, wondrous, and obscure. On one end of the spectrum, we try to understand why anyone would give up *anything* for a moral commitment. Yet on the other end, we wonder how anyone could give up *everything* for a moral commitment. These are not the same questions, of course; but we suspect that they will share at least some of the same answers. There are important connections—developmental ones, we believe—between the minimal and elevated ends of the moral spectrum.

One of the themes that we shall explore later is what we call the "developmental continuities" between everyday acts of morality and the enlarged commitments of moral leaders. Great moral acts, we believe, spring from the same sources as lesser ones. Enduring moral commitment is available for all to acquire. This is because there are many commonalities between how ordinary moral conduct and extraordinary moral commitment develop. The differences between them tend to be of degree rather than quality. We do not mean to belittle the noble acts of moral heroes but simply to demystify them a bit. We wish to capture the essence of extraordinary moral commitment in ways that make apparent the fundamental continuities between it and the more ordinary moral responses that the majority of people feel.

Part of our task in demystifying moral commitment is to see beyond the myths and stereotypes that are often used to characterize moral leaders. Popular culture tends to dramatize moral heroism as if it were a magical fantasy set apart from the dog-eat-dog daily life. Such dramatizations may be appealing in a Hollywood sense, but they can discourage common identification with moral excellence (not to mention aspirations to such excellence). This can stand as an unnecessary impediment to the normal moral strivings of most people. Exploring the developmental roots of moral excellence reveals its true connections to the possibilities of growth inherent in everyone.

Our exploration will also show moral excellence in a less remote and forbidding light than many have realized. Among the stereotypical features that we did *not* turn up in our study were the notions that moral exemplars endlessly reflect on what is right or wrong; that they constantly struggle with temptation, fear, and doubt; that they lead grim, joyless, or dreary lives; that they fight many of their battles in splendid isolation; that they are harsh and unforgiving with themselves and their followers; or that they provide their followers with a definitive, fully formed vision as a kind of "moral marching order." The truth, as we shall see, places moral exemplars far closer to the center of a collaborative support group. It is a picture of striking joy, great certainty, and unremitting faith; one that results in both high standards for the self and charity toward others. It is a story of self-development that extends the boundaries of personal morality beyond most people's imaginations, and yet it is one that draws on developmental processes shared by all.

We aim in this book to explain these developmental processes and to show how some highly moral people have managed to maximize them in their own lives. As we became immersed in their stories, we found them to be deeply moving ones with a message of hope for individuals and society alike. In order to capture this message, we explore the origins of moral commitment in the life histories of twenty-three extraordinary people: How did these people find the causes and concerns that come to dominate their entire lives? We also explore the growth processes responsible for transforming their early moral awareness into a lifelong calling: How do such people develop their firm and enduring dedication to moral causes? There are many temptations and fearful risks along the way: What makes them stick with their commitments without regard to the personal consequences? How do they maintain their personal integrity in the face of demands to compromise? Beyond maintaining a commitment, growth often means expanding the commitment to encompass ever new moral concerns: What triggers such growth, and what feeds it?

Some of these questions have been raised by religion and philosophy, not surprisingly without much hope for final answers. In the social and life sciences, they have been broached all too seldomly. To be sure, there have been some empirical studies of morality's psychological origins, but these studies have produced little agreement or shared understanding.

In recent years, social scientists have offered up a cacophony of languages worthy of the Tower of Babel to explain the origins of moral commitment. Some child psychologists have pointed to the influence of natural emotional responses such as empathy, while others have pointed to invariant processes of cognitive functioning,[1,2] cultural psychologists have pointed to the communication of values across generations,[3] psychoanalysts to dramatic personality-shaping events in the early years of life,[4] sociobiologists to species-preserving instinctual dispositions, such as an inborn tendency toward altruism,[5] and social psychologists to mechanisms of attitude change.[6] These answers diverge radically, with cataclysmic fault lines and little common ground between them. The questions continue to elude and intrigue us.

To be fair, the field of moral psychology has not positioned itself to address the question of how either character or long-standing moral commitment develops. Much of the research on lifelong moral development has been heavily influenced by Kohlberg's moral judgment work, or by the work of Kohlberg's critics (such as Carol Gilligan) who share many of the same cognitivist assumptions and methods. Generally, such approaches focus on people's theoretical reflections on real or hypothetical moral dilemmas. Moral reflection certainly has its uses: In any society, citizens must reason about complex issues of right and wrong every time they make important social choices. But moral reasoning alone does not tell us much about a person's actual social behavior. After decades of moral judgment research, we are still highly uncertain about the connection between reflection and everyday social conduct.[7]

Character and commitment are played out in the realm of action, not reflection. Pondering moral problems is not the same as dedicating one's life to their solution. The capacity for single-minded dedication to a moral cause may have little to do with the capacity for reasoning about abstract moral principles. The will to take a stand may derive from a source entirely different from the ability to arrive at a sophisticated intellectual judgment. It may even be that some people who live out strong moral commitments tend at times to be impatient with extensive reflection, as if they instinctively fear that it may lead to hesitation and doubt. In other cases, reasoning may contribute but still be only part of the story.

Beyond its focus on moral reasoning, the psychological tradition has produced some experimental studies of actual altruistic behavior. These have usually been limited to young children and generally have been done under artificial laboratory conditions. Some have been informative for the field of child development. Most, however, have represented altruism in disembodied and trivial ways. For example, one popular paradigm has been for an experimenter to "accidently" drop some paper clips and see whether the subject will spontaneously help by picking them up. In general, such studies have not been able to tell us much of note about the course of moral life outside the lab.[8] The overriding problem is that social behavior created for an experiment cannot replicate the complexity, depth, longevity, or vital spirit of human morality in the world at large.[9]

More promising are studies that begin with people who have already accomplished moral deeds in the broader arena of real life. In a recent study by Sam and Pearl Oliner, for example, a unique and truly inspiring group of people were selected to represent "the altruistic personality": European rescuers of Jews during the Holocaust.[10] These were people living in Nazi-occupied countries at a time when even a hint of dissent meant certain imprisonment and possible death. Despite the terrible risks, these people—themselves Gentiles—sheltered and aided the Jews fleeing Nazi persecution. The measure of altruism, therefore, was taken at the study's outset, and it was far from trivial.

The Oliners' study was done within a fairly traditional psychological framework, implemented through a series of personality tests and other psychometric instruments. These measures yielded some informative facts about these remarkable people. Yet we wonder whether these facts have brought us any closer to the roots of moral commitment. According to the study's findings, the personal qualities of the rescuers included a strong sense of control over events in their lives, strong attachments to others, feelings of responsibility for others, a history of family closeness during childhood, greater empathy for pain, a willingness to see different types of people as essentially similar to themselves, and an inclination to befriend others on the basis of personal qualities rather than religion or status.[11]

This characterization may constitute a partial explanation for the rescuers' behavior, but we must keep in mind that we are referring to people who routinely risked their lives to shelter despised outcasts, *often wholly unknown to them,* in a climate of the most virulent hatred and terror. To capture the mystery of what these special people did, we surely need to go beyond their happily ordered childhoods, their sense of control over their lives, and their empathic natures. Many people share these fortuitous life conditions and personality attributes, yet not many extend themselves in the noble and courageous manner of the Holocaust rescuers. These people showed a quality of extraordinary dedication that, unfortunately, is not widely found in society, even among good-natured people raised in felicitous family conditions.

How is this rare quality of dedication developed and maintained? What, if anything, does it have to do with early experience? In asking these questions, we start with the realization that many people raised in secure, warm, and ordered family environments do not acquire this quality. We also start with the belief that some unusually dedicated people come from backgrounds quite the opposite. For all these reasons, we are skeptical about analyses that reduce extraordinary moral commitment either to social factors such as family background or to personal ones such as a tendency to have close relationships.

We are in fact skeptical about the role of *any* early experience in determining the course of moral commitment. One of the characteristics of highly moral people is their ability to learn from their experience all throughout life, and we shall have more to say about this quality as we describe the moral exemplars in this book. For now, we simply note that personal integrity often requires one to keep an open mind and a receptive outlook: This is a fundamental part of the personal commitment to truth that constitutes character.

In order to explore the depths of moral commitment—its origins in a person's life, its meaning to that person's life, its development and sustenance throughout the person's life—we need to go beyond laboratory experiments, personality assessments, or discrete bits of family background. We need to understand the person's life and how the person makes sense of it. The method of investigation must set the moral commitment in the context of a life history. It must establish the person's own perspective on both the commitment and the history.

With this in mind, we look to biographical and autobiographical material for better sources of information about the development of moral commitment. We believe that the best source is an autobiographical statement systematically structured around questions about how the individual's moral commitment originated, grew, and was sustained. The account is founded upon the person's own recollections and beliefs. The recollections are prodded and focused by a sympathetic interviewer, the beliefs are explored and challenged, and the resulting interpretations are negotiated between investigator and subject. To this end, we arrived at what some have called an ''assisted autobiography'' method of case study, to be described in the next chapter and more fully discussed in Appendix B.

Something, of course, can be learned from spontaneous autobiographies left by historical moral leaders, as well as from intelligent biographies done by scholars interested in similar kinds of developmental questions. Historical accounts such as these helped us prepare for this study, suggesting questions, hypotheses, even general principles. Because of such accounts, we already had in mind a prefiguration of some key themes when we began interviewing those profiled in this book. Had we not, it would have been far more difficult for us to draw out their life stories in ways that would have given us the critical insights we were seeking.

As two cases in point, the life histories of Andrei Sakharov and Mahatma Gandhi are rich in information about how moral leaders acquire and sustain enduring commitments. We discovered Sakharov's writings early in our study and published a speculative analysis of what they revealed about moral development.[12] The Gandhi account that most intrigued us is part of a work in progress by Howard Gardner on "creators of the modern era."[13] We had a chance to read Gardner's manuscript as we were finishing our book and found his Gandhi case study redolent of many of the themes that we were working on, as well as enormously suggestive in its own right.

Of course, neither Sakharov nor Gandhi was available to us as a subject for study. Gandhi had long been dead and Sakharov was exiled to remote Gorki for most of his final few years. In any case, we had decided to limit our study to moral exemplars who had done their main work in the United States, the only society that we knew from the inside.

Yet we remain struck by how closely the patterns that we found among our twenty-three moral exemplars resembled those in biographical accounts of Sakharov, Gandhi, and other extraordinary men and women. Clearly, we cannot examine historical accounts in anywhere near as great detail as we can cases where we are able to sit down with our subject and ask questions and discuss interpretations. But the historical cases help place the patterns in the perspective of another time and place, and they are illuminating because the life details of historical figures are already common knowledge. Because the lives of Sakharov and Gandhi are widely known and revered at the current time, we cite them here as a means of introducing some themes in this book.

THE DEVELOPMENT TRANSFORMATION OF MORAL GOALS

Sakharov's memoirs are particularly revealing on the question of how moral commitment develops throughout one's life. Without doubt, this great crusader for human rights and world peace was a moral exemplar by the standards that we shall establish in the following chapter. Yet until age thirty-six, he seemed little more than a sturdy, albeit brilliant, pillar of the Soviet establishment. Sakharov was the inventor of the Russian H-bomb and the youngest person ever elected to the USSR Academy of Sciences. He was considered both a patriot and a brilliant scientist of unique stature. With these achievements, he enjoyed unparalleled comfort and privilege as a Soviet citizen of the highest order. He had distinguished himself in many ways, but societal concerns were not especially high on his agenda.

Then, beginning in 1957, Sakharov began a series of activities that permanently altered his role in Soviet society. Over the next three decades these activities became progressively more challenging to the Soviet order, and their progression reveals some features of moral growth in one exceptional adult life. The following is a rough chronology of significant events:

1957:
Sakharov became concerned about radioactive contamination following nuclear weapons tests and issued internal memoranda urging caution.

1961–62:
Sakharov personally contacted Soviet premier Nikita Khrushchev in an attempt to halt further nuclear testing. He was rebuffed and told to cease "meddling" in affairs of state.

1964:
In a meeting of scientists, Sakharov criticized the enduring influence of Trofim Lysenko (Stalin's science adviser) in Soviet scientific theory.

1966:
Sakharov went public with his dissent. In an open letter to the Soviet congress, he and others warned against the reintroduction of Stalinism. Later that year, he protested a new antislander law used to silence criticism.

1967:
He wrote Leonid Brezhnev to plead the case of two dissidents who were harshly sentenced under Soviet law.

1968:
Sakharov allowed a "self-published" work entitled *Progress, Coexistence, and Intellectual Freedom,* to be published in the West. The text argued mildly for détente but contained little criticism of the Soviet system. Nor did it contain secret information. In fact, Sakharov refused (as he had done before) to speak with Western news reporters because of his access to military secrets. Nevertheless, he soon lost his clearance for scientific work, effectively ending his government career. Later that year, his first wife died.

1969:

With more time on his hands, and with the termination of his family life as a result of his wife's death, Sakharov broadly expanded his circle of friends, seeking out other intellectuals and dissidents.

1970:

With two of his new acquaintances, Sakharov started the Moscow Human Rights Committee. This group at first met to discuss civil rights and to establish links with international organizations. But as word of the group spread, it attracted countless pleas from people to whom injustice had been done. In response to these pleas, the group began functioning as a legal-aid society, conducting appeals and advocacy for persecuted people throughout the Soviet Union.

1973:

Sakharov broke with his practice of working within the Soviet system and reached out to the United Nations and other international agencies for help. He asked Westerners to intervene on behalf of Soviet citizens assigned to psychiatric hospitals, and he began granting interviews to Western correspondents. Shortly thereafter, he was officially warned to stop communicating with foreigners.

1974–86:

As the official press and other state channels sharpened their attacks on Sakharov, his criticism of state policies became increasingly broad-based and direct. This escalating cycle of repression and activism led finally to his exile from Moscow to the industrial city of Gorki.

1987–89:

During the Gorbachev era, Sakharov was gradually redeemed in the eyes of the state. He was returned from exile and even assumed a legislative position in the Supreme Soviet. At the time of his death, he was broadly accepted throughout the government as well as the populace as a man of admirable principles and unimpeachable integrity. Increasingly, the official Soviet rhetoric began to emulate ideas that Sakharov had put forth in his visionary statements.

Even this brief sketch of dramatic events in one moral leader's life reveals some intriguing things about the growth of moral commitment. For one thing, it shows an ever-expanding course of development, not at all limited to childhood influences. Sakharov transformed himself in mid-life from a distinguished scientist to a great ethicist. His concerns and actions became more pointed, more effective, and more directed toward the broadest of moral ends.

The course of Sakharov's transformation is informative. His first deep ethical concern—the dangers of nuclear testing—arose out of his own work on the hydrogen bomb. Sakharov came by his subsequent concerns less directly and more as a part of new social relationships. For example, his active engagement in the civil rights issue occurred only after he had had frequent communications with a group deeply concerned with this matter. Sakharov was initially drawn into contact with these people because his nuclear testing concerns matched theirs. As his new colleagues shared information and insights with him, he was introduced to a broader set of issues and induced to extend his activism accordingly.

One of these transitions came after he had finished a successful petitioning campaign aimed at freeing a biologist who had defied Stalinist dogma. His collaborators in this campaign then initiated the idea of forming a committee to observe dissident trials generally. (Sakharov recalls being told by a friend at the time, "One of the problems in getting involved with us is you do something and we're right on top of you to do something else.") This idea was to become Sakharov's Committee on Human Rights. It is clear from Sakharov's account that the committee was a venture developed jointly with his new associates. This collaboration provided Sakharov with an intimate form of social guidance, which gave birth to a new and broader set of ethical goals.

Through all of this, there was an intricate relationship between Sakharov and the many followers that he attracted and inspired. And the direction of influence went both ways: Sakharov was as much affected by his colleagues as they were by him. Although he was clearly the leader who galvanized support for the cause of human rights, Sakharov continued to learn from his "followers" throughout his career as an activist. We shall see a similar reciprocity of influence in the stories of all our moral exemplars.

It is also significant that Sakharov's original plans for the committee were simply to study and "witness" the trials, not to advocate directly on anyone's behalf. Studying, of course, was a course of action quite familiar and comfortable to Sakharov the scientist. Only later, and under the influence of compelling urgings and observations, did he himself take direct public action. His transformation was gradual and his actions always measured. But he came a very long way from where he started, largely because he was always receptive to change and growth.

What makes some extraordinary individuals receptive to lifelong moral change while others "shut down" developmentally at some point in adolescence or adulthood? This is one of the central questions of our study. Because we did not have the opportunity to interview Sakharov, we cannot answer this question in the context of his life. But from what little we do know, we can see a striking openness to moral change that we might call an "active receptiveness" to particular sorts of social influence.

There are two things we can say about this active receptiveness. First, as we noted, the simple fact that it existed signifies a propensity toward ethical growth even late in life. Second, it is not a blanket receptiveness toward just any sort of social influence. Witness, for example, Sakharov's strenuous resistance to Soviet governmental pressures to conform. Sakharov's active receptiveness was predirected toward a moral influence that he could not yet define but was prepared to recognize.

It is important to emphasize that, at each step in his evolving moral engagement with the Soviet dissident community, Sakharov actively chose to move forward rather than to withdraw. The direction and shape of his moral growth was forged by the continual interplay between him and his chosen community. The social influences in Sakharov's life cannot be understood without knowing what both he and his chosen colleagues brought to the process.

In Sakharov's case, we know from his writings that he brought to this social process an ethical framework for interpreting events through certain key moral values. For Sakharov, the values of truth and justice were so central to his own personal identity that he could not allow himself to draw back from the challenges he encountered regardless of the conflicts and risks they presented. The new people in his life posed these challenges for him, directing him toward actions that accorded with his ethical framework. His friends and colleagues did not create Sakharov's moral potential, but they certainly broadened it and helped him realize it.

If Sakharov's colleagues provided him with a kind of positive social guidance, the Soviet system of sanctions did just the reverse. As he became an "enemy of the people," Sakharov began losing the incentive to sustain a connection with the social order. During the bleakest, pre-Gorbachev days, he almost gave up hope of working within the system, and as a consequence, his actions became more radical. He began to think of his mission as one of creating ideals rather than actually effecting changes in an almost immutable system. He said: "There is a need to create ideals, even though one can't see a route by which to achieve them; because if there are no ideals there can be no hope, and then one is completely in the dark, in a hopeless, blind alley.''

The system, through its punitive rigidity, led him to a state of detachment from it. In its place, Sakharov substituted a system of moral values that one can only call universal. In his Nobel Peace Price address (delivered in Stockholm by his second wife, Elena Bonner), Sakharov wrote, ''Peace, progress, human rights: these three goals are indissolubly linked. It is impossible to achieve one if the other two are ignored.'' Yet even at these lofty heights of insight, Sakharov's moral search for still more worthy goals did not come to rest. At the end of the address, Sakharov wrote, ''We must make good the demands of reason and create a life worthy of ourselves and of the goals we only dimly perceive.''

It was fortunate that Sakharov lived to see some of his ''dimly foreseen'' goals introduced into his nation's civic consciousness. Many moral leaders are not that lucky. They must take their contributions to human goodness on faith.

There are many mysteries in the lives of moral exemplars such as Andrei Sakharov, and they cannot be contained by simple normative formulae that connect early events or ingrained tendencies to later moral excellence. Moral commitment is a continually evolving process that implicates every part of one's personal and social world. Gaining a good view of this process means taking into account the person's whole life. As part of this, it also means obtaining—and taking seriously—that person's moral perspective.

The life of Sakharov exemplifies developmental patterns that run throughout the lives of the exemplars in this book. The adult transitions of every moral exemplar chronicled in our study have been marked by a quality of active receptiveness to progressive social influence as well as by the process that we call the developmental transformation of goals.

THE RECIPROCAL NATURE OF SOCIAL INFLUENCE

Both Sakharov and Gandhi, like all our moral exemplars, communicated actively with small groups of supporters throughout their entire careers. The relations between the exemplar and the group are reciprocal in their influence and are mutually transformative. Initially, there is a partial match of goals between the two. Then there is a communication of new information and concerns, followed by an engagement in new activities, followed finally by the adoption of broader moral goals. In this manner, transformative social influence continues through one's life span. It is not contained alone in early experiences, in onetime dramatic incidents, or in determinative personality characteristics, although any of these may play a role. The chief operative force is social communication and support. In the course of such communication, the leader paradoxically draws developmental benefits from the feedback of followers.

Gandhi's innovative use of nonviolent methods (a fast and a labor strike) during a dispute with the British drew heavily upon the network of support that Gandhi had established with his faithful followers. As Howard Gardner explains it, "From one perspective, Gandhi may look like the creator who invented himself; but from another perspective, he benefited from the most family-like support system during the moments of his most daring and decisive breakthrough." All throughout Gandhi's creative moral odyssey, Gardner writes, "His experiments were carried out partly inside his own head but partly in consort with other individuals, whom he attempted to engage in his several missions." Writing generally of Gandhi as well as all of the modern "creators" that he studied, Gardner concludes, "the creator required both affective support—someone with whom he or she felt comfortable—and cognitive support—someone who could understand the nature of the breakthrough."

As for the nature of Gandhi's relationships with his supporters, there was the same peculiar mix of directedness and receptiveness that we found among many of our twenty-three exemplars. Gardner describes the quality of Gandhi's social communications this way: "Gandhi got away with [his] dictatorial arrogance because he at least listened carefully to what others said, because he had a sense of humor about himself, and because he could openly admit mistakes and change his mind. . . ."

Sakharov and Gandhi were both influenced by historical moral figures as well as contemporaries. A distinguished American educator recalls Sakharov telling him on a visit to Moscow that his (Sakharov's) greatest personal debt was to Martin Luther King, Jr., whom he had never met.[14] Gardner writes that Gandhi adapted his highly effective nonviolent techniques from writings and sayings of Christ, Thoreau, Tolstoy, and Socrates.

CERTAINTY AND MORAL COURAGE

The lives of Sakharov and Gandhi also demonstrate a combination of great certainty about moral principles—combined, as noted above, with an open-mindedness about new facts and their implications. Perhaps this seems a curious combination on its surface, but it is a highly effective one for moral leadership, for it enables one to be both steadfast and adaptive.

Like all the exemplars in this book, both Sakharov and Gandhi subjected themselves to great risks. It is noteworthy that, in his *Memoirs*, Sakharov seldom (if ever) remarks on his own moral courage. It is as if he assumes that he has no choice in matters of principle. Courage seems moot, even unnecessary, in such a light. This, too, is a pattern that we observed in our twenty-three exemplars.

As for Gandhi, Gardner notes: "Not infrequently, Gandhi placed himself at risk. . . . Yet he refused to sacrifice his principles. Indeed, far from intimidating Gandhi, these encounters with harsh and sometimes unyielding reality strengthened [his] resolve."

POSITIVITY AND FAITH

Despite the dismal events that he had witnessed, Sakharov's public lectures expressed unremitting faith in humanity and its future. For Gandhi, such faith was an integral part of his moral, religious, and personal self. This quality of positivity—a capacity for finding hope and joy even while frankly facing the often dreary truth—was a striking characteristic in most of our moral exemplars. It is a capacity that enables them to endure circumstances that would be dispiriting for others.

We find such positivity in Sakharov's Nobel Peace Prize acceptance speech, in which he affirms "our sacred endeavors in the world" while fully recognizing the dreary failure of his native civilization. We do not, however, find this spirit of positivity throughout the memoirs themselves. The tone is more angry, defiant, and bitter than we should have expected—although, as we shall see in at least one of our chapter profiles, such sentiments dominated the tone of a few of our exemplars as well. Similar to Sakharov, these were people whose moral commitments forced them to spend their lives fighting great injustices.

THE UNITING OF SELF AND MORALITY

Beyond these general themes, moral leaders such as Sakharov and Gandhi show a unity of self that we find remarkable as well as informative. There is little separation in Sakharov's writings between his moral life, his personal life, and his professional life. Unlike most people, he does not compartmentalize his concerns. Gandhi renounced all personal pleasures other than his moral mission, pursuing, as Gardner writes, a "life of saintlike simplicity" in which "he shrugged off worldly possessions, ate and drank abstemiously, wore few pieces of clothing, lived with as few creature comforts as possible." One of Gandhi's close supporters described Gandhi's "irresistible" quality this way: "He said what he believed and put into practice what he said, so his mind, spirit, and body were in harmony." There was a quality of intended fusion between moral and personal in both Sakharov's and Gandhi's lives. Personal concerns became inseparable from moral ones. In many instances, they were by choice perceived as the same concern.

In his *Memoirs,* Sakharov himself does not reflect upon this fusion, nor upon any of the common themes that we have identified (we have not examined Gandhi's writings on this score). Why would he? These are *our* themes, extracted by *our* interpretive framework for the purpose of answering the social and psychological questions that drive us. Because our access to Sakharov's life is limited to his unadorned autobiographical statements, we cannot get his direct feedback either on our specific questions or on the themes that we have detected. We have only an incomplete data source and no means through which to verify our impressions.

Life histories of moral leaders such as Andrei Sakharov and Gandhi can yield speculative insights concerning certain developmental patterns, but they cannot suffice for a full or definitive account of how lasting moral commitment is acquired and maintained. There are many direct questions that we need to ask a person if we are to come away with a sense of the individual's moral experience and moral perspective. There is much that we must know about how fears are conquered, how challenges are approached, how choices are made, and why other choices are not made. Only an in vivo methodology can explore such issues adequately. Historical studies cannot fully address issues such as the development of moral commitment, because, to put it simply, their subjects are dead. As such, they are unavailable for participation in the study's mission. No matter how rich the historical record, there is no substitute for questioning, probing, and counterprobing the subject of an investigation.

What is more, the direct questioning becomes especially powerful when the same questions and probes can be directed toward a number of people. This provides a standard of comparison that can validate the investigator's interpretations. In the absence of any firsthand questioning, and without any standard of comparison, the interpretations are very difficult to evaluate or generalize. This is the case even when the interpreter is brilliant and imaginative. Erik Erikson's studies of Martin Luther and Gandhi, for example, are brimming with insight, but they are also marked by a speculative and idiosyncratic flavor that inevitably reduces their value.[15] In the end, they tell you more about the creative gifts of their author than about the developmental processes responsible for the subjects' moral commitment.

In Chapter 2 and Appendix B we discuss the in vivo methods that helped us gain more direct access to the lives and perspectives of our twenty-three moral exemplars. Ironically, the major inspiration for our choice of methods came from a thirty-year, in-depth exploration of the lives of nine hundred Belgian murderers—not, one would think, a sample that has much in common with American moral exemplars.[16] The director of the Belgian study, criminologist Jean-Pierre DeWaele, refined a method of "assisted autobiography" that does rare scientific justice to the lives and perspectives of the study's participants. The aim of an assisted autobiography is to gain access to a person's own interpretations of his or her life as an invaluable source of insight. Recognizing that all of us are unavoidably subjective about our lives, one does not rest there; instead, in a sense, one begins there. We devised the interview procedures in our study with this aim in mind.

Our true beginning, though, was not in the questioning of moral exemplars but in finding some to study. What is a "moral exemplar"? How can one be identified? In a study such as ours, how can we be sure that we are not just selecting people whom we personally admire or who simply match our own biases? Are there any objective criteria for moral leadership? These difficult questions are crucial for understanding what moral commitment is and how it develops. We address these questions in Chapter 2.

THE IMPORTANCE OF MORAL LEADERSHIP IN AMERICA TODAY

No psychological study can be dissociated from the social and cultural context in which it is set. We noted earlier the questions that drove us as developmental psychologists to this study. But we are also Americans who care about the moral future of our country. Like many, we see our democratic republic as a "work in progress." This gives us further interest in American moral leaders, beyond our focus on the dynamics of their individual development, for we believe that the course of any society is largely determined by the quality of its moral leadership.

Our investigation by choice focuses on those who have lived and worked in the United States. It is a diverse group, drawn from across the ideological, religious, ethnic, and economic spectra of contemporary American society. Despite the group's diversity, the moral leaders all have at least two things in common. First, they all have acquired, developed, and maintained firm commitments to moral causes over decades of social engagement. Second, they have done much of their work in the United States. It is in this country that they have touched many people with their dedication and talents.

Now there are those who believe that contemporary American society provides a barren climate for sustaining a moral life, and much public discourse in recent years has supported this view. Increasingly during the past decade, the media has portrayed the American cultural landscape as being a terrain overgrown with hedonistic values. Television shows highlight the "rich and famous" single-mindedly pursuing flamboyant life-styles. Newspaper columnists have used the phrase "decade of greed" so often that it has become an unquestioned symbol of our recent past—a past supposedly dominated by acquisitiveness, self-promotion, and materialism. In this vein, major social analyses of the day have portrayed a "culture of narcissism" in which altruistic community engagements have become the exception rather than the rule.[17]

We have some doubts about this view. From the perspective of history, our recent past has continued the moral traditions that have existed in American society from the earliest days. Naturally, it is true that, as in any society at any time, there are self-serving people who promote themselves to social prominence. But there are also those who dedicate their lives to ethical principles and noble pursuits; and these people also contribute importantly to the cultural climate.

Fortunately, we get some sense of this, even from the daily news. The media from time to time give us glimpses of courageous people dedicating their lives to the common good. In fact, no doubt as a reaction to the most extraordinary demonstrations of blatant greed in the 1980s, there recently have been special attempts to highlight the activities of highly altruistic individuals. The work of such people, though, is rarely glamorous enough for much in-depth or extensive coverage. So the glimpses we get are brief and occasional, leaving the impression of isolated life rafts floating in a sea of indifference.

Still, there may be more here than meets the eye. In his book *Local*

Heroes, community psychologist Bill Berkowitz paints a very different picture.[18] Amid all the squalor and corruption of modern life, there are many ordinary people, "local heroes," struggling against the tides of decay and misery. Most, perhaps all, communities have such people. They are the ones who create and sustain the bonds essential for civilized social existence. Without them, in fact, there could be no true communities in the first place. Through a simple one-year search, Berkowitz was able to identify over four hundred such people throughout the United States. He interviewed some twenty of them about how and why they do what they do and presented these interviews in his book in fairly undigested form.

Reading what Berkowitz's "local heroes" have to say about their lives, one cannot help but think of the word *character*. Berkowitz himself calls it "old-fashioned virtue." He cites qualities such as (his words) "commitment . . . hard work . . . persistence . . . considerate treatment of others . . . riskiness . . . tolerance . . . optimism."[19] Berkowitz's heroes exemplify these abstract qualities in the sense that these people bring the qualities to life with their own actions. It is precisely these qualities, along with some important others (honesty, integrity, fairness, humility, faith) that constitute personal character.

Exemplary character of the sort Berkowitz has chronicled is, in fact, part of our national heritage. American history is full of women and men who have spent their lives selflessly ministering to the poor and forgotten, fighting tyranny and injustice, healing the sick, teaching the ignorant, enfranchising the powerless, and serving spiritual values through their deeds and words. With songs, national holidays, stamps, and displays we celebrate the great moral leaders of our past: Harriet Tubman, Abraham Lincoln, Susan B. Anthony, Florence Nightingale, Martin Luther King, Jr., and others. Many more were known only locally and are now largely forgotten. At certain historical junctures, ethical concerns may be submerged, but public respect for exemplary character is deeply ingrained in the American tradition and never far from the surface. Our recent past, it is true, has been portrayed as one of rampant, unashamed avarice. The unscrupulous and power-hungry have captured the spotlight with their misadventures. But perhaps now we can look back upon this purportedly unexalted epoch and see that naked greed was never the all-encompassing theme. Genuine moral heroes have remained active and effective in many walks of American life, however quietly and off center stage. The journalistic accounts by Berkowitz and others provide glimpses of such people. During our own travels, we have made many additional sightings. In fact, before our study even began we were surprised by an unexpected finding: As we met and interviewed people across the United States in preparation for this book, we discovered in virtually every place we looked many more dedicated moral leaders than we could ever study. They are by no means an endangered species.

The moral exemplars that we encountered are wrestling with classic societal problems in contemporary guises. They strive to find shelter for homeless families in communities where housing has become unaffordable. They campaign against racism and bigotry. They educate the illiterate. They feed the hungry. They work for peace. They introduce moral and religious values into communities torn by drug wars. They hold themselves to uncompromising standards of integrity. They set inspiring examples for others by conducting their affairs with exceptional honesty and decency. Such moral exemplars can be found in business, civil service, education, religious organizations, and community action groups throughout the land. They are widely distributed throughout our ethnic, socioeconomic, and religious subcultures and across the ideological spectrum of American political belief.

We want to know more about how exemplary "character" of the sort demonstrated by Berkowitz's local heroes is formed. And it is all the more intriguing to think about how it is formed in a cultural climate so widely characterized as materialistic and narcissistic. How may exemplary character be formed and how may it be sustained throughout a contemporary American life?

Berkowitz's treatment cannot answer this question for us. It gives us rich but wholly unstructured interview material. With no systematic questioning about the past and present influences that may have shaped his heroes' moral character, Berkowitz can do little more than fall back on uninformative truisms in his analysis. He concludes that his heroes are distinguished by a "belief in and reliance upon . . . virtue, the kind instilled by parents, taught by Sunday Schools and scout troops."[20] Parents, church, and scouts may well have played key roles in his heroes' early lives, but they certainly were not the only important ingredients in the development of their moral character. As for even these key influences, we need to know much more about how they worked in these particular lives. After all, many of us have been exposed to parental teachings, church, and scouts without going on to assume a lifelong moral commitment of heroic proportions. What makes the difference? Where do such values and personal strengths come from? What are the challenges and temptations that arise and how are they conquered? What makes some individuals stand out from the crowd in their determination to live a moral life?

We do not ask such questions in order to deify or glorify certain people. We do not wish to promote a new canonization ritual. Rather, we are interested in persons of exemplary moral character because we believe that, in the long run, they exert an extraordinarily beneficial influence on civilization. If one believes at all in the tortuous course of the human race toward a finer moral sensibility (and we do), one can hardly imagine any progress toward that end without the critical contributions of moral leaders. The milestones of moral history are marked most of all by the words and deeds of highly dedicated individuals. We also believe, as we said at the outset, that there are developmental continuities between ordinary and extraordinary moral achievement. The difference is a matter of degree rather than kind. Understanding how some individuals acquire great moral strength can help bring some degree of moral excellence within everyone's reach.

The sight of a highly virtuous person living a life dedicated to moral causes can have a powerfully influential effect on other people's moral behavior. As a rule, people are far more captivated by the example of a human life than by an ideational treatise. The extraordinary influence of moral exemplars is due in large part to this natural human preference for personal embodiments over abstract notions. When a human life comes to represent a virtuous quality, that quality gains an appeal that could never be realized through ideas alone. The quality becomes "personified," a symbolic process not unlike metaphoric or rhetorical thinking. Like many other symbolic processes, personification is a powerful mover of human feeling and action. By bringing abstract ideas literally to life, it not only communicates elusive notions but also spurs their implementation. Its symbolic force can compel action just as a great poem or song can compel deep emotion.

In the course of human events, moral values have been most convincingly demonstrated and communicated through the personification of good in individual lives. Moral behavior and moral influence of every kind rely heavily on such personification. This may be inevitable, because moral choices are constructed in relationships with real people, and moral ideas have behavioral meaning only as they are actively interpreted in human relationships. Moral personification is a ready-made means of creating such interpretations, since it brings with it direct illustrations of human action as well as an inspirational example of virtue embraced.

Adding to this interpersonal force is a widespread human tendency that social psychologists have called "minority group polarization." Dramatic and extreme forms of behavior capture people's attention. By definition, behavior that seems dramatic and extreme will be the work of the few, because if everyone did it, it would no longer seem very dramatic and would certainly not be perceived as "extreme." When a few people, a minority of the populace, capture the attention of the majority, a number of things can happen. The majority can ignore the minority; it can repress it; it can choose to encourage the minority; or it can even emulate the minority. Social scientists have found that, when the minority's behavior is perceived as both extreme *and* virtuous by the majority, sooner or later the majority will move in the direction of the admired minority. The eminent European social psychologist Serge Moscovici has written: "It is also well known that when an individual adopts a behavior that most individuals would themselves like to carry out, *he serves as an example and has a liberating effect*" (emphasis in original).[21]

Of course, it takes a highly unusual person to pursue virtue in the extreme, especially when the majority is busily pursuing less noble goals. Swimming against the tide for any extended period of time is a stressful and debilitating experience for most. But there are individuals in every walk of life who willingly shoulder the lonely burdens of uncommon efforts. Without this kind of minority effort, it is hard to imagine progress in any field of human endeavor. In the long run, such minorities, when right, generally do reshape the majority rather than vice versa. A Christ or a Galileo can be persecuted during his lifetime; a Susan B. Anthony can be ignored and ridiculed for long, lonely stretches of years; even a Winston Churchill can be relegated for a time to a political wilderness—but eventually, if there is truth to the message, stubbornly maintained, the majority will listen. It is the ultimate hope of humanity that this process will slowly transform our moral affairs for the better, just as it has moved us forward in science, the arts, medicine, and so on. From this hope is born the realistic expectation that there will be moral innovation and progress in each generation as well as new solutions to enduring social ills.

What kinds of people will lead this movement? Who will keep alive our hopes for the moral improvement of the human race? What are they like and how did they come to be that way? What gives them their special sense of mission? How do they stick with it in the face of hardship, opposition, and social indifference? What gives them their capacity to lead? Their courage? Their moral insight?

It is urgent that we search for answers to these questions. For all of the fascination of the existing journalistic portraits, we rarely get far enough beneath the surface to obtain the answers that we need. Nor are the studies that attribute moral excellence to upbringing, good family background, or early experience particularly convincing.

To answer questions about the genesis and course of moral commitment through one's life span, sustained moral accomplishment must be examined as the dramatic and heroic occurrence that it is, and not just as another benign by-product of a decent conventional upbringing. We must appreciate the lives and perspectives of moral leaders in a way that captures the uniqueness and integrity of those lives and perspectives. We must try to understand what is special about such people and how they got that way.

CHAPTER 2

Identifying Moral Exemplars and Studying Their Lives

When we began this study, we were aware that everyone, including the two of us, has ideological biases that influence how he or she construes morality. We were determined not to let our own biases dictate our choice of subjects, choosing only people we happened to like or agree with. Instead, we wished to study a group of people who would be recognized as highly moral even by those who disagree with their beliefs or approach life with different ideologies.

In order to accomplish this, we needed to develop formal criteria for identifying moral exemplars. We also needed to establish a nominating process that allowed input from individuals with a range of religious, cultural, and ideological perspectives. It was through this nominating process that we were able to distance our personal values from the selection of the study participants and cast a broad net that went beyond the limitations of our own circles of acquaintances in terms of class, race, occupation, and political perspective.

Our efforts to develop nominating criteria were guided by our desire to frame the notion of a highly moral person in a broad yet coherent manner. This was a challenging task. Who could possibly be in a position to call another person "moral"? Wouldn't people with different values make entirely different determinations? Unquestionably, all through history, one person's hero has been another's villain. Even revered spiritual leaders such as Jesus or Mohammad were reviled by many of their contemporaries. Such a phrase as "moral exemplar" will always provoke skepticism, because people not only disagree about the nature of moral standards but also about how to evaluate whether a particular individual's behavior reflects such standards.

Part of the inevitable controversy reflects social, cultural, and political differences among people. Values vary widely within and across societies. Beliefs vary in important ways across religious, political, and cultural groups. As for moral heroes, most people naturally tend to admire those who share their beliefs and to judge harshly those who express opposing opinions. There are not many pro-choice advocates who will select their moral heroes from the ranks of the pro-life movement, or vice versa.

Moreover, people differ not only in their values but also in their assessment of the facts about other people. There are multiple sources of information about any individual, and such information may be interpreted in a multiplicity of ways. Often the selection and interpretation of facts about a person are shaped by, and further exaggerate, one's evaluative biases. This can greatly influence one's attitude toward candidates for moral heroism. For example, a free-enterprise corporate executive might dismiss Ralph Nader as a self-promoting careerist, whereas a regulation-minded lobbyist would see him as acting out of concern for the welfare of others. Were both to share the same perception of Nader's real motivation, the two would find themselves in agreement on the moral worth of Nader's actions. How people read the facts is as important as their values in determining how they size up another's behavior.

Another source of dissension concerning moral heroes is the inevitable problem of human imperfection. Perhaps heroes and saints do not *always* have feet of clay, but they all have occasional lapses. No matter how great their contributions in some areas, there will be other areas where someone can find fault. The most revered public figures— the Mahatma Gandhis and Martin Luther Kings of this world—have been accused of improprieties in their private lives. Observers differ in how important they consider such faults to be when compared to the virtues these great figures stand for. Again, such assessments may well be linked to the observers' moral and political preconceptions.

The variety in people's moral values, and the differences among those who are revered for moral excellence, suggest that the term *moral exemplar* should be used with caution. We would argue, however, that the notion of morality is not entirely arbitrary or subjective.[1] On the central question of what constitutes a moral act, there is a broad range of consensus within our culture, and perhaps beyond. This is not to say that there is agreement about the moral worth of every act or person. But even contending parties in social conflicts are subject to certain shared standards of truth and justice. However much disagreement there may be about values and beliefs, there is a shared consensual core, at least within the Judeo-Christian tradition, that most would endorse.

Our initial assumption was that any set of criteria for identifying moral exemplars within American society should reflect the consensual core of our culture's morality: the pursuit of truth, the avoidance of harm, the upholding of responsibilities and obligations, the concern for human welfare, the respect for legitimate authority and human rights, the spirit of justice or fairness, and so on. Criteria deriving from such ideals would not necessarily confine us to people whom we just happen to admire; nor would they necessarily lead us to the best-loved people in the United States today. Rather, the criteria should lead us to people whose lives have exemplified a widely endorsable set of moral standards.

Let us consider now what we mean by the term *moral exemplar,* in contrast with how others have used the phrase. Some philosophers, for example, John Rawls, have defined a moral exemplar as a person whose actions exemplify any putative system of morality, whether admirable or not.[2] The term, as Rawls uses it, is morally neutral. Other philosophers have used moral exemplar to designate those who have shown exemplary virtue in the sense of *ideal* moral living.[3] Our use of the term is different than either of these. In calling someone a moral exemplar, we mean to imply that the individual exemplifies some widely shared ideas of what it means to be a highly moral person (and we do not mean in a neutral sense), but not that the individual is morally perfect or ideal. We were not seeking the occasional saint who lives a pure and unblemished existence, however much we might revere such a person. Rather, we wished to understand the more common life stories of highly dedicated persons who, through their sustained commitment and talents, labor to make the world a better place. Our interest was in people who have shown long-standing commitment to moral purposes, thus exemplifying good principles and virtues. We did not seek or expect perfection from our moral exemplars.

In order to identify the individuals that we would study, we worked with a group of twenty-two "nominators," one at a time, to define criteria and suggest people who fit the criteria. Because we wanted to be sure that the criteria reflected a broad view of morality, we chose a nominator group that was diverse in its political ideology, religious beliefs, and sociocultural background. Because articulating and implementing criteria for the purpose of making nominations required some facility with moral reflection, we decided to work with nominators who had experience engaging in systematic thinking about morality.

Why use a group of "expert nominators" instead of simply sampling the public at large for its choice of moral heroes? Most people, of course, have ideas about moral goodness and can readily provide examples of what they consider to be good people. However, most people do not distinguish carefully between the characteristics they like and admire and those they consider essential to being a good person. People who have not had a great deal of experience doing so cannot be expected to explain clearly the assumptions underlying their moral judgments or to make careful distinctions and define their terms precisely. In contrast, people who reflect systematically about moral ideas as part of their professions—theologians, philosophers, historians, social commentators, scholars of ethics and morality—engage in precisely these efforts daily.

Our decision to rely on expert nominators rather than laypersons, therefore, reflected our desire to solicit the opinions of people who have already thought long and carefully about the definition and nature of morality. We expected that they would be able to identify definitional and interpretive problems in our tentative, initial set of criteria. They would be careful to communicate any disagreements that they might have with our preconceptions. Most importantly, they would explain fully the reasons and logic behind their selections.

Although a highly select group professionally, the individuals in the nominating group were diverse in other ways, including both race and gender. The group included people: with both liberal and conservative political beliefs, with a wide variety of religious beliefs and affiliations, and from varied geographic locations across the United States. (We stayed mostly within U.S. borders because we wished to focus our study on American moral exemplars.) By ensuring that the nominating group was diverse in ideology and background, we hoped to limit the biases inherent in any nominating process and to cast a broader net than our own expertise would make possible.

Our goal in working with the nominators was to develop a general definition of a moral exemplar that would include morally committed people while excluding fanatics, hypocrites, and self-promoting careerists. Our purpose was not to identify the *best* set of moral exemplars in the country, but to identify a group of living people that we could be confident met a set of clear and relatively impartial criteria for a morally outstanding life.

We interviewed each of the twenty-two nominators individually, presenting them with a preliminary list of criteria that we believed offered a tentative basis for identifying moral exemplars. The nominators were given the opportunity to modify our criteria, to add new ones, and delete those with which they disagreed. During the remainder of the interview, nominators were asked to suggest and describe living people who fit the revised criteria and to comment on the appropriateness of exemplars suggested by other nominators.

Our preliminary list of criteria (see Appendix A) established a satisfactory initial framework for the nominators. All twenty-two nominators endorsed at least some part of the preliminary list, and all were willing to suggest revisions or additions that would make the list acceptable to them. There was some variation in these suggestions but not as much as one might expect, especially considering the diverse backgrounds, disciplines, and ideologies they represented.

In fact, the degree of consensus that we found in this diverse group was striking. We encountered a solid core of shared belief about what constitutes morality as well as what kinds of lives exemplify it. Even across an ideologically divided group, there were some basic elements in the definition of the highly moral person with which all could agree.

Once the nominators' suggestions had been incorporated, a final set of criteria could be established. The resulting five criteria were used to determine those people who were moral exemplars. Each of those chosen demonstrated all of the following characteristics:

1. a sustained commitment to moral ideals or principles that include a generalized respect for humanity; or a sustained evidence of moral virtue
2. a disposition to act in accord with one's moral ideals or principles, implying also a consistency between one's actions and intentions and between the means and ends of one's actions
3. a willingness to risk one's self-interest for the sake of one's moral values
4. a tendency to be inspiring to others and thereby to move them to moral action
5. a sense of realistic humility about one's own importance relative to the world at large, implying a relative lack of concern for one's own ego

In order to understand these criteria better, let us consider each more closely. Criterion 1 centers around the notion of *sustained* commitment or virtue. This distinguishes people who have shown continued moral activity over long periods of time from those who have performed isolated heroic acts. Of course, heroes who risk their lives to save others on a single occasion are praiseworthy exemplars of a sort, but not necessarily the same as those who have pursued long-term moral commitments over decades of dedicated work. We were interested in the special developmental processes that account for sustained commitment rather than the single noble act.

Another key element in the first criterion is its specification that exemplars' principles reflect *a generalized respect for humanity rather than a discriminatory regard for particular groups at the expense of others.* Not just any principle counts as a moral one: Principles that cause harm or injustice to some people are excluded. The wording of the first criterion implies that moral principles must be compatible with concerns for people in general. This aspect of criterion 1 is designed to weed out fanatics who are passionately dedicated to immoral goals.

Criterion 2 focuses on consistencies of other sorts: between principles and conduct; between actions and intentions; and, most importantly, between means and ends. Not only do moral exemplars hold noble moral ideals, but they also act on them *in a manner that reflects the same values as their ultimate purposes.* This eliminates those who espouse high ideals but rarely do anything about them. It also eliminates those who carry out ostensibly noble actions for ignoble reasons, and it eliminates those who resort to violent or corrupt tactics in pursuit of their goals. The last qualification—the means/ends issue—is especially important. The world is full of people who are ostensibly dedicated to noble causes but do more harm than good because of the destructive means they employ. Moral exemplars, in contrast with tyrants or fanatics, are rigorously principled about their methods as well as their objectives.

Criterion 3 indicates that moral exemplars are willing to risk their self-interest for the sake of their moral values. This does not require a moral exemplar to be a martyr. In any particular life, the degree of risk or cost attached to the pursuit of moral goals may be minimal or very great, depending upon one's life circumstances. Many moral exemplars bear relatively little personal risk during their years of dedication. In fact, many report rewards that far outweigh the costs. Many others, of course, have been called upon to make great personal sacrifices, although they often do so without even perceiving them as hardships.

Criterion 3 does *not* mean that moral exemplars neglect their own welfare. Rather, it means that, when self-interest and morality collide, a moral exemplar will be steadfast. Should a personal sacrifice become necessary, the exemplar will be undeterred by economic risks, physical hardship or danger, or the loss of time and family satisfactions. This criterion is designed to eliminate those who live socially responsible lives but for whom moral commitments occupy peripheral rather than central positions in their affairs. It should also eliminate those who use ostensibly moral pursuits mainly to advance their careers. Such persons typically compromise on their moral concerns when these begin to impede their chance of personal success. For moral exemplars, the moral concern is primary and, should the need arise, their personal advancement is readily sacrificed.

Criterion 4 implies that moral exemplars will have some salutary influence on those around them. Morality is by nature a socially embedded phenomenon: One does not perform moral acts in isolation. Through processes of observation, communication, and social influence, moral exemplars serve as sources of inspiration, at least for people who share their fundamental values. This may happen on a small scale—within a family, perhaps, or across a community of friends and coworkers—or on a worldwide scale, as in the case of international spiritual leaders. Whether the influence is local or global, it is an inevitable legacy of the exemplars' relations with society. In our study, we were interested in the dynamics of this influence and the personal qualities that facilitate it. We were not concerned about the scale of the influence: For criterion 4, the exemplar's inspirational power may have affected few or many.

Criterion 5 points to the sense of perspective moral exemplars have about their own contributions. Even the most powerful and effective world leader has limited opportunity to accomplish all that he or she aims for. Some realize this, others do not. Moral exemplars have some humility about their own importance in the world. They maintain a sense of perspective about their goals and their ability to accomplish them. Moreover, morally exemplary people are dedicated to missions, values, or persons beyond their own self-aggrandizement (see criterion 1). They are not taken, therefore, by the majesty of their own power or the sweep of their own influence. They are oriented to the task at hand and realistic about their expectations for success. Criterion

5 does not imply that exemplars show false modesty about their often impressive achievements. But it does rule out those who are egotistically directed, who glory unduly in their own honors, or who set themselves above "less worthy" members of society. Moral exemplars may well express pride in their own good deeds, but they do not look down contemptuously at those who have accomplished less.

One of the nominators described this characteristic as a "cosmic humility": "Some of the philosophical literature would call that 'wisdom.' There is a modern equivalent that would say 'perspective.' The old term is really humility. It's a basic humility . . . it's a kind of sense of one's own limitations. Perhaps it has to do with a sense of human limitations, human boundedness, human finitude . . . a sense of the limitations of human wisdom and human knowledge."

The final set of five criteria does not exactly constitute a scientific "operational definition" of moral exemplariness. They are, instead, somewhat indeterminate guidelines for choice. We had to rely on the nominators' judgments of whether the people being nominated typically acted out of intentions consistent with their moral goals and showed a consistency between moral means and ends. In addition, the criteria are intentionally quite general. Taken as a whole, they rule out morally undistinguished and morally objectionable persons. But there is a broad range of morally exceptional people who match the guidelines. The criteria allow considerable latitude concerning the kinds of moral causes that will engage a moral exemplar. They also leave unspecified the precise nature of the principles or virtues that a moral exemplar can personify—although they do rule out antihumanitarian, corrupt, or self-aggrandizing people. Using the criteria, one can generate a diversity of clear cases. It is also possible to imagine numerous marginal or ambiguous cases. For the purposes of our study, we urged our nominators to suggest individuals who would match all the criteria with a high degree of certainty and to describe those people's lives fully enough to make clear why they qualify.

After offering us their suggestions about the criteria, the nominators proposed individuals who, in their opinion, were a good fit with the entire set. In all, they nominated eighty-four people. Not surprisingly, these eighty-four nominees constituted a highly diverse group. On the surface, they had little in common beyond their match with the five selection criteria. They varied greatly in occupation, income, gender, race, ethnicity, religion, education, political orientation, moral mission, and public visibility.

Some of the nominees were impossible to locate, because the nominators did not know how to reach them and we were unable to obtain their addresses from other sources. We wrote to the remaining people, inviting them to take part in the study. Twenty-eight people agreed to be interviewed.[4] Of these, one died before the interview was conducted and three found it impossible to find time for the interviews and so were dropped from the study. One other, a prominent public figure, asked to leave the study partway through; he had become concerned that sensitive details of his life could not be disguised sufficiently. The final group consisted of twenty-three men and women who were willing to take part in our extensive personal interview process.

The final group was no different in composition from the original nominee group of eighty-four. The "self-selection" did not alter the sample's makeup in any noticeable way in regard to age, race, education, or area of contribution. Educationally, the final group ranged from completion of eighth grade to M.D.s, Ph.D.s, and law degrees. In terms of occupation, the group included religious leaders (a Catholic priest, a Buddhist monk, a Catholic bishop, a Protestant minister), businessmen (the founder of a giant corporation, a wealthy entrepreneur), physicians, teachers, charity workers, an innkeeper, a journalist, lawyers, heads of nonprofit institutions, and leaders of social movements. Ages ranged from thirty-five to eighty-six, with most of the group being at least in their late sixties. The group included ten men and thirteen women; seventeen whites (of various ethnic backgrounds), four African-Americans, and two Latinas. Although about a third of the group have operated on the national level, the majority were known primarily in their local communities. The exemplars with high degrees of national visibility did not differ from those known locally on any of the dimensions that characterized the sample as a whole.

The twenty-three exemplars who participated in the study have made important contributions in the areas of civil rights, civil liberties, the fight against poverty, medical care, medical ethics, education, business ethics, philanthropy, journalism, the environment, peace, and religious freedom. The largest number concerned themselves with poverty, focusing on food, housing, clothing, health, and other issues. Among those dealing with poverty, there was a range of views about how to remedy poverty. Some felt that the American economic system is inherently unjust and must be radically changed, whereas others felt that the system is fundamentally sound but that poor people must be drawn in for fuller participation. Some of the antipoverty workers

came from poor backgrounds themselves, while others had affluent
upbringings. The exemplars' personal histories were not related to
their perspectives on poverty in any obvious way. Within each of the
other areas of contribution, we also saw a diversity of views and little
obvious relationship between the nature of the exemplars' views and
their backgrounds.

Table 2–1 indicates the occupations, religious affiliations (if any),
geographical locations, ages, and moral missions of the twenty-three
exemplars. Some of this information is presented in general terms, and
pseudonyms are used for the eighteen exemplars not focused on in
depth. This reflects our wish to preserve the anonymity of all exemplars except the five whom we studied in greater detail and discuss in
chapters of their own.[5]

We asked five of the exemplars to spend additional time with us
so that we could explore their lives in greater depth. The five people
chosen for this treatment possessed the same diversity of educational,
religious, ethnic, and occupational backgrounds as the sample as a
whole. Although all five are Christian, they hold religious beliefs that
range from fundamentalist Pentacostal to Quaker to secular humanist.
Their political views vary from conservative (Valadez), to moderate
(Brand, Waddles), to liberal (Coleman, Durr) in social and economic
matters. Educationally, the five include two who did not complete
high school, one with some college, one with a college degree, and
one with a Ph.D. The occupations of the five include Christian ministry, charity, entrepreneurial business, innkeeping, and civil rights advocacy. The ages of these five men and women range from sixty-eight
to eighty-six, overlapping with the predominant age range of the
larger sample. These five were chosen for in-depth treatment in part
because they were among the twelve or so who gave us full permission
to use their names and all the information we had about them.

All twenty-three exemplars participated in an initial round of interviews that focused on key personal and moral events in their lives.
We conducted the interviews ourselves, asking them questions about
their goals, values, world views, and life assumptions. We asked them
about their life histories, and especially about the events, relationships,
and experiences they saw as having been influential in shaping their
lives. We focused especially on the question of how they had developed their moral commitment and how they had sustained it in the
face of inevitable difficulties. Throughout the interviews, we solicited
the exemplars' own understanding of their lives and work. We probed
for their own explanations for the choices they had made as well as

Table 2.1

Name	Age*	Occupation	Religion	Geographical Location	Mission	Sex	Education
Bowles	72 (1916)	Religious educator	Baptist	Mid-Atlantic	Poverty	F	Ph.D.
Brand	67 (1923)	Businessman	Presbyterian	South	Poverty	M	B.A.
Burchell	49 (1938)	Physician	Nonsectarian	Mid-Atlantic	Peace, environment	F	M.D.
Coleman	68 (1921)	Economist, college and foundation president	Quaker	New England	Education, philan-thropy	M	Ph.D.
Coll	48 (1941)	Volunteer	Catholic	Southwest	Sanctuary movement	F	High school GED
Crandall	40 (1947)	Lawyer	None	South	Civil liberties	F	B.A. law
Davis	58 (1928)	Organizer	Christian	West	Poverty	F	High school
Donaldson	68 (1918)	Catholic bishop	Catholic	New England	Poverty, alcoholism	M	M.S.W.
Drake	54 (1934)	University professor	Catholic	Mid-Atlantic	Religious freedom, education	M	Ph.D.
Durr	86 (1903)	Volunteer, legal secretary	Protestant	South	Civil rights	F	Some college
Ehrlich	46 (1943)	Organizer	Catholic	New England	Poverty	F	B.A.
Goldberg	35 (1953)	Physician	Jewish	Mid-Atlantic	Health care, poverty	M	M.D.

(continued)

Table 2.1
(Continued)

Name	Age*	Occupation	Religion	Geographical Location	Mission	Sex	Education
Green	84 (1904)	Businessman	Quaker	Mid-Atlantic	Business ethics	M	B.Sc.
Hardie	57 (1929)	Teacher, journalist	Episcopal	Midwest	Foster care, journalism	F	B.A.
Hayes	40 (1948)	Farmer	Buddhist	West	Environment	F	B.A.
Henry	86 (1901)	University professor	Quaker	Mid-Atlantic	Peace	M	Ph.D.
Johnson	82 (1905)	Head of center for ill children	Baptist	Mid-Atlantic	Care of ill children	F	High school
Linsky	75 (1913)	Businessman, statesman	Jewish	Mid-Atlantic	Business ethics, peace, and international relations	M	Law
McCrea	62 (1927)	Organizer	Catholic	New England	Poverty	F	B.A.
Stinson	67 (1921)	Physician	Catholic	New England	Medical ethics	M	M.D.
Thomas	46 (1940)	Physician	Methodist	Midwest	Medical ethics	M	M.D.
Valadez	66 (1925)	Missionary	Assembly of God	Southwest	Poverty	F	10th grade
Waddles	76 (1912)	Missionary	Pentecostal	Midwest	Poverty	F	8th grade

*Age at time of interview

for their own interpretations of their critical life experiences. We wanted to know how they viewed their commitment to the enormous social problems they had taken on and what meaning they had given to the challenges and obstacles they encountered.

Our first-round interview schedule is presented in Appendix B. During the actual interviews, we added to these basic questions numerous probes, challenges, countersuggestions, and other follow-ups. In this manner, the interview procedure was grounded in a standardized list of questions that all exemplars were asked, but it was always supplemented by a more individualized exploration of the particular issues surrounding the moral commitment of each.

With the five people about whom we wrote full chapters, we conducted at least one further interview session on a later occasion. At the second session, we conducted a more extensive personal interview designed to fill in the gaps in our understanding of the exemplar's life. We then gave the exemplars our written accounts of their stories, complete with our interpretations about how they had formed and sustained their moral commitments. We discussed these interpretations with them and probed for any discrepancies between our interpretations of their lives and their own.

CHAPTER 3

Suzie Valadez
"Queen of the Dump"

The hills surrounding Ciudad Juarez look especially bleak on a frigid January day. The great garbage dump for Juarez (or *socosema*, as it is known locally) is placed among the hills, and a number of ragged people regularly forage there for things that the cityfolk below have thrown away. Those without homes camp out on the fringes of the dump; others have small, one-room houses full of children but with no running water, heat, or refrigeration.

One of the drearier places in this bleak landscape is a low, two-room schoolhouse with paper-thin walls. The school serves about fifty of the neighborhood children. On a chilly, windswept day in January it might as well be a one-room schoolhouse. All fifty children and both teachers are huddled together in the only room with a heater—an old wood stove running precariously low on fuel.

School staples—chalk, books, paper, and pencils—are also in short supply. The parents in the community are responsible for making sure there is wood for heating the school and practically everything else besides the building, desks, and teachers. There are no school lunches. The teachers say that few of the children arrive with good breakfasts in their stomachs. The families are simply too poor to provide even the basic necessities for the children and their school.

But there is a bright spot in the children's day. Late in the morning, a gray-haired bundle of energy named Suzie Valadez appears on the scene. She bustles into the room with two assistants, laden with sandwiches and sweaters. Immediately, her smile and greetings light up the children's faces. She and her assistants pass out the food and clothing. Before the children are allowed to dig into their lunches, Suzie becomes serious and asks for their attention. All eyes turn respectfully to her as she leads the group in a prayer of thanks for the Lord's gifts.

This is a day much like any other for Suzie Valadez. Early in the morning she and her assistants in El Paso, Texas, make hundreds of sandwiches from food donated by a local supermarket chain. Then they pack several boxes with the sandwiches, other food, and an assortment of used clothing. After loading the boxes into Suzie's rickety van, the small group makes the bumpy trip across the Rio Grande, through the old streets of the Mexican city, and up into the hills near the dump.

Their first stop is the dump itself, a windswept, dusty stretch of barren hills. As soon as the van pulls in, cries of welcome arise from little bands of men and families who have been roaming the hills in search of anything that could sustain their meager existence. Suzie and her assistants pass out food and clothing, carefully doling out the supplies so they can reach as many people as possible. With each donation Suzie passes along a word of hope, a greeting, a smile of encouragement. She does not blanch at approaching the toughest of the lot, a bedraggled contingent of desperate-looking men. Her assistants say that there are many days when Suzie must make the trek alone. She doesn't fear for her safety, even among the most hardened outcasts in the most isolated situations.

When she has given out all the food and supplies, Suzie gets back in her van and moves on to the school. After that, she visits a new medical building for which she had raised funds and her son Danny had volunteered his services as a professional builder. This is the third medical facility Suzie has provided for the *socosema* community: the first was a small mobile van, the second a more permanent nurse's station, and now, finally, the crowning achievement, a comprehensive medical clinic, complete with doctors and medicine. In a coordinated effort, Suzie also brought nutritional and health education to the *socosema* families. Along her journey, Suzie greets the people warmly. Old and young alike seem cheered by her good words, the sparkle in her eyes, her quick, bright smile.

At the end of the morning, Suzie and her assistants head back to El Paso. The van is stopped at the border by a severe-looking young customs officer—perhaps looking for drugs, perhaps for illegal immigrants. However, before the old van is dismantled (like the one in front of it), a more senior border officer begins talking to Suzie. After a few words, the senior officer waves the van on, saying, "It's no good interfering with God's work." One of the assistants comments that this is the kind of treatment Suzie gets now that her work has become known. Earlier it was different, and crossing the border was a challenge to be negotiated skillfully.

Hoping that it won't break down, Suzie coaxes the antique van along as it chugs its way back to the small storefront office that serves as headquarters for her mission. She is barely back before it is time to rush off to a fund-raising meeting with the mayor.

In all, Suzie will put in a fourteen-hour day. This is no different from the day before or the day after. At the age of sixty-six, she shows not a trace of exhaustion at the fast-paced life she leads. Nor does she express any irritation at her material discomforts or humble surroundings; nor any worry about the obvious hazards of her trips through the squalor of urban Juarez up to the desolate *socosema* hills. Through it all, she shows only a love of life, a love of God, and a tangibly shining presence.

Suzie Valadez is known in south Texas as the "Queen of the Dump." She came by this title after years spent feeding, clothing, and providing medical care to thousands of poor Mexicans living in the surrounds of the huge Ciudad Juarez garbage dump. Her operation is run through Christ for Mexico Missions, a charitable religious organization she started in 1963 and now manages along with three of her four children.

The purpose of Christ for Mexico Missions is to serve the people of Mexico, especially the children. "We minister the word and we clothe them, we feed them physically, and help them with their families, and we encourage them, you know, that they're not by themselves." The mission feeds and clothes thousands of people a year. Its health clinics offer free medical care, pharmaceuticals, and vitamins; and plans for a sparkling new orphanage are under way.

Because the people live in terribly unsanitary conditions with little knowledge of modern health practices and no access to physicians, the mission's medical services are critically important to their welfare. As Suzie describes, "You find out about dysentery in the summer, you find out about sickness because of the flies. There's thousands of flies. Sometimes you cannot even talk because of the flies. Sometimes the people find tortillas, they find vegetables, they take them home, they wash them and they eat them. That's all they have."

In addition to teaching the people hygiene and other basic health practices, Sister Suzie and her missionaries "try to show the children that there's a better life than they're living now." Crime, alcoholism, and drug abuse are rampant in the areas served by the mission. Suzie's goals are to give the people hope, to help them finish school, find jobs, keep their families intact, and escape drug addiction and alcoholism. During the twenty-eight years that she has worked in Juarez, she has followed a generation of children from age three or four through early adulthood, and she has tirelessly repeated her message of wholesome living to them. Observers remark that she has made a marked difference in their lives.

The mission also supports the community public schools in many essential ways. Even public schools in Juarez require the payment of fees—in amounts that seem nominal to middle-class people but are beyond the reach of families who need to scrounge for their very survival. The mission helps provide these fees for the families of the dump. It also provides other urgent material aid. Without Suzie's daily sandwiches, the children of this community would have no lunch—and many go to school with little, if any, breakfast.

As important as the food and clothes Suzie gives to the poor is the message of God's love she offers them. "The most important thing is telling them that they're not alone. See, when I started this work here in Mexico, their faces were so hard, you know, because of their problems, circumstances they had, and there was no help for them. And so when I came in I told them that there was somebody that really loved them, and that was Jesus, and that they were not by themselves. And they didn't know that Jesus was in that place; it's horrible, you know. So this is why we told them that they weren't all by themselves, just to be encouraged, that there was somebody that was going to send help. And this is how we got working with them." She was giving them a belief in their own value as precious children of God, a sense of hope, and a feeling that someone cares and will help. Even those who may doubt the theological doctrine behind Suzie's message must acknowledge the literal truth of it. She was telling the people that someone loved them, that they were not alone, and that someone was going to help. Suzie meant to suggest that the "someone" was Jesus. Many of the people seem to accept this message, but even those who do not can see another "someone" in the form of Suzie herself.

Over the twenty-eight years since she established the mission, Suzie Valadez has accomplished a tremendous amount. As a single individual, she has been able to develop and maintain an organization that makes a world of difference in the lives of thousands of people. With no training or prior experience, she took on the monumental task of dealing with these desperately poor people—collecting the food, medicine, and clothes herself; taking these supplies across the border into Mexico; and finding her way alone or with one or two volunteer helpers to the worst areas of Juarez where she personally gives out what she has collected. In doing all this she has confronted a seemingly bottomless pit of need, but she does not become discouraged or give up, and she has stuck with her exhausting task for almost thirty years now. She doesn't seem to worry that what she does, as impressive as it is, can never be more than a drop in the bucket of the overwhelming poverty of Mexico.

Even more incredible is the fact that when Suzie moved from California to Texas in order to start the mission she was a single mother of four young children with no money at all, not even a car, a tenth-grade education, only slight knowledge of Spanish, and almost no work experience. She brought her four children with her to El Paso and had to find ways to provide for them while she was also fully devoting herself to the missionary work.

Accomplishing all this would in itself be more than most people could handle. But Suzie was able to raise her children to be well-functioning adults even though they had very little materially throughout their childhoods.

What was it that allowed Suzie to begin with nothing yet accomplish so much? The answer to this includes all of the important elements we have identified in our exemplars, but most salient in Suzie's case is her certainty. Once she decided that she was called to missionary work, it took her only a few weeks to pack up her family and move to Texas. Then, too, she was not deterred by the harsh conditions she faced in El Paso, her difficulty in finding a job, the fact that she was not eligible for public aid to help feed her children. Through all this she stuck to her purpose. As the mission developed, she maintained a steadfast commitment, never having enough money or supplies but always with plenty of energy to go out and raise money and gather what she needed. Although many of the places she went were dangerous and she often went alone, she set aside any feelings of fear and eventually became immune to them.

Yet the certainty of Suzie's beliefs and the rewards that she found in her work have not always shielded her from the temptation to become discouraged and to give up the work. Like other moral leaders, Suzie set aside her own pressing needs and those of her family as she directed most of her attention toward helping others. This is not a trivial issue. Suzie's children were required to make real sacrifices in the interests of their mother's cause, as were the children of another exemplar, Virginia Durr, a civil rights activist. The Valadez children grew up with little beyond the bare necessities. It was not unusual for Suzie to give away her children's shoes if she saw a Mexican child with bare feet. For Suzie, as for others, the conflict between her concern for her own children and the social cause to which she had dedicated her life was sometimes very painful. Suzie talks about many moments of serious doubt when she found herself depriving her children of things they needed:

> And a lot of times I cried because I said, ''Father, what do I have to do?'' My $35 that I got for working at the hospital I couldn't spend more of it on my children because it was going for the orphans. But a lot of times I cried. A lot of times I thought I was in the wrong field. And I used to get away from the house and away from my kids and I used to ask the Lord ''Am I in the right place? Is this where you send me?'' Because if I didn't have that vision I would have gone back because of what I was going

through. But now my faith is stronger. See, at that time when
I started it was weak. I was just going by that vision.

Still, the fact remains that during these very difficult times and in
the face of the challenges that followed, Suzie did not go back to
California. In fact, in spite of her anguish, she maintained a strong
conviction that she *had* to help the poor. Her commitment may at
times have come into conflict with other things she felt she had to
do, but the mission did not seem to be an optional activity that could
be dropped if the cost was too great. This is the sense of certainty and
conviction that we have seen in all our moral leaders. It does not mean
that there is never conflict. It certainly does not mean that there is
never anguish. But in the midst of the conflict and anguish a basic
conviction remains, a conviction that makes it impossible to turn one's
back on the problem.

In response to our question about moral courage, Suzie, like all
the others, denied its relevance while admitting that in the early days
of her work she often felt afraid. The risks that she confronted during
her trips to the slums, the prisons, and the dump were too obvious
to escape even her optimistic vision. She went ahead with her trips in
spite of her fear, and she attributed this more to her faith than to
courage: "Well, I guess it did take courage, but at the same time
inside of me I didn't know how I was doing it or why, but I know
the Holy Spirit was leading me." It was her feeling of certainty that
she was answering the Lord's call, and that she had to do it, that
carried her through. Later, she stopped feeling afraid entirely, and
with good reason. As the poor of Juarez came to know her and know
about her, she felt protected by the trust that existed between them
and her.

In Suzie's case, the key to understanding certainty is her faith in
Jesus Christ and her conviction that she was "reborn" in adulthood
by her conversion to the fundamentalist Assembly of God branch of
Pentecostal Christianity. Moral certainty need not be religiously based,
as we shall see in Virginia Durr (Chapter 5) and others. But Suzie
Valadez's moral certainty is inextricably linked to her strong religious
belief. She sees her work as a religious calling: "The Lord put that
spirit in me to be, to have mercy with the needy who don't have
nothing. . . . So once you know Jesus as your personal savior, you
are stronger, because He's the only one that gives you the strength,
that gives you the wisdom, that gives you the guidance. He is the
only one." She sees her religious conversion as the origin of her mis-

sionary work. She believes that it is also the source of her stamina
over the difficult years, and that it is the means by which she has been
able to accomplish her work. Her sense of personal responsibility for
the poor of Mexico also derives directly from this religious belief. The
sense that she has been called by God to serve the people of Mexico
is the basis of her unwavering certainty about what she is doing. As
she puts it, "I didn't know how I was doing it or why, but I know
the Holy Spirit was leading me, saying, 'You *have* to help them, you
have to help them.'"

Suzie believes that, beyond providing the inspiration for her work,
God also provides the means through which the work is accomplished.
If materials are needed with which to build a mission, if funds are
needed with which to buy food and medicine, Suzie's first approach
to solving the problem is to pray for God's help. "Prayer, prayer—
it's the only way I can do it because I cannot knock on doors, but
I'm sure that the Lord can do it. He knows everybody and I know
that through him it has to be, because He is my source. This is faith
work." Any successes Suzie has she attributes to God's grace. "So
this is how we minister the word, because it's not of ourselves. The
Lord has permitted all this for their service" or "I know that everything is because of the Lord."

Her reliance on God as the source of everything does not mean
that she waits passively for solutions to the problems she encounters.
On the contrary, she is tremendously resourceful as she attempts to
deal with each new challenge as it arises. Working on her own with
no financial resources, she had to figure out how to feed hundreds of
children, how to take medications past immigration authorities into
Mexico, and how to bury the children who died despite her efforts.
"And so after that year of '63, I made twelve coffins. I used to make
them. I had twelve babies dead. . . . I was not used to that. So what
happened, I made my own coffins from cardboard or thin plywood
and I covered them with contact paper. And you see me going to the
cemetery in a van that I borrowed."

It was her abiding faith that God would provide for her and her
family that allowed her to give so much to others, trusting that she
and her children would be all right. "When the Lord called me, when
he gave me that vision, he told me that if I dedicated my life to serving
He would take care of my children. And He has. So I have a beautiful,
beautiful family and I thank the Lord for it." Although during their
childhood Suzie's children had ambivalent feelings about their mother's overriding dedication to the mission, they were left with no bit-

terness and as adults have joined their mother in her work. Her son Danny has been most explicit about this, calling his mother's devotion a "great gift" that more than compensated for his materially humble childhood.

Closely tied with Suzie's religious faith are the personal qualities that most vividly represent her approach to life. These are compassion, love, and a sense of the holy preciousness of all people. It is clear from her recollections that her love for children and her generous spirit predate her religious conversion, but she prefers to discuss their meaning in the context of her current religious beliefs. "These are precious people. But I love everybody, I mean love. The Lord has given me a love for these people that I myself don't understand." We will discuss later the social process through which the experiences of helping the children of Juarez serve to deepen Suzie's love for them.

Suzie's generosity, which was so evident even at the time that she was barely able to feed her own children, is very much like the ever-present concern for others that we will see later in Charleszetta Waddles (Chapter 8). As Mother Waddles said, "You're never too poor to help someone else," and this was exactly Suzie's attitude. Neither of them felt a need to attend to their own security before helping others, because they believed that God would provide for them and their children. Both women also attribute their generosity to a love of people and an "openheartedness" that had been with them as long as they could remember. This lifelong love of people is an example of a personality characteristic that is shaped and enhanced through a process that we will discuss in Chapter 7 as interactional continuity. Briefly, we argue that when people behave toward others in generous and friendly ways, this often calls forth from the people with whom they are interacting behaviors that further reinforce the initial gregarious tendency. This notable ability to engage with people has served both Suzie Valadez and Mother Waddles well in the work they do. As Suzie puts it, "And so, when I had the calling with the children, I started going through the neighborhood and asking for clothing and groceries and things like this. And I went to the produce, to the Piggly Wiggly, I remember talking to the manager. And he says, 'Why do you want this produce?' I said, 'We have a lot of people there that don't have anything to eat.' And he would give me a lot of produce. He would throw in something good. And so this is where my personality really has been, how should I say it, a wonderful, wonderful thing because it is through the Lord."

Suzie's love for people leads her not only to help the poor but to do so with unmitigated joy. The constancy of Suzie's buoyant attitude is rare among those who regularly confront the grimier sides of human life.[1] But it is not rare among the moral leaders chronicled in this book. As we shall discuss in Chapter 10, one of the striking things that virtually all have in common is their positive spirit in the face of severe challenge. We believe that this is intimately connected with the inspirational leadership they exert. It also gives them considerable staying power.

A stubbornly positive attitude in the face of hardship can function like a Midas touch, turning lead into gold. Difficulties and challenges can become their own reward. Like the other moral leaders in our study, Suzie loves her work and talks often of the joys it brings. Of course, Suzie has also known unhappiness. She describes herself as having been especially joyful as a young child, but she has also suffered her share of life's pain: the loss of her sister and the abandonment by her husband, not to mention the misery that she witnesses in her daily rounds. In particular, during the difficult days just before and after her move to El Paso, Suzie remembers herself on the edge of despair. Yet she was determined to see the potential for doing good even in the darkest situation. This determination enabled Suzie to muster a positive emotional response and create a constructive solution even when things were at their bleakest. It made possible the resourcefulness and stamina that gave her tools to overcome the obstacles that she faced.

Such an orientation can be critical for those making a long-term effort against poverty. Otherwise, the magnitude of the problem relative to what any one person can accomplish may seem too forbidding. Suzie copes with her awareness of this inescapable reality by taking pleasure in the help that she can give to the children she gets to know. She does not focus on the many thousands who fall outside her capacity to help.

This positive attitude is also critical in dealing with the unpleasant fact that many of the poor do not know how to say thank-you. Nor do they normally respond to charity in storybook fashion, straightening out their lives and becoming totally self-sufficient. As Mother Waddles told us, to be able to do this kind of work you must be able to "forgive seventy times seventy."

This positive attitude in Suzie's case derives from the same religious source as her sense of certainty, although the two are not the same. Certainty refers to an unwavering conviction and sense of responsibility. Positive attitude refers to the ability to take joy in one's life and work and to make the best of whatever happens. Although for many people they may occur together, they can be distinguished as two different qualities. In a few of our exemplars we saw a great deal of moral certainty but little of the joyful, positive approach to life that characterizes Suzie Valadez. For example, Aline Burchell, an influential peace activist whom we discuss in Chapter 10, was pessimistic and angry but very sure of both her beliefs and her responsibility. Her moral conviction was unwavering but her attitude was negative. None of our exemplars lacked moral certainty, so we cannot tell from this group whether one can have a strong positive attitude without a sense of certainty. It seems plausible, though, that some people might take joy in life and be optimistic and yet lack a strong sense of responsibility or moral conviction.

In seeking an explanation of Suzie's deep conviction, love for people, and joyful attitude, we must look to the continuities in her character and to the transformations she has undergone. The most important transformation, of course, is the religious conversion that led to and sustained her call to missionary work.

Suzie began life in very modest material circumstances but within a strong family that provided the context within which she developed the religious convictions and love for people that form the basis of her missionary work. Her mother, Beatriz Azucena Flores, was born in Mexico. Her father, Pablo Flores, was born in Texas, his parents having moved there from Mexico before he was born. By the time Suzie came along, the Flores family had become assimilated to their new home and Suzie grew up speaking English, learning Spanish only after she began ministering to the poor of Juarez.

Born in 1925, Suzie Flores was the first of five children. Her mother was a homemaker and her father held various jobs, including selling shoes and running a small grocery store. She describes her family as having been quite poor but very close, loving, and happy. "So we had a beautiful, could you say 'fellowship,' with our parents. I was even thinking this morning, I was thinking about my parents, how they raised us, how they gave us so much love and respect, and being where we are, we owe it to them, besides the Lord of course. And so we were very happy though we didn't have much. I remember I used to sing in school with a very faded dress on. My dress was so faded you couldn't even tell the colors. I don't remember having many dresses, many clothes to change."

Although Suzie was close to both of her parents and to her grandmother, she remembers being especially influenced by her father. She recalls him as someone who was scrupulously honest and always ready to help others, qualities that came to characterize Suzie as well:

> "He used to love to help other people in need. If on his way home he found somebody in need, he would stop to help them. . . . He taught us that. And then the other thing he said, "If you find a penny that's not yours, you just put it in the desk." He was very well known as an honest man. He used to sweep the floors, he used to work on the grounds, and every time he found a penny he put it in the register or the desk and then they would tell him, "This is not ours." He said, "I found it. It is your store, so it's yours." And so he taught us that. He said, "Never take a penny, because from the penny you go to the nickel, from the nickel you go to the dime, you go off and steal what is not yours."

Suzie is proud of her father, remembering him as having been widely respected and trusted within the communities in which they lived. In the small town of Del Rio, Texas, in which Suzie grew up, her father was someone to whom people looked for leadership in a crisis, he was a key figure in the Catholic organization Knights of Columbus, and a grand juror on many occasions. As Suzie put it, "He was very special for the Mexican people there." She felt that she was treated as a special child by her teachers because of their high regard for her father, and even many years after the family had left Del Rio people would say to her when she visited the town, "You mean this is Pablo Flores's daughter?" When the family moved to California, Mr. Flores continued to be a highly respected person within the communities he joined there. Soon after converting to the Assembly of God, for example, he became treasurer of the church and was regarded as a key member of the congregation.

Having grown up in a close family, Suzie was an unusually outgoing and happy child. "I was always joyful, always singing, always doing things, you know. I was very active. I had a lot of friends. I loved people; I loved people regardless of their color, whatever, I love them. And if they don't talk to me, I talk to them. And my husband used to tell me, 'My goodness, if you're by yourself I guess you'd make the stones talk to you.'" This gregariousness and love for people was a key element of Suzie's later engagement with the poor of Mexico.

Suzie was raised until mid-adolescence as a Catholic. Although she attended church regularly, she felt no particularly strong spiritual sense at that time. When she was about fifteen, her younger sister Irma became seriously ill with pneumonia and was not expected to live. Mrs. Flores was extremely distraught and when an acquaintance from the Assembly of God church offered to bring the pastor to pray for Irma, she accepted immediately. The friend flew out of the house and returned with the pastor and several members of the congregation. They prayed for the girl and she recovered, much to the amazement of her doctor. After that incident, Suzie's mother left the Catholic church to join the local congregation of the Assembly of God, "a very, very poor church. It was just like a little room with maybe just ten to fifteen people in it."

Although Irma's immediate health crisis had passed, she required follow-up treatment that was not available in Del Rio, and the family moved to California to be closer to the medical treatment she needed. Because Suzie was afraid to start school in the big-city atmosphere of San José, she dropped out of high school after tenth grade to pack fruit for Del Monte.

Three months after the move to California, Irma became acutely ill again and died. The family was torn by grief and turned to their new religious community for solace. It was at this point that Suzie's parents felt a deep emotional conversion to born-again Christianity. The moment of real emotional and spiritual conversion for Suzie came several years later, though, after her marriage and the birth of her children. It is this later conversion that she refers to when she speaks of being spiritually reborn.

At age twenty-one, Suzie married Jesus Valadez, an electrician. They had four children. While the children were still very young, Jesus started drinking heavily and returned home only sporadically. He finally left for good soon after their last child was born: "He just went away and never returned," leaving Suzie a single mother with four children, very little money, a tenth-grade education, and virtually no job skills.

At age thirty-six, when her youngest child was still an infant and her husband had been gone less than a year, Suzie underwent the spiritual conversion that was to profoundly affect the direction of the rest of her life. The conversion was triggered by an experience that Suzie considered to be a miracle. When her youngest child, Danny, was an infant, he developed serious, chronic asthma. By the age of eight months he was having life-threatening episodes in which he was unable to breathe. At that time, the doctors recommended a radical and painful treatment that frightened Suzie and her parents, so they decided against it. "I fell on my knees by his little bed where he was having a spell. I said, 'Okay, they say there is a God.' So I just fell on my knees and I said, 'Okay God, if there's a God, I want to know right now.' So I lay him there, eight months old, and to this day he has never had another spell. See, I was desperate, I was desperate because I was by myself with the four children . . . so I didn't know what to do. But at that time, I rejoiced."

Following this episode, the minister from the local Assembly of God church visited Suzie. Someone had told him about the miracle and he wanted Suzie to come to his church to talk about it. She did so, and soon thereafter "surrendered her life to Christ and was baptized with the Holy Spirit." "It was a big, big auditorium, and I was there when the minister made an altar call. I went and surrendered myself. If I'm a sinner, I confess all my sins and just give them to you. And the Lord filled me with the Holy Spirit."

Within a few months of joining the church, Suzie was asked to teach Sunday school. In her view, the minister saw her special talent with children before she did. "He knew, I didn't know, but he knew that there was a gift in me with children. And he said, 'You're very good with children. Children love you.'" Suzie was a great success as a Sunday school teacher, and the class grew from eight to thirty-two children in a period of two or three months.

Thus, the church gave Suzie an opportunity to develop her first exceptional talent. While teaching Sunday school in California, Suzie discovered her gift as a minister and proselytizer to young children. She attributes this to an inherent magnetism of personality that goes back to her childhood and is linked to her love for all people, especially children. "With the love of Jesus in me, I feel like a magnet." Later, the children of Juarez were strongly drawn to her, even before she had any food or clothing to give them. Her initial mission work in Juarez grew directly out of this new discovery of her special attraction for children. She began there with a Sunday school, modeled on her recent California work. This soon led her to pursue a far broader range of charitable activities; but however ambitious her program, there always remains a sense of continuity to her original success as a magnetic Sunday school teacher. Even today, when she hands out lunches to hungry Mexican schoolchildren, the prayers come first. Suzie leads and the children join in with rapt attention.

Before Suzie moved from a Sunday school teacher in California to a missionary in Texas and Mexico, however, a life changing incident was to occur. One day, while sitting in church with her Sunday school

WHERE YOU HAVE MADE A DIFFERENCE

Sister Suzie & The Staff Of Christ For Mexico Mission

This is an artist's rendering taken from a greeting card used by the Mission. The subscript of the card is the Mission's message to those who have helped the Mission's work over the years. In Suzie's original vision of the children, they were more ragged, thinner, and barefoot.

class, she saw a vision of a line of dirty, barefoot children carrying a banner saying "Ciudad Juarez." She described the vision to the pastor, and he told her that it meant she had a calling to Mexico. Suzie felt unprepared to move to Mexico with her four small children and resisted the call. The pastor replied by saying, "Don't say no. Let's wait for the confirmation." When Suzie asked him what he meant by confirmation, the pastor replied, "If it's from the Lord, He'll give us some more signs." The first sign was in fact followed by two more, and after the third Suzie decided to go to Mexico. The second sign was a nighttime dream with the same vision. Suzie describes the third and final sign in the following way:

> I was in Sunday school again and somebody came running, running and he said, "Sister Suzie, your house is on fire." All my house totally, totally got burnt—clothing, food, everything. So we didn't have nothing left. So the following day our pastor came in and I said, "Pastor, what does this mean?" He said,

"The Lord wants you to come to Mexico." So I said, "But I don't have any money, I don't have a car." He said, "Well, don't worry, we're going to have a shower for all of you, your family, and we're going to give you clothes." So I said okay. So my daddy said, "You're not going to go alone. The children are very, very small for you to handle them and then to minister whatever you're going to do." He said, "We'll go with you. Your mom and I will go." So he had a station wagon, and he rented a trailer, and maybe three weeks to the day after my house got burned we got ready, and they had some furniture, and so we came, we came to El Paso.

Suzie Valadez arrived in El Paso in June 1963, along with her parents and her four children. The whole troupe stayed together in a $5 per night motel until, some weeks later, they were able to find an affordable apartment with a landlord willing to let so many people live in one small place.

Suzie started her missionary work by teaching Sunday school to a small group of Mexican children in Juarez. As in California, her class quickly grew to many times its original size. Soon she had over three hundred children in her tutelage, and during the summer of 1963 she began to feed and clothe the poorest of them. Thus began the charitable engagements that were to be the centerpiece of her life.

Helen Haste, a British developmental psychologist who has written about moral commitment, believes that the lives of many dedicated people are affected by "triggering events"[2]—sudden, unexpected occurrences that create powerful emotional responses that "trigger" a reexamination of one's life choices. This in turn can lead the way to a new moral perspective and a new sense of social responsibility.

More than any of our other moral leaders, Suzie Valadez seems to have experienced triggering events. Without question, these occurrences changed her life radically and permanently. In fact, Suzie's life, like that of many people of religious faith, has been marked by sudden and dramatic conversion experiences. In such cases, there indeed seem to be triggering events of a watershed nature.

But such events do not happen in isolation. They occur amid a continuing interplay of personal and social forces that can become, in some individuals, agents for progressive moral change. This is the process that we refer to in Chapter 7 and throughout this book as the transformation and elevation of moral goals. It is this process that gives triggering events their moral meaning and their dynamic effect on a person's life. In Suzie's case, as in any transformation of moral goals, there was a necessary component of social influence. For Suzie, this took the form of guidance and support from those close to her in California.

Suzie's immediate source of guidance during the "three calls" episode was her pastor, who urged her to pack her family, move her home, and become a missionary in Mexico. One might even see his advice as a rather aggressive recruitment of Suzie into a missionary role. The Assembly of God denomination is, in fact, known for its evangelistic zeal and is the fastest-growing church among American Latinos. Other people played a part by offering crucial social support for the pastor's advice. Members of the church rallied when the house burned, holding showers at which they donated clothes and other household goods, all of which made possible Suzie's move to Mexico.

Perhaps most critical was the extraordinary cooperation of Suzie's family. Her parents not only supported the move in principle, they offered to go along and join her in her missionary work. In the early years, they provided desperately needed financial help and took care of her children while she worked at the hospital or with the children in Juarez. They later became Suzie's first volunteers in the mission.

Suzie's children, too, went along with remarkably little fuss and did not grow bitter about the time and energy their mother gave to her work. One very important reason for this is that Suzie's parents lived with them and took loving care of them. Danny recalls going with his grandparents to take his mother to her nightshift job at the hospital. "My grandpa was actually my dad, in a sense, because he helped raise us. And my grandmother was very sweet to us and she was my second mother, so none of us had any real resentment. One of the things I do remember was when Mama first started the ministry, we would go drop her off downtown. She used to work at a hospital and I remember that she used to work the graveyard shift. I remember my grandfather, we had a truck with a camper and me and my brother would get in the back and Granddad and we'd just go drop off Mom downtown. And that was just like, it was part of our routine, you know? Time to go drop off Mom, at about eleven o'clock at night."

Later, Suzie's children enthusiastically pitched in with the missionary work. While all four children helped from time to time, it was the youngest, Danny, who made the most lasting commitment. Danny was trained as a builder, learning drafting, masonry, and carpentry, and he had established a career in the business when he felt the pull to join his mother's work full time. Danny had always helped out in his spare time, but increasingly he felt a desire to do more. Like his mother, he had developed a passionate faith in evangelical Christianity. Finally he left his job and dedicated his services wholly to the mission. Danny has applied his training to the mission's activities, directing the construction of the new medical building and planning the design of the orphanage. His work with the mission has not been without financial consequences. The inevitable reduction in income that followed his decision to leave his business has hampered his ability to provide materially for his family. Although Danny believes that his children's lives are invaluably enriched through their association with the mission, he acknowledges that they have felt the sting of material want. Knowing they do without because of their father's noble choice does not at all times still the children's discomfort or complaints.

Suzie's pastor, parents, children, and friends all offered her a network of social support and guidance leading in the same direction: Ciudad Juarez. But neither the triggering events nor the social network that supported it would have meant much if Suzie herself had not been prepared to recognize the moral message and follow its dictates. She was ready for a morally significant life change. The sources of her readiness were both personal and religious. They included her awareness that she was in desperate life circumstances, her intense spiritual awakening, her talent for teaching Sunday school, and her love of children. Her religious fervor permeated all of this, providing its own source of longing for a more devoted life. Suzie's visions, of course, were her own. But their meaning and effect upon her came entirely from her sense that they were the word of God.

Suzie's early family life had oriented her toward a love and concern for others as well as toward a commitment to honesty and other moral values. This was important, but by no means was it the whole determinant of Suzie's remarkable story. Her attraction to spiritual values, her passionate religiosity, her interest in helping children, and her deep sense of personal responsibility owe at least as much to events and persons later in her life as to her early family experience. Most telling of the later influences was the church that Suzie joined in a spirit of charismatic conversion. The church offered her support, direction, and inspiration all at the same time. It provided the interpretive context through which her "three signs" could take on the significance of a true triggering event. Suzie brought her own history, interests, and values to the event. But it was the instrument of change, providing the critical social guidance leading to the transformation and elevation of Suzie's moral goals.

Hispanic Pentecostalism, within which the Assembly of God church is included, is well suited to provide just this kind of guidance. It is known as the church of the poor, with a particular commitment to outcasts, the poor and oppressed of inner-city barrios. The church not only seeks out the poor and uneducated as members but welcomes them to leadership positions as well. The doctrines and practices of the church are egalitarian, in the sense that anyone can experience a spiritual awakening or rebirth and thus become a highly valued member or leader of the church community. As a recent treatise on Hispanic Pentecostalism notes, "The sense of holiness and the endowment of power for service . . . contributes greatly to an understanding of calling and ministry/leadership which is no longer the exclusive province of the trained professional or of an elite. One now finds that the most humble member, who has been baptized in the Spirit, has a new spiritual status—so important, given the denial of status by the society at large."[3]

As we have said, the Pentecostal church is characterized by intense evangelistic zeal, and all members are called upon to proselytize, or be "witnesses for God." As Grant McClung has noted: "Evangelism and pentecostalism could be said to be synonymous terms. It is expected, especially in the Third World, that to be a pentecostal Christian one is to be a witness. Pentecostals feel an obligation to reach all men [sic] with the gospel. . . . Pentecostals see aggressive evangelism in the pages of the New Testament and feel that they must respond accordingly."[4]

In this evangelism or missionary work, women have played a significant role despite the tradition of "machismo" within the Latino culture. Edwin Villafane argues that "Indigenous Pentecostalism could not have survived without the leadership of women, especially 'la misionera' (the local church missionary) ever present in the visitation of homes and hospitals."[5] Within the Latino community, the Pentecostal church is an important source of social services, and many of these services are provided by women in the context of their missionary work. Thus, Suzie's work can be seen as following a long-standing tradition within the church.

Within Pentecostalism, a conversion experience such as Suzie Valadez underwent is not unusual. Such a conversion provides believers with a clear break from their past lives, identifies them with other participants in the movement, sets them apart from the larger social context, and provides strong motivation for personal change.[6] As Villafane notes, "The paramount commitment experience in Pentecostalism is personal conversion to Jesus Christ as Lord and Savior. It is a life-transforming experience."[7] This was certainly the case with Suzie Valadez. Her initial experience with the "miraculous" healing of her son (while she was still a Catholic) was picked up by the Pentecostal pastor, who encouraged her to come to his church to speak about the miracle. She was then given responsibility for teaching Sunday school, which served to draw her more fully into the church. Her vision of the ragged children was interpreted for her as a call to missionary work in Mexico and the pastor, along with members of the congregation, kept this idea alive until she eventually accepted the call herself. This kind of dramatic life transformation involving "burning one's bridges" and devoting oneself fully to a new way of life was not especially unusual or strange within Suzie's social context. Evangelism was expected, social service was highly valued, and movement into a leadership role by a poor and relatively uneducated woman was acceptable if not commonplace.

Another aspect of Pentecostalism that is helpful in understanding Suzie Valadez's life is the "certitude" that characterizes its believers. The conversion experience, often called "Baptism of the Spirit," results in "a sense of finality—of having gotten firm hold on a belief system or a conceptual framework that fully satisfies the human need for explanation and meaning."[8] What outsiders may see as dogmatism is experienced by insiders as a certainty that they now understand the truth. Villafane points out that this certitude "brings along a strong sense of meaning and hope to the believer in an otherwise meaningless and hopeless barrio."[9]

Suzie's belief that she has direct personal access to God, that she is striving to fulfill the will of an omnipotent God, and that she will be protected by God's transcendent power are central features of the Pentecostal doctrine. A belief in the power of God to heal the sick is typical of this ideology. It is not unusual for these beliefs to result in a greater willingness to take risks and a paradoxical simultaneous increase in both sense of control over personal destiny and fatalism toward personal and world events.[10] Insofar as she remains within the context of like-minded believers, she is fully supported in these interpretations, which have been so critical in determining and maintaining the direction of her life. Because of the way she sees her own relationship to God, she is led to feel both greatly empowered (with the power of God working through her) yet consistently humble (it is not her own strength but God's that is empowering). This combination of a sense of effectiveness with a deep humility is one of the most characteristic features of many of our exemplars and can be seen especially vividly in Charleszetta Waddles (Chapter 8), who is also a Pentecostal. As Suzie Valadez says, "The ministry is in my heart and I'll never leave it. I'll never want to leave it just because it keeps me humble. It keeps my perspective of life in the right order, and it keeps my priorities in line."

Another defining feature of devout Pentecostalism, as Villafane describes it, is "the rejection of the ideal-real gap." As we have seen in Suzie Valadez and will see in Charleszetta Waddles, the Scriptures are taken as a direct guide to one's life with the expectation that one should strive intensely for the ideal. Their belief in the power of God and one's access to that power provides a way to overcome the gap between the ideals of the creed and its actual practice. According to Villafane, "The aggressive nature of Pentecostalism noted in evangelism and mission, risk-taking, and reinterpretation of any negative feedback as positive affirmation of his/her ideological position, are all indicative of the rejection of the ideal-real gap."[11]

Along with this effort to live the Gospels as perfectly as possible goes a perception of the world as sinful or evil and a rejection of the secular values of society. Although Suzie recognizes the pragmatic value of money for her missionary work, her personal values are explicitly antimaterialistic. She foreshadows similar words of Mother Waddles when she says that "God's not against people having money. It's just when money has the people, when you crave it, when you desire to have it and you lust for it. That's when money can get in your way."

Although recently some Pentecostal scholars have called for a more politically situated and radical vision, by and large Hispanic Pentecostalism, like African-American Pentecostalism, is apolitical, offering a spiritual and personal solution to the problems of poverty and oppression. Thus, the work that Suzie does with the poor of Juarez focuses on giving them the means to realign their lives according to the values of evangelical Christianity.

During her early years as a missionary, Suzie gradually and with a strong sense of continuity shifted the primary focus of her activities from Sunday school teaching to healing, clothing, and feeding the poor. This transition is a clear instance of goal transformation. Like other goal transformations, the changes were induced by new activities that introduced Suzie to an ever-broadening set of social concerns. The new activities followed directly from her original goals, thereby preserving her sense of continuity, but they also required her to consider new goals. As long as Suzie looked and listened, she found new obstacles to overcome, new miseries to remedy, new children to save, new "ways to serve the Lord." Her receptiveness to these new problems—her willingess to consider them challenges rather than frustrating defeats—explains a great deal about her enduring capacity for moral growth. She did not go looking for unending pressures to do more, but she was willing to take them on when they arose.

It was inevitable that running a large Sunday school for desperately poor children would lead to an open-ended barrage of demands. The mark of Suzie's response was that she invariably welcomed the demands rather than retreated from them. The children were hungry and looked to her for food. To the best of her ability, she fed them. The children were ragged and barefoot and looked to her for clothes. Once again she responded with whatever she could get her hands on. And once begun, Suzie's work engaged her more deeply than she had ever expected. Yet she found rewards in the engagement: "And all the children have told me 'Sister Suzie, since you've been giving us this peanut butter sandwich, you have to give me bigger pants because I'm getting fat.' Oh, it's wonderful. It's very, very encouraging work. When you give them an old used pair of shoes they make a dance right in front of you. They welcome everything that we do, everything, everything."

Many social scientists have commented that depersonalizing the poor is an effective way to disengage from them and hence deny responsibility for helping them. If one relates to the homeless man on the sidewalk as a shapeless lump, the theory goes, one can easily pass by without much psychological cost. Suzie points to a related phenomenon: people's tendency to focus their attention on crises far from home, such as famine in Africa, rather than on the problems in their own communities. Although some people may be very effective in helping with such geographically remote crises, for most, the remoteness exacerbates their feeling of powerlessness and thus leads them to do nothing.

In contrast, Suzie's mode of operation could almost have been calculated to hook her in more deeply at every step. She regularly formed personal connections with the people she was helping. Her involvement increased her awareness of their problems, and she took on these problems as her own. No sooner was one child fed than thirty more sprang up in her place. No sooner was there enough food than disease would strike, making the lack of medical care painfully evident. Each of her engagements led to a further engagement. She was always pressed to do more, to move ahead to the next level of commitment. For many people, these ever-expanding demands, this inexhaustible need, would lead to discouragement and a sense of futility. But the pressure to do more simply increased Suzie's energy and enthusiasm because of her deep conviction that she had to help and the joy she took in the work.

The road to this destination, however, was not easy. During her first months in El Paso, Suzie and her children received welfare; but when it came out that she had been in Texas less than a year, her payments were stopped. "So I went to the home service and they denied food, and I went to welfare again and I asked them if I could borrow some money, that I had no food for my children, and he said, 'No, we cannot do that.' So I said, 'Well, could you find me a job?' He said, 'There's no openings right now.'" She prayed for help and eventually found a job as an orderly in a hospital. She made $35 a week, spending $5 on food for her children and using the rest to pay for the assistance she gave to the Mexican children.

These were the days of despair that we referred to earlier, days when Suzie could barely feed her children and when she wondered whether she had made the right decision in moving to El Paso, whether she ought to leave her missionary work and move back to California. Suzie was able to set aside the despair that she felt and move forward with her work. She was resilient, and the loss of her welfare payments did not immobilize her. She was determined to find a job and was willing to work nights at low wages in order to stay in Texas. The support of her parents was crucial in making all this possible, since they cared for her children while she worked. But even more salient in her mind was the vividness of the vision she had received and her belief in God. She prayed when she fell into doubt or despair, and felt at those times a direct communication with God.

In thinking back on this time of extreme hardship, Suzie sees it as having helped her to understand true hunger and need, all the better for her efforts later to serve the poor of Mexico. Rather than causing her to turn her attention away from other people's problems, her own family's poverty prompted her to redouble her charitable efforts. She began to collect discarded produce and clothing. She and her helpers cooked big pots of stew and carried them across the bridge to Mexico despite the initial resistance of customs and immigration authorities.

It was not long, though, before she had won over the government officials of both countries and began receiving their active cooperation.

Gradually, over the years, Suzie attracted help for her work from many sources. She organized the Christ for Mexico Mission and successfully solicited contributions from local business leaders. The El Paso press discovered her and ran regular feature stories about the "Queen of the Dump." Volunteers pitched in to help collect donated goods and cart them over the border to the Mexican poor. By the late 1980s, the national media became interested. Suzie was profiled in network news blurbs. Large foundations gave her awards and offered her financial support. But no matter how generous the support, there was always more to do: No one who works for the poor expects to end poverty. The more outside help Suzie received, the more she intensified her efforts—and in a steadfastly personal way. Throughout the building of her substantial organization, Suzie never drifted from her hands-on approach. Crammed between meetings with mayors and funders, her own daily visits with the children of Juarez are still her first object of love and dedication.

Suzie Valadez's sustained commitment, its endurance during periods of extended hardship, its influence on her family and followers, its many victories, its very existence—all would seem improbable by any usual yardstick. This is even more true if one considers the position from which she began. If anyone would be likely to feel powerless in relation both to her own life and the world outside, it would be a woman with little work experience, an incomplete education, no money, no husband, and four small children. This is the situation in which Suzie Valadez found herself in 1962. But instead of overwhelming her, Suzie's desperate condition provided a turning point in life, leading to almost thirty years of effective work on behalf of the poor.

Given this remarkable life, it would be easy to forget that Suzie's certainty was not always as strong as it later became. In spite of the vividness of her visions and her communication with God, she speaks of her faith as having been weak in the early difficult days and as having strengthened later as she developed the mission. Suzie Valadez at age sixty-six is a person of exceptional clarity and commitment. How did that commitment develop, that faith strengthen over time?

In thinking about this question, it is important to remember that we see in this book only those whose commitment, or faith, has strengthened or remained steadfast over long periods of time. Many people start down this path but few stay on it for decades. In order to understand our exemplars, we must ask what it is that keeps them on the path.

In the early days, setbacks such as the loss of her income led Suzie to question, at least briefly, whether or not she should pursue her vision. Later, the inevitable challenges of running the mission did not lead to this kind of questioning. Things that would have been powerful enough to sway her in the beginning couldn't sway her later because by then her commitment had grown and solidified. She had made a tremendous investment in this work and through the years of experience she developed a single-mindedness of purpose that is intimately linked to her sense of who she is. In the beginning years of her mission, her life was still somewhat open. She could conceive of alternate routes. But after years of work in Juarez, the mission had become her life.

One may still ask how Suzie maintained her commitment during the many years between her initial days of "weak faith" and the later period of steadfast certainty. The process seems to be a kind of snowball effect. Suzie experienced some anguish and doubt, but she also believed in her calling and in God and she found tremendous satisfaction in her daily contact with the children of Juarez. Although she faced setbacks and experienced doubts, her religious perspective allowed her to treat the doubts as illegitimate and avoid dwelling on them. She was determined to stay and act in spite of them. Having done this, she most often found that things got better, and her belief that she was doing the right thing reinforced. If the results of her actions were less successful, she found ways to construe them as a challenge rather than a defeat.

Suzie approaches her work with joy in the activity itself. She does not define her own value in terms of the success of her efforts but rather by her continuing effort to do the right thing. Thus, she does not feel bad about herself if things do not go smoothly. This allows her to keep going, and the harder she works, the more she experiences the power of transforming defeat into success. Over time, she has developed a history of success and good feeling on which she can draw in more difficult periods.

For almost thirty years, the work of Christ for Mexico Missions has been Suzie Valadez's consuming passion. When asked about the relation of the goals of the mission and her other interests or life goals, she replies, "It's very hard to explain, because my life—it's all there." The work is hard, it is draining, sometimes it is discouraging, but in the final analysis, "It's a very exciting ministry, calling, that the Lord gave me. I just love it. And I could keep on until I'm one hundred, if the Lord permits."

In Suzie Valadez, as in the other exemplars, this implies a fundamental identification of the self with the values and beliefs that are at the heart of the work. She has become consumed by the work, fully and completely engaged. For Suzie, her work *is* her life. It makes her more alive, yet it doesn't distract her from other things that she is trying to do. With the occasional exception of her concern for her children, it does not present her with difficult conflicts. As she sees it, the work with the poor of Juarez is what she is here for, what she most wants to do. This kind of wholehearted desire to pursue one's moral goals is what we mean by unity of self and morality. In Suzie, this unity is the key to her stamina, her certainty, and her joy.

CHAPTER 4

Courage and Certainty
Amid Risk

Never look down to test the ground before taking the next step. Only
he who keeps his eye fixed on the far horizon will find the right road.
—Dag Hammarskjold

The lives of moral exemplars often are full of risk, sacrifice, and
material hardship. Some exemplars in this book have received
threats of physical harm, even death, while defending controversial
causes such as civil rights. Others have endured impoverishment, with
all its attendant hazards, as a lifelong condition. Some have given up
jobs, affluence, and high social status for the sake of the principled
positions that they have taken. What is more, several have had to
forsake not only their own material comfort but that of their families
as well. As a result of either selfless dedication to charitable causes or
unpopular moral stands, many exemplars have seen their families
forced to give up ordinary middle-class privileges and security. For
highly responsible people, the specter of not being able to provide
fully for loved ones can be particularly haunting.

Now it is important to note that not every moral exemplar lives
a life of deprivation or danger. Some of our subjects have gained great
wealth and prestige while steadfastly pursuing their moral ends.

But even those who have not faced serious risk or hardship have
still resisted constant pressures to forgo their goals or compromise
their integrity. They have still been forced to confront the difficul-

ties—perhaps impossibilities—of the social challenges they have taken
on. They have still risked the peril faced by anyone who dares tackle
the world's most impenetrable problems: the sense of spiritual and
moral discouragement that accompanies the lack of a final resolution.
This is a risk that "goes with the territory." For struggles against
prejudice, human corruption, disease, poverty, violence, and environmental degradation are rarely winnable in a lifetime. Nor are such
lengthy fights waged without real personal costs. In accepting such
struggles, moral exemplars willingly take on such costs, with little
assurance that their efforts will prove the least bit successful.

By all rights, society should reward those who take on daunting
challenges for the welfare of all. In rare moments of societal rational-
ity, this may indeed take place. But more often, it is in the nature
of moral commitment to assume risk and sacrifice—and, even more
stinging, to receive ingratitude from the very people and society that
one is laboring to salvage.

Why should moral commitment expose one to such adversities?
One reason is that moral commitment leads to a focus on causes and
concerns broader than the self. As moral commitment grows, one
inevitably turns away from self-protection or self-promotion and
toward concerns of the broader social good. It is not that morally
committed people necessarily seek martyrdom, nor do they become
abjectly defenseless as a matter of principle. But as they vigorously
pursue their moral aims, they often forgo a self-protective stance. The
preservation of self becomes a less primary mission than their other
moral purposes.

This characteristic was striking in all our moral exemplars. It
could not, in fact, have been otherwise, since it was embodied pur-
posefully in one of our nominating criteria ("a willingness to risk
personal well-being for the sake of one's moral principles"). This particular criterion reflected our fundamental assumption (and that of our
nominators) that people who place their own fates above their cherished moral beliefs may be acting in a perfectly understandable way
but not in a morally exemplary one. People who regularly do the
opposite are truly exceptional among human beings.

Forgoing self-protection as a primary focus can leave one vulnerable to the vicissitudes of fate. Moreover, the objective state of risk
that this creates may often be compounded by the added dangers inherent in certain types of moral commitment. This is because moral commitment often leads to actions that provoke social conflict and feelings
of resentment in others. Strong dedication to justice and human rights

is commonly greeted by antagonism because of the nature of these causes.

Struggles for justice and human rights go hand in hand with conflict, because they inevitably generate discord over who deserves what share of the world's resources. Claims of unfairness have always been instigators of heated emotions, because they inevitably threaten someone's established privileges. Conflicts over justice and rights are among the primary causes of anger in human affairs, and anger, unfortunately, all too often turns into threats, denunciations, and violence.

Among our moral exemplars, some of those who have taken up causes of justice and human rights have lost their jobs, encountered legal troubles, faced violence to themselves and their families, and suffered smear campaigns in their home communities. Virginia Durr and other civil rights workers in the South received death threats frequently and saw such threats materialize for less fortunate coworkers. Others in our study have faced severe forms of antagonism while campaigning for the safety of Central American immigrants, for the causes of peace and environmental preservation, or for the rights of the homeless, the sick, and the dying.

Not all of our exemplars have engaged in contentious struggles for human rights and justice. Most, in fact, have focused their energies on the less controversial works of charity, healing, and education. They minister to the needy, tend the sick, educate the ignorant—and rarely, if ever, engage in conflictual battles over justice and rights. Others in our study have committed themselves to lives of honor and integrity, again in ways that allow harmonious rather than conflictual relations with their communities.

But even those exemplars who have led these less combative lives have encountered risks stemming from their willingness to sacrifice their own interests for the sake of their principles. These are risks of a different sort. Often they entail the abnegation of material comfort and financial security. Generally they entail the sacrifice of leisure time, family time, friendships, and other interests outside their moral goals. All of our exemplars have devoted a great share of their energy, time, and resources to their moral commitments. Some have given up secure jobs or important opportunities for career advancement because these did not fit into their moral plans.

Jessie Bowles, for example, gave up a lofty position in the National Council of Churches—as well as the comfortable life that the position made possible—in order to return to Harlem and found the Harlem Youth Guidance Center. She now serves as their full-time, unpaid director. Allison McCrea quit her successful career in advertising to start a shelter for the homeless. In doing so, she gave up a well-paid, middle-class life and now lives close to the poverty line herself. Matthew Goldberg, a pediatrician, devotes his potentially lucrative practice to the care of indigent children, including some for whom there is no possibility of medicaid reimbursements. And so on down our list. A great many of our moral exemplars have turned away from opportunities to enrich themselves when they have felt these opportunities stood in the way of their moral goals.

Whether intentionally or not, moral exemplars inevitably bring their families along with them on their journey of devotion. The risks as well as the rewards of the journey are shared. The choice to renounce material gain for oneself may not especially trouble a person whose whole life has been dedicated to the common good. But when this choice means that one's family must go without things they need or want, the choice is bound to cause pain. We saw this vividly in Suzie Valadez's decision to serve the poor of Juarez even though it meant her own children had to suffer as a result.

Some of our exemplars' moral choices ultimately meant that their families had to give up the affluent life-styles they would otherwise have enjoyed. Sometimes this amounted to losses that the exemplars considered trivial and perhaps even beneficial—for example, their children would not be able to accumulate little-used, fancy toys. Suzie Valadez and her son Danny expressed this sentiment during our meetings with them. But many times the losses caused genuine regret, as when a child had to endure periods of real privation or social isolation. When Virginia Durr became a pariah for her civil rights work in the segregated South, she had to endure watching her children lose friends and privileges as well. At still other times, it was the exemplar's parental energy or attention that was sacrificed. The time-consuming demands of a moral quest often meant that the parent was less available than the child would like. What is more, the social turmoil surrounding the parent's activities too often draw the parent's energies and attentions away from the family. The inevitable draining of time, energy, and resources were most acutely experienced through the eyes of the exemplar's dependents.

In the end, we found that there was one and only one central area of our exemplars' lives about which they commonly expressed regret: their relations with their children. Even at age eighty-six, Virginia Durr suffers anguish at the memory of what her civil rights battles cost her children in lost advantages, childhood security, and parental attention. Suzie Valadez speaks poignantly about needing to take food and clothing from her own four children when they were young in order to aid the much poorer children of Juarez. A doctor who dedicated his energies single-mindedly to medical ethics was unable to find the time to start a family or to sustain a close relationship with a treasured nephew. He says his childlessness is an unfilled hole in his life.

It is nothing new that some people are willing to bear risks and sacrifices, for their loved ones as well as for themselves, in order to carry out their deepest convictions. History, after all, is full of such stories—typically celebrated well after the great sacrifices have been made. But the psychology of such choices remains something of a mystery. How does a person muster the courage to take on the risks? How does one fend off the temptation to return to a safer way? How are the burdens of hardship borne?

A common notion among psychologists is that moral action is a choice that one makes after sorting out one's options and weighing the consequences of action or inaction to the self and others.[1] A number of information-processing models have been offered to explain this sorting and weighing process.[2] The common theme in all of these models is the notion that individuals bring a number of evaluative frameworks to bear on problems of moral choice. There are frameworks of moral judgment, frameworks of social and personal responsibility, frameworks of self-interest, and so on. When these frameworks operate in unison (as when one decides that duty to one's family serves society, one's loved ones, and oneself simultaneously), moral action becomes a relatively simple affair. Often, however, frameworks collide, as when one becomes aware that speaking the truth will offend one's boss. In such cases, according to psychological theory, one is placed in a moral conflict that can only be resolved by cognitively sorting and weighing one's moral and nonmoral priorities.

The picture of human morality that follows from such theories is a picture of well-intentioned people constantly in the throes of decision (or indecision, as the case may be). Moral choices are seen as products of inner battles with oneself, wrenched from never-ending crises of conscience. It is, we believe, a picture not too distant from our everyday intuitions about moral behavior. It may well fit some instances in which individuals struggle with their fears or temptations in order to "do the right thing." Or it may be a mistaken stereotype, a myth that we hold about the agonized heroism of moral behavior. In any case, *this picture most certainly does not describe the manner in which our moral exemplars approached their moral choices.* Among our exemplars, we saw no "eking out" of moral acts through intricate, tortuous cognitive processing. Instead, we saw an unhesitating will to act, a disavowal of fear and doubt, and a simplicity of moral response. Risks were ignored and consequences went unweighed.

In order to explore how our moral exemplars have approached the risks that accompany their moral commitments, we asked each of the twenty-three to explain his or her views on moral choice, risk, sacrifice, and courage. We probed especially for the origins of their determination to persevere in the face of difficulty and doubt. We were interested in their views on how one avoids becoming discouraged when encountering formidable challenges, and we were especially curious to see how they account for their own evident bravery. We were hoping for answers that might reveal how moral courage is acquired and experienced by those who have a history of consistently demonstrating it.

The special features of the moral exemplars' views are immediately apparent throughout our interviews. Most striking is their lack of attention to the risks and sacrifices that accompany their moral actions. As a rule, they almost never calculate the personal consequences of their commitments. At times they note certain adversities, particularly when they see these affecting their children, but even then the adversities do not weaken their determination to pursue their chosen courses of action.

In disregarding the costs and consequences of carrying out their moral goals, the exemplars avert the familiar process of strategically weighing their options while making moral decisions. If there are perceived risks, the exemplars generally consider them to be inevitable companions to living according to one's beliefs and thus an inevitable part of life itself. The exemplars consistently report that they do not question the necessity of doing what their principles dictate.

Because the exemplars do not weigh the pros and cons of their decisions, they usually do not experience their moral actions as a matter of choice. They are not tormented by fear or paralyzed by the agonies of indecision: There is nothing Hamlet-like about this group. They are people who translate their principles into action directly, with little indecision or hesitation. There is a sense of great certainty, and a conspicuous absence of doubt, in their moral conduct. We saw this in Suzie Valadez's conviction that she "had to help the poor," and we will see it again in others—for example, Virginia Durr, who felt that "there were no choices to make" when she confronted the issues of racial segregation in Alabama.

The exemplars' great sense of certainty was most clearly expressed in their views on fear and moral courage. With but two exceptions, our moral exemplars gave us a remarkable and singular reply to all questions about their bravery. Twenty-one of the twenty-three exemplars disclaimed entirely the experience of moral courage. For them, our questions about courage seemed somehow beside the point. By and large, they rejected the idea that bravery was critical for moral action, at least insofar as their own efforts were concerned. Even the two who did not follow this exact pattern were exceptions closely compatible with the rule.[3,4]

In general, the exemplars claimed that the notion of courage simply did not capture anything that they had felt or done. Their overwhelming response was that it had never been necessary for them to muster their bravery once they had determined the right course of action. Their feelings of moral necessity had given them their great sense of certainty, and this in turn had relieved them of their fears and doubts. Courage became irrelevant, an unexercised affective appendage.

The links between moral necessity, certainty, and the disavowal of courage are apparent throughout virtually all of our twenty-three cases. For example, Allison McCrea, a tireless advocate for the homeless, doubted whether bravery played any role in her service despite numerous threats and public vilifications that she has withstood. She told us:

> I don't think I'm a particularly courageous person. I mean, I wouldn't run away from a fight. But, again, I tend to look at things far more simplistically than perhaps they are. And it's either right or wrong. And I don't know if courage plays as much a role in it as a fundamental knowledge that things are right or wrong and, you know, an abiding commitment to what you think is the right way to go. I don't consider myself a courageous person. No, I don't, I don't.

The sense of compulsion simply to do the right thing runs throughout our interviews. It is as if the exemplars are rhetorically asking, Why does one need courage when one has no morally acceptable choice in the matter? The right path seems so clearly defined that it rules out all alternatives. Virginia Durr told us: ". . . I did what I

felt I had to do but I never felt that I was doing it from courage, that
I was being so brave about it. It was just doing something I had to
do. But I didn't feel any great sense of exultation about it.''

Another exemplar, David Linsky, used similar terms to describe
his bravery. Mr. Linsky, the founder of a major U.S. corporation,
left his business to become an international statesman working for
diplomatic solutions to long-standing conflicts in the Middle East and
Central America. He is known for his record of uncompromising integrity as well as his ability to stand firm in the face of withering
pressure. He told us:

> I don't think of it as courage. In my case, I didn't have to say,
> as Nixon used to, ''I could do this, but I'm going to do that.''
> For whatever reason—thank God whatever that reason was—in
> important choices in my life, I knew for me the right answers
> without sleepless nights and indecision. . . . In my own experi-
> ence, I don't see myself as meriting applause for moral courage
> because I never was tempted to take a contrary course.

Later, when asked about some unwelcome public positions that he
had once taken:

> No, it's funny. I don't remember ever being deterred from doing
> what I felt would be the right thing because it would be risky.
> It's funny, but I can't recall that particular situation. I do remem-
> ber taking on positions which I need not have taken on because
> I believed it was right. But not with any sense of self-congratula-
> tion—''Aren't I the plucky fellow.'' It was just that I felt as
> though it was right, and I had something to say and I would say
> it, or something I ought to do and I ought to do it. And follow
> that course. People say to me, and have said to me, ''that's
> courageous''. . . but I never saw it that way.

Luisa Coll, an immigrant from Central America with a far less
privileged position in our society, dismisses her own bravery in much
the same way. Mrs. Coll has devoted her efforts to creating sanctuaries
for recent immigrants fleeing persecution. For her efforts, she has received direct physical threats. On several return visits to her native
country, she has witnessed firsthand violence to her associates as well
as to families that she is aiding. She has also been warned—possibly
disingenuously—that some of her activities may bring her afoul of
repressive laws in that country and that if she continues she may end
up a political prisoner if she tries to return again. Under the circum-

stances, her denial of courage seems incredible. It has the same ring to it as statements by our other moral exemplars:

> No, you know, I don't see it as being very courageous, because I don't feel that. I don't stop to think about that. I see it as something that I am called to do and I need to do. It's not anything to do with courage or fear. It's . . . I guess it has more to do with obedience. Obeying the call that I hear, and doing what I hear I am asked to do.
>
> As far as facing jail, I don't know what I will do when the time comes, but at this moment, I know that it's a possibility in my future. But I'm not afraid of it. And I don't doubt that I am willing to do it, because I am doing what I am doing, which means that it is a consequence. No, I don't see any doubt at all in any of my decisions, in terms of doing what I have to do for people.

Jessie Bowles, herself the subject of repeated racial discrimination, denies any courage in her stands for justice. Her answer expresses her determination that fear must not stand in the way of what is legally and morally right. When fear stands in the way of following the law, she in effect banishes it from the emotional landscape:

> I don't think of myself as a person who has had to exert excessive courage, because I was taught that there are laws either on the books or can be put on the books that protect citizens. And so I usually am very conscious of the legal opportunities and the legal rights. . . . And people would meet me on the street and say, "What a courageous act!" I say it didn't take any courage to help a person operate according to the law.

Dr. Bowles's assurance is interesting in two ways. First, as she herself notes, sometimes good laws must be put on the books. This, of course, can be conflictual and uncertain, and does not exactly confirm the stated source of her confidence (that the law is *already* behind her). But she has confidence that, if it's right, it eventually can be done, and so she treats the good law as if it is already in place. Second, Dr. Bowles knows perfectly well that standing up for civil rights can be a conflictual process, one in which many people (including some of her close friends) have been hurt or killed. In the tumultuous days of the civil rights movement, there was plenty to fear and plenty of need to call up courage. But she did not let herself dwell on the danger. As a consequence, she did not experience the need to call up bravery.

Not dwelling on the adverse consequences of moral commitment is a common way moral exemplars sustain certainty and deter doubt. In fact, many experience the hazards and hardships of their lives as an inevitable part of their life choice. One of the primary reasons behind their disclaimers of bravery is their feeling that they were taking the one path that their moral commitments had made available to them. The sacrifices are inevitable, many of them say, because their commitments had engendered them. Many of the exemplars deny that harsh, self-imposed conditions that most of us would view as severe sacrifices are sacrifices at all.

Allison McCrea, who abandoned a lucrative advertising career for a low paying job serving the poor in a Catholic parish house, speaks of her choice this way:

> I didn't really think all that much about it. I only knew that this [the parish house] was where I belonged, this was home. Before that, there was something missing in my life. I really didn't know what it was, because by our popular standards, I should have been pretty content. You know, I had a decent job, I had a decent apartment, I had money. I had things. I could move pretty much as I wanted to. So, by our popular reasoning, there was no reason in the world that I should change my life-style from what I had, which was very, very comfortable. But something was missing, the core something was missing. When I moved to [the parish] house, there was a security like nothing else I ever knew in my entire life. And on the face of it, there was no security. I had to raise the funds for the church, including my own salary. I had to scratch around so that we could pay the rent, the gas bill. So there was no economic security at all. We never knew if we were going to be thrown out by the archdiocese. We never knew when the call would come in, saying, "Get rid of the broad."

Jessie Bowles gave up the comfortable life of college professor and top administrator in the National Council of Churches to help found the Harlem Youth Guidance Center. She has remained there ever since—the full-time executive director of a financially struggling community agency that cannot even provide her with a salary. In order to sustain herself, Dr. Bowles does some free-lance preaching and an assortment of odd jobs. She is aware of the toll that her hard life has taken, but she celebrates her situation nonetheless. Dr. Bowles's overall assessment of her life lacks any sense of regret for the ease and material rewards that she has forgone:

> The struggle is sometimes almost unbearable to carry your many roles of program developer, funder, administrator, but the need is so great that you try to make your contribution to the problem. But it can take health tolls, energy tolls, and social tolls, but you still persist. As one of my friends years ago said, "You're crazy, you can't earn the salary a good educator can earn in religious education or community development. You need to get out there and exploit the system." That was never my interest. But I have never suffered as a result of that decision. I traveled around the world three times, because the doors have been opened.

Far from bemoaning the risks they have exposed themselves to or the sacrifices they have borne, our exemplars accepted them without any sense of loss or suffering. What is more, many spoke of the hazards to which they would have exposed themselves had they *not* pursued their moral aims. Implicit in this concern is their sense that psychological hazards can be at least as debilitating as physical and material ones. The exemplars were concerned about such dangers as guilt, self-doubt, and loss of personal integrity—all of which they saw as risks of inaction in the face of compelling moral duty. As one exclaimed, representative of just about all the rest: "I think it would take more courage for me not to do it because, basically, it would be more difficult for me not to do it . . . How could I live with myself afterwards? Not to say what I want to say? It meant really nothing at all. It wasn't a courageous act. It was a *normal* act."

This kind of statement became exceedingly familiar to us in the course of our interviews. We found it reminiscent of a passage in Victor Hugo's great moral book *Les Miserables*. After wrestling with his conscience, the protagonist Jean Valjean forces himself to reveal his identity as a criminal in order to prevent another man from being punished for Valjean's past misdeeds. By so doing, Valjean gives up his comfortable life and faces a return to prison. At the moment of his fall from social grace, Valjean exclaims: "I presume that all of you consider me worthy of pity? Great God, when I think of what I was on the point of doing, I consider myself worthy of envy."[5]

Such sentiments naturally culminate in the sense of great certainty that we observed in the moral exemplars' interviews. It is the certainty of one who has little patience with compromise or half-truth, and it evokes a quality similar to numerical necessity, as when one realizes that two plus two must equal four and therefore simply cannot be convinced to say that it equals something else. Virginia Durr expresses this certainty when she says that all people must be treated equally, and that this must apply to blacks as well as whites. Cabell Brand (Chapter 9) expresses it when he says that it is wrong for poor children to have less opportunity than rich children. These and other exemplars cannot imagine wavering from the core beliefs that they hold to be fundamentally true. To do so would be to step away from their dedication to these beliefs. This would impair their abilities to act with the urgency and vigor the beliefs demand. It would diminish the decisiveness that sharpens their words and deeds.

Great certainty when carried too far can turn into dogmatism. Yet we found little dogmatism in the statements of our twenty-three moral exemplars. We believe that the quality that distinguishes great moral certainty from dogmatism is persistent truth-seeking—an eagerness to learn more about the world combined with a willingness to examine one's ideas when they are challenged. This "open receptivity" to new ideas, as we will discuss in Chapter 7, is an orientation that characterizes the moral exemplars in this study. It is the reason they continually modify their goals and strategies, remaining developmentally "alive" even late in adulthood. It is the primary catalyst for the frequent creative transformations in their modes of moral action. Such dynamism in orientation is not the hallmark of highly dogmatic individuals. As we shall see in the next chapter, Virginia Durr was a strong-minded and outspoken person. She never feared taking a stand for a position she believed in. Yet she was also open-minded and willing to learn from experience and from other people. This allowed her to undergo in middle adulthood a dramatic transformation from racist to civil rights activist.

The great certainty that we observed in our moral exemplars was the certainty established by logical necessity once the truth is found. It is the certainty we feel when we reason that a straight line is the shortest distance between two points, or that a dead animal will not come back to life again. But it is not a certainty that precludes further questioning or blocks out further information, any more than certainty about confirmed scientific principles should preclude a scientist from remaining open to legitimate revisions in those principles when truthful new insights are realized (places indeed may be discovered where a straight line is not the shortest distance). The spirit of this is that truth, when determined, must be vigorously asserted, defended, and acted upon. Yet this should not deter us from remaining open to new truths and, where necessary, revising the old ones.

The kind of certainty we observed was not just certainty about anything the exemplars happened to believe in. Rather, it was certainty about their most central values and assumptions. These core tenets of belief were matters of faith—often, though not always, religious faith—and not themselves subject to doubt. Typically the exemplars had maintained a lifelong commitment to these central values and assumptions. But it is crucial to note that this commitment did not rule out their openness to reexamining other, less central opinions that they held. To the contrary, their value commitments encouraged such a reexamination. We will see this in Cabell Brand, a successful businessman who established and leads the antipoverty program Total Action Against Poverty (TAP). Mr. Brand had a stable, long-standing belief in equality of opportunity and in the importance of helping low-income people take advantage of that opportunity. Yet in the early days of the program he questioned the ability of such people to play a significant role in determining the shape of TAP. Due to the regulations of TAP's federal funding source, he was required to include representatives of the low-income communities on the board of the organization. As a result of working together on the board, Mr. Brand soon developed tremendous respect for their input and now sees them as indispensable to TAP's success.

Most of the exemplars expressed a core commitment to honesty. They were as rigorously honest with themselves as they were with others. (Indeed, this was one of the most striking qualities that distinguishes the exemplars from other well-intentioned people trying to do good in the world: Unlike other social leaders, who often feel they must compromise the truth in order to accomplish their presumably beneficent goals, the exemplars generally rejected this and all other means/ends contradictions.) When a commitment to honesty is sustained throughout life, it paradoxically creates fluctuation in one's other beliefs. In fact, the greater the truth commitment, the more uncertain the commitment to other attitudes and opinions—although not to *all* other beliefs, since, as our exemplars demonstrated, a core commitment to honesty can coexist with other central articles of faith. Inevitably, the ardent truth seeker shakes up comfortable presumptions, including those of the truth seeker herself. A stable belief in honesty thus injects a vital dynamism in all other belief systems, possibly leading to their revision or, in some cases, even their overthrow.

We will see this clearly in the life of Virginia Durr, who carried a
consistent dedication to honesty throughout her entire life. This spirit
of honesty with both herself and others caused her to reexamine her
views on racial discrimination and other social problems many times
over a period of decades.

Along with honesty, the other core articles of our exemplars' certainty were justice, charity, harmony, and religious faith. Often these
were interconnected, as for those who saw all their moral concerns as
emanating from their belief in God; but for others, a particular concern was preeminent and grounded more in a set of secular assumptions than religious ones. The former, however, were by far the more
common among our group: almost 80% of the exemplars attributed
their core value commitments to their religious faith. This was an
intriguing and unexpected finding—our nominating criteria, after all,
reflected nothing that was directly religious in nature.

We will examine with special attention the role of religiosity and
faith in Chapter 10. For now, we note that it would be a mistake to
blur the distinction between commitments based on religious faith and
those based on secular conviction. There are many special spiritual
qualities that spring from strong religious faith. In Chapter 10, for
example, we discuss the unwaveringly positive interpretation of life
events that, for many of our exemplars, can be traced directly to the
affirmative spirit that they take from their religious traditions.

Nevertheless, despite the irreducible qualities of the religious and
the secular, there are still many ways in which the two can play similar
roles in shoring up the exemplars' sense of certainty. And in many
cases secular conviction makes its own particular contributions, such
as in lending a sense of logical, social, or political necessity to the
exemplars' beliefs.

Virginia Durr and Cabell Brand, both Southerners, rejected racism
primarily on secular grounds, each developing an abiding conviction
in the equality of people. From such a conviction flowed a determination to treat everyone, regardless of station in life, with absolute respect. Invidious racial distinctions were simply incompatible with this
determination, and both Mrs. Durr and Mr. Brand eventually recognized this—for her not until middle adulthood, for him as early as
childhood. Once achieved, this recognition carried with it the full
force of logical necessity. It became an evident truth not subject to
denial or compromise. Both exemplars have been forced on many occasions to defend this truth—sometimes at considerable risk to their
own social status—and they have done so with unblinking certainty.

A third exemplar, who devoted herself to the fight for civil liberties, came to her own fierce certainties about racial equality from an equally secular perspective.

Apart from these three, we interviewed for our study six other exemplars who have fought extensively for the rights of racial and ethnic minorities, and all six credit their determination to their religious faith. Yet their religious traditions are diverse. They are Catholic, Baptist, Pentecostal, Quaker, and Jewish. Despite this diversity, each maintained a similar view of God's word and their obligations under it: They must live according to the will of God without regard to personal consequences. They each maintained a willing sense of faith with regard to these consequences. In Suzie Valadez's almost mantralike phrase, "God will provide."

There was, however, variation in how literally the religiously oriented exemplars' took such faith. Some strongly believed that God would in fact protect them, whereas others had a more general sense that doing God's will would work out for the best in the end—the time, location, and beneficiaries of this salutary end being possibly remote and necessarily indeterminable. But whether God's beneficence was seen as directly or indirectly engaged, in either case the belief in it bolstered the certainty of the exemplars' determination. It gave them a powerful, deeply felt reason to pursue their convictions regardless of personal risk.

Psychologically, the two mental dispositions that made possible our exemplars' great sense of certainty were their belief in the moral necessity of their position and their "willing suspension" of fear and doubt. Whether these dispositions were based on religious or secular conviction, they seemed to provide certainty in much the same way. The belief in moral necessity precluded a sense of behavioral choice (much as would a belief in logical necessity preclude a sense of intellectual choice). When pushed, one might even say that one must follow one's fate in matters where there is only one right way.

But the willing suspension of fear and doubt makes such an attitude of dejected fatalism unnecessary. God will provide. Or, life takes many unforeseen turns; when people do what's right, things have a way of working out; you create your own future by sticking to your principles; no one ever comes out ahead in the long run by doing something one is ashamed of; a coward dies a thousand deaths; and so on through all the multiple ways of establishing the rewards of virtue and the dangers of turning away from it. We heard echoes of these rewards and dangers throughout the interviews. Many of them function psychologically as the secular equivalents of "God will provide." They offer compelling real-world reasons against shrinking from one's obligation to follow one's deepest convictions. Our secular exemplars had an arsenal of such reasons at the ready, and its effect on their determination was perhaps as powerful as the spiritual supports that we observed in those with religious faith.

Aline Burchell, a peace activist, had grown away from her religious background and barely mentioned it in connection with her moral values. She considered peace to be a self-evident moral concern for anyone with the most elementary feelings for the human race. As a physician, she had made a decision to spend her life promoting human health. Campaigning for peace and nonviolence was no more than consistent with this decision. Much like the others, she saw her conviction as a logical and moral necessity: How could she work for health as a doctor while tolerating human destruction as a citizen? She considered peace to be a moral cause well worth dying for. Consequently, she feared the failure of her efforts—or the possibility that she might let up in these efforts—far more than she feared any difficulties that her peace work might bring her.

Our three other antiwar exemplars were religious: two of them were Quakers and the third a mid-life convert to Zen Buddhism. All three directly tied their pacifist sentiments to their religious beliefs. All were able to elaborate in detail the philosophy behind the nonviolent creeds of their churches. The necessity of peace was clear to them on an assortment of grounds—their reverence for their religious tradition, their sentient adoption of the Friends' pacifistic philosophy, their own creative and critical consideration of contemporary human conditions. Each of these grounds was sufficient to impart a sense of certainty to their pacifism. As a consequence, none of the three gave much thought to the controversies or risks raised by antiwar actions. All three concentrated to a far greater extent on the search for spiritual fulfillment.

Charitable work—feeding the poor, healing the sick, educating disadvantaged children—is less contentious than political action on issues such as peace or civil rights. But it can carry with it extensive privation, particularly for those who dedicate themselves single-mindedly to serving others. Eleven of our exemplars took charity for the poor as their primary moral mission. Ten of these eleven were deeply religious, a fact that we take to be significant and one that we shall discuss in Chapter 10. For the present purposes, suffice to say that all eleven pursued their charity work and dismissed their personal sacrifices with the same quality of certainty that characterized our other exemplars' campaigns for peace and human rights.

The exemplars devoted to charitable work saw poverty as an unacceptable state of existence for any member of the human race. Once they had adopted this as a necessary truth (necessary because it was consistent with all of their other core assumptions about right and wrong), the exemplars took the course of action that inevitably followed. There was no room for doubt and no reason for hesitation. The only fear that any of them mentioned was the worry that they might become discouraged in the face of their enormous task. They all knew that no matter how heroic their efforts, there would be more poor people on this planet when they died than before they started their work. Most often, for the exemplars dedicated to charity, it was their religious faith that pulled them through. A belief in a benevolent God's plan appeared necessary to sustain their certainty in the face of the grueling hardships and disappointments encountered during a lifetime's work with the poor. But the certainty was there, as surely as in the rest of our twenty-three.

In a recent study of British social activists, Helen Haste has noted similar characteristics of "certainty, conviction, and lack of doubt" among her subjects.[6] Another revealing parallel can be found not in an account of moral commitment but rather from an exploration of artistic and creative experience. Mihaly Csikszentmihalyi has described a process of optimal psychological functioning that he calls "flow."[7] During such experiences, people become so engrossed in their activities that they are able to tune out the more mundane concerns that might distract them from achieving their present goals. They lose consciousness of self, including many of the self's interests in material gain, personal advancement, security, or self-protectiveness.

The artist working feverishly on a masterpiece, the scientist approaching a new discovery, the athlete on the verge of setting a new record—all are likely to be concentrating on the task at hand rather than the rewards they may soon garner. If so, they are prototypes of persons experiencing flow. Csikszentmihalyi describes flow as "the state in which people are so involved in an activity that nothing else seems to matter; the experience itself is so enjoyable that people will do it at great cost, for the sheer sake of doing it."[8]

We believe that moral commitment has much in common with artistic and creative work, and that morally committed individuals often experience sensations akin to "flow," much as do other intensely dedicated people. We are not alone in this belief. In the closing chapter of his recent book, Csikszentmihalyi himself harbors speculations along these lines: "The hero and the saint, to the extent that they dedicated the totality of their psychic energy into an all-encompassing goal that prescribed a coherent pattern of behavior to follow until death, turned their lives into unified flow experiences."[9]

Dedicated moral work is certainly as engrossing as any other challenging activity, and the captivating "flow" state that one experiences during moments of peak performance are no doubt the same. Although of course we were never able to directly enter our subjects' consciousness, we observed many of them in action; and their joyful absorption with their work was readily recognizable as what Csikszentmihalyi has called flow. In addition, many of the exemplars reported, in their own language, affective experiences strikingly akin to Csikszentmihalyi's descriptions. The phenomenology of optimal experience, we believe, is pretty much the same in the moral realm as elsewhere.

Beyond its special experiential state, there are certain positive mental conditions that derive from flow; and these can be found as much in the moral domain as elsewhere. Most important of these mental virtues is a direct concentration on one's dealings with the world rather than on oneself. The individual becomes able to focus all energies on the task at hand, improving his or her performance on the task as well as the enjoyment of it. This can enhance the person's self-confidence without necessarily leading to misguided arrogance or conceit. For this reason, Csikszentmihalyi calls this fortuitous condition the virtue of "unself-conscious self-assurance." It no doubt contributes to the certainty with which dedicated people carry out their missions.

Because flow is characterized by an unself-conscious immersion in activity for its own sake, it can diminish one's anxieties over the immediate results that one is able to achieve. This in turn can alleviate some of the frustrations that inevitably follow from taking on difficult (and sometimes impossible) challenges. Satisfaction is gained from the attempt more than from the end results. When one takes on great moral causes such as poverty, this can preserve one's spirits and one's determination. Who could ever hope to make a dent in the world's poverty? Yet morally committed people enter the fray wholeheartedly, knowing full well that their contributions will not conquer the problem for all time. They find a way to take satisfaction from their service despite its ultimate limits. Were they to dwell instead on the success or failure of their efforts, they likely would experience frequent discouragement rather than the exhilaration that they report.

We saw just this kind of absorption in Suzie Valadez, as one example. We asked in the context of her life what might lead to a strengthening of commitment, certainty, or faith over time. A part of the answer is that she was fully absorbed in her work and consistently derived flow from it. This extremely gratifying experience protected her from becoming discouraged by challenges and setbacks. It helped to keep her moving forward with the work year after year. Then, as the years of experience compounded, she became less vulnerable to the inevitable vicissitudes of the struggle to fight poverty.

Csikszentmihalyi notes a number of other flow conditions that may contribute to the enactment of moral commitment. He mentions a readiness to discover new goals and solutions, clearly a precondition for the kinds of lifelong developmental transformations that we discussed in the previous chapter. He also discusses the joy that flow makes possible, even in the grimiest undertakings. The thrill of the immersion can inure a person to much of the unpleasantness that would seem salient under less engaged circumstances. This includes the debilitating fear that might otherwise accompany a dangerous mission—a form of unpleasantness that can be especially severe in the case of moral action. (In fact, as we discuss below, coping with the extended risks of moral commitment probably requires mental and character strengths that go well beyond the capacity for flow.)

Finally, Csikszentmihalyi's profile of flow "exemplars" (our word, not his) has much in common with the twenty-three subjects of this book. In fact, his description fits our exemplars perfectly, as will be especially apparent from the chapters on Virginia Durr, Charleszetta Waddles, and Cabell Brand: "Such individuals lead vigorous lives, and are open to a variety of experiences, keep on learning until the day they die, and have strong ties and commitments to other people and to the environment in which they live. They enjoy whatever they do, even if it is tedious or difficult; they are hardly ever bored, and they can take in stride anything that comes their way."[10]

But moral commitment is more than just flow. However much it has in common with artistic, athletic, and other intense activity engagements, moral commitment draws on psychological and characterological resources all its own. As a force for the good, it remains a special condition in human affairs. It may share the exhilaration and sense of immersion of other flow experiences, but it always directs itself to a special set of human goals, and it confronts challenges that are found nowhere else. Although in some respects ardent moral commitment may be the *non plus ultra* of flow, in other respects it is a world apart.

The key difference lies in the nature of moral goals as opposed to other human aspirations. Moral goals transcend the self: They are not primarily self-serving, almost by definition. In contrast, Csikszentmihalyi's "autotelic self"—a self able to generate "flow" through regular consciousness control—can be directed toward practically any personal or social ends. ("Autotelic self," Csikszentmihalyi writes, simply refers to a self with "self-contained goals.") Among the goals mentioned as potential instigators of flow are mastering an occupation, learning tennis, performing a dance, and reading a book. As long as the goal is self-chosen and the attempts to attain it engrossing, the state of flow can be readily achieved.

Moral goals also are self-chosen, at least eventually and in the context of considerable prior social influence. But moral goals are not wholly self-derived, nor are they at all arbitrary. Rather, moral goals are drawn from considerations extending well beyond any individual's personal inclinations and interests. These considerations may include concerns about another's welfare; about the welfare of society as a whole; about one's duties and responsibilities; about cultural rules and regulations; about matters of honor, honesty, and integrity; or about a number of other norms and principles. Although such concerns are always influenced by one's subjective interpretations of situational reality and the "right" moral course, nevertheless they are not discretionary. There is always an obligatory element in moral goals, and they are always attached to social reality, spiritual sentiment, or religious tradition. Morality always will remain elusively hard to define. But this does not mean that its meaning is altogether up for grabs at the idiosyncratic penchants of an individual.

Missing in the notion of an autotelic self is the commitment to a prescribed set of particular moral values. This commitment may not be critical for "flow," but it is essential for the development of moral character. If moral goals are to be unified—one of Csikszentmihalyi's prime criteria for optimal flow—they must be unified around an abiding concern for the good.

In the case of a moral exemplar, this commitment creates the enduring theme that ties together the changing goals and strategies that are developed as the years pass. Even as new goals are discovered, there is still a sense in which the new goals report to the same fundamental concerns. So Virginia Durr will turn her attention from voting rights to desegregation out of her abiding concern for justice; or Cabell Brand will launch a new organizational program in pursuit of his continuing attempt to raise the poor. The original moral aim remains primary and stable. Unity is achieved because all new systems of action are derived from that aim rather than upon the changing interests of the individual. For this reason, unity of goals comes quite naturally for a person with moral purposes. Coherence is readily attained.

The goals themselves, however, may not be so readily attained. In fact, it is fair to say that persons dedicated to moral goals encounter levels of resistance unknown in other sorts of human endeavor. For one thing, there is the frustration that always accompanies problems that can never be wholly solved. For another, there is the great and sustained personal risk that moral exemplars inevitably face. As discussed earlier, moral choices can endanger the lives and personal welfare of both those who make such choices and their families. Ignoring safety for a civil rights cause has a whole different meaning than it does for an artist experimenting with an unconventional form of expression. In pursuing their aims, moral exemplars often meet grave tests and face unparalleled obstacles.

This brings out a final point of difference between sustained moral commitment and Csikszentmihalyi's notion of flow. People who have embarked on a course of dedication to moral goals must steel themselves for hardship, resistance, risk, and possibly even danger. They are willing to sacrifice their own comfort and that of their families for the pursuit of their moral aims. Personal happiness is not a central focus. In fact, happiness was rarely mentioned in any of our moral exemplar interviews. Nor did any of our twenty-three speak of trying to "control psychic energy" in order to gain a state of "optimal experience." Yet these are the central considerations in Csikszentmihalyi's theory—as if flow, optimal experience, and happiness were in themselves adequate goals for living. A commitment to the moral life is less concerned with individual fulfillment. It is difficult indeed to imagine our moral exemplars reading a book on how to have an optimal experience. Moral work can and does lead to a deep sense of satisfaction, but the satisfaction comes as one makes one's contribution to the needs of others. Not just any exhilarating activity will do. An optimal moral experience is always in the service of, responsible to, and in large part defined by the social good.[11]

If flow is not a sufficient explanation for moral certainty in the face of hardship and risk, what other psychological processes come

into play? We have discussed the steadfast dedication to moral principles that guides the exemplars' choices—and indeed often makes them
feel that they have little latitude of choice. Such a spirit of dedication
is often found in the moral realm of human affairs but not in moral
matters alone. In fact, people can feel this kind of dedication to any
number of causes that they are committed to, *once they are so committed.*
The key is the volitional act of commitment.

In recent years, research by German psychologist Heinz Heckhausen identified what he called "the Rubicon effect."[12] As the phrase
implies, the effect describes a single-mindedness of purpose that follows from a commitment to a certain intent (a mental "crossing the
Rubicon"). Heckhausen distinguished between *motivation,* the state in
which one makes a choice, and *volition,* the state in which the choice
has already been made and all energies are directed toward the question
of how to implement it. (Perhaps a clearer designation of this distinction was made earlier by Kuhl, who called the two processes "selection motivation" and "realization motivation," respectively). "In a
state of motivation," wrote Heckhausen and his colleagues, "we
should be open to a broad range of information which we probe im-
partially, whereas in a state of volition we should turn into narrow-
minded partisans of our action and become correspondingly preoccupied."[13]

With respect to their moral commitments, our exemplars have
long since crossed their "Rubicons." This occurred long before we
had a chance to observe them. For most of their lives they have operated in the state that Heckhausen calls "volition," focusing wholeheartedly on courses of action aimed at accomplishing the commitments that they have already made. Not surprisingly, the exemplars
demonstrate the single-minded mental dedication that characterizes
volitional states. What is exceptional about the exemplars is the longevity of their commitments as well as their moral basis.

We have also noted our exemplars' determination to discount adversity and to celebrate the rewards of their choices. This determination acts as a key support system for their sense of certainty because
it protects them from the real risks of discouragement and doubt.
How, psychologically, do they manage it in the face of repeated trials
and setbacks? Not, as others might, through denying or romantically
distorting the often insurmountable problems that they struggle
against.

Certainty in the midst of risk need not imply denial, nor need
it spring from a foggy obliviousness. The moral exemplars that we

interviewed were by no means naive, or even casual, about the dangers and difficulties they faced. They were not wholly insensate when it came to feelings of fear. But they were able to manage such feelings so the fear did not emerge in consciousness as a formidable emotion to be reckoned with. They at times experienced what we would call *intimations* of fear and doubt. Their success lay in not allowing those intimations to become full-blown emotional forces capable of deterring moral action.

Emotional management of this sort requires resolute self-control. Sometimes this is accomplished quite consciously: Several of our exemplars spoke of how they regulate their feelings in times of stress, and it is clear from these accounts that moral certainty oftentimes is an active, intended process.

Emmylou Davis, like Charleszetta Waddles, is a black woman who came from a poor background. In adulthood, as she witnessed the Watts riots of the 1960s, she felt a responsibility to do something to combat her community's turmoil and desperate hopelessness. Watts was not an easy place to build a community organization in those days. Mrs. Davis told us about how she handled her own intimations of fear in the many difficult situations that she faced as the founder and director of an active community center in Watts:

MRS. DAVIS: Is there something I do that seems frightening sometimes? Oh, sure, some [things] I do seem frightening sometimes. Places I go sometimes seem frightening. It's something that'll come over you quickly. Something will say, "You better not go there." And something will say, "I can do all things through Him that strengthens me." And you go on.

So, just as sure as you have a negative answer, you're going to have a positive [one]. If you don't have the positive answer, you'll get the negative answer. *You* have to give yourself the positive answer. And it happens so quickly. It happens so quickly in the mind. I can sometimes feel a pain, maybe get a headache, and I have to say right quickly, "It's OK." Otherwise this frightened part will come. Frightening to me is death. I just don't allow it.

INTERVIEWER: So you shut it off, you shut it down as soon as it comes up.

MRS. DAVIS: Exactly. Just like that.

INTERVIEWER: How do you do that?

MRS. DAVIS: Number one, you've gotta be aware that it can happen, that it do happen. Then you listen for it. It's in the mind—you listen for it. And every time something comes in the mind, if you listen for it you can put it back as fast as it comes up. You can feed it back. But you have to listen for it. It's a gift I think.

INTERVIEWER: So you generally don't stop doing something because of fear.

MRS. DAVIS: I shut the fear out, and when I'm doing it the fear is not there. 'Cause if the fear was there, I don't think I would be able . . . the fear wouldn't allow me to do it. So the minute the fear comes, I shut it out and keep going and so there is no fear.

What we have learned from Emmylou Davis and the others in our study is that the roots of moral courage are not so much to be found in wrestling with fear as in preventing it, which can be done in a variety of ways, all of which stem from a fundamentally moral perspective on life. Such a perspective places priority on core moral values like truth, justice, peace, and charity. It establishes the moral necessity of decisions based upon these values and demands rigorous adherence to the implications of these decisions. Once such a commitment is made, already the specters of fear and doubt have taken a backseat in consciousness. When further discouraging intimations arise, they are dampened before they develop.

Self-control of this sort must draw on inner strengths and resources that some people do not have. In our exemplars' lives, there have been social resources that have come from their special communities and there have been personal resources that have come from deep within their own characters. We shall discuss both in Chapter 7, but here we take note of the most central resources of all: those that come from their values and their faith.

We end this chapter with a quote from Allison McCrea, who, like our other exemplars, has managed to maintain her stamina and commitment to fight homelessness and other aspects of poverty over several decades. The way she thinks about what she is doing is a large part of what makes her persistence possible:

One, I have enormous faith that somehow it's going to be OK. I also know that I am a part of a struggle. I am not *the* struggle, I am not leading any struggle. I am there. And I have been there for a long time, and I'm going to be there for the rest of my life. So I have no unrealistic expectations. Therefore, I'm not going to get fatigued.

Along the way, there are those moments that I'm willing to settle for, those tiny moments of grandeur, you know, that we are together and we can breathe together, and we can hold each other and somehow we're going to make it. There is a story that the sky is falling and all the animals were running through the village, the lions and the tigers. In the middle of this dirt road, there was a sparrow with his little legs up in the air. And the zebra runs by and says, "Hey dummy, the sky is falling. Do you think with your spindly little legs, you're going to hold it up?" And the little bird says, "One does what one can."[14] That's me.

I have no illusions. I have absolutely no illusions about who I am or what I can do. I mean, I love the work we do and the thing that keeps you going is that the dragon doesn't win all the time. I think that there are . . . there are moments in your life when you instinctively know that you are where you're supposed to be.

I know who I am and what I do. As far as I'm concerned it makes sense to me. It doesn't have to make sense to other people. I think that when you become committed to some kind of an idea or a vision or a faith or whatever you want to call it, it doesn't matter that you have a lot of detractors or that people say "Oh Jesus Christ, here she comes again!" And you know, you do what you can and you grab your laughs where you can find them. And you find them. I mean you find them in impossible places, but they're there. And that's good enough for me.

But again, we're simply part of that struggle. That's what it's about. And I don't feel bad about it. I mean, not to have unrealistic expectations of yourself is a fairly adult way of looking at life, I think. And most of us are not . . . many of us are not satisfied with anything. And the more we have, the less we're satisfied. So, I mean, I certainly consider myself ahead of the game. I'm a reasonably happy woman.

CHAPTER 5

Virginia Durr
Champion of Justice

O ur conversations with Virginia Durr took place in surroundings as genteel as her upper-class Southern upbringing. She had come North for a summer visit with her daughter and son-in-law in their antique seaside retreat. The scene had that odd mix of restfulness, bustle, and civilized rusticity found only in the most well-established vacation spots of this country.

Framed by the quiet, elegant charm and the lively summer socializing, Mrs. Durr made a striking figure. She stood out sharply, not so much in contrast to the setting, for she was warmly comfortable with the many family members and friends gathered around her, but in the same way that a splash of color in a finely crafted painting merges with the design yet leaps out at the viewer. In the end, the splash of color may make its own statement, apart from all the rest, and it may be the main thing that one remembers.

In fact, Mrs. Durr's visual presence is almost as distinct as her moral and personal one. On that summer day, she was dressed in bright white, and this, in combination with her head of thick white hair, gave her a brilliantly flashing look that matched perfectly the blaze in her eyes and her voice. It was startling to us when we realized that this impeccably mannered, friendly, gently humorous eighty-six-year-old lady with a lovely Southern accent is most truly described by a single word—a word not usually associated with such a refined and pleasant person: *fierce.*

The fierceness of Mrs. Durr is apparent in every opinion, every judgment, every determination she makes. It is apparent in the astonishing sweep of her awareness and in the intellectual rigor with which she appraises all matters of interest. It is apparent in her unwillingness to compromise, to let up on the truth in even the slightest degree— or to let up on those who find it difficult to face the truth so unwaveringly. Above all, it is apparent in the strength of her convictions and in her steely commitment to carry these convictions through to the end.

Many of our conversations with Mrs. Durr concerned civil rights, the area of her own seminal contribution to American society. We had quite expected her to be informed and insightful in this area, and indeed she was. Exploring contemporary race relations with Mrs. Durr opened our eyes to issues and problems that we had not previously understood. The depth of her thinking in this area proved powerfully instructive for us. This delighted but did not particularly surprise us for, after all, we were talking to one of the civil rights movement's great historical leaders.

We were less prepared for Mrs. Durr's incisive reach into the other major political and social debates of our time. The one that stays with us most vividly came up during our last visit with her, in the summer of 1991. At that time, the "political correctness" wars were raging on American campuses. Coming from major universities, we were not far from the front lines ourselves and had become accustomed to the predictable arguments for one or the other side of the controversy. Mrs. Durr's reasoning was subtle and more difficult to categorize. She examined the reported incidents individually, sorted through the issues on their merits, and came to conclusions independent of any party line. Perhaps most noteworthy was her searching curiosity. She asked and listened more than she spoke, wholly receptive to new information and alternative points of view.

Probably because we have been influenced too much by a youth-oriented culture, it is tempting for us to remark that Mrs. Durr's acuteness and openness seem incredible for a person of eighty-six. But the fact is that Mrs. Durr's present intellectual and personal capacities would distinguish a person of any age. They clearly are at the heart of her magnificent life achievements stretching out over six decades. The way that Mrs. Durr has sustained her energies, her intellectual acuity, her moral commitment, and, yes, her fierceness is as much a part of her story as the manner in which these qualities grew out of her Southern plantation origins.

Virginia Foster Durr comes from aristocratic Southern lineages on both her mother's and father's sides of the family. Her paternal grandfather, for example, was both a physician and a successful plantation owner in Alabama. Through wise investments he had come to own a great deal of land around the town of Union Springs, where his plantation was located. Virginia's paternal grandparents had had slaves, and during the time Virginia visited the plantation "the system . . . was just the same as before the slaves were freed except that they were paid a little something. Granny Foster still had the same number of servants, and they still lived in the backyard."[1] In this setting, Virginia was imbued with "the romantic traditions of the benevolent slave system."[2]

Some of Virginia's most powerful memories of her childhood concern visits to her paternal grandmother's plantation. (Her paternal grandfather died before Virginia was born.) She loved the rural beauty and the atmosphere of abundance and grace, an atmosphere that she later realized could exist only because of the exploitation of the black servants.

Visits to the plantation were absolutely blissful. Everything was beautiful and we'd get off the train and there would be the car-

riage to meet us and they had a driver named Washington and
he would be there in a tall silk hat. We would come to the house
and it would be full of fires, you see they heated and lit it by
fireplace and my grandmother would be there to receive us and
there would be a fire in the bedroom. And then the food was so
marvelous and my grandmother was so warm and welcoming.
And then the servants were the best part of it. They were as
pleasant as they could be and kissing and hugging and loving
you. You see, everything was done for you. We didn't have any
running water or anything. We didn't have any electric lights.
But I've never been so comfortable because you would wake up
in the morning and there would be a person—a black person—
bending down doing your fire. And by the time your fire was
bright, she would have brought up the water for you to bathe
in and then help you get dressed. Then you go downstairs and
there would be a delicious breakfast waiting for you. And everything was done for you.

Beginning with this antebellum plantation atmosphere, Virginia
Foster grew up surrounded by individuals who believed that black
people were innately inferior to whites. Yet Virginia Foster Durr
become a central figure in the fight for civil rights for African-
Americans. In adulthood, Virginia came to see the racial attitudes that
she had grown up with as inconsistent and irrational as well as degrading to blacks. She talks of the close and loving relationships that white
children of that era and class developed with the black servants and
the servants' children. This closeness is later forbidden, as prohibitions
against familiarity between the two races are imposed. It becomes
unthinkable to eat at the same table with the beloved black woman
who used to rock one to sleep. The implications are insulting and
degrading to black people—that they are dirty or diseased. To Virginia, this psychological degradation was as important as the economic
and political oppression that the whites imposed on the blacks.

Mrs. Durr also distinguishes between benevolence and respect in
whites' treatment of blacks. Some of the white segregationists, including the families of both Virginia and her husband, Clifford, were
benevolent and protective toward the blacks with whom they had
contact. They felt responsible to care for them, as one would in relation to children. Virginia saw this patronizing attitude as destructive
in that it undermined the sense of self-respect and self-determination
of black people. Whereas her friends and family thought it was suffi-

cient to hire black men and women for nonliving wages and then extend the kindness of giving them cast-off clothing, she believed that the black citizens of the South had a right to an equal voice in government, a good education, good jobs, and fair wages. This may seem obvious to us today, but in Alabama in the 1930s this was a rare and important insight.

Virginia Foster Durr spent over thirty years leading the struggle to outlaw the poll tax, which had been used for many years to prevent women, blacks, and poor people from voting. She worked to desegregate the restaurants and hotels in Washington, D.C., and all the public facilities, including schools, in Alabama. Because of the principled stands on race and civil liberties that they took, she and her husband lived most of their adult lives with very little money, sometimes so little that they could not afford to maintain an independent household. For more than twenty years, Virginia worked in Clifford's law office, the two of them serving primarily poor, black clients who were fighting discrimination, segregation, and other forms of exploitation.

How did this happen? How did a woman born to such privilege in a segregated and pervasively racist society end up spending her life fighting for the rights of the outcasts of that society? In order to understand this, we must examine the origins of Virginia Foster Durr's commitment to equal justice and trace the formation and subsequent transformation of her life goals. As we have seen in all of our exemplars, Virginia Durr was open to moral change and exhibited a broadening and ennobling of her goals as she engaged with the experiences and people she encountered. We can trace the resulting changes across the course of her life, including important transformations that occurred in middle adulthood and beyond. In addition, we must look to see how she sustained her commitment through some trying times, including material hardship, social stigma, and physical danger, all the while drawing upon a deep sense of certainty in the rightness of her cause.

Some of the qualities that are most characteristic of Virginia Durr throughout her life are evident in the earliest stories she tells about herself. She is a strong-willed individual, and in the family lore she is seen as having been so from the very beginning. "My mother said that from the beginning I was an extremely greedy and red-faced yelling baby. I was considered the bad child of the family. I was the youngest and evidently was demanding from the beginning."[3] She describes herself as having been very different in this respect from her ladylike and compliant older sister.

We can see Virginia's characteristic defiance at age seven as she fought the forces of racial segregation for the first time at her birthday party on her grandmother's plantation. As a young child, Virginia was devoted to her black nurse and played frequently with her nurse's daughter and the children of the other black servants. This harmonious situation was disrupted for good on her seventh birthday when she was forbidden to include the black children in her party. The subsequent family argument resulted in the loss of Virginia's nurse:

I was told none of the black children could come to the party. Only white children—perfect strangers they had picked up in Union Springs. So I had a temper fit early that morning and they finally agreed that I could have a barbecue in the morning and the party in the afternoon. The barbecue would be in the backyard with the black children, and the party would be in the front yard with the white children. We had the birthday barbecue and everything was going fine. One of the little black girls was tearing up the chicken, and she offered a piece to Elizabeth [Virginia's cousin]. Elizabeth, who must have felt like an outcast in this group, all of a sudden said, "Don't you give me any chicken out that black hand of yours. I'm not going to eat any chicken that your black hand has touched, you little nigger." I told Elizabeth to go to hell. I was just furious. You see, the black girl was Nursie's little girl, Sarah. She and I played together all the time. I was raised with her. When the afternoon came, I went to the birthday party with all these strange white children. I had another temper fit and screamed and yelled. I bashed the cake in and was put to bed again. . . . That night at the supper table, my aunt said I was the worst child she had ever known. She told my mother, "I really think you have got to do something about her because she's so high-tempered, such a bad child." I was sitting right there listening to her, so I took a knife and threw it at her. Well, I was really a disgrace then, so they sent me away from the table. I went out to the back porch and sat in Nursie's lap. We could hear Aunt May through the window saying, "Annie, the trouble with Virginia is that nurse. She spoils her to death. And besides, I think it's terrible that you let her sit in her lap and sleep with her and kiss her and hug her. You know all those black women are diseased." My mother defended me, but she didn't try to defend my nurse, and neither did my grandmother. Nursie had been spending the summer in Union Springs

all my life. She had been with our family for seven years, caring
for me and my brother and my sister. They knew how kind she
had been to us and what a faithful servant she was. Yet they
did not defend her from Aunt May's charges. . . . Nursie was a
dignified woman and she was, I am sure, highly insulted. She
put me to bed that night and the next morning she was gone.
She took her child and left and never came back. She got a job
somewhere in the neighborhood in Birmingham, and I would go
and cry and beg her to come back, but she never would. She
never forgave the insult. That was a terrible trauma in my life.[4]

Although Virginia's defiance cannot be seen as a mature instance
of standing up for her convictions despite the consequences, it is no
coincidence that she was growing up in a family, indeed in a culture,
which valued this kind of courage. In the same year as the birthday
party incident, Virginia's father stood up to authorities in a much
more serious way and suffered severe repercussions as a result. Sterling
Foster was a Presbyterian minister, educated at Princeton and Edin-
burgh. When Virginia was seven, Mr. Foster was thrown out of the
church as a heretic. The Presbyterian church in which Mr. Foster
served was fundamentalist, and some of the more powerful members
of the church began to suspect that he was heretical. "They asked
him to declare on oath before the Session that he believed the whale
swallowed Jonah and Jonah stayed in the whale's belly for three days
and was spewed up alive. He had to swear to that as the literal truth,
God given. They gave him a week to make up his mind, and they
told him if he didn't agree to do it, he would be denounced as a
heretic. . . . At the end of the week, he went back and told them that
he didn't believe the story of Jonah and the whale. He was dismissed
from the church and brought before the Presbytery and the Synod as
a heretic. He never got another church."[5]

Following this incident, Mr. Foster had a nervous breakdown, and
his wife was left alone for a time with her three children. After his
recovery, he began to work for a big insurance company that sold
insurance primarily to blacks. His mother died soon after his expulsion
from the church, and he inherited a part of her plantation, along with
a significant amount of money. The family was prosperous for a time,
but Mr. Foster was not a particularly successful businessman and the
inheritance was gradually lost through mismanagement and the boll
weevil crisis in Southern agriculture. By the time Virginia reached
adolescence, the family income was greatly reduced. During the de-

pression, the Fosters lost what little they had left and became financially dependent upon their two daughters and their daughters' husbands.

Virginia's defiance, as shown in the birthday party incident, can be seen as a precursor of her deep belief in standing up for what she believes in, whatever the consequences might be. This is a theme that recurs at critical points throughout her life story and is inextricably entwined in her sense of who she is. In this area we see a continuity with rather than a departure from her family's values and traditions. Her most dramatic memory of her father concerns his willingness to risk and lose his entire career in the ministry rather than to deny his beliefs about the literal truth of the Bible. He never fully recovered from the incident, and the implications for Virginia were very grave, leading to a prolonged separation from her father and to financial difficulties throughout her girlhood. Given these dire consequences, it would have been reasonable for Virginia to conclude that it is very dangerous to stand up for what you believe in and to avoid doing so herself when faced with such a choice. Clearly, this was not her reaction. Although she seems to have been puzzled by her father's soul-searching and decision to take a stand, she had a vague sense that he had made an honorable choice. This fell into place more firmly when she later studied the Bible as literature at Wellesley College. ''So I learned that my father had been right about Jonah and the whale. You can't imagine what that meant to me. I had always felt that Daddy did a very noble act by saying he did not believe the whale swallowed Jonah. He refused to lie and be a hyprocrite. But I had always been uneasy that my father had been thrown out of the church for being a heretic as a result of that. It was a great relief to learn that he had been not only noble but also right about the Bible stories as symbolism and myth.''[6]

Clearly a strong will and independent mind have characterized Virginia throughout her life. Her early opposition to the imposed racial segregation of her birthday party should not, however, be taken to mean that she failed to internalize the prevailing views about race relations. Her behavior at age seven simply signifies that she was, even at that early age, fiercely determined, tenacious, and unwilling to give in to social pressure. In a sense she was fighting for justice even then. She would not allow Nursie's daughter to be treated unfairly. She would not allow her childhood friends to be excluded from her party because of their race. Her actions were not based on any general principle of racial justice—that concept developed some thirty years later—it extended only to the particular children who were her friends.

A later incident illustrates how limited her early perspective on racial equality was and how successfully she was educated in racial prejudice by the culture in which she grew up. Upon entering her sophomore year at Wellesley College, Virginia went down to the dormitory dining room for dinner. "The first night, I went to the dining room and a Negro girl was sitting at my table. My God, I nearly fell over dead. I couldn't believe it. I just absolutely couldn't believe it. . . . I promptly got up, marched out of the room, went upstairs, and waited for the head of the house to come. . . . I told her I couldn't possibly eat at the table with a Negro girl. I was from Alabama and my father would have a fit." The head of the house calmly explained that the rules of the college required her to eat at that table for a month, and if she did not comply she would have to withdraw from college. This was the first time Virginia's values had ever been seriously challenged and she stayed awake all night worrying about the dilemma. She was afraid of angering her father, yet she enjoyed Wellesley and very much wanted to stay. "Now, I was having the time of my life at Wellesley. I had never had such a good time. I was in love with a Harvard law student, the first captain of VMI [Virginia Military Institute], and life was just a bed of roses. But I had been taught that if I ate at the table of a Negro girl I would be committing a terrible sin against society. About dawn, I realized that if nobody told Daddy, it might be all right. That was the only conclusion I came to. I didn't have any great feeling of principle. I had not wrestled with my soul." Virginia stayed at Wellesley and spent a month eating at the table with the black girl, whom she came to like and respect. "That was the first time I became aware that my attitude was considered foolish by some people and that Wellesley College wasn't going to stand for it. That experience had a tremendous effect on me."[7]

This incident illustrates the transformation of goals as it applies to Virginia's development. Her goal in agreeing to sit at the dining table with the black student was very clearly to be allowed to remain at Wellesley and continue her active and entertaining social life. It was not an immediate awakening to a new perspective on race relations and civil rights, but it did move her a perceptible step in that direction. She was forced to interact with an educated, middle-class black girl for the first time, and she realized that the girl was intelligent and civilized. Virginia became aware of the fact that her views on segregation were not shared by the community she had joined, a community she prized very highly. Although this incident did not change Virginia's racial views overnight, it did sow the seeds of doubt about the beliefs she was raised with.

There are distinct threads of continuity connecting the different periods of Virginia's life and connecting her with her family and Southern heritage. But overall, her life is more dramatically a story of change than one of continuity. The two years she spent as a student at Wellesley College constitute the first really important period of change for her. The awakening she experienced there included an incipient feminism and an awareness that she could use her mind and "get pleasure out of it."[8] She studied the Bible as literature and began to rethink her religious beliefs. She learned about social conditions in the United States and became interested in issues of social justice. In regard to the latter, she said, "I began to realize that people had a hard time living and didn't get paid enough. I began to get some inkling of economics."[9] Later this inkling was important to her ability to interpret the poverty she saw around her as the depression hit Alabama.

Virginia was not able to return to college after her sophomore year. As she put it, "The boll weevil ate my education." Her father could not afford the expenses and was too proud to send her back as a scholarship student. Virginia returned to Birmingham to make her debut and look for a husband. When one did not materialize immediately, she took a job in the law library to help with the family expenses, much to the humiliation of her parents. Soon afterward she met Clifford Durr at church and asked her brother, who had been Clifford's fraternity brother in college, to invite him to dinner with the family. Clifford courted Virginia enthusiastically, and they were married within a year, in 1926. Virginia's marriage to Clifford was considered an excellent match, since he had been a Rhodes Scholar and president of his fraternity at the University of Alabama. In addition, his family was well off, and he held a good position as an attorney in a corporate law firm in Birmingham.

Virginia became pregnant soon after the wedding, had a daughter, and lived the comfortable life of a young married woman in Birmingham. Like most of the women in her position, she was active in the Junior League, the church, and other social groups. The depression was very severe in the South at that time, and Virginia became more and more aware of the desperate poverty surrounding her. In response, she became quite active in providing assistance to the poor. For example, she organized a program in which the Southern Dairies Association delivered surplus milk to feeding stations run by the Red Cross. There was no public welfare or relief at that time and many families in Alabama had nothing. In order to provide some diversion from the misery they felt, Virginia created recreational programs, with free concerts and shows every Sunday. She also began to work with the Red Cross. Once families were certified as completely destitute, they qualified to receive $2.50 a week in aid from the Red Cross. Virginia's job was to drive Red Cross women around so they could certify more families as eligible. In the process, she was exposed to the extent and depth of the poverty and the cruel treatment of the workers by the mine and mill owners. "I would go in these houses and they would be cold. There was no heat. [When the people were laid off, the owners] would let them stay, but they wouldn't supply them with any heat or electricity. And the children had protein deficiencies and other deficiency diseases. And then some of them lived in coke ovens, and it was just a horrible thing to me. . . . That's what aroused my anger against the corporations—the absolute lack of sympathy they showed."

Virginia also became aware that some people felt the poor had only themselves to blame for their condition and that the poor blamed themselves as well. "The preachers would come to see them and would say they had sinned and that's why they were suffering; if they hadn't sinned, they wouldn't have suffered. I thought that it was awful for them to come into a freezing cold house with children that were trembling from some kind of deficiency disease and the people out of work." Even President Harry Truman used the fable of the grasshopper and the ant[10] to express his belief that if the poor had been more prudent, they would not be in such trouble. This attitude was very much at odds with the more societally oriented perspective on poverty Virginia had developed at Wellesley, and it disturbed her greatly.

The kind of work Virginia did in response to the poverty she saw in Birmingham was well within the accepted range of behavior for a genteel Southern matron. It did not signify a departure from the prescribed role. It did, however, give her a new perspective on issues of social justice and experience in actively creating solutions to social problems.

Not long after their marriage, Clifford Durr lost his job in an incident reminiscent of the same kind of determination to hold fast to a principled stand that we saw in Virginia's father. This was one of many such stands Clifford took, at great cost to both himself and his family. During Clifford and Virginia's early years in Birmingham, Clifford was a partner in the law firm of Martin, Thompson, Turner, and McWhorter, and his future with the firm was secure. But as the depression brought financial strain to the firm, the senior partner, Logan Martin, began to fire people without notice or explanation. When a young stenographer with a small child and no husband was fired, Clifford protested and suggested that the more senior members of the firm take pay cuts in order to retain her and prevent more layoffs. Mr. Martin reacted very negatively to this suggestion, and as a result of the conflict Clifford's continued association with the firm became untenable. As Clifford Durr's biographer notes, ''Whether he was fired by Martin or resigned before that could happen is beside the point. What is clear is that he suddenly found himself in the depths of the depression, with a young family to support and no job, having taken a stand, as he was so often to do, on principle.''[11]

Clifford was soon rescued from his joblessness by his brother-in-law. Back in 1926, at the time of Clifford and Virginia's marriage, Virginia's sister Josephine's husband, Hugo Black, ran for the U.S. Senate and won. While the Durrs were living in Birmingham, he ran successfully for a second term. At that point, President Franklin Roosevelt took office and, through Hugo Black's influence, Clifford Durr was called to Washington to head a program to recapitalize the banks under the Reconstruction Finance Corporation. The Durrs moved to Washington in 1933, settling in the genteel suburb of Seminary Hill, right outside Alexandria, Virginia, and began an important new period in their lives.

Many of the men living in Seminary Hill were political appointees or elected officials, and the Durrs socialized with many of the key figures in the Roosevelt administration. In 1935, Virginia began to go with a friend[12] to sit in on congressional hearings and to the Supreme Court to hear the ground-breaking New Deal cases being tried. Over several years in the mid-1930s, Virginia's fascination with legal cases and congressional hearings provided her with a sophisticated understanding of politics and the law. In the spring of 1938, the Durrs' three-year-old son died of appendicitis. Virginia was terribly depressed and in order to distract her thoughts from the tragedy, she spent almost every day during the summer of 1938 at the historic LaFollette hearings on civil liberties. Some of the most dramatic of these hearings focused on the labor movement and the often violent management opposition to union organizing, including the famous Harlan County United Mineworkers case. Virginia later commented about these hearings. "This is where I got my education."[13]

It was at the LaFollette hearings that Virginia first heard about Joe Gelders, a leftist labor organizer and former college professor who became her dear friend and an important influence on her. While organizing a union for steelworkers in Birmingham, Gelders was badly beaten by the head of U.S. Steel's private police force. He was left for dead on a backwoods road and then hospitalized. Gelders did not testify at the hearings because he was still in the hospital, but there was extensive testimony about him and his work. Virginia, moved and impressed by this testimony, told us that "He was the hero of the hearings." Virginia was greatly shocked when she came to understand that not only the steel company but also many of her friends' fathers and other "fine gentlemen" she knew in Birmingham had teamed up to keep the unions out of Birmingham and were using blatantly violent methods. Virginia had seen hardship in Alabama, but she had never been aware of this kind of violence. Looking back on it later, she sees this experience as having been the first time she understood the connection between civil rights and economic issues. Mrs. Durr later sought out Joe Gelders, to whom she attributes her important awakening, and they became close friends until Gelders's death years later.

As she came to know more about the New Deal and the people who were making it happen, Virginia Durr began to want a role in it. "I lived in a lovely, quiet neighborhood that I adored. But I also wanted to be in Washington in the midst of all the excitement, because to me the New Deal was perfectly thrilling. Cliff was saving the banks and the telephone was ringing all the time. It was an exciting time to be there."[14] She had met Eleanor Roosevelt and admired her greatly, so she decided to volunteer for the Women's Division of the National Democratic Committee, since she had heard that Mrs. Roosevelt worked closely with that group.

Because of the availability of low-cost servants (an irony she later came to appreciate), Virginia was able to leave her three young children at home several mornings a week while she volunteered at the Women's Division. Mrs. Roosevelt did come to the office quite often, along with a number of other interesting women, and Virginia loved the work. One of the primary goals of the Women's Division at that time was to get rid of the poll tax so that white Southern women could vote. Virginia had long resented the sex-stereotyped roles that

Southern women had to play, and she "plunged into the fight to get
rid of the poll tax with greatest gusto."[15] She soon began going to
the headquarters every day, answering the phone, putting out literature, and trying to persuade someone in Congress to introduce a bill
to abolish the poll tax.

This was the beginning of what would be for Virginia a thirty-
year campaign to abolish the poll tax in the southern United States.
Beginning in the early 1900s, the poll tax was used by the Southern
states to disenfranchise black and poor white men, making the legal
right to vote dependent on their paying a tax they could ill afford
each time they voted. This effectively prevented them from voting.
After the passage of the Woman Suffrage Amendment in 1920, the
poll tax was used in the same way to prevent women from voting.
As Virginia Durr puts it, "If a poor tenant farmer had scraped up a
dollar and a half to pay his poll tax, he sure as hell wasn't going to
pay a dollar and a half for his wife. And the women themselves never
had any money. In Alabama, the poll tax was retroactive to age twenty-
one even if you started voting when you were forty-five. . . . Missis-
sippi had the lowest [proportion of people of voting age who voted]:
12 percent. As a result, much of the South was run by an oligarchy
composed of white, usually middle-aged, gentlemen, or men—some
of them were gentlemen and some of them weren't."[16]

From the very beginning, however, this work encountered serious
political opposition. About a year after Mrs. Durr joined the fight,
the chairman of the Democratic National Committee, James Farley,
in response to pressure from Southern senators and representatives
within the Democratic party, forbade the Women's Division to continue work on the poll tax issue. The men holding political power in
the South at that time wanted to maintain the poll tax because the
entry of blacks, poor whites, and women into the electorate
threatened their control in a time of considerable economic and social
turmoil. Labor unions were just beginning to become powerful and
were seen to threaten the South's only economic advantage over the
North—cheap labor. Because the Democratic party needed to maintain
some unity across the rather disparate elements of Southern conservatives and Northern liberals, pressure from powerful Southern Demo-
crats was a formidable force in preventing the success of the anti-poll
tax movement.

Although the Women's Division was forced to stop its anti-poll
tax work, Virginia maintained her commitment to the issue and soon
resumed the struggle within the framework of another organization,

the Southern Conference for Human Welfare, which was created, with the backing of Franklin and Eleanor Roosevelt, as an organization that would bring together the New Deal elements in the South. The first meeting of the conference, held in 1938, brought together the New Dealers, the labor unions, and the groups working for black civil rights. The meeting was held in Birmingham, Alabama, and, by including both blacks and whites, challenged Alabama's segregation laws. Only the presence of Eleanor Roosevelt prevented the participants from being arrested by the notorious police commissioner Bull Connor. Mrs. Durr describes the meeting as follows:

> The conference opened on a Sunday night in the city auditorium. . . . Oh, it was a love feast. There must have been fifteen hundred or more people there from all over the South, black and white, labor union people, and New Dealers. Southern meetings always include a lot of preaching and praying and hymn singing, and this meeting was no exception. The whole meeting was just full of love and hope. It was thrilling . . . and we all went away from there that night with love and gratitude. The whole South was coming together to make a new day.[17]

At that meeting, Mrs. Durr became the vice president of the anti-poll tax committee. The fact that the committee was a part of the Southern Conference for Human Welfare gave her a sense that her work was part of a larger movement and provided a very powerful feeling of support:

> All of a sudden you felt that you were not by yourself. There were all these other people with you. After all, when the wife of the president of the United States and a Supreme Court justice and John L. Lewis [founder of the Congress of Industrial Organizations (CIO)] are on your side, you have a lot of support. And the Negro people, like Mrs. [Mary McLeod] Bethune, certainly gave me a feeling of support. Almost everyone who came to that first conference in Birmingham had the same feeling of finally getting together.[18]

Many Southerners, however, including friends from Virginia's childhood, were opposed to the liberal movement represented by the Southern Conference, and Virginia encountered intense pressure to step back from her involvement. For example, "Some childhood friends of mine—sweet, dear people—took me out to lunch. One had been in my wedding, and both were very devoted friends. One of them said, 'Now, Jinksie [Virginia's nickname], I think I should tell you frankly that I think it's awful for you to come down here and encourage this rabble to take over. You are going to go back to Washington and we are left to deal with it. I don't think you could possibly know what you are doing.'"[19] Many of the people with whom Virginia had grown up were very much afraid of the opening up of race relations. While they may have been benevolent toward their black servants, they believed strongly in the separation of the races and had no wish to see the current social order disrupted. The participants in the Southern Conference were also denounced as Communist sympathizers, as were the Roosevelts and the New Dealers generally. And, in fact, some labor unions in the United States did have close ties with leftist political forces, so the charge was not entirely without substance. As Virginia Durr points out, "The Communist party at that time was much more open and had organized many of the unemployed. The young Communists were not welcome in the South and were often beaten up and held in jail incommunicado. A number of them were even killed."[20]

Following the meeting of the Southern Conference, Virginia returned to Washington to continue her efforts to abolish the poll tax. The committee put out a newsletter, persuaded a congressman to introduce a bill, arranged hearings on the bill, and lobbied for support. Over a period of many years, the fight against the poll tax was an obsession for Virginia, despite the fact that she now had four children at home. Eventually (in 1942), a limited bill was passed abolishing the poll tax for people in the armed forces, for federal elections only. Broader anti-poll tax bills were introduced year after year, but they were defeated by Southern senators over and over. Because of the small electorate in the South, many Southern senators and representatives had been in office for thirty or forty years and controlled most of the important committees. Particularly in the Senate, the anti-poll tax bills were filibustered by conservative Southern senators to prevent passage. Although the anti-poll tax committee was not successful in achieving a legislative abolition of the tax, they did make it a national issue of considerable visibility, and the poll tax was finally abolished for federal elections by constitutional amendment in 1964. (It was abolished for state elections by the Voting Rights Act, signed by President Lyndon Johnson in 1965.)

Just before and during World War II, the anti-poll tax work lost the backing of the Roosevelts, since obtaining the broad support needed to enter and then win the war was FDR's highest priority. To make matters worse, the committee also faced bitter opposition from anti-Communist groups. The financial and political supporters of the committee threatened to withdraw their backing if the committee was not purged of suspected leftists. Mrs. Durr and the other committee leaders had always maintained the policy that they would work with any group that shared their goal of abolishing the poll tax regardless of the group's political orientation. Among the groups that had offered the most support were labor unions. The voting rights issue was linked with labor organizing because antilabor groups maintained political control in part through preventing low-income workers from voting. Some of the labor unions and other organizations that supported the Committee Against the Poll Tax may, in fact, have been associated with socialist or Communist groups. When the leaders of the anti-poll tax committee refused to cooperate in the purge, the committee lost the support of more moderate groups and was unable to continue. The committee closed its doors in the summer of 1948, and the Southern Conference for Human Welfare did the same in November of that year.

During the time that they lived in Seminary Hill, Virginia and Clifford were close to Josephine and Hugo Black and friendly with many of the other key political figures of the time, and Virginia was very much influenced by the experiences she had with them. Hugo Black, in particular, influenced the political thinking of both Virginia and Clifford Durr very deeply. Virginia also rekindled some college friendships at this time, most notably her friendship with Clark Howell Foreman, who had been a Harvard student from Atlanta when Virginia was at Wellesley. As two Southerners up North, they had become very close friends. Mr. Foreman later became a central figure in the New Deal and a leader of the Southern Conference.

When Virginia Durr and Clark Foreman renewed their friendship in Washington, she found that he had undergone important ideological changes since his college days. He had witnessed a lynching and had traveled and studied in England and Russia. As soon as he arrived in Washington to work for the Public Works Administration, Foreman had hired a black woman for his secretary. This caused a tremendous outcry, since at that time Washington was still segregated. Foreman believed very strongly in racial equality and was willing to risk public disapproval for the sake of integration.

Virginia describes an incident with Clark Foreman concerning his relations with blacks that was no doubt a turning point for her:

> That Sunday afternoon when he came out to our house, he began
> telling us what he was going to do and what he was doing. Well,

my Lord, I just fell into a fit! I couldn't believe it. We got into the most awful fight you have ever known in your life. Clark is not tactful at times. He said, "You know, you are just a white, Southern, bigoted, prejudiced, provincial girl." Oh, he just laid me out. I got furious and I said, "You are going back on all the traditions of the South. You, a Howell of Georgia, going back on all of it. What do you think of the Civil War? What did we stand for?" White supremacy, of course. When they left, Cliff said, "Well, I don't think you'll ever see him again." Amazingly enough, they called us up the next week and invited us to dinner.[21]

The Durrs became very close to the Foremans and through them began to socialize with some distinguished African-Americans. Virginia describes, for example, an occasion on which she was asked to pour tea at a reception that the Foremans were giving for Mattiwilda Dobbs, the black opera singer from Atlanta. "I don't know how many Dobbses were at the Foremans' the night of Mattiwilda's concert; there must have been fifteen. I served the tea—quite a reversal of roles for me, as you can imagine."[22]

Through her involvement with the Southern Conference and the poll tax committee, Mrs. Durr worked with many black organizations since the NAACP, the Council of Negro Women, the Black Elks, and many others were strong supporters of the anti-poll tax work. In part through her association with the leaders of these organizations, Mrs. Durr also became involved with other civil rights issues, especially desegregation. The activities of the committee itself often violated prohibitions against blacks and whites working or eating together or staying in the same hotel. Virginia was chair of the District of Columbia branch of the Southern Conference on Human Welfare (the Washington Committee), which became one of the most active local chapters. By the 1940s, the primary emphasis of the Southern Conference had shifted from labor union issues to race, and since D.C. itself was still segregated in many respects, the Durrs became involved in efforts to integrate the District. In one memorable incident, the Washington Committee organized a dinner for Virginia's brother-in-law, now Supreme Court Justice Hugo Black, in order to integrate the Washington hotels. Justice Black's colleagues on the Supreme Court were all invited, along with prominent black leaders. "Cliff and I went, of course. Poor Cliff was really caught between a rock and a hard place there. His mother was mad at him for attending an integrated dinner.

She wrote him that she had lived for many years under the shadow of his grandfather's brief defection to the Republicans during Reconstruction and she couldn't bear another cloud over her sunset years. 'The South has a tradition to preserve,' she wrote, 'and preserve it we shall with bloodshed if necessary.' Cliff went despite his mother's plea. The dinner was the first big breakthrough on the hotels in Washington."[23]

The poll tax fight provides an especially illuminating example of the transformation of goals because it took place over such an extended period of time. Virginia's goal in joining the Women's Division of the Democratic party was to have some part to play in the excitement of New Deal Washington, to have an opportunity to work with Eleanor Roosevelt, and to meet some interesting women. She soon became intensely involved in the fight for women's right to vote but was not at first sympathetic to blacks' struggle for equal rights.

When she began working with the National Democratic Committee in Washington, she was still, from her own subsequent point of view, "an absolute Alabama racist." Although she very much admired Mrs. Roosevelt and the other women on the committee, she initially disagreed with them completely on the race issue. She worked closely with these more liberal white women over an extended period, and also became acquainted with such important black women leaders as Mary McLeod Bethune and Mary Church Terrell. "And I'm absolutely positive that the reason I changed is because I was working with all these women in the Democratic Committee—women whom I loved, whom I admired, certainly. And I was, all of a sudden, you know, here I was working with women who thought my whole tradition was wrong. I admired Mrs. Roosevelt tremendously, but she thought I was wrong."

Because of the coalitions that formed around the voting rights issue, Mrs. Durr soon began to work closely with black organizations and distinguished black women such as Mrs. Bethune. The activities of the committee itself violated segregation laws because the committee held integrated meetings in cities that outlawed them. Mrs. Durr describes an encounter with Mary Church Terrell that was typical of the kind of experience that contributed to her awakening.

> I worked with Mrs. Mary Church Terrell in an effort to integrate Washington, D.C. Now, she was much older, she was as old as I am now, if not older. And she came from Memphis and she wore a high frilly collar and pearls in her ears and she looked like

a really high-class Southern lady. And so she and I got to be quite friendly, and she asked me one day if I knew anybody in Memphis. And I said yes, my mother had come from Memphis. And she said, "Well, who was your grandfather?" And I said, "A congressman, he was Congressman Patterson." And she said, "Well, he was my guardian." Well, it was quite a surprise to know that my grandfather was Mrs. Terrell's guardian. And her grandfather was Colonel Church, who had been my grandfather's best friend and they had fought in the war together and so Mr. Church had two families—he had a black family and a white family. And she was part of his black family. And my grandfather was her guardian. . . . So you see, it goes in mysterious ways. When you change your mind, you don't do it overnight unless you have a bolt of lightning. You go along your way and things change and all of a sudden you realize it's wrong. You think it's just terrible. And then you do feel, certainly, a sense of shame that you were blind so long.

Combined with an intellectual awakening on these issues stimulated by her more liberal friends in Washington, such as Clark Foreman, the opportunity and need to work closely with black people on the poll tax issue led to a transformation of Virginia Durr's goals that changed her life dramatically; indeed, it changed fundamentally who she was.

After World War II, the anti-Communist feeling in Washington began to escalate. The House Un-American Activities Committee (HUAC) had operated throughout the war; after the war, President Truman instituted the loyalty order, according to which everyone working for the government had to be examined for possible Communist ties. The loyalty oath was required of all government officials. Clifford Durr, who in 1941 had been appointed commissioner of the Federal Communications Commission (FCC), was in deep disagreement with the loyalty order and felt that the procedures used to investigate people were contrary to the most basic civil liberties. In these investigations, the accused were not told who had accused them, and people lost their jobs on the basis of unproven allegations of Communist ties. As commissioner of the FCC, Clifford Durr was asked to investigate employees of the FCC accused of having Communist ties or sympathies. Durr fought against the HUAC and the loyalty order, speaking out and writing about the issue frequently. He eventually decided, however, that he could not continue to work for the government in the current climate of fear and suspicion and resigned after his seven-year term expired, refusing an offer of reappointment from President Truman. As Clifford Durr's biographer puts it: "Durr's opposition to the president's loyalty program took three main forms. He refused to cooperate in its implementation within the FCC, he attacked it publicly whenever he could, and he decided to leave government service rather than compromise with the changed climate of opinion."[24]

Virginia did not want to go back to Alabama, so in 1948 Clifford opened a law office in Washington. He expected to do very well, because he had developed a very strong network of associations during his years in Washington and was considered impeccably fair and highly competent.

Clifford's first client was Roy Patterson, who had been suspended from a government job for disloyalty. Patterson had been wounded in World War II and decorated for valor and bravery. On his return he took a government position and later joined a Marxist bookshop that held discussion groups on political issues. Clifford Durr argued the case, and Patterson was reinstated the first time he was accused of disloyalty; however, soon afterward he was accused again and lost his job. The case got a lot of publicity, being one of the first loyalty cases. As a result, the big corporations and radio networks with whom Clifford had connections took their business elsewhere. So, almost by default, he became one of a small handful of attorneys who specialized in defending people accused of having communist ties. Clifford was unusual even within this group in that he was willing to defend people who had in fact been communists, belonged to Marxist discussion groups, and the like.

At this point, the Durrs' income dropped precipitously. Since individuals accused of disloyalty were fired and immediately taken off the payroll, even if reinstated later, they had tremendous backlogs of bills to pay. Legal bills were often the last to be paid. Perhaps even more problematic were the emotional tolls of Clifford's work. At the height of McCarthyism, the fight against the anti-communist witch hunt appeared to be a losing battle. Clifford was disillusioned to see how many of the people he had admired and in whom he believed caved in under pressure. "Cliff felt that he had no support at all. Hugo [Black] and Bill Douglas dissented in the cases that went to the Supreme Court, but all the cases were confirmed anyway. Even the great liberal Felix Frankfurter went along. The Court upheld faceless informers; it upheld loyalty orders; it upheld people being fired because some FBI agent, whose name wasn't revealed, said they had been at a meeting of the Spanish War Relief. It just got worse and worse."[25]

Clifford became more and more depressed and discouraged by the political climate in Washington and decided to leave. Virginia was opposed to returning to the South because she feared living in a climate of racial bigotry even more than she disliked living in the anti-communist climate of Washington. She told her daughter Ann that she was "frankly terrified of going to Alabama" and thought the social pattern there "utterly evil."[26] So, in 1950, Clifford Durr took a position in Denver as general counsel for the Farmers' Union Insurance Corporation. During the drive to Denver from Washington, Clifford's long-standing back problem was exacerbated so that he had to have surgery when they arrived in Denver. He was hospitalized for over a month, and the Durrs had to spend all of the profits from the sale of their house in Seminary Hill to cover the uninsured costs of his illness.

To make financial matters worse, while Clifford was in the hospital, Virginia became involved with an incident that was to cost Clifford his job. The Korean War was going on at that time and Virginia received a postcard from Linus Pauling and several other eminent scientists asking her to indicate on a return card whether she favored or opposed bombing above the Yalu (River) in Korea. Since bombing above the Yalu was seen as risking a war with China, Virginia indicated on the card that she opposed the bombing. She signed it and sent it off.

Soon after Clifford returned to work, still on crutches, the *Denver Post* published a prominent story with a headline that read "Wife of General Counsel of Farmers' Union Insurance Corporation Signs Red Petition." In response, Clifford's boss demanded that Virginia sign a retraction that would be published in the *Denver Post*. If she refused, Clifford would lose his job. Since she was unable to reach Clifford on the telephone, Virginia called the chief justice of the Utah Supreme Court, who had also signed the petition. After talking with Mrs. Durr about her family's financial situation, the chief justice advised her to sign the retraction. "[He said,] 'I think you will just have to do what people do when they are forced to do things they don't believe in. You'll just have to do it. You'll just have to do it and say you are doing it under duress.' 'But I don't see how I could keep my self-respect if I signed a letter like that.' 'Well, sometimes you have to give up your self-respect. You have three children [at home] and no money and a sick husband.'"[27] This presented a serious dilemma for Virginia. Whereas she did not want to jeopardize her husband's job and her family's welfare, she was well informed about the Korean War and strongly opposed to it.

Before Virginia had time to resolve her dilemma, Clifford came hobbling down the walk on his crutches. He had been threatened with dismissal unless he talked Virginia into signing the letter. He told the head of the Farmers' Union that he would never allow his wife to sign such a letter and walked out of the office without a job. In a letter to her daughter Ann, Virginia said that the incident in Denver had taught her a valuable lesson: "The struggle is the same everywhere."

Faced with no income, no savings, and Clifford's serious health problems, the Durrs decided to return to Alabama to live with Clifford's mother. For the first year after they returned, Clifford was too ill to work, and Virginia supported the family with a low-paying job as a secretary for an insurance company. During this time, she became less politically engaged in deference to Clifford's parents, who were being very supportive of Clifford and Virginia despite their political and ideological differences. This was not a happy time for Virginia, although she was grateful for the love and kindness Clifford's mother showed them. She missed very much the "sympathetic political companionship" she had become used to in Washington and missed being "in communion with people that believed and worked for a solution to the ills of the world." She felt very isolated from the Montgomery community, writing in despair to her old friend Clark Foreman, "I think we are going to be doomed to the same isolation that Aubrey lives in [Aubrey Williams, one of Virginia's closest friends, was an Alabama man who was assistant administrator of the New Deal's Works Progress Administration and later the head of the National Youth Administration. He was considered a political radical and shunned by Southern conservatives.] We have gone outside the tribe and broken the taboos and they won't take us back in unless we do penance and confess our sins."

Virginia also disliked very much being financially dependent on Clifford's family and experienced considerable tension in living with Clifford's strong-willed mother and aunt. Although their political differences were one source of the tension, Virginia did not really blame the Durrs for their racial and political beliefs. "You see, you have to realize one thing about being a Southerner, which is that you know you felt the same way. And you felt the same way for, say, thirty years, as I did. So how in the world can you blame other people for feeling the same way you did? I can't say 'You're a terrible racist and you ought to be ashamed of yourself,' when, for thirty-odd years, I was exactly the same way."

When Clifford had recovered, in 1952, he opened a law office in Montgomery, and Virginia worked with him as his secretary. Although she enjoyed the work, these were difficult years, both financially and emotionally. Clifford became known as someone who was willing to represent poor blacks, and frequently their cases involved serious exploitation by "respectable" white citizens of Montgomery. His cases included police brutality, loan sharking, and insurance scams. Clifford, although in favor of integration by this time, was not yet as sensitive as Virginia to the extent and consequences of Southern racism. "The people who were charging the Negroes tremendous rates of interest—sometimes 500 percent—were some of the 'best people' in Montgomery. That shocked him and made him ashamed. He thought it was shameful for white men who had a good background and were gentlemen to take advantage of Negroes. He felt the same way about some of the insurance cases he had—where some poor black person would pay on an insurance policy for years and years and get sick and find that the fine print said that the policy didn't apply."[28]

Although Virginia devoted most of her energy to her work in the law office and her family during the early 1950s, she remained involved with civil rights issues and was active in the very early efforts to integrate Montgomery. For example, she worked to integrate the United Church Women, which was a coalition of churches with separate organizations for black and white churches. Following the leadership of Mrs. Clara Rutledge, Mrs. Olive Andrews, and others, Virginia Durr worked to bring the black and white church women together. The difficulty of the transition to an integrated group is illustrated by an incident in which the white group asked Mrs. Cooper, a black woman prominent in the national organization of United Church Women to speak at a meeting to be held at the YWCA Campground, which had a rule forbidding blacks and whites to eat together. With a hypocrisy that was appalling to Virginia, most of the participants felt that the group ought to obey the camp rule and ask Mrs. Cooper to leave at suppertime. In response, Mrs. Rutledge, Mrs. Durr, and several others went outside the property and ate supper together.

> So we had to go off the grounds of the camp and sit down and eat our supper. By this time Mrs. Cooper and some of the other

ladies were crying, and nobody ate much. We told Mrs. Cooper
we would take her home, but she said, "No. You are not going
to take me home. I'm going back there and I am going to stay
till the very end." She dried her eyes and we took her back and
stayed until eleven o'clock that night. It was a very embarrassing
evening for everybody concerned. One lady got up and said,
"Mrs. Cooper, I don't want you to think we are prejudiced on
account of color. We want to stay separate, but you see I am
almost as black as you are, so it's not color." She rolled up her
sleeve and she was very sunburned.[29]

Eventually an integrated prayer group was formed: "We used to
meet and pray and sing and hold hands and have a cup of tea afterward. We always met in Negro churches. Mrs. King lived in Montgomery then, Mrs. Coretta King, and she and Mrs. [Ralph] Abernathy came."[30] the group grew to include about one hundred women
and stayed together throughout some of the most difficult times of
Alabama's desegregation until it was finally broken up by white rac-
ists.

During this period, John Crommelin had a group of people in
Montgomery who were fighting integration, and they took all
the license numbers of our cars at the meeting. Crommelin . . .
who was known for his right-wing and anti-Semitic views, published the names and telephone numbers and addresses of everybody at the United Church Women meeting in his paper, *Sheet
Lightning*. The women began to get terrible calls at night and
were harassed in other ways. That broke the group up. We never
met after that. The women became frightened when their names
were publicized. Even their husbands began getting phone calls
from people who threatened to stop doing business with them if
their wives went to any more integrated meetings. Several husbands took out notices in the papers disassociating themselves
from their own wives.[31]

In 1954, just before the Supreme Court was ready to rule on *Brown
vs. the Board of Education*, Mrs. Durr was called to testify before the
Senate Internal Security Subcommittee. The subcommittee was the
Senate's version of the House Un-American Activities Committee.
The chairman of the committee was Senator Jim Eastland of Missis-
sippi, who was running for reelection. His platform argued that if the
Supreme Court voted to desegregate the schools, it would prove that
the Court was part of a communist conspiracy. Eastland hoped that

by portraying Virginia Durr as a communist and publicizing her relationship with Hugo Black, he would strengthen his reelection campaign. Mrs. Durr was subpoenaed because of her involvement in the
Southern Conference, which had ceased to exist several years before,
and she was asked questions about people she had known who may
have had communist ties. She was furious and refused to cooperate.
She drafted a statement that she gave to the press, which ended with:
"I stand in utter and complete contempt of this committee." Despite
the fact that refusing to answer questions and thus being in contempt
was a criminal offense, Virginia never considered cooperating. Instead,
she remained silent no matter what was said to her, every now and
then taking out her compact and powdering her nose.

On the last day of the hearing, Eastland vowed to cite Mrs. Durr
for contempt and have her jailed but in fact did nothing. The press
coverage of the hearing was sympathetic toward Mrs. Durr, and public reaction in Montgomery was relatively mild. One reason for this
was that the hearing did not tie the anti-communist issue to the race
issue, which was much more sensitive in the South at that time. Furthermore, as Virginia Durr points out, "There was hardly anyone we
knew in Montgomery whose grandfather hadn't tried to overthrow
the government by force and violence, and they still were revered as
great heroes. A few people were nasty to us, but as a whole the
hearing didn't cause as much of a ripple as you might think."[32] Although the hearing did not seriously damage the Durrs' personal reputations, Clifford's law practice was affected. His few middle-class clients slipped away as people came to fear that they might suffer from
their association with so controversial a family. This meant that Clifford's practice was even more exclusively devoted to representing the
poor, especially poor blacks.

Fearing possible attacks as a result of the Eastland hearing, Clifford
and Virginia decided to move out of Clifford's parents' house. For
Virginia, this was a tremendous release, for she had suppressed her
political activities while living with the Durrs so as not to offend
or embarrass them. When Clifford and Virginia moved to a nearby
apartment, Virginia felt that she could reclaim her real identity. "In
a way, I was grateful that my cover as a nice, proper Southern lady
was blown by the hearing, because then I could begin to say what I
really thought. . . . It's ironic that, by and large, political people were
very quiet during the fifties, either because there was nothing to be
active in or because they just had to watch themselves, as I had been

doing earlier. The hearing changed all that for me. It put me into the fray, and I loved it. I felt freed.''[33]

It was an opportune moment for Virginia Durr to "reenter the fray," since soon after the hearings the Brown decision came down and "all hell broke loose. There was no choice. You had to stand up and be counted or move. We didn't move."[34] Virginia joined the Council on Human Relations, the only integrated group in Montgomery, and devoted herself to the desegregation of Montgomery. As always, she valued very highly the opportunity to work closely with other people who shared her beliefs. "It was a tremendous relief to me to be able to join something like that, where I was with people who were against segregation."

The atmosphere in Alabama at that time was extremely hostile toward integration. In Washington, Virginia had been surrounded by people who agreed with the liberal views she had come to hold. Now back in Alabama, they were part of a tiny minority and isolated from most of their former friends. This was painful for Virginia, who had grown up a Southern girl, expecting to be loved and admired by everybody. It was even more painful for her to watch the suffering inflicted on her children, and eventually two had to be sent to school in Massachusetts because their social isolation had become so intolerable. The children were treated with hostility by their teachers, who associated the school desegregation they were facing with actions of the children's uncle, Hugo Black, and resented the Durrs' support of desegregation. The parents of the children's friends also forced their children to stop associating with the Durr family.

> I think one of the most painful moments in my life was when Lulah had just started school. She was in the first grade. The Brown decision came down in May of 1954. Lulah was invited to a birthday party. I'd gotten her all dressed up in a little white ruffled dress with a big sash. She tied up her present, but she couldn't remember whether the party was at three-thirty or four. It was right around the corner, so I called up and the husband answered the telephone. I said, "I'm Mrs. Clifford Durr, Lulah Durr's mother, and Lulah has been invited to your little girls' birthday party"—two little twins—"and she doesn't know whether the party's at three-thirty or four." "Now what is the name you said you were?" he asked. "Mrs. Clifford Durr." "You're Hugo Black's sister?" "No," I said. "I'm Hugo

Black's sister-in-law. He married my sister." "Well, I don't know myself," he said, "but I'll ask my wife." I waited and waited. I heard them talking in the background and I waited and waited. Finally he came back to the phone and said, "Mrs. Durr, there will be no party this afternoon as far as your daughter is concerned because I wouldn't have a child of yours in my house."[35]

Although the Durrs were isolated from the white establishment in Montgomery, they were by no means working alone in the struggle for racial justice. By the time of the bus boycott in December 1955, Virginia had gotten to know many of the black leaders in Montgomery, including Martin Luther King, Jr., and his wife, Coretta Scott King. Virginia also knew Rosa Parks well, and it was Clifford Durr who was called in to get Rosa Parks out of jail when she was arrested for her historic refusal to move to the back of the bus. Clifford explained to Mrs. Parks that he could probably have the charges dropped or get her off on a technicality if she preferred. The other alternative would be to test the constitutionality of the bus segregation law. Mrs. Parks's husband feared greatly for her safety if they pushed the case to the limit, but she showed no reluctance. They decided to go forward with the case with the financial backing of the NAACP Legal Defense Fund. Although Clifford did not represent Mrs. Parks in the case, he acted as an adviser to her attorney and was very much involved with the case. The NAACP organized the famous Montgomery bus boycott in support of Rosa Parks. The boycott lasted an entire year and required the support not only of the blacks who refused to ride the buses but also of the white sympathizers like Virginia Durr who drove the protesters to and from work, risking fines and harassment in doing so. The boycott ended when Rosa Parks won her case, and the Supreme Court declared the ordinance unconstitutional in 1956.

Clifford Durr assisted the NAACP attorneys on the legal aspects of the Parks case throughout the boycott, working without payment and behind the scenes. Although his direct involvement in the case was not recognized at the time, Clifford was well known to sympathize with and support the boycott. As a result, the Durrs were even more socially ostracized and Clifford's law practice further damaged.

Resistance to the integration of Montgomery was intense, with bombings of Ralph Abernathy's church and the houses of Martin Luther King and many of the other black leaders and their white sympathizers. It was a difficult time for the Durrs, and it was at this point that they decided to send their two younger daughters to school in the North to remove them from the constant taunting that they endured from both teachers and other children. Although Clifford Durr received attractive job offers from universities and law firms in the North, he felt that Alabama was his home and refused to leave. According to Mrs. Durr, there were times when the isolation was so painful and the children were suffering so badly that she would have left Alabama if Clifford had been willing to do. Clifford, however, had a deep sense of responsibility for the South and would not be driven out of the land that he loved and felt was his own.

Having stayed in Alabama, the Durrs remained very active in the civil rights movement throughout the 1960s. Among other things, they housed and fed dozens of students and other protesters who passed through Montgomery on their way to Selma and other protests. During this period, Virginia felt she was living "in the middle of a storm." But in spite of the violence and turbulence of the times, the overriding feeling was that the battle for civil rights was slowly being won, as were most of the important segregation cases that Clifford tried. Virginia was left with a profound respect for the law, "when it works," and to her it seemed that by and large the law was working.

Despite this faith in some aspects of the American legal system, Virginia Durr is not naive about the power of law as a complete solution to racism and poverty. In reflecting back on the gains, she is acutely aware of how far we have to go and how difficult it will be. "I wish I could be more cheerful and end on an upbeat note and say, 'We're going into the land of Canaan now. We've been through the desert and we've crossed the Red Sea.' But I'm like Moses. I glimpsed the promised land, but I never got there, and I never will. It's sad, because I would like very much to live long enough to see a change come about, a really fundamental change. I don't think I ever will, because I think it's going to take an awfully long time."[36]

Clearly, Virginia had come a long way from her plantation heritage. Her moral development occurred gradually over the course of her life, with noteworthy changes occurring as late as her thirties and beyond. A history of openness to moral change leads some individuals to continue developing in the moral area while others do not progress much after early adulthood. Although Virginia's emerging new values were not entirely self-initiated, they do reflect what we might call an "active receptiveness" to social influence of particular sorts.

Mrs. Durr's openness to change was not a blanket receptiveness toward just any sort of influence—witness, for example, her strenuous resistance of the pressures to give in to Jim Eastland or to go along with the prevailing racial views of her friends in Alabama. When she arrived in Washington, Virginia already had some liberal ideas in the economic and political areas, a real concern for equality and respect for others, a deeply valued honesty, and the Wellesley experience with the black classmate. These things no doubt contributed to her receptiveness to new ideas about racial equality when contradictions were pointed out between her views on race and her values and ideologies in other areas. The fact that some of the people she admired most, for example Eleanor Roosevelt, disapproved of her views on race also helped motivate her to rethink her beliefs.

It is therefore important to emphasize that, at each step in her evolving moral engagement with the civil rights movement, Virginia Durr chose to move forward rather than to withdraw. Consequently, we must conclude that the direction and shape of her moral growth was "co-constructed" by the continual interplay between her and her chosen community. The social influences in Mrs. Durr's life cannot be understood without knowing what she herself brought to the process.

Excerpts from the interview with Mrs. Durr illustrate the way in which her social experiences interacted with her values, beliefs, and character to result in the developmental path she took.

INTERVIEWER: Now, before I start asking the questions that I came with, I would like to hear a little bit more about your experience of not having made choices, as you put it. Maybe you could just talk about that a little bit. You've mentioned that a couple of times . . .

MRS. DURR: You make . . . I suppose you make choices every day of your life. But the thing is, as far as the decisions I made concerning my part, say, in the racial struggle in the South, it wasn't a decision, it was something that grew over a period of years and one thing led to another. But I never—like Paul on the road to Damascus, was it?—thought that I saw a revealing light and just all of a sudden saw the light. But it was over a period of a number of years that I began to change my feelings. And the same thing was true really about the . . . well, in a way, it was true about so many things. I changed as things happened. Rather, things happened and I changed because they happened.

Social influences play a central role in both transforming Virginia Durr's beliefs and goals and in sustaining her motivation and energy.

We have already discussed the influence of her exposure to the liberal New England attitudes of the Wellesley College faculty and administration. While at Wellesley, Virginia chose Southerners as her closest friends, thus softening the impact of the "culture shock" she faced. These Southern friends were, of course, somewhat unusual in that they had chosen to attend such schools as Wellesley and Harvard and, furthermore, were themselves being influenced by the new environment. Virginia's relationship with Clark Foreman illustrates the gradual nature of the transformation. She and Clark became close during their college days because both were from the South and considered their Southern heritage a very important part of their identities. While she was again living in Alabama, however, Clark was living abroad and undergoing profound personal changes. When she encountered Clark again in Washington, he was able to influence her racial views as no Northerner could because she knew he came from a similar background and understood her point of view.

Although acting according to what she believed in often required standing up to intense social and political pressure, Virginia did not experience herself as a lonely hero or nonconformist. She felt very keenly not only her links with others fighting for the same causes but also saw the positions she took as unremarkable and taken for granted by the majority of people elsewhere.

> And actually, you see, I never have felt . . . it's only due to the circumstances of the U.S. that what I did ever seemed to be of any historic value. In others words, integration and now the right to vote, which were the two things that I especially worked on, were commonplace in almost every other civilized country which didn't have segregation and certainly gave everybody the right to vote. So I really was identified with an extremely small part even of the United States, which was the South. And therefore, I have never felt that I myself was any great radical. Although I seemed radical to other people, and was considered radical, I never thought of myself as being radical because I was simply doing what was common everywhere else. So I always felt that I was the one that belonged to the majority, that I was the one that was going by the laws of the United States, I was the one that was conforming to the majority.

Mrs. Durr was energized and sustained by her sense that she was fighting a critical battle and that she was fighting alongside powerful and admirable people. She compares the role of people in her life with the role religion often played in the lives of others.

> I've gone to church all my life and I am religious in a way in that I believe in a power in the universe beyond my comprehension, but I never have been able yet to feel, as some people do, the intimate power of God. I've had people tell me they felt that God was there. I've never been able to feel that. Well, I've felt always it's more people being with me, supporting me. People— I'm a great people person. I like to be around people, and I like to be with people, and I believe in that. I think it's the people that stick together who can accomplish great things. The difficulty is getting them to stick together.

Without a doubt the most important influence in Virginia Durr's adult life was that of her husband, Clifford Durr. She deeply respected, even revered, her husband, seeing him as a figure of absolute integrity. Clifford's and Virginia's racial views evolved in synchrony, and they supported each other fully at each step of their deepening commitment to civil rights and opposition to the anti-communist movement. In the Korean War incident in Colorado, Clifford fully supported her decision to sign Linus Pauling's protest letter and her refusal to issue a retraction. They shared equally the conviction that one does not go back on one's word or compromise one's principles for the sake of expediency.

After Clifford resigned from the FCC, he had some trouble finding another position. Yet when he was offered a very lucrative job with a Wall Street firm dealing with communications, thus using his political contacts in ethically questionable ways, Clifford turned it down without hesitation. In describing this incident, Virginia remarks, "The idea of Cliff's going back on his principles is just unthinkable. It never was a question. It was something he never even thought about. Cliff was a man of absolute principle, and he never cared much about money."[37] Later, during the most turbulent times of the fight to integrate Alabama, it was most often Clifford who insisted that they stay and fight rather than retreat to the North. No doubt each learned a lot from the other at every point in their long relationship. Clifford's biographer speaks of Virginia's influence on Clifford's political beliefs during the early years in Birmingham as Virginia struggled to make sense of the terrible poverty of the depression. Virginia tells of the long talks the couple had about their work and the moral and political issues with which they were struggling.

For example, Clifford would "wrestle over [legal] cases tremendously" with Virginia as they lay in bed at night. These conversations
must have stimulated Virginia to think through the moral and political
assumptions of her own work as well. Clearly, throughout their forty-
nine-year marriage, the moral influence was mutual and positive, with
each reinforcing and supporting the other's highest values.

It is important to note that the social influences that shaped and
motivated Virginia Durr came not only from her supporters but also
from her opponents. She talks often about the importance of working
closely with like-minded people in her poll tax and desegregation
work, but also evident, although less explicit, is the energizing effect
of mobilizing against opponents. Virginia often felt intense anger
toward those who sought to preserve the racial status quo in the South
and those who violated civil liberties in the name of anti-communism.
She felt their pressure to conform in a very personal way, and this
pressure strengthened her will to resist. The emotions revealed are
reminiscent of those aroused over her seven-year-old birthday party
in which increased pressure to conform led her to more and more
unacceptable behavior in response.

In thinking back on these difficult times and what it was that kept
her going, Virginia Durr talks most about her absolute certainty that
what she was doing was right.

> I knew that the things we were working for were right. When
> times get bad, you only have one thing to fall back on—that you
> believe in what you are doing. My children, as they reached
> young adulthood, would sometimes say they wished I had stayed
> at home and baked brownies as other mothers did. But what
> good were brownies in a society that tolerated poverty and denied
> people the education that enabled them to get out of poverty.
> What good were brownies in a society that denied people the
> right to vote?[38]

Like so many of the other exemplars in this study, Virginia Durr
denies having questioned or struggled with her beliefs. She knew what
was right to do and knew that *she* was responsible to carry it out. To
a large extent, she disregarded the costs and dangers, although she
was well aware that they existed, after all, when issues of principle
were at stake. As a result, like our other exemplars, she did not experience herself as courageous. Again, in this regard, she is prototypical:

INTERVIEWER: When you were working on all these things and so on,
were there some times when you weren't sure what you should do? It

seemed that many times it seemed very obvious what you needed to do and so on, but were there times when you really felt in a dilemma, you had trouble making decisions or you found it difficult?

MRS. DURR: No, I can't remember that. I remember people saying, "You can't be self-righteous, you're so self-righteous. You know you're right." Well, I did know I was right and I felt that denying anybody the right to vote was wrong. I felt to segregate people was wrong. I never had any doubts about it. You see, you're terribly criticized when you do these things that are against the majority. If you don't know you're right you have nothing to fall back on. I knew I was right. I was actually certain of it; I never had any doubts.

Later,

INTERVIEWER: It seems that you attribute courage to other people a lot, but then you didn't attribute it to yourself. You would say that the black children that were going to school . . . talking about them showing courage and your husband and so on and all these people, but you don't attribute yourself as having acted . . .

MRS. DURR: Well, no, because I did what I felt I had to do but I never felt that I was doing it from courage, that I was being so brave about it. It was just something I had to do. I didn't feel any great sense of exultation about it.

Like our other exemplars, Virginia Durr exhibits a positive approach in many aspects of her life. Also like the others, she loved her work, "enjoyed being in the fray," and was not preoccupied with self-pity in regard to the difficult conditions of her life and her modest financial circumstances.

Virginia Durr was often able to turn a difficult situation into a positive one, as she did in relation to the Eastland hearings. Not only did she use the incident to gain sympathetic press coverage, but she also used it to her personal advantage, as a catalyst to move from Clifford's parents' house to a home of their own.

In spite of these similarities to the other exemplars in her approach to her life circumstances, Mrs. Durr differs from many of the others in some of the feelings that she expresses. First, although she accepts the costs and consequences of her commitment to social justice and is not deterred by them, she fully recognizes the sacrifices she and her family have had to make and looks back on them with some regret.

Many of our exemplars describe their lives as extremely happy, fortunate, and satisfying despite the economic and other sacrifices they have made. In contrast, Virginia Durr is left with the sense that standing up for what you believe in, fighting for social justice, exacts a heavy toll and that people have to be willing to pay the price if they are going to enter the fight:

INTERVIEWER: It seems that freedom of speech and honor and sticking up for what you believe in and so on seem to be part of the values of your family and your heritage.

MRS. DURR: Well, certainly, my father did that, but the thing is that I never saw anybody profit from it. My father lost his church, lost his home, and had to go out and sell insurance. And my husband for years showed extreme bravery and being exactly right and then in the end, you know, had nothing whatever. And so I do believe in honor and I believe in standing up for what is right, but I think people have got to realize that they are not going to be rewarded for it. The thing I want to impress on people is that if you do what you think is right it gives you a great deal of satisfaction. But on the other hand, people rush into things, and they don't realize the price they have to pay. They're not prepared to pay the price when they see it. And it's a strange thing but the people that you help, very few are very grateful. Most people that you help in this world resent it. They don't want to be in the position of being helped. I think that's just a human characteristic. It's just the way I didn't want to have to live on charity and borrowed money. You don't like to be in a dependent position.

INTERVIEWER: Does that make you want to stop helping them?

MRS. DURR: Oh, no. It's just . . . what I'm trying to say is . . . don't live in a world of fantasy. Try to see things as they are and not go into a fantasy. . . . It certainly was a terrific struggle, but we did win it, so that's the main thing.

Among the costs that were most painful to Virginia were the social isolation that she and her family endured when they returned to Alabama and the criticism of her political activities by relatives and friends. She was still very much a Southern lady and the disapproval of her former friends meant more to her than it might to someone who had more fully renounced the culture. The criticisms that hurt the most were those that accused her of neglecting or harming Clifford and the children. She was especially vulnerable to these attacks, because she feared that they were valid.

Virginia recalls an incident in her adolescence that reveals the prevailing attitude toward women who devote themselves to social change:

> When the women's right to vote was passed, I was a teenager. And one of the ladies who had led that struggle, Patty Jacobs, was a friend of our family. She lived nearby so I saw her a great deal. She would come by the house all the time, and my mother would say, "There's Patty Jacobs. Oh, my goodness, I feel for those children! She's *never* home." And my father would say, "Oh, I feel for her poor husband! She's out trying to lobby the men while poor Saul's at home cooking and so forth." So I got the idea that a Suffragist was somebody who neglected her children, who abandoned her home, who left her husband to wash the dishes while she lobbied the men. Well, it turns out she was a very brave woman who did play a big part in getting women the right to vote.

Although Mrs. Durr is critical of her parents' attitude toward Patty Jacobs, she was herself vulnerable to the charge of neglect. In looking back on her life, Mrs. Durr does not regret the lack of money or ease in her life or the turmoil of being "in the fray." But she does regret not having spent more time with her children, and she regrets the suffering the younger children had to endure during the hardest times in Alabama. This is a source of considerable pain for her, even at age eighty-seven. She looks back on what she contributed and what it cost her and feels that the children's suffering and the need to spend so much time away from them are the most painful sacrifices she had to make:

> My children certainly don't look back on Montgomery with happiness. Too hard, and too many threats, and too poor and didn't feel any sense of real pleasure. And that's sad in a way, that your children have such a large number of years that they look back on as unhappiness. And you feel kind of guilty that you got them in that position.

And later:

> [The worst thing] was to have people say, "Well, now here, Virginia, I really don't see how you *can* do this. You *know* it's going to hurt Cliff and the children." And it *did* hurt the chil-

dren. And I had to send them off to school. They were perfectly miserable. And none of them wants to come back to Montgomery now. Not one of them will even come back for a visit. That is the most painful part of the whole thing. . . . And so when your children feel that way about their home, it's very sad.

In spite of this regret, as she looks back on her life, at the time that she was embroiled in the anti-poll tax and desegregation work, Virginia Durr did not feel that removing herself from the struggle was a viable option. She was aware of the costs to her family but felt the urgency of her fight against injustice left her no choice but to go forward. Her certainty about the importance of the issues seemed to justify the sacrifices she and her family made. Although she feels deep regret in relation to her children, when she thinks back on the pressures of the times, Virginia Durr realizes that if she had it to do over again, she would no doubt do the same thing. As she said: "Well, there were no choices to make."

Virginia Durr contrasted with some of the other exemplars in the anger she felt toward her opponents and her inability to forgive those who had wronged her and her family. At age eighty-seven, Mrs. Durr was still struggling to come to terms with the intense anger and bitterness that she felt toward Clifford's colleagues in Washington who had turned their backs on him during the worst of the McCarthy era. She felt a need to make peace with these painful memories but was unable to do so: "I have no kind feelings toward them. I don't forgive people sometimes and I do not forgive those three boys that we knew so well [Abe Fortas, Thurman Arnold, and Paul Porter]. And then I don't forgive a lot of them, though I try to. I try not to hate and despise the people that let Cliff down. But I still feel it. And I have to fight it because it not only makes my blood pressure go up, but you know, there's so many of them that you can't be mad at all of them."

Mrs. Durr's feelings of bitterness and regret contrast sharply with the attitudes of Suzie Valadez and Mother Waddles, who find it possible to forgive over and over those who betray them. In some sense, then, Virginia Durr did not have a "positive attitude" of exactly the same variety that we saw in most of our exemplars. The difference in orientation may have something to do with differences in the nature of their work. Mrs. Durr's primary contributions involved fighting against a powerful establishment, whereas Mrs. Valadez and Mrs.

Waddles are extending charity to the poor. Although both tasks involve some relationship with both the oppressor and the oppressed, Mrs. Durr's primary focus is the oppressor, and the primary focus of the others is the oppressed. Anger must have a target, and if Mrs. Valadez and Mrs. Waddles had allowed themselves to feel angry for any significant period of time toward the objects of their charity, it would have completely undermined their work. In contrast, anger toward her opponents might even contribute positively to Virginia Durr's work.

In a sense, one may wonder whether people like Virginia Durr, who spend their lives fighting for social justice, need the harder edge that anger provides. Mrs. Durr's attitude toward issues such as the exploitation of women, blacks, and the poor are energized by anger, as are her relationships with her political opponents. The outrage at the injustice she encountered was a powerful motivator for her. She talks, for example, about the first time she became aware of the unfairness of the poll tax and of the fury it aroused in her. Virginia paid her poll tax when she first voted, at age twenty-one, but somehow avoided paying it again for the next eight years under the mistaken assumption that only one initial payment was required. She was shocked and outraged to learn, at age twenty-nine, that she must pay retroactive taxes back to age twenty-one if she was to vote. It was immediately clear to her that making a payment of that size would be impossible for most women and many men. As she commented later, "It made me perfectly furious. . . . But that got me stirred up on the right to vote." Mrs. Durr was strengthened by her anger at the Eastland hearing as well. During the hearing, she was able to be defiant in the face of a possible jail term because she experienced no fear, only anger at the injustice of the outrageous accusations being made.

Another source of the difference between Virginia Durr's approach and that of Mother Waddles and Suzie Valadez may be in the role religion played for each woman. Mrs. Valadez and Mrs. Waddles are deeply religious, trusting in God's goodness and explicitly aspiring to be Christ-like themselves. Virginia Durr, on the other hand, approached her work and her life from a secular orientation. She describes herself as having lost her faith in the goodness of God while still a young woman.

Since her father was a minister, Virginia had grown up in a very religious household. She went to church, Sunday school, Sunday afternoon religious education meetings, and Wednesday prayer meetings. In addition, the family held morning services at home before breakfast each Sunday. Sterling Foster preached hellfire and damnation, and during her early childhood Virginia believed all that he said. Virginia's mother held a gentler view of God as a kindly father, which she conveyed to Virginia.

Virginia's belief in a powerful and benevolent God lasted for many years, but did not withstand her exposure to suffering and evil in the world. In Birmingham during the depression, she was exposed to terrible poverty and cruel and callous treatment of the poor, of prison inmates, and others without power. This experience led her to question the belief that a kindly God would protect the powerless of the world:

> The only philosophy I came to [based on that experience] was that I could not depend on God to do it. That was the one thing I had learned. He wasn't going to save me or anybody else that I could see. So that then I came to the conclusion that maybe the only way that God could do anything was through us, through human beings. That all that magic didn't exist; that maybe [it was only] through people He could do, that was the only way He could get anything done. So *we* had to do it.

This realization did not give Virginia a sense that in her political work she was doing God's will, as we saw in Suzie Valadez and as we will see in Charleszetta Waddles. On the contrary, she became more and more alienated from religion over time as she endured and confronted suffering and faced evil in the world. She connects her inability to forgive those who hurt her and her husband with her inability to believe in a benevolent God. As she reaches the end of her life, this is an important struggle for her, and she wishes that she could return to her earlier faith in the goodness of God.

When asked whether faith had been a support to her in difficult times, as it was for many of our exemplars, she responds that it had not:

> I'm afraid that my faith in the goodness of God is very weak. I mean I just don't, I cannot imagine a beneficent God, you know, letting the innocent suffer, that's the thing that just . . . when our little boy died, you know, that was so hard to understand. You know, it was just . . . oh, I believe there's an infinite being and I believe that there's a consciousness in the universe but it's hard to forgive a God that lets all this viciousness happen. I mean, of course, you shouldn't be the one to forgive God, but it's so hard to believe, to have faith.

Instead of the steadfast faith in God that sustained many of our exemplars, Virginia relied on solidarity with other people fighting the same battles, on an intellectual framework that was organized around a recognition of basic human rights, and on some deep values of honesty, integrity, and honor that had roots in her family and Southern culture.

The values of honesty and honor were strong in both Clifford's and Virginia's families and were consistent with a Southern tradition of honor and willingness to take a stand. In Virginia's childhood, the Civil War was not remote but instead proudly remembered as a time when Southern men were willing to die to defend their way of life. The defiance of desegregation orders by people like Governor George Wallace, who personally blocked the door of a school, can be seen in the same light. Although Virginia came to see the way of life that the Confederates and segregationists defended as destructive and unfair racial domination, she drew on the tradition of Southern honor that prized such acts of defiance, while changing radically the content of the beliefs for which she stood.

Other Southerners exemplified for Virginia Durr a less brutish version of this tradition of honor. She describes such a person as follows:

> Dr. Randolph, an Episcopal minister, had been head of an Episcopal school somewhere in south Virginia and he had failed the sons of some very prominent people in the Episcopal church. The board of trustees warned him . . . but he was a man of total integrity and honesty, and he kept on failing the students who did poorly, so the board fired him. He came up and lived in the little house next to us . . . on Seminary Hill. During the war he got a job in a torpedo factory. He'd go off in the mornings with a lunch basket in his hands. And Mrs. Randolph would come out and empty the garbage. . . . There are a lot of Virginians I didn't like at all, but there is a strain in Virginia of men of integrity, men like Cliff who insist on doing right in spite of hell or high water. Dr. Randolph was one of them. And he did it in such a matter-of-fact way.[39]

Virginia Durr's enemies in the extended battle for civil rights were the industrial and political leaders who opposed change. She saw some of these, the "gentlemen," as benighted but essentially worthy opponents. She saw the others as corrupt and "dishonorable" and approached them with anger and outrage. For example, she considered

Jim Eastland, who presided over the Senate's Internal Security Committee, to be "lower than a rattlesnake." In making these judgments, Mrs. Durr exhibits a perspective that combines concepts and images drawn from the culture of the South with beliefs about race and social justice that are in complete opposition to those she was taught as she was growing up.

Thus, the concept of honor is one that is linked to Mrs. Durr's Southern heritage and remains central to her thinking about morality throughout her life. To Virginia Durr, honor means first of all "honesty, being true to yourself, being true to what you believe in," even in the face of pressure to conform to an opposing majority, or politically sanctioned, opinion. In Virginia Durr's mind, her husband, Clifford, was the embodiment of this kind of honor. "I think the kind of honor I'm talking about is the kind of honor that my husband had, who I think is the most honorable man that I ever met in my life. Which is that he was absolutely true to himself. Never spoke or did a dishonorable thing."

In further defining the meaning of honor, Mrs. Durr goes beyond the idea that it involves being true to oneself to a less relativistic statement, that it involves doing what is *right*, not just what one believes in, in spite of pressure to do otherwise. According to this expanded definition, it is possible for people to be dishonorable even while they are acting in accordance with their own beliefs. "But now you see, I think that during the period of Clifford's life when he was a Southern segregationist as I was, we both were engaging in dishonor without even recognizing it. We were committing acts and doing and saying things and believing things that were dishonorable."

Even as she retains such Southern (and basically elitist) language as the term *common* to refer to vulgar or disreputable people, in adulthood Mrs. Durr uses revised criteria for classifying someone as common. In her youth the term would have referred primarily to breeding or taste. Although breeding and taste retain central roles in the way she thinks about people, moral integrity and humanity are the important characteristics that separate the people she admires from those she disdains.

The intellectual framework that Mrs. Durr brought to her later life experiences and choices began to develop at Wellesley as she studied economics and political theory and was deepened as she pursued these subjects further in a later attempt to understand the poverty that surrounded her as a young married woman in Birmingham. Even before she and Clifford moved to Washington, Virginia Durr became

interested in new and radical ideas as she began to question the moral
validity of the system that generated or at least tolerated the kind of
suffering she saw around her.

> So that [the Red Cross work in Birmingham] was the beginning
> of my interest in communism. I began to try to find out what it
> was. I remember going to a bookstore in a little town in Alabama
> to ask for a book on communism and they didn't have any. They
> had a book on socialism but not one on communism. I was inter-
> ested in communism because, well, my goodness, just to hear
> about it, the idea of providing people with a living, you know,
> sounded wonderful, particularly coming there from the depres-
> sion.

Despite her initial interest in communism, Virginia never joined
the Communist party, because she perceived it as limiting the freedom
of expression of its members and this was something she would not
tolerate.

> The thing that kept me from ever even thinking about being a
> member of the Communist party was that the only time I was
> asked to join, they said you've got to remember that if they take
> action at one meeting, then you have to support that action at
> the next meeting. You can't disagree. And I knew I never could
> do that. You see, I think that really the basis of both Cliff's and
> my political viewpoints was the First Amendment. And that's
> what we fought for and that's what we believed in.

In this context, as elsewhere, we can see the importance of her
belief in basic human rights such as free speech and self-determination,
combined with a concern for social justice and the welfare of the least
advantaged members of society. Durr's belief in human rights served
as the centerpiece of her philosophy of life. For her it is, in a sense,
the moral equivalent of a deep faith in God.

For Virginia Durr, as for the other exemplars, moral growth resulted from an interplay between the influences and demands of the
circumstances and situations she put (or found) herself in and the values, beliefs, and intellectual framework she brought to these situations. At least by the time of her serious involvement in the civil
rights movement, she approached the moral issues she confronted with
an intellectual framework that stressed the value of law and due process in protecting fundamental civil rights, along with an awareness
that many laws were unjust and had to be broken and then challenged

through the courts. She clearly understood her anti-poll tax work in this framework, and the strength of her opposition to Joseph McCarthy and his sympathizers was based in large part on her awareness that the anti-communists continually violated basic freedoms and the right to due process of the law, thus betraying the very liberties they claimed to stand for. And, of course, her work in Clifford's law office frequently involved challenging the constitutionality of segregationist ordinances and laws. It is impossible to understand what Virginia Durr's work meant to her without seeing it in the context of this intellectual understanding of the issues. This does not mean, however, that she lays out all of the assumptions of the framework when she is asked why she acted as she did. Her interpretation of the situation and what is right and wrong within it are closely tied to these assumptions, but when asked why she took the actions she did, she answers more simply, saying that she did it because it was right, because everyone should have the right to vote, or because people should not be segregated by race.

INTERVIEWER: When you were spending so much energy on the fight against the poll tax, what was driving that . . . from your point of view? What was really the energy behind it inside you?

MRS. DURR: I thought the right to vote was something that everybody ought to have.

It is this simple truth, this conviction, that guided Virginia Durr in the fight for civil rights that consumed her life.

CHAPTER 6

Jack Coleman

Seeker of Personal Excellence

J ack Coleman, past college president, former head of a large philanthropic foundation, ex-ditch digger, garbageman, short-order cook, and voluntary homeless person and prisoner in a tough city jail, now runs an inn in bucolic Chester, Vermont (pop. 3,508). To get there from Boston we drove several hours through green hills and picture-book villages. Coleman's place, a cheerful sight no matter how long the ride, has its name fittingly inscribed above its porch on a carved wooden sign with a picture of an old-fashioned, horsedrawn sleigh: The Inn at Long Last.

We arrived in the evening, too late to meet with Jack, so we scheduled the first interview for the next day. In the morning, over breakfast, we encountered what seemed at the time to be an unbearably awkward situation. The man that we had traveled so far to meet, our distinguished interviewee, came up to us in cook's garb to take our breakfast orders. He then proceeded to serve us a multicourse meal of fruit, cereal, eggs, pancakes, coffee, and an abundance of wholesome trimmings, all with a straightforward and humble manner. Jack's demeanor, of course, was probably not much different from that of countless waiters in countless eating places worldwide, including our own when we took our turn at similar jobs during student days. But under the circumstances, considering Jack's repute and the nature of the relationship that we were there to establish with him, we found the occasion to be embarrassing and uncomfortable.

The feeling passed by the end of our first day. Looking back on that visit—the first of two extended stays—our initial discomfort in the presence of this unpretentious man now seems incredible to us. In fact, it took very little time for us to accept his service for no more or less than it was. After less than half a day, we came to accept as natural his transitions between distinguished interviewee and inn-keeper, gracious host and breakfast chef/waiter. In retrospect, the ease with which he made us accept these transitions is worth noting, for it says something about Jack's personal demeanor. It is, we believe, a small testament to his matter-of-fact, unassuming style as well as to the absolute seriousness of purpose with which he comports himself. It is as if his purity of purpose so permeates the large and small missions in his life that for him the roles of innkeeper and distinguished college president emeritus are more alike than different.

During a lifetime succession of one high-powered job after another, Jack brought to each position a characteristic humility, integrity, and concern for other people. In each of these positions, and in the unusual activities he pursued while on leave from these positions, he found ways to express his deep belief in the worth of every human

136

being and to use his varied roles to pursue the implications of this belief.

At the age of sixty-five, Coleman chose to become an innkeeper at least in part for the same reason that he chose to live temporarily as a laborer, homeless person, and prison inmate—"because that is where my heart and my head told me to go." A quotation from George Orwell represents to Jack Coleman the central theme of his life: "The fact to which we must cling, as to a lifeboat, is that it is possible to be a normal, decent person, and yet be fully alive." Coleman's goal is to lead his life in such a way that he can say "I'm glad I did" rather than "I wish I had." What prevents this from being a self-indulgent or irresponsible orientation is that it is combined with the deepest respect for the dignity of others and with an exacting demand for personal integrity, cast in ethical terms, as in the Orwell quotation.

Where does this personal quest lead Jack Coleman? For Jack, following the heart and the head means "being able to do those things that seem most important to me, to be able to think my way through a new opportunity, which is a very frightening one each time, but be able to see that this is something I *could* do and I really want to do." For Coleman, as for many others, the heart and the head do not always urge him in the same direction. But he believes that if you go slowly until you get them together, most of the time they will unite, often in the still hours of the night. He offers as an example his friend Douglas McGregor, who had two very attractive job offers, teaching positions at Stanford and MIT, and was having trouble deciding which one to accept. After hours spent analyzing the pros and cons of the two situations, McGregor finally decided to make the decision by flipping a coin. The coin toss came out Stanford. McGregor immediately said to his wife, "Let's make it two out of three." And as soon as the words were out of his mouth, he knew that the whole thing had been a rationalization, that he had been wanting to go to MIT all the time.

The lesson that Coleman draws from this story and from his own experience is that most of us know "when we wake up at 2:30 or 3:00 in the morning"what we really want to do. The head gets pulled away by rationalizations, fears, and outside pressures, but on some level, if we can set aside those distractions, we know what it is we *really* want to do. Coleman is talking here not just about intuition but about inner harmony, "the sense of wholeness in which the pieces come together."

This inner harmony, in which the head and heart come together, is not itself a moral dimension except insofar as "being true to your-self" is for Coleman a quasi-moral imperative. Becoming an innkeeper is the fulfillment of a dream for Coleman, but he does not see the ambition in moral terms. The moral neutrality of this work appears to contrast with the activities he pursued in earlier stages of his life—work on behalf of the poor, contributions to the fights against racial discrimination and for gender equality, prison reform, and bringing the best of values and social conscience to educational administration.

Although Coleman's current role as innkeeper may seem to be morally neutral, his life as a whole certainly does not. A guiding theme that ties together Jack's diverse contributions is respect for the dignity of every person. Jack Coleman is a Quaker and, for him, this concern for another person's dignity is best expressed in the Quaker belief that "there is that of God in every person." It is this theme of concern for the dignity of all that has colored and shaped his search for personal fulfillment. For Jack, being true to yourself, living so that you can say you are glad you did, is inextricably bound up with living in a way that expresses this belief. As a young academic, Jack volunteered for the Urban League in Pittsburgh, working toward the goal of fair housing practices for blacks. He moved from this to a full-time posi-tion at the Ford Foundation working on programs to open job oppor-tunities for racial minorities. Later, as president of Haverford College, a prestigious men's school, he put his position on the line over the issue of the admission of women. Coleman then moved back to foun-dation work, as president of the Edna McConnell Clark Foundation, a philanthropy devoted to aiding the severely needy. In this position he developed programs for job training for disadvantaged youth, women's access to traditionally male occupations, and prison reform. He was an early spokesman for the homeless, living himself as a home-less person in New York in order to better understand the conditions of their lives.

The respect for another person's dignity and humanity that guides and unites all these efforts is closely tied in Jack Coleman's mind to his conviction that one must act in each encounter, in every one of life's contexts, honestly and with the highest possible personal integrity. The inner harmony that represents self-knowledge and self-direction for Jack is closely related to this more ethically charged version of inner harmony that is integrity. Integrity, for Coleman, includes both internal consistency, the absence of compartmentalization, and a con-sistency between means and ends in action. "There isn't a part of you that says 'I hate this aspect of me over here and what I've done there, and yet I go ahead and do it,' while the rest of you is pursuing the other." He equates this kind of internal consistency with wisdom. Coleman's approach to life exemplifies a kind of moral ideal we have not seen in the others profiled here: to follow his head and heart, to fulfill his most cherished dreams, to be personally fulfilled, but to do it all in a way that is thoroughly imbued with moral concerns that become for him the pursuit of personal *moral* integrity.

Honesty and respect in all dealings with others and a consistency between means and ends are crucially important to Jack Coleman. In illustrating their importance, Coleman recalls an incident that occurred fifteen years before the interview but remains very vivid in his mind. The incident was one in which he felt that his "integrity was less than complete." As president of Haverford College, Coleman was, of course, charged with raising money for the programs of the college. He described the incident as follows:

> It was a situation of taking advantage of a potentially very generous donor to Haverford College . . . and this was the night, a night on which alcohol had flowed freely, when we were really going to push her and her husband hard on a commitment. They had said lovely words but still no commitment yet. And late in the evening she made a commitment of a million dollars, and I— this is the point I am embarrassed about—I told her, "You know, if you don't make a larger gift than that a very large amount of your money is going to go to the government. It's just going to go into welfare programs." And she went up to 4.5 million dollars. And I really am embarrassed about it. I knew this aspect of her character. I knew that she dreaded the idea of money going to welfare. And I don't like the fact that I used that. I was playing up to something in her which I didn't like and which is at odds with my own set of beliefs.

Many might consider this a very adroit move to allocate significant resources to a worthy cause, but to Coleman it is a source of real shame. Part of his objection to his own behavior in the incident is the dishonesty, part is that he had "failed to treat the other person as you would want to be treated." Thus, the standards being applied here are distinctly moral ones, not simply the personal or psychological precept to be true to yourself.

Although Coleman has pursued many of the same goals in his life that we have seen in our other exemplars, he represents the nature of his quest very differently from the way the others do, and the pattern of his life has differed from theirs. His life, thus, illustrates a kind of moral dedication that is somewhat different from that of the others we have described and an important piece of a full picture of morally committed lives. Throughout his adulthood, Jack Coleman held a series of positions that could have been treated as morally neutral occupations (or even ambitious moves up the career ladder), but with each one his primary orientation was to the moral issues, the values, and the potential for doing good that the role offered. As a college president he was deeply concerned with the moral climate of the campus and with issues of justice raised by college policies. As a foundation officer and later president, he sought to contribute to the solution of some of the country's most pressing social problems. As an innkeeper, he is acutely sensitive to the moral aspects of his responsibilities toward the town, his employees, and his guests and contributes to the local community in important ways. Thus Coleman is notable for having carried out with unusual integrity, moral awareness, and social responsibility roles that in themselves do not necessarily require exceptional moral commitment. (Perhaps, however, they do require this moral component to be done really well.) People who are corrupt or callous in such roles often attract the attention of the press and are widely recognized for the harm they do both to other people and to the moral climate of the country. Thus, it is important to examine here the life of a man who has operated with integrity and social conscience in positions of leadership.

Jack Coleman also differs from many of the other exemplars we have studied in the degree to which he is self-consciously pursuing personal integrity and growth. The belief that one ought to be "true to oneself," and the guiding role of this belief in Coleman's life, is unusual in our sample, although it can be said to represent an important moral type that ought to be included in a study of enduring moral commitment.

John R. Coleman was born in 1921 to a middle-class WASP family living in a small town in northern Ontario, Canada. His father, Dick, was the smelter superintendent for the International Nickel Company and Coleman describes the town they lived in, Copper Cliff, as a company town. Dick Coleman's position was an important one in the company, and the family was moderately well off. Dick Coleman came from a very proud old Church of England family. His ancestors had been United Empire Loyalists in upstate New York who immigrated to Canada in 1784 and founded a town in Ontario, which they named Coleman's Corners. He was brought up in what had been Coleman's Corners (after its name was changed to Lynn), and his family continued to be very prominent members of the community. After graduation from the University of Toronto, Dick Coleman went north to work for the International Nickel Company in Copper Cliff, with the expectation that he would be back within a few years. But he didn't leave Copper Cliff until near the end of his life, when he moved to Sudbury, four miles away.

Jack's grandfather on his mother's side, John Lawson, was first a cook in a lumber camp and then a laborer in the smelter in Copper Cliff. His wife, Mary, ran a boardinghouse right next to the smelter and cooked wonderful meals for the residents of the house. Jack's mother, (Mary) Irene Lawson, did not finish high school and never left Copper Cliff from the time of her arrival there at age three to the time of her husband's retirement. But Irene Lawson was an intelligent, widely read, and self-educated person. She knew everybody in town and was considered a truly good person, someone to whom anyone could turn for help. "Hoboes who went through town knew that our house was one where they'd find food. People in town who had trouble knew that Mother would help."

Jack Coleman considers his mother to have been the most influential person in his early life.

> My mother was not an educated person, but she was just an amazing woman in terms of the respect that she had for every single human being she met, up to the point where that person put on airs and pretended to be something he or she wasn't. Then, I'm sorry to say, she was unforgiving. So if you were the garbageman and you did your job well and you didn't go around griping about the thing all the time, then that's fine. If you were the mayor and you went about your job in what, for her, were ethical ways and realized that you were very, very privileged and used your privilege to help other people, then that was just fine with her. And that's been a large part of it. Decency has been, I think, for me, this respect for all human beings [that I got from her].
>
> My mother was a paragon of excellence in motherhood. Knowing that my brother had a number of doubts about himself, my mother did just a terrific job of patting him on the back and building him up. And with me, in very kind, loving ways, cut-

ting me down in ways that were just right. I remember in particular, at one point I was nine or ten years old and didn't have a
girlfriend. And I told her and she said, "Oh nonsense, there's
always somebody, no matter how unattractive you are." Or a
time when, much younger—I was only four—and a big electrical
storm came up and I ran in the closet. I was crying and crying
and she found me and she asked me what I was crying about and
I said I was afraid the lightning was going to hit our house. She
said, "Well, why do you think it would hit our house, rather
than the O'Connors?" She just named a house of some people
who lived across the field from us—there were eight or nine
houses over there, she picked one house. But I used to watch the
O'Connors' house in a storm. You know, from that moment on,
I never worried about lightning. She had this way of . . . she
just created security in the way she talked.

Jack's father was a very reserved, private person, and he helped
the needy in Copper Cliff in a quiet, behind-the-scenes way. Jack
found out only many years later about many of the altruistic things
his father had done:

A very good example was in the middle of the depression, I remember one night we were listening to the radio just before
Christmas and there was a story on about a woman who had
come into town with her money to go Christmas shopping and
somebody stole per purse. And I remember [the] impact it had
and I also vaguely remember my father getting up and going out.
I found out years later, when I worked for the radio station for
a brief period, that my father had come into the station that night
and had given her the money.

Jack was the second of three children. He had a competitive and
conflictual relationship with his older brother, Richard, who was
physically powerful and athletic and would beat Jack easily during
their frequent childhood fights. Richard was similar to his father in
many ways, reserved, straightforward, and unpretentious. He followed the same career line as his father, becoming the superintendent
of smelters worldwide for Noranda Copper Mines. Jack was much
closer to his younger sister, who died of emphysema and alcoholism
in her late fifties.

Jack was recognized early as talented and self-confident. While
growing up, he read "literally every book that was in the children's
section of his small town library," recalling especially Tom Swift,

Horatio Alger, the Hardy Boys, and even the Bobbsey Twins. As a bright and highly motivated student in a very small town, Jack was usually at or near the top of his class and "knew success before I came up against really tough competition." Perhaps as a result of this success, he developed a strong sense of his own effectiveness to go along with the sense of security provided by his mother and the protected environment in which he grew up. He won the oratory prize, and the fact that there were only two other competitors did not detract from his pride. He was the valedictorian of his high school class of fourteen. "So, by the time I went to Toronto [to college] and met students who had, by some standards, a better education than I had and had more experience and so on, I had success in my background and I had a sense of self. While I was scared, and I'm scared every time I do anything new, I still thought I could do it."

As a student at the University of Toronto, Coleman chose to major in economics and political science, in part because his real love, English literature, was not "macho" enough to be respectable in the mining town of Copper Cliff. Jack was a leader in student government but was having too much fun to be especially successful academically. The one area of economics that deeply interested him was labor economics. He cared very much about "the questions that were being raised about why people work and what it takes to make people satisfied on the job and how organizations like unions can play a part in articulating that and in helping achieve the satisfaction, or in defeating the satisfaction." As a graduate student at the University of Chicago, Coleman became intoxicated with the excitement of his discipline. The faculty and courses were powerful, and he developed a close relationship with Frederick Harbison, who played an important role in his professional development. Upon completion of graduate school, Jack looked for a teaching position in Canada, but the field of labor economics was much more active in the United States, so he accepted a post at the Massachusetts Institute of Technology.

The sense of security and efficacy Jack had developed early in life stayed with him as his career developed. After teaching for six years at MIT, Coleman took a faculty position at Carnegie Tech, where he remained for ten years as a specialist in labor economics. In looking back over his career, Coleman recalls that "I have really spent very, very little time thinking about job security." He was barely aware that he was up for tenure at Carnegie Tech in 1960 and was surprised and "moderately happy" when the dean told him he had been granted tenure (i.e., a lifetime post at the university). Being considered for tenure was not a source of anxiety for him, because he thought then, as he did at other points in his career, that there were other places he could go and other things he could do if he was not granted tenure.

Coleman shows in this and other incidents a sense of basic security, the sense that things will work out all right, that he need not exert much effort looking out for his own interests, because he trusts that his needs will be met without such effort. We have seen this same sense of security in many of our exemplars. For most of them, the belief takes an explicitly religious form, some version of "God will provide." Coleman's sense of security, however, is not framed in religious terms. His religion provided a set of ethical principles but no relationship with a personal deity. In Coleman's case, the confidence that things will work out may come partly from his mother's ability to impart a deep sense of basic security, but also from his lifelong habit of confronting himself with challenges and then overcoming them. The result is a sense that "if this doesn't work out, I can always do something else."

In addition to this strong sense of security, we have seen in all of our exemplars a related sense of personal effectiveness, the opposite of powerlessness. The importance of this sense of effectiveness for exceptional moral behavior has been evident in this study and others. Put most simply, it is unlikely that people will consistently put forth the effort, and take on the risks, that moral action entails without some sense that they have the power to make a difference.

Jack Coleman himself attributes his strong sense of effectiveness to the influences of his mother and the small town in which he grew up. No doubt these early factors did play a role in his initial tendencies to feel confident and capable. His personality exhibits important consistencies across time; we do not see in his life the dramatic changes that we saw in Virginia Durr's life. We can trace the evolution of his goals, values, and beliefs, but the changes that he exhibits in adulthood appear to be elaborations and intensifications of characteristics that were present earlier. This more subtle kind of evolution is important, however, in better understanding the processes by which moral commitment is deepened and expanded as the individual engages with transformative life experiences.

Even though we can see the roots of Jack's efficacy and security in his childhood, the question remains as to why the characteristics persisted and developed over time. We do not believe that an individual's personality is formed in childhood and remains fixed and immune to later experience. In Coleman's case we can see a process at work that functioned to maintain and heighten these characteristics. It seems plausible to assume that through his childhood experiences Jack Coleman developed the qualities that led him later to be especially likely to take on challenges, often despite feelings of fear. As we shall see, each time he took on such a challenge and succeeded, his sense of efficacy was further reinforced.

Jack's tendency to put himself into situations that would test the limits of his effectiveness illustrates the active role he played in the process of his own development. He repeatedly and deliberately placed himself in new and challenging situations. Each time he did this he was faced with fear and some degree of doubt, but he set these aside and rose to the occasion. The result of this series of trials or self-imposed challenges is an ever-stronger sense of efficacy. In this he is very similar to another of our exemplars, Cabell Brand, who is the subject of Chapter 9. Both men welcomed challenges and by taking on and meeting these challenges they became more confident and more willing to take on other difficult tasks. This kind of developmental process has been called "cumulative continuity," which refers to people's tendency to choose environments or situations that reinforce the personality characteristics that led them to choose those settings. (We will talk more about this in Chapter 7.)

Coleman's sense of security, efficacy, and control of his life's direction have led him to feel that he could achieve whatever he needed or wanted to do without compromising his values "in order to make it." "I have had enough security and enough willingness to speak my mind and enough willingness to get up and walk out, that I have not had to make that kind of compromise." As indicated by the example of the Haverford donor he felt he had misled, Coleman is fully aware of his fallibility, but this is not in conflict with "a very deep conviction that people can, in fact, in spite of *all* the pressures that may be on us, that people can lead honest lives and can deal with one another in an honest fashion."

Jack Coleman's feeling that he can "get up and walk out" of a situation rather than compromise his deepest convictions led him to act in ways that reinforced and further developed this tendency. Approaching people with this degree of confidence is likely to evoke respect and even deference such that usually it will not be necessary to walk out. Likewise, Coleman's tendency to treat people with respect is likely to elicit a response that will reinforce that tendency. People who are treated with respect are more likely to behave in a way that seems worthy of respect. This process by which personality characteristics are maintained and developed has been called "interactional continuity." This term refers to the tendency of individuals to evoke, through their own styles of social interaction, particular sorts of responses from others. (We will explore this concept further in Chapter 7 as well.)

As is true for many people, Jack Coleman's religious orientation also went through a gradual transformation across the course of his life. His development in this area can again be described as a transformation of goals resulting from the interplay of his intellectual framework with the social and institutional situations with which he engaged. As a child, without any particular encouragement from his parents, Jack became very interested in one of the local Protestant churches, the United Church of Canada. He went to church every Sunday morning and to Sunday school in the afternoon. He joined the church's youth organization and other church activities, and many people thought that he would become a minister. Jack especially loved the ritual of the church and the music. He also responded to the values that were discussed, remembering vividly the lessons about the Golden Rule.

While in college, Coleman turned away from the religion of his boyhood, maintaining the humanistic values but denying what he saw as the myths of his earlier religious beliefs. He began dating and later married Mary Irwin, the daughter of a minister and Old Testament scholar; she had joined him in wanting nothing to do with organized religion. In rejecting organized religion, they were following the socially accepted practice for young intellectuals eager to demonstrate their independence of thought. However, Jack never questioned the values that he had associated with his earlier church involvement. "I certainly am not aware of any time in my life when I questioned the values of honesty or doing good to others. The period when I was making fun of the church, the organized church, and of the people who are in it, I don't think I was ever behaving in any way that suggests I wasn't buying the very values they were talking about in that church on Sunday."

Later, when they had children, the Colemans joined the Unitarian church, thinking it the "least harmful thing we could do" to provide the children with some religious education. At that time, Coleman took his religion fairly seriously as a reminder of ethical values. "God was for me a god who set the standard by which men and women could lead their lives—it was not a helping god but was a god that simply said, 'Hey, here's what people *can* be when they strive hardest to relate to the people around them.' '' Somewhat to his own surprise, Coleman became very deeply involved in Unitarianism.

Coleman's church memberships illustrate the way transformation of goals works. He joined the United Church of Canada primarily in order to enjoy the music and ritual and the fellowship provided by the Sunday school and youth group. During the years that he was a member of that church, he developed solid humanitarian values that stayed with him for the rest of his life. Later he joined the Unitarian church for the sake of his children's moral and religious education. After joining that church, he became an active member of the congregation, eventually taking on such leadership roles as trustee of the Meadville Theological Seminary and as chairman of the board of the Pittsburgh church he attended. Through this active engagement with the church, his life developed a central religious core that remained from that point on very important to him.

Entering (and later leaving) the marriage with Mary Irwin also played a part in the direction of his growth. By marrying Mary, he was joining his life with someone who shared his values, and over the years they reinforced those shared values with each other. During their twenty-three-year marriage, Jack and Mary Coleman had five children.

When the Coleman's oldest child was fourteen and the youngest was five, Mary left her husband. In Jack's view, she left him for another man, and he was devastated. Twenty-four years later, he still cannot tell the story of the divorce and his children's reactions without tears. Perhaps most poignant is the memory of his youngest son handing him a note as he moved out of the house. The note said, ''I love you, Dad. I hope I'll see you again.'' Jack remained in close touch with his children after the divorce, seeing them frequently and becoming the custodial parent for two of them during their high school years.

In spite of the pain the divorce caused him, in retrospect, Coleman sees it as having been an important growth experience for him. Although at first he was too angry to do so, in time he came to understand the part he had played in the failure of the marriage. ''The breakup of the marriage and other very painful experiences have been very important in making me take stock of myself. I have an enormous ego and I can very easily forget the limitations on myself—on what I can and can't do. As a result I am more at peace, more sensitive to others, more able to show that sensitivity by every action.'' The divorce also freed Jack to pursue some activities that would have been much more difficult within the context of the marriage, particularly the many episodes in which he worked in blue-collar jobs or lived as a prisoner or homeless person.

During their marriage, Jack and Mary Coleman worked together as volunteers for the Urban League and the NAACP. They had first become aware of racial discrimination while graduate students in Chicago and were especially concerned about the injustices of unfair housing practices. According to Jack,

> What really galvanized me into action was a very biased survey conducted by the realty board of Allegheny County. They did a door-to-door survey which showed that people were overwhelmingly against racial integration in neighborhoods. And what I did with a fellow over at the University of Pittsburgh was devise a questionnaire which was equally biased on the opposite side. What ours said was, "Do you believe that you should be free to buy a home wherever you wish? Do you believe other people ought to be free to buy homes where they wish? Do you think that applies to blacks?" And they're trapped by then—yes, yes, and they're trapped. We went to one house with the realtors' questions, we went to the next house with our questionnaire, and what we showed was that an overwhelming majority of people support the idea of blacks being able to buy houses on our questionnaire, and a small majority favor discriminating against blacks on their questionnaire. And that was the end of their survey. We published the results and they withdrew theirs right away.

While in Pittsburgh, Jack also helped create an organization called Negro Equal Education Development (NEED). The purpose of the organization was to raise scholarship funds so that black men and women could go to high-quality colleges and universities.

This volunteer work in Pittsburgh, combined with his professional experience as an economist, led (at about the time of Jack's divorce) to a position at the Ford Foundation in New York, working on programs to develop job opportunities for minorities. Looking back, Jack sees himself and his colleagues then as having been idealistic and very naive about the magnitude of the problems of racism and poverty in the United States. The War on Poverty was being launched on the federal level, and Jack found the work very exciting.

Because he enjoyed the work at the Ford Foundation so much, he turned down the presidency of Haverford College the first time it was offered. Becoming more honest with himself about the appeal of this kind of leadership position (as he puts it), he accepted the position when it was offered again a year later. Coleman became president of Haverford in 1967.

When Coleman went to Haverford, he met large numbers of Quakers for the first time since it is the oldest Quaker college in the country, and the campus environment is still laden with Quaker values. In fact, Coleman was the college's first non-Quaker president. After having been at Haverford for a short time, he started going to Quaker meetings and felt more at home than he had in any other religious setting. He joined the Society of Friends and is still a member. At that point, Coleman still saw God as a standard, a set of ethical principles by which people could live. The move from Unitarianism to the Society of Friends represented an elaboration of these principles and a concern for spirituality rather than a move toward a more theistic conception of God. Most importantly, Coleman was drawn to the Quaker teaching that "there is that of God in every person," which he felt expressed so well his long-standing concern for the dignity of every person. Along with this teaching go the beliefs that "every one of us is a minister, and that each of us has the capacity to minister to others and to learn from others."

The Quaker faith also puts a great deal of emphasis on scrupulous honesty in people's dealings with each other. In fact, Quakers do not swear oaths of honesty, since this would "imply the existence of a double standard of truth. Thus on all occasions when special statements are required, it is recommended that Friends take the opportunity to make simple affirmations, thus emphasizing that their statements are only a part of their usual integrity of speech."[1] This special focus on the importance of truthfulness and personal integrity was something that very much appealed to Jack.

Unlike the Pentecostalism of Suzie Valadez and Charleszetta Waddles, both Unitarianism and the Society of Friends have strong traditions of social action and social reform. This aspect of both denominations was important to Jack, and the concern for social justice went with him as he left the Unitarian church to become a Quaker. In contrast to the Unitarian church, however, Jack felt that the Quaker meetings offered a kind of spiritual comfort that was lacking in the Unitarians' intense, almost exclusive, focus on social issues. In the Quaker meetings, "there was this very strong sense of social concern, but there was never a time when we were not made mindful by those who spoke of the religious tenet that underlies this, the belief that there is that of God in every person.''

While president of Haverford, Coleman was acutely aware of the moral tone of the college and felt a sense of responsibility to contribute to it. The values that the college stood for were central to its unique identity. ''I used to say to students that no matter how sordid, ugly, nasty the world becomes, you know it doesn't have to be that way. Once you lived in a place where it wasn't so—Haverford College. We made mistakes, we were thoughtless in a variety of things, but, by God, this was an honest, decent place and you were part of it.''

This emphasis on the defining values of the college was very much related to what became a consuming struggle for Coleman. The issue was his conviction that the all-male college should become coeducational and his unsuccessful fight to convince the governing body of the college, the board of managers, of this. As Coleman put it,

> The reason I believed it deeply was because whenever I got on a public platform, I talked about the values of Haverford, which go beyond the fact that it has educational strength. Lots of places can match it in educational strength, but the particular values that permeated that campus, respect and dignity, those things have *nothing* to do with whether you're talking about male or female. If I had been president of Bryn Mawr [Haverford's ''sister college''], the talks I would have made about the values there would have been different. They would have been values that largely took a very important part for women. That is the value of having a place where women are in the majority, where they are fashioning that particular institution, they're shaping it, they've got the leadership roles, and so on. That's a different thing entirely. And the values I was talking about were not ones that had to do with the sex of the person.

Coleman did not feel that he could back down on the conflict with the board of managers, although he recognized the need for compromise in the short run in order to achieve the long-term goal. The issue concerned fairness to women who wanted to attend Haverford, and Coleman could see no moral justification for denying them admission. He saw a compelling rationale for an all-women's college as a means toward empowering women in a society in which men and women are not equal. But in his mind there was no parallel argument for justifying the existence of an all-male college. He felt that women were being unfairly excluded from Haverford and continued to fight for their admission throughout his presidency. In the end, his decision to leave Haverford was linked with the failure to resolve this conflict. (Two years after he left, the decision was made to admit women, and Haverford is coeducational today.)

The extent to which Coleman's approach to administration was imbued with a sense of moral values and social responsibility is illustrated by an undertaking that he describes as "one of the best things we ever did." In 1970 a student had created a plan, which the college adopted, to protest and learn about the Vietnam War and the bombings of Cambodia by having the entire college go to Washington—all the faculty, students, and staff, including clerical workers, kitchen workers, grounds crew, president, and board of managers. They went "as a symbol of protest and also to learn." They saw and talked to anyone they could who was in a position of leadership in the country, including members of Congress and other political leaders.

At the time that the Vietnam protest was being planned, a student came to the president's office to speak to Coleman about the deep disappointment he felt at having been forbidden by his father to take part in the protest. The young man cried bitterly at the thought of being left out of this important event. The fact that he was able to be the kind of college president to whom a student could show his feelings in such an honest way is, to Coleman, one of the proudest achievements of his presidency. Coleman solved the problem by asking the student to cover the switchboards while the rest of the students and staff were away. This allowed the young man to play an important role in the protest without leaving campus. Coleman sees this solution as prototypical of his goal as a college president to respond to an individual's need within the framework of the needs of the institution.

We can see the transformation of goals in Coleman's life again in his experience at Haverford. As a result of his decision to take the job as president, Coleman was immersed in a context in which moral values are very salient and where there is somewhat greater agreement on beliefs and values than at a large and heterogeneous university like Carnegie Tech. His leadership role at Haverford demanded that he articulate the values of the institution both to himself and publicly. The picture of values he presented as representing those of the institution were bound to be an amalgam of what was really there in the culture of the place and the particular emphases and interpretations he brought to the values already a part of the Haverford culture. His involvement with the Society of Friends resulted from his move to Haverford and resulted in a further refinement and reordering of his values and goals.

Even more unusual than the dramatic antiwar protest he organized was a series of "blue-collar sabbaticals" that Coleman began while president of Haverford. There were a number of reasons he chose to spend time disguised as a ditch digger, garbage collector, and short-order cook. The most obvious, although not necessarily the most important, was professional. As an economist, Coleman's specialty was union-management relations, job satisfaction, and personnel administration. In trying out the blue-collar occupations, he was, in part, testing some of the things he had written as a labor economist. Other reasons for his sabbaticals were personal. In line with the guiding principle of following his head and his heart, Coleman wanted to experience the freedom of heading out of town with wide open choices before him. "The opportunity is there and, damn it, I have the freedom to do this. So why not go where the heart and the head say to go? What's holding me back? When I started down the driveway, I could turn left, I could turn right. First time I know of that I came to a place where it didn't matter one bit which direction. It was scary but it was also exciting to know that I did have that freedom."

Another personal reason for these adventures was a desire to test himself:

> I really wanted to see whether I could make it with my hands, my back. I had made my living, ever since I got my doctorate, with the fairly glib tongue and connections . . . so I wanted to know, can you do it without your name and without those connections, and where your tongue may be a disadvantage, the desire to test it out. And this brother I spoke of is physically very strong and can do all kinds of things that I can't do. Not only can he do heavy work, but he's very skillful. I'm not. And I wanted to match him a little bit, and I wanted him to see that I could do some of the things he had done. But the biggest reason of all was simply that I wanted to find out what it's like when you do that day after day. What do people talk about on their job, what are the satisfactions they find, what *is* it like to be a garbageman, for example. In our society, we say, I've heard this all my life, that any job is a good job, respected job, as long as it's an honest job. Well, it turns out not so. When you're a

garbageman, you're automatically looked down on, particularly if you're my age. I was in my fifties at that time. A woman watched me carrying the very sloppy garbage out of her motel shed at the back, an elderly woman watching me for quite some period of time, I became very uneasy and I looked back at her and she said to me "Will you ever amount to anything?"

Whatever the personal and professional reasons Coleman had for choosing to try out this series of diverse roles, an important result was a testing and deepening of his core moral values and beliefs:

I really wanted to know how other people lived. And from it came an increasing concern about this word *dignity* that I love so much and realizing that I didn't really know much of what I was talking about, that I can mouth the words about "that of God in every person" very easily because of the glib tongue, but I didn't even know what it meant. And certainly going to the prisons and going as a homeless person was to try and learn more about that. Where is the dignity and where is your worth, what is there to believe in in your life when you're completely ignored by everybody, you're a nonperson.

Taking very seriously the idea that there is that of God in every person and truly respecting the dignity of even a homeless person or prison inmate, treating them as you would want to be treated yourself, is what Coleman means by decency. If we recall that his central life goal is to "be a decent person and yet be fully alive," we can appreciate better the significance of his role playing. In some cases the role playing was carried out in connection with long-term involvement in organizations dealing directly with the issues he encountered and resulted in specific actions. Also significant, however, is the sense of having learned through these specific experiences how to be more consistent and sincere in approaching with respect everyone he encounters. The role playing, in this sense, contributed to Coleman's development as a "normal, decent person."

Another result of the role-playing episodes was that he developed long-term friendships with many of the people he met in these diverse settings. At first, as he attempted to maintain the friendships he had made while a sanitation worker in New York, the men were suspicious and did not trust his interest in them to be sincere. With time, however, they came to understand that he genuinely enjoyed their company. "We have a friendship. We talk about all the things that really matter in considerable depth with one another. They come to the inn, but it took a while for me to persuade them that this is for real.'' These friendships have deepened even more Coleman's convictions about the importance of work and people's ability to find satisfaction in a wide variety of situations. One of these friends, a sanitation worker in New York, came into the foundation for a week-long internship. Afterward he expressed astonishment at the fact that the foundation staff seemed to work very hard, saying, ''I never knew until I came here that other people in jobs outside of the sanitation department work so hard.'' This was a man who loved the department, loved his work, and was very proud of it.

Despite the results of his experiences as a blue-collar worker, the role playing was not originally motivated by a desire to help others or to become a better person. Coleman specifically denies the importance of such motives. Here again, as elsewhere, he combines a pursuit of the purely personal with an appreciation of the moral implications.

> Why do I do these things? It's meeting my selfish needs. It's taking advantage of an opportunity that's there for me to do something I've wanted to do, which I can do and not hurt anybody in the process. I am not aware of how I've hurt anybody by doing any of those things I've done. And if I can meet my need, if I can learn more about other people on the job, which I think is a very important part of each person's life, if I can learn more about that and test myself a little bit, test my physical endurance, test my ability to learn quickly, what kind of cardboard is the best cardboard to keep out the rain on a wintry night and so on. If I can do all that—great!

The ''blue-collar sabbaticals'' are, of course, a dramatic example of someone choosing a context and a role and then being influenced by it. For example, Jack's original motives for posing as a cook, construction worker, and sanitation worker did not include a conscious desire to deepen his understanding of the Quaker principle of reverence and respect for people. This was, however, a salient result of the experiences.

After leaving Haverford, Coleman became the president of the Edna McConnell Clark Foundation, a major philanthropic organization with assets of almost half a billion dollars. The mission of the foundation, as defined by Mrs. Clark, was to help those not served by the other institutions of society. This was to Jack Coleman a ''dream assignment, because I'm proudly a do-gooder. And here was an opportunity to do good with somebody else's money and do it on a fairly big scale.'' The board of the foundation was looking for a president who would bring a coherent focus to the foundation's programs and chose Coleman as someone ''who's going to come in with some enthusiasm and with some ability to inspire people around him and make a difference.'' Coleman developed an agenda around a few important target areas. His intent was to reach out to issues that were unpopular in society, either because the problem group was unattractive or because the problem seemed intractable. He was most personally committed to developing programs in two areas. The first concerned imprisonment—particularly prison reform, overcrowding, and alternatives to imprisonment. The second focused on jobs for the very hard to employ, including inner-city high school dropouts.

Jack posed as a prisoner for the first time shortly after taking the position at the foundation and subsequently posed as a prison officer in a maximum-security prison in Texas and on a chain gang in South Carolina as well as a prisoner in other prisons throughout the country. The foundation had a preexisting program in prison reform, an area that Coleman knew little about. He decided that before working in this new area, he ought to get some firsthand experience of prison life. ''Again, I wanted to walk in the shoes of other people. I wanted to get some sense of what it is to be an inmate, to be in a situation where you have no control over your life.''

These experiences confirmed and added depth to his belief that incarceration was overused and most often destructive in its effects on the inmates. One obvious reason to consider alternative forms of punishment that has achieved some visibility in recent years is the soaring cost of building, maintaining, and staffing prisons. Whereas this economic concern played a role in Coleman's thinking, a more important concern was the belief that imprisonment does grave harm to those who undergo it and may not be necessary in many cases if there are other ways of controlling crime. Coleman was concerned not only for the prisoners but for the victims of crime as well. He believed that programs should be developed to deal directly with the losses of the victims and their families rather than offering them nothing but the pleasure of retribution. ''One of the saddest things about imprisonment, or even more capital punishment, is that sometimes it seems to be all we can do for the victims. And if the most that we can say to somebody who has lost a member of their family through murder, if the most we can say is 'OK, we'll take the life of the person that did it,' that's pretty small, that's pretty miserable. So in part, prison is a substitute for dealing more humanely and genuinely with the victims as well as the perpetrators.''

Coleman continues to be interested in prison reform and, at age seventy, finds time in his busy life as an innkeeper to work with the state of Vermont on prison issues. He served on an advisory committee to Governor Madeleine Kunin on prison overcrowding and is currently a member of the council on criminal justice for the state. He is also a supporter and spokesperson for a halfway house in a nearby city.

In order to address the issue of joblessness among the hard-to-employ, the Clark Foundation focused especially on the situation of inner-city youth. Among other things, the foundation's programs sought to integrate into the academic curriculum of inner-city high schools concepts and skills relevant to the world of work. The importance of these issues to Jack Coleman was underscored by his belief that people are shaped to a considerable extent by the work they do.

While president of the Clark Foundation, Jack also became concerned with homelessness and decided to live for ten days in midwinter as a homeless person on the streets of New York. He wrote a diary during that period, from which we quote:

Friday 1/21/83
On the northwest corner of Eighth Avenue and 33rd Street, there was a blocked-off subway entrance undergoing repair. I curled up against the wall there under some cardboard sheets. Rain began to fall, but I stayed reasonably dry and was able to get to sleep. At some point, I was awakened by a man who had pulled back the upper piece of cardboard. ''You see my partner here. You need to give us some money.'' I was still half asleep. ''I don't have any.'' ''You must have something, man.'' ''Would I be sleeping here in the rain if I did?'' His partner intervened. ''C'mon. Leave the old bastard alone. He's not worth it.'' ''He's got something. Get up and give it to us.'' I climbed to my feet and began fumbling in my pocket. Both men were on my left side. That was my chance. Suddenly I took off and ran along 33rd Street toward Ninth Avenue. They gave no chase. Good thing, too, because I was too stiff with cold to run a good race.

Saturday 1/22/83
A man I squatted next to in a doorway on 29th Street said it all: ''The onliest thing is to have a warm place to sleep. That and having somebody care about you. That'd be even onlier.'' He had what appeared to be rolls

of paper toweling wrapped around one leg and tied with red ribbon. But the paper, wet with rain by now, didn't seem to serve any purpose. I slept little. The forecast was for more rain tomorrow, so why wish the night away?

In thinking about his experiences as prisoner and homeless person, Jack Coleman is well aware of the critical differences between the reality of these situations and the temporary and unreal versions that he experienced. He says,

> The danger in these things is that you begin to think you know what it's like to be a homeless person, or prisoner, or a dishwasher fired after one hour. And you don't, as long as you have the comfort of the things you can go back to and you have the contacts that I've got and all the rest of it. When you have those things, these experiences are all phoney. But, if you're mindful of that, you can still learn things there that you couldn't learn any other way. I don't think that there's any way that I could have sensed that feeling of helplessness, being completely under somebody's control had I not been in that prison. Or take the other side. I put on the guard's uniform. Until I did that I didn't know sides of myself. I didn't realize the extent to which I would play the game and go along with the others. What I told myself

was that if I stayed long enough, that I would go along long enough to show the other guards that I am capable of doing the job, and once I'd shown that and won my spurs, then I'd speak to the decent, good side of myself and let it come out. Is that a boast? Is it true? Is that just a bromide I'm using?

Coleman notes that while working at the Ford Foundation on issues of job discrimination, he was completely unaware of discrimination against women and did not think to include women as a target group in his programs. As we have said, while at Haverford, Jack became acutely aware of issues of equal access for women and fought a long and very difficult battle to open Haverford to women students. Bringing this new concern from Haverford to the Clark Foundation, Jack was eager to fund programs in the jobs area that provided access for women to traditionally male occupations. He remembers especially a successful program funded by the foundation to train women to be firefighters:

> We provided the support for some special physical training programs for women who wanted to become firefighters in the city of New York. What was happening was that there were programs available for anybody who wanted to go through the physical training and scarcely anybody applied to be a fireman without taking that special training. They were crazy if they didn't take it. What happened to women when they went to it was they were harassed in the training, and life was made so miserable that a large number of them dropped out right at that point, never even got to the point of taking the test and doing the rest of it. And what we funded was a separate program for women. The same instructors, the same stuff exactly except the women were on their own. The result was that when they went into the examination, they were on a level with the men. Fortunately, there wasn't any harassment in the exam room itself, and they passed the exam. The story from then on is not necessarily smooth at all. The harassment might come up later on the job. But at least they got the entry as a result of this program. That's the kind of thing we were doing that again I think is consistent with the same concern about the dignity of every human being.

Coleman left the Clark Foundation after ten years, in part because he felt that holding such a position for longer than that could lead to a corrupting arrogance. "You begin to think it's your money you're giving away. And you begin to think, 'Gee, I'm really a pretty good fellow—I'm doing these things for you.'" He had hoped that while at the Clark Foundation he could communicate with presidents of other foundations about their role in America and the more personal topic of how to avoid being corrupted by their power. He was disappointed in this hope and was left with a lingering sadness about the reticence of foundation presidents to talk openly with each other about both the opportunities and risks of their positions.

Upon leaving the foundation at the age of sixty-five, Coleman made an unconventional choice about his next career move. Following an old dream (and once again following his heart), he bought a beautiful antique inn, renaming it The Inn at Long Last. He had for a very long time felt that when he was sixty-five he would do something different with his life. Having a long-standing interest in and love for good food, one possibility he considered was starting a restaurant. When he shared this vision with a friend, she responded by saying, "Jack, you're talking about a Vermont country inn." He realized at once that she was right:

> The reason why the inn idea made so much sense has been borne out by the experience, and that is that it's a far, far better opportunity to get to know people. It's a far better opportunity to share the things that I have, the things that I like with people. And to be able to share and to celebrate what I have here with other people is just enormously satisfying—and that's innkeeping. And then the inn also has the food. And I do love the food. [Being an innkeeper] offers the opportunity to be a leader, to be an employer, and I enjoy being an employer. I enjoy the times when I feel that I have helped people associated with me to grow, to develop, to see more strength in themselves than they realized before. Those things are all here.

It is not a coincidence that Coleman is running a *small* business. Just as he enjoyed being president of a small college, he prefers running a small inn rather than a hotel or a chain of inns. The fact that the organization is small makes possible an intimacy, an immediacy in the relationships between the head of the organization, all layers of the staff, and the clientele. His love for small organizations is consistent with his belief that in many areas, smaller-scale programs are both more effective and more humane than larger, less personal programs.

In describing his work as an innkeeper he says, "I've never done anything that has been so completely absorbing in my life as this is. I've never been as single-minded in my life as I am right now in just keeping this place afloat and trying to make it what I'd like it to be." In fact, the inn loses money and Coleman has given up an easy retirement with generous pensions to pour himself into this demanding task. He sees the inn as a new challenge, an expression of his goal of living in such a way that you look back with satisfaction, not regret about lost opportunities.

Although other people see the move from academia and the foundation world to running an inn as a radical break, Jack experiences a strong sense of continuity across the different phases of his career. "I'm still doing the same thing I was doing. As president of the college and president of the foundation I was setting a tone, I was setting a direction for the place, I was creating a vision and then trying to make that vision become reality. I was trying then and trying now to practice on the job what I believe about the dignity of people and treating them with respect." In his role as innkeeper, Jack Coleman is trying to "create an environment in which people can feel at peace and be comfortable and at the same time feel stretched, become more than they have been, to create an environment that is a growing environment."

During the five years since he bought the inn, Jack has become a very active member of the local community. He is justice of the peace and auditor of the school board and has organized a number of memorable community events. Twice he produced Thornton Wilder's *Our Town* with a cast of local residents. He also wrote a play about a mysterious figure in the town's history, Clarence Adams, a respected citizen by day and burglar by night, which he produced with the townspeople as cast. In these and other ways, Coleman has sought to make the Inn at Long Last a force for cultural vitality in the town.

In addition to the usual recreational activities, the Inn at Long Last provides workshops that grow directly from Coleman's conviction that people can and ought to live so that they can later say "I'm glad I did." These workshops have grown out of the tendency for people to see Coleman as an example and from their desire to talk about what this has meant for them in their life choices. Coleman is ambivalent about his influence on other people. He feels great confidence in his general message that it is possible to achieve what you most want while also acting with integrity, honesty, and decency. He is wary, however, of people trying too literally to follow his example. "I have no desire, in fact I have a fear of having followers in the sense of people who try to do what I did. If you take these words seriously and go where *your* heart and *your* head tell you to go, [your choices may be very different from mine].''

What Coleman sees as one of the most important things that he can share with others from his own experience is the fact that each time he confronts a new challenge, he feels afraid. The message here is that we all feel afraid, but that we need to set the fear aside and move forward. In Coleman's words, ''If you don't have courage, you have to fake it.'' If people considering a difficult life choice or challenge think that others who have faced such challenges have not been afraid, they may retreat from the challenge and thus fail to follow where ''their heads and hearts lead.'' If they realize that others are afraid and move forward effectively in spite of it, they may be more successful themselves in setting aside the fear.

When asked about moral courage, Coleman responds at first in a way that is indistinguishable from the pattern we have seen in our other exemplars. ''When I talk about going and doing the blue-collar things and going to prison and going homeless, I talk about how lucky I am and I'm often interrupted as if 'No, it takes a lot of courage.' It doesn't seem like courage to me. What it seems like is meeting a selfish need in myself and finding that there's no good reason why I can't do what I really want to do.'' What Coleman is saying here is that his role-playing episodes have not required moral courage in the sense of having to muster the strength to do what he feels he *should* do but doesn't really *want* to do. This absence of conflict between one's self-interest and one's moral goals characterizes everyone in our sample, however different they are in other ways. The identity of self-interest and morality results for most in a lack of attention to the risks or dangers entailed by their activities. In this area, Coleman differs from the others, at least in degree.

On a related dimension, we see similarities between Coleman and others in their reaction to our query about moral courage. Like the others, Coleman denied that he had exhibited courage. The typical response of the majority of exemplars was some version of ''What I did did not involve courage. It had to be done, so I did it. I didn't think about the consequences so I didn't need to muster courage.'' In Coleman's case, the response was

> The reason I back away from the word *courage* is that I don't feel courageous when I go out, I feel scared. But I felt scared the first day I walked into a class at MIT to teach. I felt scared the first

day I was in the presidency at Haverford—nothing's prepared me
for this day, why did I take this job? Obviously I felt terrified
the day I signed the papers and owned this inn. And I feel scared
when I go into a prison. The fifth time is no easier than the first
time. So that what I have done is acting *in spite* of fear, or with
an awareness that fear is there. And, to me, that is not what I
think courage is. . . . I don't think that I had courage. I think
that I faked it. If you don't fake courage you aren't going to do
those things that you really want to do, you are going very
quickly to develop the reasons why you can't do that which your
heart and your head say you should do.

However afraid he may feel, we see that Coleman moves toward
the things he believes in despite the risks his choices may entail. In
this he is exhibiting the pattern we saw in the group of exemplars as
a whole. He differs from the others in that his awareness of the risk
is more acute and his fears are more salient. He must make a conscious
effort to set them aside. It is clear, however, that this dimension is a
continuum. All of our exemplars show some awareness of the risks
they have taken and some moments of doubt or conflict. Several of
them spoke of making a conscious effort to set aside the doubt and
fears. As Coleman himself points out, it is useful for those who are
not as relatively immune from doubts and fears as some of our exemplars seem to be to see that one can "fake it" and move forward in
spite of them.

Coleman shares with most of the other participants in this study
a positive attitude toward his life, a sense that he is fortunate, and
gratitude for that good fortune. When asked what kinds of things
have made it most difficult to pursue his goals and live out his ideals,
he responds by saying that he has not experienced it as difficult and
attributes the absence of inner struggle to good fortune. "I used the
word *lucky* before, and I'll go back and use it again. I have not been
put in situations that I can think of anyway, right now, where I had
to compromise in order to make it." Indeed, in comparison with
many of our exemplars, Coleman's life circumstances have been fortunate. This does not mean, however, that his life is lacking in material
for self-pity were he inclined toward such feelings. The extent to
which people see their lives as fortunate or not is not closely related
to an objective assessment of the difficulty or ease of their circumstances. We see this dramatically in some of our other cases.

When it comes to the issue of certainty and wholehearted identification of moral values and goals with the self and self-interest, Coleman in some ways fits the dominant pattern we have identified and differs from it in others. The similarities and differences are revealed in the observation that Coleman sets as his goal—and is quite successful in attaining—the achievement of congruence between his deepest values and his life as it is actually lived. He is self-conscious about trying to do what is most important to him rather than settling for an "inauthentic" life. One might say that he aspires to achieve what the others have without self-consciously pursuing it. To the extent that he achieves his goal, he is like them. To the extent that he must consciously strive for it, he is unlike them.

In spite of the real satisfaction Jack found in becoming an innkeeper, soon after he took on that task a long-standing drinking problem he had had since the years following his divorce reached a crisis point. His openness about this period in his life is indicative of his general tendency to be unusually honest with both himself and others about his weaknesses. It also underscores the fact that all of our exemplars are human. As Jack tells the story, he had been drinking too much for years, but the drinking had not interfered with his work, and he had not considered himself an alcoholic. But as an innkeeper, he found it all too easy to have screwdrivers at breakfast instead of orange juice and to keep drinking all day. He found himself making promises that he later did not remember, using poor judgment in personnel matters, and generally becoming unable to function. Not wanting to look at his drinking, Jack decided that he must have a brain tumor and began to feel seriously suicidal. At about that time his family, who were aware of the trouble he was having, held a family "intervention." For it, all of his children gathered at the home of his son Paul. His son John used a ruse to bring Jack to Paul's house, and when Jack walked in and saw the gathering, he knew immediately why they were there. Each child presented a written statement about the pain Jack's alcoholism had caused, and they all told him that they felt he should enter treatment. Although his initial reaction was to resist their advice, within forty-eight hours he had agreed to enter the hospital for treatment. The hospitalization had a very dramatic impact on Jack and he found it "a painful growing experience, but a good one. The pain I went through, the things I had to learn about myself, has all been worth it."

When Jack first entered a recovery program, just after the family intervention, he worried that the spiritual focus of that program was inconsistent with his religious beliefs as a Quaker. "I thought, 'Boy, this doesn't fit at all with me and I want to be awful careful about this stuff. . . . My God was simply a standard, a set of ethical principles by which men could live if they wanted to. Then, how do I accept the fact that the core of this program is that you admit that you're helpless and that only this God that you understand, only God can save you." As his involvement with the program continued, Jack's view of God changed and became more personal. "Today I am a Quaker and I am in a recovery program and I have a different picture of God now. I feel that I am, in fact, dependent upon God. I don't know how else to explain the miracle of my recovery. So for me it's now more than a set of ethical principles. We believe that there is a power in our lives that shapes those lives and that is there to help us, if we will simply give that power the opportunity."

Although this involvement changed the meaning of God for Coleman and resulted in a shift in the role of God in his life, he does not see the conception of God he developed there as inconsistent with his earlier view of God as a standard for human behavior. Although he does not think of God as in any sense like a person, Coleman does see God as a personal force. "The human adventure at its best is God for me—the attainment, the achievement of higher values, of shared values in the community and that God for me is personal in the sense that there is some force beyond anything that we understand. . . ." The change through the program was not so much in his conception of what God is, but in his own relationship with God. Whereas previously he had felt that these standards of right and goodness are there for those who wish to turn to them, in the program he came to feel that in order to live a healthful life, in fact in order to live at all, he had to rely on that God:

MR. COLEMAN: For me, there is a mystical force, a trust, that makes it possible for human beings to lift themselves above the most mundane things, to see in these broader terms, to relate to others in more loving ways. That trust is God. That trust has expectations that go with it, but in accepting it now, there's also help. If you really believe that, you'll find that there's help in dealing with those issues that come most pressingly home to you—for me, my alcoholism, and at another point in my life, another set of circumstances, there would be another kind of an issue. In a way, this is not completely different from that point that I made over and over again, that 2:30 in the morning voice, that knowledge of what is right, of what you could do, put aside the rationalizations of the day. It's the same kind of thing. God's will for me is the simple, commonsense knowledge that, "Damn it! This is what I should be doing!" That I should not be drinking. I am one of those people in the world who cannot handle it, and I should not, I must not, do it.

INTERVIEWER: So it's really, on some truest, deepest level, you really knew that about yourself, that you weren't being true to what you knew to be right for you?

MR. COLEMAN: That's right. Exactly. That's exactly it. I went through all these rationalizations. . . . I think all that's changed—and it's enough—is a realization that I had no choice but to strive for that standard. The standard is more than something about a good life. For me, it was life itself. That's a different meaning for God, for the power of God, than the one of saying, "It would be nice if I were better than I am," which was sort of the way I looked at it before. Now I know I have to lead that kind of life in order to stay alive, that's all.

For Jack Coleman, the basis for the certainty he feels about how he should live and what he ought to strive for come not from faith in a loving and omnipotent God, as we will see in several of our other exemplars. For him, the certainty revolves around the basic values according to which he believes he must live, especially honesty and uncompromising integrity. His faith is not so much in the goodness of God as in a transcendent force within human beings, a faith in the power of the individual to live a full and decent life.

Personal control and efficacy are also a conscious and explicit part of Coleman's philosophy of life as well as being perceptible in his behavior. As we have seen in reviewing his life, a guiding principle has been the belief that he *can* do those things that he wants to do. This is not only a characteristic that he attributes to himself but also something that he feels it is *right* to do, that one *should* do. One *ought* to accept life's challenges, set aside groundless fears, and "follow where one's head and one's heart dictate" regardless of the difficulties that may entail.

A related tenet in his personal philosophy is the belief that one seldom needs to cheat, cut corners, or otherwise compromise one's integrity in order to achieve one's ends. Coleman believes that too often we excuse our lack of integrity by claiming that our freedom is limited by circumstances, pressures, the need to make a living, feed our family, or get by in a corrupt world. This is a central message he has wanted to give to students and to others on whom he may have an influence. Another of our exemplars, David Linsky, has said much the same thing: "And what I've seen happen in my life not only supports my optimism but reinforces my conviction that you can do well by doing right, that you don't have to cut corners and indulge in sleazy tactics. . . . When my book came out, what most delighted me was the number of letters I got from young people. And these youngsters said, 'You've given us reason to believe we can achieve what we want without having to do some of the [corrupt] things people do.'" Linsky and Coleman are both affirming the individual's responsibility and denying the validity of the most common kinds of rationalization.

The feeling that it is not necessary to compromise one's integrity, that one can succeed without such compromise, presupposes a sense of efficacy. And this feeling may further enhance one's sense of efficacy if accepted as a guiding principle of life. Many of our exemplars exhibit a similar stance in relation to the issue of responsibility and what counts and does not count as an excuse for morally questionable behavior. We will see in our discussion of Charleszetta Waddles, for example, that she wanted to take away people's excuses for criminal behavior by feeding them and providing them with clothes and housing. Coleman's message is somewhat different, because he is reluctant to make judgments about others who have had much more difficult life circumstances than his. He feels that it would be presumptuous for someone who has led such a privileged life to preach to others who are less fortunate that the pressures of need provide no excuse for moral compromise. This attitude is consistent with his general reluctance to influence other people's life choices or to serve as a model for them.

Throughout his interview, Coleman interweaves two sets of ideals or standards, the personal and the moral. He first casts his concept of integrity in personal terms, "I evaluate my behavior by asking whether I would be embarrassed if my children knew." When pushed on the meaning of this statement (after all, some people don't seem to mind if their children know they are criminals), he goes on to elaborate in terms of honesty and the Golden Rule, as shown in the Haverford fund-raising example, and also in terms of respect for the dignity of all people—in Quaker terms, seeing that there is "that of God in every person."

CHAPTER 7

How Moral Commitment
Develops Throughout Life

Above all, commitment implies reliability. People committed to moral goals are reliable in the sense that we have confidence in their responses to morally charged events. Was it surprising that Sakharov battled the resurgent Soviet drift toward dictatorship up until the last moments of his life? Anyone familiar with his life story would be surprised if he had not. Sakharov, like many moral exemplars in this book, sustained his commitment over decades of formidable pressure. Throughout the years, he forged a stable system of moral response that withstood the vagaries and trials of his shifting life circumstances.

One of the mysteries of moral commitment is how people develop these stable modes of behaving that endure over decades of changing life circumstances. What creates a lasting dedication to particular values and goals? How is it that some people center their lives around principles that they have believed in since youth while others have few, if any, beliefs that they hold onto from day to day? The story of moral exemplars is largely a story of extraordinary reliability, dependability, and stability in their values and in their conduct.

Yet stability is by no means the whole story. Many moral exemplars show great capacities for change and growth, even late in life. They critically examine old habits and assumptions, they adopt new strategies, and they take up unexplored challenges. They resist becoming set in their ways. The stability that they exhibit, therefore, amounts to a moral constancy that is wholly unaccompanied by cognitive or behavioral stagnation. This quality is a noteworthy developmental achievement. In one regard, it presents us with a kind of "developmental paradox,'' in that *the same processes that account for reliability and stability in the exemplars' moral commitments also account for lifelong change and growth in their manner of carrying out these commitments.*

Moreover, these processes have certain characteristics that may not come readily to mind when we think about the development of extraordinary capacities such as lifelong dedication to a cause. The processes are *gradual* in their workings and *collaborative* in nature. Enduring moral commitment takes years to forge, and it is not accomplished in splendid isolation but through extended, frequent communication with collaborators and supporters. Exploring this will bring us into other apparent contradictions, namely that *even exemplars who are widely regarded as leaders take formative guidance from others close to them, and even those noted for independence of judgment draw heavily upon the support and advice of groups close to them.* This is the second developmental paradox in the life stories of moral exemplars.

In order to understand our developmental paradoxes, we turn to a model of human change that we have adapted from a number of theories in social and developmental psychology.[1] The model describes the formation and transformation of goals through social influence. Because goals and influence are so central to moral commitment, we have found the model especially helpful for addressing the question of how people develop such commitment. Here we shall refer to the model in shorthand as ''goal theory''—with the qualification that it remains more a working model than a formal theory. Goal theory, we believe, can explain the development of moral commitment in all persons who acquire such commitment to a greater or lesser degree. Still, like many normative propositions, goal theory is especially helpful in explaining extreme cases, since such cases distill the processes that are found in less pure form in more ambiguous ones. For this reason, we believe goal theory to be especially well suited for discussing moral exemplars and the processes through which they grow and change over time.

The central notion behind goal theory is that development in a person's belief and conduct is brought about through social influence processes that gradually transform the person's goals. Goal theory focuses on *development* rather than on other sorts of psychological change. Development, in its purer forms, has a number of distinguishing features, among which are that it tends to be orderly, broad-based, and hard to reverse.[2]

Development is orderly because it bears a direct relation to what has come before it. We may, for example, speak of the development of democratic forms of governance by referring to historical conditions that set the stage for them. As we shall discuss toward the end of this chapter, progressive links between past, present, and future, found only in developmental change, will help us unravel the "developmental paradox" referred to above. Where growth derives in an orderly manner from earlier states, stability and change not only may coexist but may also unite to serve the same purpose. Development is broad-based because it affects an entire network of linked action systems: The development of scientific knowledge, for example, has changed entirely the ways in which people live, think, and organize their activities. Development is hard to reverse because, once established, it has a logical necessity to it: Once people realized that the earth orbits the sun rather than vice versa, a host of affiliated phenomena (seasons, eclipses, astronomical patterns) became better understood; and it then became increasingly compelling to maintain and build further upon this insight. Regression may be still possible under conditions of duress, as when the newly developed insight challenges a belligerent societal orthodoxy (witness, for example, the recantations forced upon early followers of Copernicus). But people generally resist giving up their developmental achievements, even at their peril.

The conditions for developmental change are set when social influence coordinates with individual goals in a manner that triggers a reformulation of the person's goals. We consider this process—the *transformation of goals through social influence*—to be the critical instigator of moral development during much of the lifecourse.[3] Most significantly, this means that social influence plays a key role in the formation of major moral commitments. Moreover, since developmental change is inevitably implicated in the formation of moral commitments, certain types of social influence are particularly crucial.

Most human behavior is susceptible to social influence. Psychologists have described a wide assortment of ways in which person's beliefs and behaviors may be changed through transactions with others.[4] But behavioral *development,* as we have noted, is a special case among the variety of ways in which human thought and behavior may be influenced and changed—that is, just as development has special properties that distinguish it from other sorts of change, it also takes place through special social influence processes. Most importantly, in order to support development, social influence processes must trigger reevaluation of a person's current capacities and must provide guidance for their further elaboration. In the moral realm, such social influence results in a gradual transformation of moral goals, along with a transformation of strategies to achieve these goals.

Of course, there are many types of social influence through which people try to alter one another's behavior. If one has sufficient authority, for example, one may simply try to tell another what to do and possibly even what to think. And even beyond unilateral power assertion, there are other, more subtle forms of coercion, persuasion, cajoling, attitude adjustment, reasoning, and so on. But for long-term *developmental* change in a person's orientation, many of these social influence strategies are ineffective. Coercion, for example, works only as long as the power assertion remains in effect. Once removed, there is a drift (or a rush) away from the enforced position. For more permanent change, the person must participate actively in the transformation. Moreover, for genuine growth, there must be an extension of a capacity that the person has already partially worked out. Development, alone among all the possible changes in a person's psychological state, draws upon the following social influence conditions:

- active participation of all parties
- an initial, though only partial, match of goals between the parties
- an initial, and partial, mismatch of goals, in which the goals of the influencing parties constitute a logical extension of the goals of the parties being influenced
- reciprocal communications about goals and strategies
- a structure of guidance providing a bridge from the matched to the mismatched goals
- a mutual receptivity to direction and feedback
- an exchange of concerns, strategies, and capacities, culminating in a transformation of goals

Developmental transformation of goals is a gradual process, occurring over months and sometimes years of communication. It may begin in a small way, as when one person induces another to entertain a new idea or to adopt a new behavior. But long-term, permanent growth does not begin until the latter party's goals are affected. In order for this to occur, the first party's rationale for the idea or behavior must be accepted. Through this route, not only a discrete action but an entire social perspective is eventually transferred.

The notion of goal transformation in human development originally arose out of what Russian psychologists have called "activity theory."[5] Child psychologists have used it to explain how adults pass on to children not only ideas and skills but also the capacity and will to pursue the adult's (or society's) agenda. So, for example, an adult who instructs a child on how to build a model imparts to the child more than just the knowledge of how to put pieces of a construction together. The adult, through a long series of negotiations with the child, also conveys the overall purpose of the venture (to build an accurate copy of something) as well as how one should organize one's activity in order to accomplish such a goal (create plans and subplans, finish Step A so you can move on to Step B, and so on). In the course of such instructional engagements (any of which may take minutes, months, or years), the child comes away with new goals and improved strategies for reaching those goals.

Some American psychologists in recent years have called this proc-ess ''scaffolding.''[6] This metaphor connotes the supportive guidance offered through reciprocal communication. It is easiest to illustrate the metaphor in an example of adult-child influence, and indeed, the metaphor was derived from watching adults socializing children through instructional coaching.[7]

In many adult-child instructional exchanges, the adult leads the child toward activities in which both the adult and child wish to engage—although they may have different reasons (or goals) for want-ing to join in the activity. Consider the ordinary activity of eating with tableware. For reasons of neatness, the adult wishes the toddler to start using a fork. The toddler eagerly participates out of a spirit of play: This is a fun way to act like a grown-up, use a new tool, and join in an intriguing game with Mom. At first the toddler's playful efforts make more of a mess than if the toddler had been simply fed or allowed to eat with her fingers. So initially, the exchange comes closer to meeting the toddler's playful goals than the adult's serious ones.

Eventually, if the parent sticks with it (and parents usually do), the agenda of subsequent exchanges slowly shifts in the direction the parent desires. Through demonstrations, assistance, cajoling, sanc-tions, and so on, the adult guides the child's original playful response into increasingly competent attempts to eat neatly. As this happens, the child's goals for the activity become transformed: The child begins directing tableware usage toward the goal of good table manners. In the course of the goal transformation, the child acquires *an entire frame-work of values.* For example, the child implicitly evaluates the eating behavior of self and others, ridiculing examples of particularly sloppy dining and feeling embarrassed when her own standards slip. When the child maintains this perspective autonomously, the adult instinctively removes the "scaffold" of support and guidance.

Scaffolding is an informative metaphor for some types of adult/child social influence, and it offers a basis for thinking about the social communication of values more generally.[8] The useful parts of it have to do with its vision of development as a guided process of communication that embodies the critical features laid out above. There is an active participation of both parties, an initial sharing of an agenda (usually around play), a partial mismatch of goals (in that the parent is trying to socialize the child), reciprocal communications over an extended period, a structure for guided exchange, and an eventual transformation of goals that brings with it a more "socialized" set of values.

Because developmental theorists have concentrated much of their attention on socialization through parenting, it is not surprising that the major existing models of developmental social influence have been most explicitly articulated through such metaphors as scaffolding. How much can we borrow from such models and metaphors in our attempt to explain the sorts of social influence processes that have affected the moral exemplars in this book?

Our moral exemplars are highly respected, mature people, many of whom are recognized as true societal leaders. By no means can they be described as subordinates in the way children may be. Still, virtually all of them have been powerfully influenced by others, whether early or late in their development, in thought and in deed. In fact, this may be one of our more counterintuitive observations: *Even the exemplars most widely regarded as leaders take guidance from others close to them.* Similarly, *even those who have been noted for their independent judgment draw heavily upon the support, feedback, and advice of groups close to them.* Throughout their lives, trusted associates played critical roles in the formation of the exemplars' values, strategies, and goals.

Here, then, we add two further wrinkles to our developmental paradox: In their transactions with entrusted groups, people who become known as leaders often take direction from their "followers," and people accustomed to autonomous, sometimes defiant determinations of right and wrong nevertheless are open to, and deeply affected by, the opinions of certain others. Moreover, even late in life, social influence continues to be an important part of the exemplars' ongoing moral development.

For moral exemplars, as for any mature adult, developmental social influence no longer retains the quality of asymmetrical subordination found in adult-child scaffolding. It does, however, share with it many of the central features of transformative social exchanges noted above. Each of our exemplars, in one way or another, has pointed to the following as influences on their moral belief and conduct:

- a collaborative relationship with people having alternative perspectives
- an initial, partial match of goals between the exemplar and the other person(s)
- an initial, partial *mis*match of goals between the exemplar and the other(s)
- an extended period of transactions between the exemplar and the other(s), during which the exemplar at first becomes engaged in actions that reflect joint goals and later becomes increasingly engaged in activities reflecting those goals that were not initially shared
- accompanying such transactions, rich and frequent communications about the values underlying the other(s) goals and perspectives
- an eventual adoption of the other(s) goals, usually modified in a manner that can be coherently integrated into the exemplar's prior perspective (even as that perspective changes to accommodate the new goals)
- an eventual adoption of the other(s) strategies for pursuing the new goals, again with whatever modifications are needed to assimilate these strategies into the exemplar's developing perspective

According to the goal transformation model, negative as well as positive social influences can play a part in the growth of moral goals. Negative social influences occur when pressure is brought to bear on the exemplar by intense assertions of values that the exemplar rejects. *When a social engagement presents values that the exemplar has determined to be illegitimate, the exemplar's resistance can lead him or her toward a transformation, elaboration, or strengthening of his or her moral goals.* Recall, for example, Virginia Durr's resistance to segregationists and McCarthyites during long stretches of her civil rights career: Far from dissuading her, the pressure helped to expand and solidify her goals. In Mrs. Durr's case and others, these repeated pressures spurred her to ever greater moral clarity. As with the more positive forms of social influence, negative forms have the greatest developmental effect when they are frequently asserted over an extended period of time. Then

the modes of resistance to which these negative experiences give rise
can gradually shape revised sets of goals and strategies.

We gave another example of moral growth through negative social influence in our introductory account of Andrei Sakharov's development. Late in life, some of his beliefs were reformulated as a result
of oppressive actions by the Soviet regime. The social pressures
brought to bear by the regime were so charged with values against
which Sakharov had determined to fight—values that represented injustice, dishonesty, human enslavement—that these social pressures led
him to develop an entirely new political orientation. We consider this
to be a converse form of goal transformation through social influence.

During our interviews with the twenty-three moral exemplars,
we asked many questions about how they had formed their personal
and moral goals. (As we soon discovered, most of them admitted very
little separation between personal and moral goals. We discuss the
psychological significance of this noteworthy finding in Chapter 11.)
In the exemplars' responses to these questions, we received multiple
accounts of goal transformation through social influence. These accounts almost invariably included the features of developmental social
influence noted above. Some of the accounts focused on early social
influences, during childhood or adolescence, deriving from a relationship with a parent or other respected adult. Other accounts focused
on the present influence of close friends, colleagues, organizations, or
other valued associations. Some described opposition that came about
through their resistance to social pressures they considered illegitimate, which enabled them to crystallize their nascent values. Through
all the various accounts, the general features of the goal formations
and transformations had much in common regardless of whether the
developmental social influence came early or late in their lives.

In Chapter 5 we offered Virginia Durr's story as a case in point.
We discussed the ways in which Mrs. Durr's moral goals developed
over the course of her highly committed life. Her extended commitment to justice has endured for literally scores of years, but she acquired many new goals and strategies during that time. When Mrs.
Durr was a student at Wellesley, she discovered the goal of equal
rights for women. When she moved to Washington and joined the
Woman's Democratic National Committee, she extended this concern
to include the rights of racial minorities. Later, she became dedicated
to nonviolence, both as a goal and as a strategy. Other moral and
political issues were included along the way: civil liberties, freedom
of speech and assembly, truthfulness, and so on.

In Virginia Durr's life, as in all of our exemplars' lives, none of these developments occurred in isolation. For Mrs. Durr, the active social agents included political associates, friends, people with whom she worked, and people against whom she fought. Her most frequent collaborator and source of influence was her husband, Clifford. In addition, many black colleagues with whom Mrs. Durr worked over the years made her aware of their painful experiences in ways that resonated with her own sense of humanity. On many occasions, Mrs. Durr was drawn into new causes by someone's impassioned testimony or compelling argument. There were also turns of events that unexpectedly engaged her in modes of personal resistance: Senator Eastland's McCarthyite hearings are one example. All of these social experiences—the positive as well as the negative—were developmental crucibles for Virginia Durr. They gave her opportunities to reaffirm her long-standing values, reexamine her beliefs, and develop new goals and strategies that would serve her long-standing commitment to social justice. Usually the crucible was formed by collaborative exchanges with trusted colleagues who challenged and inspired her. But at certain trying times, it was formed by exchanges with those trying to pressure her into positions she considered morally illegitimate.

We have seen similar kinds of social influence processes at work in the moral development of all twenty-three exemplars. Some recalled influences arising from their childhood family relations. David Linsky, the businessman and international statesman who was known for his courage and integrity, spoke of becoming inducted into a framework of charitable and ethical values early in life, mainly through the example and guidance of his parents:

> What we got from our parents was this basic, fundamental understanding that you do what's right and you don't do what isn't. I can't remember them preaching. I can't remember them laying out a chart saying, "Don't steal, don't do this or that." I can't remember them saying, "Be compassionate. Be concerned for other human beings. Don't take what does not belong to you." None of that got said, *but that's how they lived.*
>
> And everything we saw—my brothers talk about this from time to time, hoping as we all do that some of it is going to rub off on our children. And how it got through to us—each of my brothers is also very much involved with public affairs of some kind or another, in addition to his profession. Each of us would be unfulfilled without it. There was something in the atmosphere

of the home—respect for the other human being, respect for learning, concern about the welfare of the other, living a decent good life—that we started with.

My mother leaving food for neighbors she knew needed it and indignantly insisting that she had not been doing it when they thanked her. My father writing off on his books—and eventually he became bankrupt—writing off on his books the bills owed to him by others whom he knew couldn't pay. But doing it by stamping their bills paid.

Later in life, Linsky directed himself toward other highly ethical people and again profited from their examples and guidance:

I've been fortunate, I guess, that throughout my life I've been close to people who by their examples set standards for me which helped guide me without necessarily trying to force me in any way. I've already indicated about my home. When I entered law practice in a small firm in Portland, Maine, I was with a judge and his two sons who were among the finest lawyers I've ever known, and who would have rejected without the slightest hesitancy anything that wasn't absolutely straight and moral and legal and ethical. And again, by their example, by my practicing with them, I saw how they conducted themselves. And I remember instances in which they turned down representation because they didn't want to become involved on behalf of those people who wanted to be clients.

Then there were occasions that forced Linsky to reaffirm his beliefs in the face of negative social pressure. He did so in collaboration with a trusted colleague with whom he shared a fundamental commitment to moral and spiritual values:

Ed Patterson, with whom I worked so closely for so many years, was a man of highest integrity, the greatest adherent to moral and spiritual values, with whom I shared so much of my life. I never had an argument with him about a moral matter. There was never any question that you do the right thing. Our corporation decided to sponsor television programs about the United Nations. . . . And when we announced what we were going to do, and the John Birch Society learned of it, each of us received thirty thousand letters condemning us. Because everybody "knew" the United Nations was a communist organization. And they circulated it to all the stockholders and all of us were deluged with letters. And we didn't seriously consider changing our approach.

The theme of inspiration by example runs through our cases. Linsky's recollections of how his parents influenced him in early childhood suggest this inspirational process. But inspiration by example, when it is effective, can take on some interactive characteristics. This is especially striking when the inspirational figure is distant in time or place, or even personally unknown to the person being inspired. Kay Hardie, a columnist who writes about social and moral issues of the day, speaks of the continuing influence that she receives from Mother Teresa in a way that suggests an ongoing imaginary dialogue:

> And I've gotta tell you I've got a picture of Mother Teresa up on my wall. It's of Mother Teresa looking at a child and touching a child's face. And a good many of the issues that I write about have to do with children: education or poverty or whatever. And I look at her and I say, "Hey, Mother, I'm gonna write now."
>
> We don't share the same formal religion, but I admire her very much. And besides keeping a couple of little prayers taped on the inside of my desk drawer, I take a look at that wonderful face and find it inspiring when there are certain topics I'm writing about. I'll tell you what is so thrilling about that woman is that we are walking on the earth at the same moment in time as a person who's clearly a saint. She is an inspiration to me.

In a similar vein, Matthew Goldberg, a pediatrician who devotes his life to the health of poor children in inner-city Baltimore, tells us of the living message that he receives from someone whom he never met, Martin Luther King. Goldberg, like all our exemplars, has experienced many direct collaborative exchanges with friends and colleagues that have supported and shaped his moral goals. He also engages at times in more oppositional exchanges with persons who have a contrasting worldview, crediting these with sharpening his own perspective. But it is an old quotation from Martin Luther King that to this day captures Goldberg's imagination:

> Well, Martin Luther King—I still have a big quote of his up on my wall. The quote is, you know, "when they ask me at my funeral . . . if someone has a eulogy, don't tell them about all the prizes and gifts, don't tell them about the Nobel Prize. Say that I was a drum major for justice. Say that I was a drum major for peace. I may not leave a lot of riches behind. But I left a

committed life behind." That's real important. That quote's right next to where I sit when I'm working.

In many ways, the moral life of an exemplar can be considered a history of the social relationships—both positive and negative—that the exemplar has experienced. The history builds with it an enduring commitment to moral values along with a commensurate set of goals and strategies. It also builds with it a tendency to profit developmentally from further morally influential relations. This is why the early and late parts of the history often have similar relational features—as in the case of Linsky, who throughout his life found himself guided by those he trusted and admired. The early experiences clearly predispose the exemplar to seek and benefit from later relations. This developmental pattern is played out time and again in the life histories that we observed.

We see it clearly in Mary Ehrlich's story. Mary was a nun for many years and in that capacity became concerned about the problems of the desperately poor. Eventually, she left her religious order to devote herself more fully to what she describes as the struggle for social justice. She now works closely with Allison McCrea, providing shelter for the homeless and raising money to support a number of antipoverty programs. Ms. Ehrlich recounted the following sequence of social influences:

> The women in my family were very strong. There were a lot of us, first of all, and they were very strong women. My grandmother, even as an immigrant, was poor but constantly trying to start an entrepreneurial business. She just turned one hundred. So, a lot of strong women [and] sort of an atmosphere of believing in women . . .
>
> I think I got a lot of class consciousness from my mother. She had and still has a very interesting way of looking at the world. And though she had always sort of sold herself as wanting to be upwardly mobile, she also had this neighborhood [feeling] or whatever. She'd say, "Well, that's because these people are poor."
>
> I had fantastic theology teachers. I had people who were really struggling with how should the Catholic church—and, in particular, religious congregations of women—respond to, you know, racial prejudice, all the stuff that was going on—Martin Luther King and the civil rights movement and all this stuff was all going on at the same time. What was our moral responsibility

to it? And how does theology fit into it?. . . . And my own
situation being in the middle of the ferment, and having people
around who were very well versed in a particular [theology], and
committed.

And as I found other people like myself—and there were
thousands of other people who were seriously committed to issues of social justice in a very real way. And putting their lives
on the line or their reputations on the line, or whatever, to speak
out and be where they thought they should be . . . giving an
institution [the church] credibility . . . In my case, you know,
that institution really did help nurture some part of me that
brought me to where I am today.

And then I would also teach adult theology. And it was
through some of that, you know—trying to get people to look
at the political aspects of scripture and to grapple with some of
these same things. And I found more and more of my life being
drawn to more and more meetings that were dealing with some
of these issues . . . And then I ran across a woman who was also
a nun who was dragging me to more and more meetings, because
she sort of took me under her wing when I came up to this area
and was highly involved herself. And I respected her very much
and her opinion. And she dragged me to a lot of stuff around the
city.

Whether in the role of student or teacher, Ms. Ehrlich remained
open to the influence of others. Her adult social relations had the same
receptive and searching qualities that marked those of her childhood.
Even when she was instructing others in theology, she was still actively formulating her own orientation, drawing heavily upon others
for new ideas and goals. She seemed to learn in much the same way
from adulthood relations in which she was a leader or a peer as from
earlier ones in which she was a child or a student.

Allison McCrea, Ms. Ehrlich's colleague in the fight against poverty, has a vivid sense of acquiring her moral perspective from some
early family examples, some hard social experience, and some instruc-
tion by friends and colleagues. Ms. McCrea recalls a childhood living
situation and a respected grandparent that together oriented her
toward concerns of justice:

I was neither fish nor fowl. I was neither rich nor poor. I was a
poor kid in a rich girl's setting. And I can remember even as a
child of twelve, thirteen, fourteen, fifteen—recognizing that.

And a very keen awareness of how rich kids were treated. So my
sense of fairness developed at a very early age because I lived in
two worlds—the world of the haves and the world of the have-
nots, although I was not in a have-not environment.

My grandmother always provided for all of us and everybody
on the street as well. Guys used to come to our house—hundreds
and hundreds of guys during the depression—and she fed them
all. And I wondered why they were and what they were doing
there and how come they knew our house. I found out years later
that they used to put a chalkmark in front of a safe house where
they could get a meal assured them. [Laughing.] My grandmother used to give away all of my uncle's everything. They'd
come home at night and my Uncle Jimmy's shoes would be gone.
And he'd say, "Well, what happened?" And she'd say, "Well,
this guy came along and he didn't have anything, so I gave him
. . ."

Later, when speaking of her first encounters with poverty work
as an adult, Ms. McCrea's account is reminiscent of Sakharov's recollections of friends who induced him into ever broader moral awareness. She acknowledges her initial goal of curing injustice but credits
her ability to do so effectively to the influence of friends who were
more worldly wise. From these friends, she learned a broader moral
perspective and a more realistic strategy of moral action. Her fundamental commitment to the poor was shared by her new friends from
the start. It endured the necessary reexamination of belief that the
new relationships forced upon her, in fact, as a consequence of this
reexamination, Ms. McCrea's commitment gained strength and staying power.

I was a white, cocky, privileged person that had come to Roxbury figuring I was going to do like so many liberals did at the
time—be one of the saviors. And they were very understanding
of that. They said to me, "Allison, nothing is going to change
because you're here, but we're glad you're here." And it was
kind of like a relief. You know, like you don't have to carry the
white person's burden. You could simply be one of the gang and
just kind of join in the struggle. You didn't lead it, you didn't
follow it, it was just kind of there and you were part of it. And
that was a very good lesson to learn.

When I went to Roxbury, I had all the answers. Living in
Roxbury taught me what the questions were, which was far

more important than the answers, absolutely, absolutely. . . . I had to learn to listen. I never did that . . . And I think that the development of Allison McCrea really began in Roxbury. I mean everything in my life up till that time was a rehearsal for what my life was to be, and again, I'm grateful to the people of Roxbury for taking me by the hand and holding me and saying, "It's OK." . . . So I learned—they taught me a lot about myself that I never knew. And they opened the door on a world into which I walked that I have absolutely no regrets about. . . . My teachers were my neighbors.

Sometimes a fortuitous turn in a career, or even a chance event, can extend an exemplar's moral goals into new areas that are generally consistent with his or her old commitments, but they can entail some dramatically new courses of action. Suzie Valadez's sudden call to Ciudad Juarez is one of these cases. Jack Coleman's opportunity to head a philanthropic foundation that was already committed to issues such as prison reform and the "severely needy" is another. In both cases, the exemplar's goals were reinforced and expanded by the new challenge; and as a consequence, the moral goals were reformulated and more powerful strategies were acquired. New York City's Mother Irma Johnson's widely renowned shelter for babies of drug-addicted mothers in the heart of Harlem began with such a turn of events. After her husband died, she needed a way to support her family:

So then somebody said to me, "You're so good with children and they like you, so why don't you take other people's children. So I did . . . I started to keep other people's children they'd bring out to me. And the children came with me. And once the children came, they didn't want to go home again. So they'd stay. They didn't leave, five days a week. Some of them even stayed seven days . . . And the mothers went to work. They were satisfied, and their children went to school. The kids didn't fail in school or anything like that because I saw to their homework and everything and the mothers were really happy. So it made a good life for them, and that's how I got started.

Gradually, Mother Johnson offered her services to ever more impoverished children, eventually opening a home for those who had been living in the most desperate conditions imaginable. Many had been born already addicted to drugs, many had been neglected or abused, and some had been outright abandoned. As she extended her reach into these grim circumstances, Mother Johnson discovered new goals and challenges. As we discuss elsewhere in this book, one of the most astonishing concomitants to this type of discovery—for Mother Johnson as well as for virtually all our exemplars—was the unexpected joys that these new and increasingly daunting challenges brought.

Among our twenty-three cases, there were many variations on these basic social influence themes. Three of the exemplars told us of a negative social influence that they experienced in their early home lives. It may seem curious to think of young children resisting the values or the conduct of the only families they have known; yet some of our exemplars fashioned their initial moral orientations through just this sort of resistance. In all three cases, the exemplars received support and guidance from positive relationships later in their lives— from friends, spouses, or colleagues—that had at least as great an influence on their moral development as the earlier contrary ones. Still, however negative, first relationships are always marked by a special vividness. John Thomas, a doctor who works long, demanding hours in his campaign to reform policies in medical ethics, speaks this way about his early life:

> I was very independent, extremely independent at an early age.
> . . . I reacted to my home life because I didn't like that. It was
> sort of a nonentity and I reacted strongly to that. . . . At eleven
> or twelve, I was the white sheep in the family. I was very differ-
> ent. I reacted to my home strongly, and that made me the good
> and bad of what I am partially. Because I reacted, it was an anti-
> model, or whatever you call it. And so that's part of what I am.

Peace activist Aline Burchell says: "I had a pretty rough child-hood. I was battered by my mother and to a degree by my father. So I think, on reflection, that I identify very strongly with people who are in an underdog position and who are traumatized and brutalized."

Sharon Crandall, a civil liberties activist, recalls: "I grew up in what I would call a dysfunctional family. My parents weren't good to me . . . and that gives me, I believe, some comprehension of external forces rendering one disabled that I think is really the basis from which I translate out and comprehend the experience of other people."

From early to mid-adulthood, the exemplars all had some community of friends, coworkers, religious compatriots, or other intimate companions who played critical roles in the formation of their beliefs. In one case, it was an ethics committee on the job that "got me going" (John Thomas). Other times it was contact with organizations outside the exemplars' main job: "I got into the community and I began to know other agencies and began to know more and more about them . . . and I got into retardation, I got into everything else [related to disturbed youth]'' (Bishop Donaldson). Sometimes it was a religious affiliation that pressed the exemplar toward a goal or a call to service: ''I think that the fact that I have been part of a Zen Buddhist meditation community for close to fifteen years definitely . . . I am definitely influenced and affected by this choice . . . which may be just one of the hazards of people who are living religious lives—I feel like I'm not coming up to the mark'' (Anne Hayes). Virtually all the exemplars spoke of peers who prodded them, provoked them, taught them, challenged them, provided them with feedback, and otherwise inspired, supported, and sustained them through the midlife years.

Perhaps most striking is the continuation of developmental social influence very late in life. Wallace Henry, a central figure in all the American Friends peace movements since World War I, astonished us with the sentiment: ''On the other hand, there are half a dozen Quakers that I know who are giving their all. They just make me feel that I haven't begun hardly in this society. And they beckon me and make me want to go further, even though I'm eighty-six years old already.''

This quality of staying alive to social influence and moral growth all throughout life is a special mark of the moral exemplars in our study. In many cases, exemplars retain their openness to change by keeping in close contact with peers who continue to expand their horizons—as has Henry, or as did Andrei Sakharov. In other cases, the exemplars press themselves toward greater heights through imaginary dialogues with admired figures. Kay Hardie's and Matthew Goldberg's statements are two instances of this. Jack Coleman offered us yet another variation on this theme—he sustains a self-constructed dialogue with a younger generation: ''My own personal definition of integrity comes from this question: Would I be embarrassed if my children knew?''

The special ways in which moral exemplars, even in old age, keep themselves alive to social influence provides an extended ideal of developmental goal transformation. It is an extended ideal because we would not expect to find such effective means of sustaining moral growth in the advanced years of most people's lives. In this regard, our group of moral exemplars exemplifies not just extraordinary moral commitment but also the processes of lifelong moral growth. Each of the life trajectories that we have examined shows (1) an initial condition of partially shared goals between close colleagues; (2) the social influence of colleagues as a primary instigator of change; (3) a gradual move toward new or expanded goals after extended periods of joint action and rich communication; and (4) a transformation of the individual's goals, governed in part by the collaborative engagement and in part by the exemplar's moral perspective prior to the engagement. Both the exemplars and his or her colleagues are active agents in determining the shape of the transformation. All new ideas must owe their shape to some interaction between external guidance and internal belief: the transformation is, in one precise word, a "co-construction." Over an extended period of time, the new or expanded moral goals are co-constructed in the course of many negotiations between the exemplar and other persons.

Because the transformation is governed in part by the exemplar's prior moral perspective, even dramatic changes may be seen as somewhat continuous with the exemplar's deeply held values and commitments. Here we have the second developmental paradox. If our first paradox was the way in which social influence can shape the goals of independent-minded leaders, the second is the way in which these same people manage to preserve a lifelong openness to change while still retaining a core stability in their moral commitments. To understand the special character of exemplary moral growth, it is important to appreciate this unique mix of change and stability, the special way in which exemplars combine their openness to change with their unwavering adherence to essential moral values.

The twenty-three subjects of this book are, of course, extraordinary in many ways: their commitment to moral principle, their dedication to others, their talent for inspiring people to action, and their high standards of personal and ethical integrity. All of these characteristics were presumed by our nominating criteria and constituted the reasons that we chose their lives to explore. In the course of our interviews, we discovered other extraordinary features that went beyond the nominating criteria: the certainty and the quiet courage that we discussed in Chapter 4, the serene reliance on faith that we will discuss in Chapter 10, the galvanizing effects on others that we have noted throughout, and so on.

Yet perhaps their most intriguing common characteristic was the paradoxical mix of lasting commitment and sustained capacity for change that we referred to above. Even as the exemplars' grip on their core ideals remained unwavering, they continued to reexamine their most fundamental attitudes and choices at frequent intervals. Many of them expanded the nature and extent of their engagements, many took on unexpected challenges, and many dramatically altered their beliefs, conduct, or life conditions on short notice. All the while, the exemplars remained true to their overarching original values, which endured the flux of frequent change and growth, and in a fundamental sense contributed to the shape of that change and growth.

Among our twenty-three moral leaders is a top business executive who, at an age when most persons retire, founded a seminal new approach to business ethics. Another is a religious leader who became renowned for his charitable work with the poor; late in life, he unexpectedly took up a passionate fight for the humane treatment of prisoners. A corporate chieftain left his thriving business to immerse himself in an international campaign for peace. A dedicated schoolteacher decided to fill her home with wayward (and very difficult) youth.

We interviewed physicians who, in mid-career, turned the main focus of their attention to child advocacy, nuclear disarmament, environmental preservation, human rights, or the ethical responsibilities of their profession. Often there was a quickly expanding succession of concerns. One physician moved beyond concerns of peace to broader concerns of environmental safety, another began offering unpaid treatment to indigent children, another broadened his personal focus on medical ethics to begin an intense engagement in the national debate about patients' rights to live or die. As these new challenges were taken on, there was inevitably an incorporation of new values and an amplification of the moral thrust.

In yet other cases we saw even more abrupt changes of course. A deeply religious clergyman renounced an authoritative interpretation of religious creed from his own religious hierarchy, setting off a storm of controversy within his church. A nun left her order and started a shelter for the homeless. Suzie Valadez saw a vision and within a few weeks moved to the Mexican border, where she has spent the next twenty-eight years of her life ministering to the poor. People on middle-class career tracks dropped out to join monasteries, found missions, create sanctuaries for refugees, or take up the struggle for civil rights.

Alterations of this sort need to be understood in the context of how adults typically play out their lives. It is not that people never change once they reach adulthood: People of all ages, in fact, experience both change and continuity every day of their lives. But personal stability does become more the rule than the exception as life progresses. Once maturity has been reached, there are many conservative forces that preserve continuity in psychological functioning. For this reason, most people become progressively less receptive to new engagements and ideas as they grow older.

This is not a surprising or counterintuitive statement. Several recent life-span studies have shown that most people believe that aging decreases one's tendencies to change and grow.[9] It is not that older people view their own development negatively—in fact, it is normal for older people to have positive views about their own life histories[10]—but people of all ages expect that growth in their adult lives is confined to young and, to a lesser degree, middle adulthood. Aging brings both gains and declines, but there is an increasing proportion of the latter over the former, beginning fairly early in mid-life. As one prominent study found, "the nature of adult development was perceived to be multidimensional (both gains and losses coexist), although the overall conception implied increasing risk of decline and decreasing potential for growth across the life span."[11]

It seems likely that such perceptions are based at least roughly on reality, that most people indeed do stabilize their choices, skills, and goals once they have reached adulthood. The extent to which this is true, naturally, is open for debate. Psychologists have disagreed about this for generations, and different approaches have led to different conclusions. In the words of one recent summary, "Whereas social learning theories and humanistic psychology stress the malleability of personality and the potential for growth, trait theories espouse the view of long-term stability."[12] To compound the uncertainty, personality theorists have identified qualitatively different sorts of stability as well as different types of change.[13] For our purposes, suffice to say that psychological science has yet to agree on the precise nature, degree, or commonality of stability and growth during adulthood, but our own reading of the available evidence suggests that stability predominates over growth in most people's aging. Moreover, this expectation is widely shared among both laypersons and experts.

We also know that, as a rule, people's psychological functioning does not decline dramatically with age, except in the case of special impairments such as Alzheimer's disease. Since the early days of psychological testing, there have been many studies aimed at the question of whether humans lose their mental facilities as they grow older. The most recent of these attempts have corrected earlier misimpressions that human abilities begin a long and uninterrupted descent in the aftermath of maturity.[14] Methodological advances, such as partialing out historical cohort effects, have shown that many individuals retain their full, higher-order cognitive capacities late in life. Even though skills linked to perceptual and motor processes—for example, reaction time—may show some decrement, the higher intellectual functions do not. This is mostly true of functions requiring highly complex types of judgment: advanced problem solving, moral reasoning, "wisdom" about interpersonal affairs.[15]

Still, even here, the best that can be said for most people is that most capacities do not decline in old age.[16] Actual improvement in any area is always limited to a minority of the population. Again, stability is the rule.

From our exemplars' accounts of their own lives, we gained a somewhat different picture: a sense of continued openness to change and growth, an openness that is not the usual expectation in most adult lives.[17] In the interviews, it was clear that the exemplars shared a capacity to create a functional, dynamic, and expanding balance between continuity and growth in their lives.

The exemplars' lives are full of change but not of random flux. All of them have long-term commitments to principles and causes they believe in. All of them have long-standing character traits they claim have endured since childhood. All of them have attained a great deal of stability in their current lives. Yet it is stability without stagnation. In all matters of belief, action, dedication, and strategic effectiveness, our subjects have kept growing. And they have done so, we believe, through the developmental process that we discussed in the first part of this chapter. The exemplars have maintained their dynamic balance of stability and change through personal qualities that keep alive their capacities to learn and profit from social experience.

All too frequently during many people's lives, stability and change do battle with one another. It is in these instances that one finds tumult, stagnation, or some unproductive vacillation between the two. In contrast, those who continue developing all through adulthood manage a balanced relationship between stability and change. Such a relationship is made possible by the expansive (rather than restrictive) nature of certain personal qualities. These qualities, such as open-mindedness or honesty, continually expand a person's developmental horizons, because they enable the person to fully experience the world in a fruitful manner. Such qualities may be thought of as *personal continuities* that provide individuals with repeated experiences that enhance their capacities as well as new challenges that stimulate their growth.

Contemporary personality theorists have identified two types of personal continuity that can act as powerful forces for both stability and change in a person's life. The first type is called *cumulative continuity:* the tendency of individuals to create or select environments that reinforce their own personality characteristics.[18] People often channel themselves into environments that amplify the precise qualities that led them to choose such environments in the first place. To take one example offered by leading theorists, a gregarious student will be the one most likely to suggest moving a seminar to a local tavern, thus providing a platform for the further expression and extension of his own gregariousness.[19] The more opportunities one has for creating self-sustaining environments, the more one's own personality characteristics will be supported. Over time, with repeated exposure to such self-chosen environments, one's personality characteristics become increasingly resistant to change.

The second type of continuity is called *interactional continuity:* the tendency of individuals to evoke, through their own particular styles of social interaction, particular sorts of responses from others.[20] These tend to reinforce the interactional style that triggered the response so that another personal continuity is established, this time on an interpersonal level. In this manner, the quality of a person's social relations tend to be repeated as the person develops a particular way of interacting with other people.

Interactional continuities may work adaptively or maladaptively, depending upon the person's developmental history. A child with a history of secure attachments to caregivers may develop a trusting and friendly interactional style that consistently evokes warm responses from others. The warm responses further support the child's open interactional style, which in turn continues to create positive social engagement.[21] In contrast, a child with a history of physical abuse may approach others with suspicion and hostility. This often triggers aggressive responses, further reinforcing the child's guarded interactional style. With repeated experience, the self-confirming cycle of expectation and result gains strength, becoming increasingly difficult to break without dramatic, pattern-changing interventions.[22]

Table 7.1 illustrates some of the ways in which interactional continuities contributed to lifelong developmental goal transformations for each of the five exemplars whose lives we examine in detail in this book. We have also noted in Table 7.1 ways in which our interviews with these five suggested signs of cumulative continuities at work. Like all people, the exemplars in this book have stable as well as dynamic behavioral dispositions and owe their own particular mixes of stability and change to cumulative as well as interactional continuities. Such continuities affect either how the exemplars shape and select their environments (cumulative continuity) or how they structure their social experience (interactional continuity). There are many examples of both in each life. The relations drawn in Table 7.1 are representative of those found throughout our interviews.

Table 7.1
Transformation of Goals Through Cumulative and Interactional Continuities

CABELL BRAND
Cluster of Personality Characteristics

Cluster 1: Positive response to challenge, willingness to seize opportunities, "can-do" attitude, entrepreneurial spririt

Cumulative continuities: Puts himself in more challenging situations, chooses to move toward rather than away from new opportunities and challenges such as taking over his father's company, responding to the new OEO legislation.

Interactional continuities: His ability to respond effectively to challenges confirms his self-concept as someone who likes challenges (expectation-confirming interaction). It is important to this process that failures are handled pragmatically and attributed to temporary, external causes. His can-do attitude evokes energy for the challenge in others and thus increases the likelihood of success.

Contribution to moral goals: Led him to take on the original challenge in response to the OEO legislation, establish TAP; contributed to growth of TAP (adding new programs); sustained him through hard times.

Cluster 2: Love of people, gregariousness, extroversion

Cumulative continuities: Puts himself in situations where he will be with people (e.g., choosing sales-type career where he needs to be an extrovert).

Interactional continuities: Being friendly, positive, extroverted evokes a reciprocal response from others.

Contribution to moral goals: Ability to make connections and get to know key people, influence people and enlist their help.

Cluster 3: Organizational ability, ability to mobilize people, leadership

Cumulative continuities: Seeks out and accepts positions of leadership (e.g., president of TAP, chair of State Board of Health).

(continued)

Table 7.1

Transformation of Goals Through Cumulative
and Interactional Continuities (continued)

Interactional continuities: Mobilizing people helps him to achieve his goals and reinforces his self-image as a leader. He sees himself as successful and others see him as successful, so people look to him for leadership.

Contribution to moral goals: Leadership of TAP engaged him more fully, leadership of State Board of Health led to CHIP.

Cluster 4:   Energy, engagement, desire to learn and expand understanding

Cumulative continuities: Leads him to read extensively, seek out information by talking to people, to travel widely.

Interactional continuities: The more he seeks out new perspectives, the more he is stimulated to go further with it (e.g., in regard to travel).

Contribution to moral goals: Leads him to learn a great deal about poverty, race relations, the environment, the global economy, and so on.

JACK COLEMAN
Cluster of Personality Characteristics

Cluster 1:   Sense of personal efficacy and control, desire to test himself, welcoming challenges

Cumulative continuities: Puts himself in challenging situations, moves toward rather than away from new opportunities (e.g., accepts position as president of Haverford and the Clark Foundation, buys and runs inn).

Interactional continuities: Successfully taking on challenging situations and testing himself confirms his sense of efficacy.

Contribution to moral goals: Puts him in a position to have an impact, leads to "blue-collar sabbaticals" that result in moral growth.

Cluster 2:   Sense of security that gives him greater independence (willingness to speak his mind, to "get up and walk out")

Cumulative continuities: Takes on a succession of radically different careers and jobs.

Interactional continuities: Because he doesn't fear the consequences, he can be bolder in stating opinions, and so on. This may evoke deference and respect in others, which in turn reinforces his sense of security.

Contribution to moral goals: Doesn't compromise values in order to get or keep a job. Doesn't distort what he believes in to suit others. Not an opportunist.

Cluster 3:   Respect for the dignity of persons (that of God in everyone); desire to do good for others

Table 7.1
Transformation of Goals Through Cumulative
and Interactional Continuities (continued)

Cumulative continuities: Joins and takes on important roles in churches that stand for this (Unitarian and Quaker), reads books that support and elaborate this perspective.

Interactional continuities: Treating people with love and respect elicits positive response from them that in turn reinforces the original impulse. This also reinforces his self-image as a loving, respectful person.

Contribution to moral goals: Leads to a particular kind of presidency (setting moral tone); leads to work on prison reform and job programs for inner-city youth.

Cluster 4:   Honesty, integrity, decency, pursuit of personal growth

Cumulative continuities: Reads books that inspire this, takes position at Quaker college, chooses wife and friends that share these values.

Interactional continuities: If you approach people with honesty, decency, and so on, they are likely to respond positively. Acting with integrity reinforces his self-concept as a person of integrity.

Contribution to moral goals: Central to his presidencies (setting a moral tone), also to how he approaches his innkeeping. Self-development *is* a moral goal for him.

VIRGINIA DURR
Cluster of Personality Characteristics

Cluster 1:   Willfulness, strong-mindedness, defiance, honor (standing up for what you believe in)

Cumulative continuities: Joins groups and organizations that take strong positions on social issues and takes vocal, high-profile roles in these organizations; is then more likely to be called upon to take positions on controversial issues; married someone who stands by his word, who then supports her in doing this (e.g., Korean War petition incident).

Interactional continuities: If you are strong-minded and willful, people may defer to you, which can make you more willful. If you take strong stands and speak out about what you believe in, people will look to you to do that more.

Contribution to moral goals: Really engages the issues, leads to feedback that then changes her (because strong-mindedness is combined with Cluster 2—open mindedness and honesty with herself)—e.g., dining table incident). Supports sense of certainty, not deterred from course of action that she believes is right.

(continued)

Table 7.1
Transformation of Goals Through Cumulative
and Interactional Continuities (continued)

Cluster 2: Inquiring mind and open-mindedness, honesty within herself, lack of hypocrisy

Cumulative continuities: Chooses to go to a very academically strong college; chooses courses in college that will open her mind on social issues; reads extensively about socialism when confronting the depression back in Alabama; seeks out a range of different kinds of people to learn from.
Interactional continuities: She seeks out diverse kinds of people, they give her new input, and she processes the input in a very open-minded way, which leads her to become more open-minded and inquiring.
Contribution to moral goals: Leads to transformation from racism to a commitment to racial equality.

SUZIE VALADEZ
Cluster of Personality Characteristics

Cluster 1: Compassion, love of people, gregariousness, sense of preciousness of all people

Cumulative continuities: Puts herself in social situations, seeks people out, joins in the activities of the church congregation as an important social group.
Interactional continuities: When she approaches people with love and respect, they often respond accordingly. When she is met with a negative response, she discounts it, which often defuses the negative response. Her self-concept as a loving person is continually reconfirmed.
Contribution to moral goals: Leads her to put herself in situations where she can help people, they then seek more help from her. She is also able to enlist others to join her, to get them to help her help others.

Cluster 2: Special ability with and love for children, their attraction to her

Cumulative continuities: Agrees to teach Sunday school, missionary work focuses heavily on helping children.
Interactional continuities: Her kindness to children draws them "like a magnet."
Contribution to moral goals: Goes from Sunday school teacher to "queen of the dump" largely by helping children, pulled in to do more by their needs.

Cluster 3: Resourcefulness, acceptance of challenge

Cumulative continuities: Takes on the move to Texas; the mission; expansion of the mission (medical care, orphanages).
Interactional continuities: Acceptance of challenges leads to greater sense of

Table 7.1
Transformation of Goals Through Cumulative and Interactional Continuities (continued)

personal control and efficacy, which leads to greater acceptance of challenge and ability to be effective in response to challenge.
Contribution to moral goals: Led her to move to Texas, establish and develop the mission.

Cluster 4:   Security, belief that God will provide

Cumulative continuities: Puts herself in unprotected situations, doesn't keep much for herself. When she finds out that she survives that quite well, she feels even more secure.
Interactional continuities: Her sense of security allows her to be generous to others. This leads people to want to support and help her, so she is further reinforced in her belief that she will be taken care of.
Contribution to moral goals: Allows her to give herself to others rather than pursuing self-protective goals. Allows her not to worry too much about her children.

CHARLESZETTA WADDLES
Cluster of Personality Characteristics

Cluster 1:   Generosity, open-heartedness, love for people

Cumulative continuities: Puts herself in social situations, starts study group with goal of helping the poor, moves in with friend to save her house.
Interactional continuities: As Mother Waddles says, "If you give out love, you get love back." Helping confirms her self-image as a loving person.
Contribution to moral goals: Leads her to put herself in situations where she can help people, they then seek more help from her. She is also able to enlist others to join her, to get them to help her help others.

Cluster 2:   Resourcefulness, acceptance of challenge, belief in personal control (anyone can become the light of the world)

Cumulative continuities: Takes on role of household head and provider while still a child; accepts jobs for which she has no experience—success at these reinforces sense of efficacy and control.
Interactional continuities: She acts resourcefully, and people respond by giving her more responsibility. She then does well with the new responsibility and this confirms her sense of efficacy.
Contribution to moral goals: Led her to start the mission—was able to get free space, able to start and keep the mission going with very few resources, able to expand services of the mission.

(continued)

Table 7.1
Transformation of Goals Through Cumulative and Interactional Continuities (continued)

Cluster 3:   Belief that God will provide

Cumulative continuities: Puts herself in unprotected situations, doesn't keep much for herself. When she finds out that she survives this quite well, she feels even more secure.
Interactional continuities: Her sense of security allows her to be generous to others. This leads people to want to support and help her, so she is further reinforced in her belief that she will be taken care of.
Contribution to moral goals: Allows her to give herself to others rather than pursuing self-protective goals. Allows her not to worry too much about her children.

It is easy to see how personality characteristics of the sort noted in the table can create the conditions for their own endurance and amplification. For example, early in his life Jack Coleman felt a desire to prove himself by taking on manly challenges. He sought out life situations that enabled him to "test" himself. In the process, he developed a wide array of competencies as well as a firm sense of self-assurance. This in turn sustained his drive to keep testing himself and enabled him to successfully take on additional challenges. Cabell Brand's entrepreneurial spirit, also discovered early, served much the same function in his life. Virginia Durr's strong-mindedness, along with her honesty, helped her develop the toughness of character and autonomy of judgment that later propelled her into the fray of civil rights. These characteristics also enabled her to withstand the isolation, conflict, and pressure that were inflicted upon her as a controversial champion of justice. In quite different ways, the early vivaciousness of Suzie Valadez and her love of children and Charlesetta Waddles's generosity and ready kindness established the social conditions in these women's lives that sustained their charitable work and enhanced its effectiveness.

One common theme in Table 7.1 is the five exemplars' positive responses to challenges. They all have a decided tendency to seek out problems rather than to avoid them. People who do this, of course, find their efforts rewarded when they achieve the challenging goal. In such instances, their love of challenge is directly reinforced. But what happens when they do not succeed? In order for challenge-seeking to be amplified rather than stamped out by defeat, a person must have some way of diminishing the personal significance of the defeats. We shall discuss in Chapter 10 one way many exemplars do this: briefly, by attributing defeats to external and temporary causes rather than to something endemic in the world or in themselves. In order to understand how cumulative continuity works in the case of challenge-seeking, we must look at how people explain both their successes and their failures to themselves. In order for challenge-seeking to endure and grow, its positive consequences must be cherished while its negative consequences discounted.

Love for people, another common theme for our exemplars, can be understood in a similar way. Usually a loving, respectful approach to people will be met with a positive response that serves to increase the original tendency to be loving. But some people do not respond to a kind approach in a like manner. People who have long histories of abuse, exploitation, and neglect, such as those with whom many of our exemplars work, may meet a loving approach with hostility and ingratitude. As we shall also see in Chapter 10, our exemplars explain these reactions to themselves in ways that allow them to forgive the negative responses and to continue to act lovingly rather than to turn hostile themselves. Their original kindly behavior is supported by a charitable conceptual scheme that leads to the maintenance or even amplification of the original tendency.

Some of the qualities noted in Table 7.1 can only be understood in combination with others. Sometimes it is only a particular mix that enables developmental change to occur. In Virginia Durr, for example, we see a strong-mindedness that might have become closed-mindedness if it had not combined with her deep and searching honesty. Closed-mindedness may prevent rather than facilitate developmental change. Likewise Jack Coleman's unwillingness to compromise may have turned into rigid dogmatism if it had not combined with a strong desire for self-improvement and a sincere concern for truth and personal integrity.

Continuities that periodically produce transformative experiences can be either of a cumulative or an interactional sort. For many people, cumulative continuities play the bigger role. Professional people whose enduring ambition leads them to seek new problems to conquer, scientists whose enduring curiosity leads them to keep asking themselves unanswered questions, artists and designers whose enduring creativity leads them to experiment with new forms and fashions, social reformers whose enduring tendency toward criticism leads them to discard previously accepted routes—all of these people benefit developmentally from cumulative continuities that repeatedly provide them with experiential food for growth.

The developmental power of the cumulative continuity is realized when the environments that it repeatedly creates provoke reconsideration rather than reification of habitual ideas. This pattern can serve people well in any field or enterprise that rewards innovation. Effective moral action also relies on innovation at times: witness the brilliantly original symbolic gestures of a King or a Gandhi, so effective in galvanizing mass support for their causes. Sometimes, too, a moral leader puts his or her own commitments to periodic tests, playing out a personal continuity in cumulative fashion. In our study, Jack Coleman provides the clearest examples of this pattern. Coleman, who has felt a lifelong desire to prove himself by tackling ever more difficult challenges, recounts a wealth of new insights and skills arising out of his self-imposed tests. For example, he learned how to maintain personal control in the most desperate situations by throwing himself onto the streets as a homeless person and into jail as a common prisoner.

Yet in the moral realm, perhaps unlike in the business, scientific, aesthetic, or professional realms, many of the personal continuities that promote lifelong development are interactional rather than cumulative. Morality is an interpersonal matter, even when it takes the form of a transcendent faith in a supernatural power. This is because it is inevitably implemented through the quality of a person's interactions with the social world. As the means/ends test of our nominating criteria affirm, it is hard to imagine how moral goals could be pursued through interactions that lacked honesty or integrity. Moral values are communicated and implemented through social interaction, and moral concerns are discovered through social experience and social influence. Processes that encourage moral action and spur moral development will necessarily be social-interactional in essence. Many, in fact, will be exclusively interpersonal in character.

In the moral realm, certain kinds of personal qualities, progressively enhanced by interactional continuity, can be especially powerful forces for lifelong change. The qualities that we have in mind are those that would be most compatible with the processes of social influence that lead to a developmental transformation of moral goals. Specifically, we propose that, *if the quality of a person's continuing interactional style is open, reciprocal, generative, truthful, and self-reflective, the social relations engendered by that manner will promote and sustain the person's moral growth.*

The interactional styles that spur lifelong moral development, therefore, are ones that establish open systems of feedback between the self and others. Such styles promote extended contact with others as well as rich communication in the course of that contact. Through interactional continuity, such characteristics are reinforced by the encouragement that they receive during social engagements.

Among our twenty-three exemplars, we saw many different examples of interpersonal styles that helped each individual receive rich and extensive feedback from others. Some of the varied examples included friendliness, which consistently opens the way to new relationships, and its sometime alter ego, competitiveness, which intensifies mutual attention and feedback in a relationship. Another example was a tendency toward empathy, which can engage an individual in continual sympathetic dialogue with others. A third is an intense interest in others—a quality Sakharov called (in himself) a "pesky inquisitiveness into all matters human." Such a curiosity can ensure that a person becomes a good questioner and a good listener. What all of these interpersonal orientations have in common is their facilitating effect on an individual's communications with others.

The moral import of good communication is that it can both act as a means for social learning and represent a moral end in itself.[23] Consider two standards of good communication: reciprocity and truthfulness. In the course of reciprocal and truthful communications, people learn to extend their moral concerns for one another. Further, reciprocity and truthfulness themselves represent a cluster of basic moral values centering around respect for the other and honesty. As a consequence, reciprocity and truthfulness each serves a dual moral function of facilitating moral growth and setting a guiding standard for moral conduct.

In a similar manner, any interpersonal style that promotes good communication can lead (through the process of interactional continuity) in at least two distinct paths to sustained moral development. First, *the characteristic style can establish the communicational conditions for moral learning.* Second, *it can itself set a moral standard,* a kind of developmental *telos,* that can direct the course of one's interpersonal affairs.

Our proposition, therefore, is that through interactional styles that promote good communication, individuals keep themselves developmentally alive in a moral sense. This happens for at least two separate reasons that reinforce one another's effect. First, such individuals are adept at conducting the kinds of open, mutually informative communications that continually expose them to social influence. It is this kind of social influence that creates the conditions for growth. Second, with development, such individuals become increasingly able to conduct their social relations in ways that incorporate moral standards such as reciprocity and truthfulness. This in turn sets a guiding standard for continued growth along these lines. It does so by guiding the individual toward certain people and experiences and away from others, and by helping to determine what the individual will learn from those people and experiences.

Although the exemplars in this book differ from one another in the specific nature of their personal characteristics, they all exemplify ways in which highly adaptive personal styles can lead to a productive balance of stability and growth rather than to either personal stagnation or inconstancy.

We have identified three enduring patterns in the lives of our exemplars. The first involves adamantly maintaining a moral commitment over long periods of time, even in the face of frustration and hardship. This is an impressive and rare achievement, requiring considerable adaptiveness. Yet even more powerful, in a developmental sense, is the second pattern: invigorating the commitment through processes of cumulative continuity. By repeatedly re-creating situations that stimulate their moral concerns, exemplars expand their goals, sharpen their commitments, and acquire greater effectiveness in pursuing them. The third pattern is more dynamic still and lies at the heart of the developmental paradox to which we have referred. Through interpersonal interactions that regularly subject one's ideas to the tests of challenge and criticism, the exemplar's ideas become transformed and improved all throughout life.

Now it should be evident from our discussion of interactional continuities that some people will be more disposed than others to lifelong goal transformations. We propose that it is people with the following sorts of interpersonal styles who will expand their goals and capacities throughout their life:

- a manner that encourages collaborative activities with others
- a determination to find colleagues that share one's most fundamental moral goals
- a toleration of, and interest in, the alternative perspectives of colleagues who share one's fundamental goals

- an eagerness to communicate with colleagues and others about values
- an active seeking of new knowledge and strategic skill from others
- an ability to take on aspects of the other while not losing the integrity of one's own long-standing commitments

In the moral realm, as in all areas of life, there are exceptional individuals who retain the capacity for development well into old age. But just as there are those who keep growing, there are also many who stagnate. What makes the difference? We have pointed to the importance of social influence in instigating the change and shaping its nature throughout life. This is the social component of the transformation of goals process that we have discussed.

Yet this is only one side of the story. Individuals, through their interactional styles and moral values, play a large part in selecting and maintaining their own social influences. They also decide what to make of them. Suzie Valadez brought herself to her pastor after she had her vision, and she was well prepared to heed his advice. Her subsequent life course hinged on the combination of her agency and his guidance.

In some sense, Suzie's goals and manner were there to begin with, at least by the time of the great events that shaped her life. In another sense, though, they were still in the process of formation, and still are today. Growth is as much a part of Suzie's story as is the dogged perseverance with which she pursues her lifelong moral goals. The irony is that, in Suzie's case as in all the others, the kinds of interactional styles and moral standards that create the capacity for lifelong development also contribute to personal stability over time. This is of course not true of all styles and manners: some types breed little change, others breed changes of a desultory and nonprogressive sort. But the sort we observed in the life stories of our twenty-three exemplars trigger the conditions for true developmental change.

CHAPTER 8

Charleszetta Waddles

Matriarch of Faith

Charleszetta Waddles, known in Detroit as Mother Waddles, is said to be a "one-woman war on poverty." She is a local celebrity and, like all of our exemplars, very busy. Yet when she came to meet us for the interview she was relaxed, not in a rush, and ready to spend as much time with us as we needed. She came in laughing about the fact that she had not put in her false teeth for the interview. "Boy, when my daughter sees I don't have my teeth in, she's going to have a fit." But she was not there to impress us, she was there to help us with our research and to have fun together. In spite of the fact that she had been sick recently, her energy did not flag during the long interview. When we asked her if she wanted to rest a bit after the interview while waiting for her son to pick her up, she said, "No, I'm fine. I'm not a person to lay down much."

The Perpetual Mission for Saving Souls of All Nations, which Mother Waddles established, has been a prominent part of Detroit's social welfare system for over thirty years. Mother Waddles, an ordained minister, tells her congregation that her mission is "to the young, old, black, white, rich, poor, drunk, and sober and to love the hell out of them." The Perpetual Mission serves 100,000 people a year, offering food, clothing, furniture, emergency assistance, housing referrals, tutoring, legal services, and vocational education classes. Mother Waddles has a radio program called "Radio Help" that provides information about community services to people who need help. She also runs a prison and jail ministry. For many years, the mission ran a restaurant offering meals of soul food for the body and spirit. For those who could pay, a dinner of smoked ribs, black-eyed peas, greens, and sweet potato pie was thirty-five cents. For those who couldn't pay, the dinner was free. The restaurant closed in the 1970s for lack of funds but reopened in 1988 with the same price per meal as when it first opened.

The purpose of the mission is to meet the basic needs of poor people in Detroit, to fill the cracks in the state and federal programs, and to help people find what they need in the confusing and often disjointed array of available services. The mission's services have changed over time as its resources and the community's needs have changed, but the fundamental purpose has remained stable.

MRS. WADDLES: So, our purpose is to have the kind of place that you can come to under any conditions. We are more like the liaison, the mouthpiece for people who don't know. People who come in and maybe they can't talk to the [social] worker, we talk to her for them. Maybe they don't even know how to explain to the utility company how they can't afford to make a payment. So we make arrangements for them.

Maybe . . . somebody stole their check and they got to wait five days before they can get a replacement, so we're there and give them food for the five days. . . . And many times there are women who come in and just need one pair of shoes for one little girl. Or a kid will come to me and say, "Mother Waddles, I'm going to the Job Corps. I need some clothes." So we outfit him and let him go to the Job Corps. You know, all kinds of things. We bury people. I had a bridal salon here who gave me some gowns. . . . You can just take it everywhere, and we're there. One woman came in and she had been to one of the government classes to prepare for a better job. And she had gotten hired at Ford, but she wore size $22\frac{1}{2}$ and she didn't have no bra, she didn't have no girdle, and she didn't want to go to work, because she just didn't look right. So we gave her money to buy a girdle and bra and have her go on with a clear frame of mind and go to work.

INTERVIEWER: So would you say that city- or government-funded programs are too limited in their focus . . . to really meet the total range of human needs?

MRS. WADDLES: Oh, yes. Especially if you want people to progress. If you just want to keep them alive, so to speak, well, this is fine. But if you want people to come up out of the ghetto, if you want people to reach out and be somebody, then there is more that has to be done, you know. The little girl who's going to school who can't get her hair done. The prom dress, there's no money there for the prom dress. And don't you know it makes all the difference in what happens to that girl? Completely different self-image.[1]

In establishing the mission, Charleszetta Waddles chose the name in order to convey the mission's openness to anyone in trouble, regardless of race, creed, or national origin. The mission has operated at various locations within predominantly African-American areas of Detroit, and 75 percent of its clients are black, as is Mother Waddles herself. Although she takes particular interest in the problems of low-income blacks, she reaches out lovingly to whites as well and tries to use the mission to foster positive race relations. She often chooses white volunteers to help black clients and black volunteers to help white clients.

Within the Detroit area, Mother Waddles has become well known and widely loved. She has received hundreds of awards, including the Distinguished Citizen Award from Michigan State and Wayne State Universities, special tributes by the state of Michigan, the Com-

munity Service Award from the Ford Motor Company, and letters of
commendation from Lyndon Johnson, Hubert Humphrey, and Richard Nixon. Several times the state of Michigan and the city of Detroit
have proclaimed a Mother Waddles Week or Mother Waddles Day.
In 1980 the Volunteers of America gave her a used car, her first. Stories
about her have appeared in *Time, Newsweek, Ebony, Playboy,* and *Read-
ers' Digest.* According to a 1971 story in *Time,* "For months, Detroit-
ers who called a city hall hot line at night or on weekends heard the
following recording: 'Detroit city offices are closed at the present
time, but will be open tomorrow during regular working hours. In
the event of an emergency, call Mother Waddles at 555–0901.'" This
went on until a story about it in the *Detroit Free Press* embarrassed city
officials. When the story about the Perpetual Mission came out in
Ebony in 1973, a young man in Africa read it and wrote to Mrs.
Waddles, expressing his interest in setting up a branch of the mission
in Africa. In 1974 he began operating a mission in Ghana that followed the same philosophy as the Perpetual Mission in Detroit, and
it has now grown to include branches in Nigeria, the Ivory Coast,
Togoland, Cameroon, Zambia, Benin, Liberia, and Kenya.

It is easy to see that Charleszetta Waddles has taken on an extremely difficult task. And she has done it without government support—indeed, without any significant funding source—and has had
to weather numerous periods of near bankruptcy both personal and
institutional. Mrs. Waddles has been able to achieve all this, even as
she struggled to raise ten children, with only an eighth-grade education and a background of poverty and hardship herself. Throughout
it all, she has not only maintained her commitment and stamina but
has approached life joyfully, expressing tremendous gratitude for her
deeply satisfying and fulfilling life.

How has she managed to do this? Many of our exemplars are
sustained in their work by their real enjoyment of what they do, by
their resourcefulness and ability to forgive, and by their capacity to
see things in a positive light and make the best of whatever happens.
This positive attitude toward life is dramatically evident in Charleszetta Waddles. She has managed to sustain a generous spirit and a
joyous approach to life through decades of hardship, rising from
within the poor community to become a leader in helping others to
cope with and emerge from poverty. Guided by a clear vision of the
kind of life she wanted to live, the teachings of Jesus Christ, she was
able to transform her personal, individual acts of charity into a broad-
reaching organization that has touched the lives of thousands of poor

people in the Detroit area and beyond. The conditions of her life have included, among other challenges, the ill health and early death of her parents, betrayal by her fiancé at the time of her first pregnancy at age thirteen, great financial hardship, the effects of racism on herself and her family, and the loss of one of her sons to mental health problems and subsequent death in the aftermath of the Vietnam War. Despite all this, she shows no bitterness; rather, she approaches her life with gratitude and good humor. Hers is the quintessential positive attitude. Together with resourcefulness, intelligence, and a great deal of hard work, this approach has enabled her not only to lead a rich and fulfilling life but to contribute a great deal to the lives of many, many others.

Charleszetta Waddles is an extremely happy person, full of energy and enthusiasm and always laughing. She responds to even the greatest challenges and bad fortune with resilience, humor, and a desire to learn. While well aware that life is a tangle of good and bad, she always finds a way to focus on the good. This is not simply her characteristic response; it is a part of her explicit philosophy of life. "And so, I look at each one of those experiences [as a teen mother, widow, and so on] as a blessing because I finally found a way to make it a blessing. And I think that one of the things we have to do with our life is know that each thing is a learning experience and, whether it's good or bad, always reach for something better, then you can achieve."[2] This ability to see the good in everything has been important in sustaining her endurance in her missionary work in the face of the numerous challenges that have confronted her.

> I think my greatest achievement has been my stick-to-itiveness, my ability to see nothing but the good coming my way in spite of whatever happens. I remember walking into the mission, and we had thirty thousand gallons of water in a tower on the roof. And they flushed it and water was just pouring all over. And I had to take an umbrella to go in the door. And I looked, and oh, there was this blinking, maddening water pouring all over, and some of your papers getting wet that were on your desk, and you've got to be moving, and you can't see. And I looked at that and I said, "Well, God's just putting up a smokescreen. He's got something good for us." And it worked out, because we were financially having problems, and by the time the press came and taking pictures of all of us, hasn't God sent the money? So God's got all kinds of ways.[3]

Like Allison McCrea, the advocate for the homeless, and others, Mother Waddles believes in the importance of having fun in her work and maintaining a sense of humor in the face of the grim reality of poverty. After recounting a number of jokes she had told in recent speeches, she went on to say, "I have a lot of fun. If you can get a little humor in where you're going . . . Keep your humor in there, you know, because otherwise it can get all sad, hard, pitiful. . . . But if you can make them laugh, it will work."

The same sense of perspective that makes humor come so naturally to Mother Waddles provides the basis for her charming humility. She attributes her effectiveness in part to this lack of hubris.

INTERVIEWER: I always find these interviews very inspiring, although I always feel kind of unworthy, you know.

MRS. WADDLES: Well, I do, too. I feel unworthy. And as long as you keep that unworthy feeling, I believe that we can make it. Once we get to feeling worthy (laughs), we might miss something.

Mother Waddles is fully engaged in what she is doing and "loves every minute of it." When asked what she would like to do for a hobby, she responds by talking about her dreams of extending her missionary work:

I would really like to travel, and especially among junior colleges, and psychology classes across the country. Somehow imploring people that "Don't forget the basics." Because the Letter can kill and the Spirit can keep alive. If you put them together, they can balance out. But sometimes we get all caught up in the rhetoric and we lose all sense of responsibility to human beings. We become a robot. I'd like to do that. That would be my hobby if I could afford it.

As all people dedicated to fighting poverty must, Mother Waddles finds a way to approach the enormous, even endless, task with optimism. This optimism is fed by the success stories of the people she is able to help and by her conviction that her life has a purpose. "One young lady . . . the prison system said she was incorrigible, she's doing fantastic today. That keeps me optimistic. . . . I'm seventy-six [i.e. as of 1988, when the interview was conducted] and almost have inexhaustible strength. My mind is fresh. I very seldom have to look at a book for a phone number. And these things did not come of themselves. I just don't believe that. And I just know that I'm here for a purpose and if I'm true to it, since I believe I have found out what it is. . . ."

It is clear that as an adult Charleszetta Waddles exemplifies just those characteristics of a positive attitude that we will describe more fully in Chapter 10. By looking at her life story we can also see that the early roots of these characteristics reach far into her past. Charleszetta Waddles has a long history of resourcefulness in the face of defeats, losses, and betrayals, a long-standing habit of making do with very little and appreciating fully what she has, and an unusual degree of generosity from an early age.

Charleszetta Campbell (later Waddles) began life in relative prosperity and ease, but a series of losses left her the sole support of her family by the time she was twelve. Born on October 7, 1912, in St. Louis, Missouri, she was the oldest of seven children, although four of the seven died in infancy or early childhood. Her father, Henry Campbell, was a barber with a prosperous business serving an all-white clientele. (At the time, barbers had to choose to serve either black or white clients, since barber shops were racially segregated.) During Charleszetta's early childhood, her father's business was very successful and the family had plenty of money and was well respected in the local community. She recalls that on her eighth birthday her father gave her a diamond lavaliere with eight pearls on it. But when Charleszetta was nine or ten years old, her father's business was hit by a catastrophe. In the 1920s, barbers were not trained in the prevention of the contagious skin and scalp diseases that can be passed readily from one customer to the next. As a result, one of Campbell's customers brought in a disease that spread to the others and permanently ruined his trade. At this point, his life and the lives of his wife and children changed dramatically.

Henry Campbell never recovered from the loss of his business. He worked for a while doing construction, then for low wages in someone else's barber shop. He was a proud man and became moody after he lost his money. "He would just go out on the corner and just stand out and look."[4] Probably as a result of the financial pressures, Henry Campbell and his wife, Ella, began to fight a great deal, and Charleszetta was "always heavy in [her] heart." Also painful for the young girl was the change in the way members of the church and the local community treated her. When her father was a man of means his children were treated as favorites; after he lost his money they were given the cold shoulder. "And when he lost his money and our clothing wasn't as beautiful, we were not able to do things the same as folks who [had money]. And I guess I was very impressionable, and I think that motivated me more than anything could ever have, you know. I can hear the tone of their voices, and see the look on their faces. And I think that's one of the things that made me study the Bible to see how could you be a Christian and come out that way."

Because Ella Campbell had a serious heart condition, Charleszetta took on the role of mother and housekeeper. From the age of about nine or ten she did the cooking, washing, ironing, and child care, having little or no time to be a child herself. She also worked "picking up numbers" (acting as a courier in the illegal gambling game called "numbers"), selling whiskey, and doing odd jobs. When Charleszetta was twelve, her father died. Mrs. Campbell was not only ill but also pregnant when her husband died. Because the family had no other source of support, Charleszetta, an A student with a keen interest in school, had to drop out and go to work full time. She worked first as a maid. At age thirteen she became a sorter in a rag factory.

When she began the factory work, Charleszetta started to associate with an older crowd and soon had a twenty-three-year-old boyfriend. They became engaged, and soon after the engagement she became pregnant. She assumed they would marry but heard from one of her girlfriends that her fiancé had married someone else the previous Sunday. In recalling this incident, Charleszetta laughs and says, "You know, I look back at it now as my preparation for the work I do today. I can certainly understand the pregnant girl. I can understand the widowed woman. I can understand the separated woman. I can understand the common-law woman. I can understand the happily married woman. I can understand them all. I've been every one of those."[5] This ability to identify with people in all kinds of difficult situations stayed with Mrs. Waddles throughout her adulthood and contributed a great deal to her capacity to personalize and care about other people's problems.

At age thirteen, pregnant and abandoned by her fiancé, Charleszetta met and married Clifford Walker. She did not know it at the time, but Clifford was "kept by women" and only pretended that the considerable money he brought home had been earned at a respectable job. When she learned the truth about Clifford, Charleszetta left him and went back home. He was arrested soon afterward on a charge of assault, became ill while in prison, and died not long after he was released from prison.

During and after this marriage, Charleszetta worked in the rag factory, then as a dishwasher in a restaurant, then as a cook. Her description of the occasion when she was hired as a cook illustrates the resourcefulness with which she approached life as an eighteen-year-old single mother:

> I never can forget when I walked in that day, I was eighteen years old, and she asked me had I ever worked in a restaurant before. I'm applying for cook now. And I said yes, but I didn't tell her I was a dishwasher not a cook. (Laughter.) And so, she hired me. And she told me she wanted eighteen chickens for lunch, brought me a bushel of cabbage, brought me a bushel of sweet potatoes. And you know, God has always been with me. I said to her, "Well, you know, everyone doesn't do the same. Would you be kind enough to show me how you cut yours?" So she showed me how to take a knife and go down the back and down through that bone and split it in half. I didn't even know. (Laughter.) And how to get this bushel of potatoes together. And believe it or not, I stayed with her. One day she left and told me that if the biscuits run out, to fix some. Oh, my God! She said, "We usually use twenty-five pounds of flour."

When she was twenty-one, Charleszetta married LeRoy Wash, who was sixteen years her senior. He worked as a truck driver for a coal company and she worked in one of the first fast-food restaurants, Liberty Sandwich. LeRoy lost his job for protesting the low wages, and the couple moved to Detroit so he could look for work with the automobile manufacturers. But when they reached Detroit, there were no good jobs available, and he took a position that paid only $11 a week. He was later laid off, and the growing family went on welfare. Over the twelve years of their marriage, they had six children.

The Washes rented rooms from a wise and helpful older woman who taught Charleszetta how to live decently without money by using ingenuity to make the most of what she had.

> A very dignified lady, a very fashionable lady, who sort of was my second mother away from home, who said, "Now look, you don't ever, ever, allow yourself to worry about circumstances." I remember one day my husband had to apply for welfare, and I went to her and I had on my welfare dress. And everybody was

wearing this kind of dresses . . . that looked like chicken sacks, feed sacks. . . . She said to me, "Don't you ever, ever, ever walk into my home again with one of those things on. You don't have to wear anything like that. You go to the Goodwill, and you find what you need, and you stay fashionable even if you are poor." From that date since, I've never had another one on. And I raised my children by going to Goodwills. And I did it so well, until the teachers would ask me where they got their clothes. But I think back at the things that she would say to me that really, really helped me. And I say to people today, "You don't have to look poor, you know. You don't have to look down. For money is a medium of exchange, that's all; but it's not a mind regulator unless you allow it to be."[6]

Charleszetta's experiences as a welfare recipient gave her a very concrete sense of the holes in the "safety net" that she would later use the mission to patch. These experiences gave her an understanding of the pressure to cheat on the system, a pressure that she has tried to remove by providing poor people with the things that give them added dignity and self-confidence. During the time when her children were young and she was receiving Aid to Families with Dependent Children (AFDC), Charleszetta began to work "under the table" and to "pick up numbers" in order to have the little extra things the children needed that welfare would not cover. She knows from that experience that the welfare system can lead people to be "devious and conniving to find not luxuries but necessities." She has a very personal awareness that dignity and upward mobility require more than the absolute necessities of food and shelter, and that welfare and other government services do not cover many of these expenses. She applies this awareness directly to her effort to help poor people to obtain these things without having to resort to the deception that is, in itself, destructive to personal dignity.

Faced with only unstable and very low-paying job options, LeRoy Wash eventually quit looking for work, becoming, in Charleszetta's words, "a welfare husband." The hardworking Charleszetta had little tolerance for this, and in time they divorced. A few years later, Charleszetta became involved with Roosevelt Sturkey, but she did not marry him for fear that she would lose her welfare payments. They lived together in a common-law marriage for seven years, having three more children.

During the years with Mr. Sturkey and then after they split up,

Charleszetta had to draw on all of the resourcefulness at her command to create a decent life for her children and herself. She worked two or three jobs at a time, kept the house and the children's clothes meticulously clean, and tried to be as creative as she could in feeding them inexpensive yet appetizing food:

> I learned rather than say "Well, I don't want any damn beans, I'm sick of this old house.". . . I didn't do that. Today, I teach not to do it. Because I learned not to do it. I didn't learn from a spiritual standpoint, but I learned from something within me that if you paint up your bed and if you paint up your walls, and if you put a decal on something, that made all the difference in the world. . . . And I've had to take colored paper, and wet it to put color on my cheeks, crepe paper. I've had to take lard and use it on my hair. I used baking soda before I could buy deodorant. But I learned that there is a way, and that if you use that way you can feel as good as the person who has access to more. It's all how you feel about yourself.[7]

In talking about her resourcefulness and the ability to appreciate what she had and make do with very little, Mother Waddles expresses concern for the materialism that has become so prevalent today.

> Whether you've got satin sheets, you get flower sheets, you get cotton sheets, foam rubber, down pillows, you can't do anything but sleep. And sleep is sleep, laying on the pillow in your bed. And if you graduate to twenty dresses, or if you're down to two, you'd better not wear but one or you gonna look silly. Twenty hats, you can't wear but one hat, you know. And when we make our priorities, these things pass away. . . . So you have to put your priorities straight that you might live long upon the earth with the Lord. And if you laugh, laughter is only laughter, no matter where it comes from. And when we find that out, the little boy who takes the broomstick and rides horses gets the same sensation as the one who has a real hobby. When we learn that, then we can grow.[8]

Later she said, "In my going, let me enjoy my life to the point of knowing that I have not sold out in my going. . . . Let me be that little pebble on the beach. Because down inside of me—no matter how all these folks you find with all this money leaving here lately [dying], there's not one of them can take a dime."

Charleszetta Waddles recalls having had a loving and generous spirit from childhood: "I think that possibly I was born with a certain something that makes for a religious activity. I always gave when I was young; I always had a kind heart. And my mother used to say to me when I was very small, 'I wish I had a heart like you.' I had compassion, I was forgiving, but at the time I didn't call it by that name. I said, 'Well, I just can't help it, I'm free-hearted,' you know. And so my mother would always look at me as if, well, you know, she's a strange girl." Charleszetta does not remember resenting the burdens placed on her as a child due to her mother's illness. "Maybe I was just born for burdens or whatever. But I never did resent it. One thing, I always worked."[9]

Even before Charleszetta started the mission at the age of forty-six, she had a long history of helping people on a one-to-one basis and making the best of difficult circumstances. For example, she recalls a time when a friend was in danger of losing her house for lack of mortgage payments. Charleszetta considered the friend to be less capable and resourceful than she was, and she wanted to help. So that she could give all her available rent money to her friend for house payments, Charleszetta and her children moved into the woman's basement, which was not even divided into rooms. They had to hang curtains in order to separate the sleeping and living areas.

During the mid-1950s, Charleszetta was becoming dissatisfied with the church she attended. She had long been concerned about hypocrisy, and felt that the church should be doing more to help the poor. "Well, one day, believe it or not, the Lord says to me, 'I want you to feed the hungry. First,' he said, 'I want you to show the preachers what to do with the churches.'" She approached her minister about these issues but was rebuffed. She joined a Bible study group in the church but was denied graduation papers at the end of the class, presumably because she challenged the prevailing views of the church's role. In response, Charleszetta started her own Bible study group, together with a group of women friends. They started with prayer meetings at different people's homes, attempting to live according to the Scriptures as well as to study them. Their goal was to provide the things that were needed in the community, following Christ's exhortation to feed the hungry and clothe the naked. "From that day on, we began to create ways to help people. I told them then that my desire was to see a group of people, no matter if we were poor—and we were all poor women with a house full of children—and I felt that you are never too poor to help someone. I suggested that we each contribute so much out of our pantries that we might have a storehouse of food; that if we couldn't give any clothes, that each one would ask their friends that we might establish a clothes closet, as well as any other things that we can help someone with.''[10] It was this prayer group that developed into the Perpetual Mission for Saving Souls of All Nations.

In the early years of the incipient mission, Mother Waddles showed the same resourcefulness and ingenuity that she had brought earlier to her struggle to survive. For example, she talked the owner of a storefront into giving her the building for two months rent free. She was ordained as a minister in the Pentecostal church in 1956 and reordained in an interdenominational group, the International Association of Universal Truth, in 1961. Some of the women from the original prayer group stayed with Mother Waddles over the many years of the mission's development. For example, one of the members of that prayer group, Alma Ruff, has since done very well in the family-care business and has provided financial assistance to the mission in lean times.

In Charleszetta's religious development we can see the processes of goal transformation that we discussed in Chapter 7. She was religious at an early age, as was usual within her community, and as early as age twelve began to be aware that many people did not practice the Christian beliefs they preached. The treatment she received as a result of her father's financial reversal brought this home to her in an intensely personal way. It was not until she reached her forties, however, that she began to challenge the existing churches in a serious way and to think of establishing an alternative. At this point she became ordained and thus took on the more formal role of spokesperson for Christian teachings. In that role she developed further what came to be a very well articulated life philosophy that she used to guide her life choices and institutional priorities and which she preached systematically to others as a central goal of her ministry. The study group that she established had as its explicit goal the living of the Scriptures, especially the passages that concern helping the poor. In this group, Charleszetta began to carry out in a more organized way the charity she had extended personally throughout her life.

We have already seen that Charleszetta was unusually generous and loving from an early age. There are many different ways of being generous. In the early years, Charleszetta pitched in uncomplainingly to help her family. She inconvenienced herself for the welfare of her friends. She was loving and tolerant to the members of her church. If her "kind heart" had continued in this vein without going beyond

it, she would have been a wonderful person to know but could not
have had the kind of impact that she has had on the low-income
community of Detroit.

With the acquisition of the storefront and the naming of the mission, Charleszetta began a gradual transformation of her personal altruism into the abilities required to develop and run a complex social
service organization. As the head of the mission, she had to plan ahead
in order to coordinate the various activities—keeping a food bank,
restaurant, clothing store, and problem assistance office going at once.
She had to develop strategies for fund-raising, convincing individuals
and businesses to donate the goods and money without which the
mission could not operate. She began to grapple with issues such as
eligibility for services. Should she require that people prove their need-
iness? Should she serve only the very poor or would an alcoholic who
was not entirely destitute qualify for assistance? She began to face the
issue of having to consider trade-offs between means and ends. If
someone offered her funding but required her to do something in
which she didn't believe in order to get it, should she take the funding
or turn it down? She had to decide how the mission should be governed. Should she make decisions on her own or should she set up a
board of directors? To what extent should she allow funders or government agencies to determine the shape and direction of the mission's
activities? As she grappled with these issues, her generosity necessarily
had to develop beyond moving into a friend's basement or making a
Thanksgiving dinner of beans a festive occasion for her children. Because we did not interview Mother Waddles at each stage of her development, as would be done in a longitudinal study, we can only specu-
late about the changes she must have undergone. It is clear, however,
that today's public figure of Mother Waddles, such a visible presence
in Detroit, was created at least in part by the demands that she responded to and the issues she had to resolve once she took on the
public and organizational roles that went with running the Perpetual
Mission for Saving Souls of All Nations.

At about the time that Charleszetta was running the prayer group
and other activities that would lead eventually to the mission, she had
the good fortune to meet Payton Waddles, who became her greatest
source of support as she established and developed the mission.
Charleszetta was selling barbecue on the street to raise money for
the church when Mr. Waddles came along. He wanted to buy some
barbecue, but just as he was paying for the food, it began to rain. He
helped the women take the barbecue tub back to the house to get it

out of the rain and in the process got to know Charleszetta. "And so we got to talking, and he decided that he would get a cab and take me home. And I guess we haven't been away from each other since, other than in the hospital or the times he went back and forth during those first two or three weeks."[11] Payton and Charleszetta were married about six months later and were happily married for almost thirty years, until Mr. Waddles's death in 1980.

Payton Waddles had steady work with the Ford Motor Company, so Charleszetta and her children were able to go off welfare and never go back on it again. Charleszetta explained to Payton "what the Lord wanted me to do and he helped me do it." Over the years, Payton stood by Charleszetta in all that she did, helping her raise the children and contributing financially and in other ways to her work with the mission. When asked how Mr. Waddles felt about her career with the mission, Mrs. Waddles responded: "Well, you know, I would say that he had a vast conviction that if a person says God wants them to do it, he is not going to fool with that. And he's been behind me on it ever since. If I need some money to pay the lights at the mission, he goes to the credit union. What more can you do?"[12]

As Mother Waddles sees it, the ultimate goal of her work is to lift the poor out of their degradation, to help them believe in themselves, and to encourage them to take personal responsibility for their lives. "You'd be surprised how a full stomach changes a person's mind about getting into trouble. When they're hungry, they think they've got an excuse." An important part of Mother Waddles's message is that there is no excuse. She often puts to work as volunteers the very people who come to her for help. Give them some good food and clean, decent clothes and some responsibility for helping others, and they are on their way to a better life themselves. "You see, most of my volunteers, people who drive, and so on, are people who others say are incorrigible. You know, you take a man who's raggedy and has no clothes but a good mind that he's just let go to waste and you put a suit on him that was give to you and you give him a clipboard that was give to you and tell him 'My gosh, look how you're cheating yourself and society,' and be begins to look at himself in a different light."

Mother Waddles offers help to anyone who asks, without trying in any bureaucratic way to determine eligibility.

Well, you know, I always take the Bible as my guideline, and the red letters specifically,[13] because those are the words of Jesus.

So I made a policy that we didn't try to determine who was worthy to receive what we had or whether they really qualified to get it, because the Scripture says you let the wheat and the chaff go together and let God separate it. And I felt that if a person should come who really didn't need it, evidently there was something else that they needed. Maybe it's a person who has no confidence in charity per se, or they don't believe anybody cares, and they come to prove that they are right. Maybe they will be touched by the fact that somebody treated them right when they needed it. Or maybe if they came for food, they might be an alcoholic and in giving them food, I might be able to get at the real problem. . . . And sometimes when people came in, and they didn't appear to really need it, but they were just playing, or maybe they said, ''Well, we don't have our credentials.'' We would say,''Well, let me tell you. You know, there is a law that we must follow, we must keep records because I don't want to go to jail. But I'm going to give you something for one day until you come back. I don't want you to say you'll be hungry tonight. So I'll give you enough to last you today, and then tomorrow you can come back and do it for the records.''

For the more than thirty years of the mission's existence, Mrs. Waddles has seldom taken any government assistance. She has felt that government grants come with unacceptable strings attached and has chosen instead to raise the money she needs by soliciting donations from private individuals and businesses. She has written two cookbooks in her efforts to raise money and has tried to market barbecue sauce and start a crafts collective. In spite of the creativity and resourcefulness of her fund-raising efforts, the financial status of the mission is often precarious. In a folder of newspaper clippings about the mission, there are several that describe the need for donations during a financial crisis. The *Detroit Free Press* ran an article in 1967, for example, with the headline, ''Soup kitchen angel can't pay her $1,000 gas bill.'' The article goes on to say, ''However high Mother Waddles stands in the eyes of the Lord, she's standing poorly with the gas company. . . . If the bills aren't paid, the utilities go off. 'God is a just God,' Mother Waddles said Tuesday. 'That's not going to happen. Help is coming from somewhere. . . . I love people. I believe that as a man is thinking, so he is. You send out hate, and you get hate back. You send out love, you get love back. Course, that doesn't do anything with the gas bill.' '' Mother Waddles takes no salary from the mission and, in fact, donates a significant portion of her $900 per month widow's pension to cover the costs. If she can't find an agency to help someone, she offers help herself, with her own money. Every month for over five years, she sent money from her pension check to a white woman in Tennessee who had no other way of getting treatment for glaucoma. She and her husband once heated their apartment for three years with their cookstove so they could afford to pay the gas bill at the mission.

It is her faith that she is doing what she was meant to do that allows Mrs. Waddles to live without fear even while giving away almost everything she has. "Well, the lack of fear is I just don't believe you have to fear anything but God and if I do something— say, for instance, if I take all of my money and go save somebody's house—I'm not going to be scared about what I've done, because I know God's going to take care of that, if I've done the right thing." When momentary fear overcomes her in a situation like this, Mother Waddles uses mental self-discipline to throw it off; she does not treat the fear as something to be taken seriously but rather as an intrusion to be pushed away as quickly as possible. "Now I can tell you that apprehension overcomes me sometimes, but I'm able to always throw it off. Get thee behind me, Satan. And that's a blessing, because I imagine that [a fear for one's own security] could be a very, very disturbing feeling."

The cornerstone of Mother Waddles's security is her faith in the goodness of God and her belief that God will provide what she needs if she lives according to His teachings. This belief contributes to the enduring sense of security that frees her from the need to focus her attention on accumulating resources for herself, and allows her to feel comfortable running the mission on an inadequate, shoestring budget. In fact, she prefers to operate the organization in a spontaneous and very personal style.

> I came to the conclusion that if I'm going to run it, then I must do it this way, like I would my family. I have to do it in a way that I'm comfortable with. So I don't get up in the morning and say, 'I've got to feed so many people.' I've got to do whatever I can. If I have enough only for clothes, well, I know that something I can do today is clothe somebody. And tomorrow, possibly, the Lord will bless me to feed them. Whatever my hand finds to do, that's what I do that day. I don't push myself to ego-tripping, to feel that because I'm Mother Waddles I've got

to have it all, you know. Because there might be the time that I don't have it all. But whatever I have, then this I can do. And many times, people have come to me and said they got a job. They show me the job referral and all that kind of thing. We check and find out they're supposed to go to work. And they need carfare to get to payday. Well, when I look over my finances and I'm not able to do it, I say, "Well, I tell you what I'm going to do. I'm going to give you enough for today and tomorrow, and you stop by when you get off from work tomorrow evening, and then I'll take you further. And if I have to give it to you two days at a time, you'll make that payday."

Charleszetta Waddles takes essentially the same shoestring approach with her personal finances. Assuming that God will take care of her, she does not feel a need to hold on to her money for the sake of future security. It is this absence of a self-protective stance that makes her generosity possible. But as we have seen with Suzie Valadez, the belief that God will provide for her does not lead Mother Waddles to be passive. On the contrary, her industry and sense of responsibility are among her most notable qualities.

When asked what she considers to be her greatest achievement, Mother Waddles answers that she is proudest of her endurance:

My ability to stick to it and not get ulcers, you know, not get bitter, or sacrilegious but to just move from one day to the other, and still be what I started out to be. You can go away twenty years and come back, and if I'm living you know you're going to find me doing the same thing. I've been reduced to go back to my home [with the mission]. I had the mission two years ago in the house. And the big eighteen-foot trailer trucks sitting all outside the gangway. But I'll still do it. Because I didn't promise that I would do it contingent upon what kind of building, what kind of clothes I could wear, what kind of money I had; just as long as I can find something I can do, I'll do it. So no matter where I'm going, people can at least know to pinpoint me in what category I'm in. Without even asking anybody, "I know wherever she is, if she's alive and well, she's a missionary." So I think that's my greatest achievement—to find yourself and know who you are, and get joy out of being you. Because that's what life's all about. . . . I'm not afraid of my age, and I'm not afraid of having to die. I'm not afraid of anything. I just live from day to day, and do the best I can each day, and enjoy.

The biggest challenge in maintaining this endurance over the course of her thirty-year mission has been to forgive, time and again, those who respond to her loving care with ingratitude or by cheating or stealing from her. It is this ingratitude that is hardest for her children to tolerate, but Mother Waddles accepts it as part of the territory and tries to bring her children to the same understanding.

> And Latheda's problem at the mission—she was at the mission every day for years—she had a yen for wanting to protect me from people, people who she thought were using me. She's just now beginning to become spiritually aware and realize that people don't use you when you set yourself up to help them. She is just now realizing that the things that I offer are the only way that you can draw a certain kind of people, to get to them so you can offer them something else. . . . And Annette was another one that could not cope with all the things that happened in the mission. If you help somebody, and then tomorrow they steal something from you. Or you help somebody, get them all straightened out, and then the next week you don't see them any more.

The way that Charleszetta Waddles herself copes with the betrayals and ingratitude is by dedicating herself ever more fully to following the teaching of Christ that one must love and forgive "seventy times seventy." If she begins to feel resentful or angry instead of forgiving, she puts such thoughts and feelings out of her mind. The same approach, a kind of mental self-discipline, was mentioned by others in the sample as a means of dealing with the inevitable failures and frustrations of this kind of work.

INTERVIEWER: What aspects of your work have been most difficult?

MRS. WADDLES: Being able to forgive seventy times seventy. (Laughs.) Because that's a large part of it. People will fail. People will make mistakes. People will cheat, you know. And one of the things I've used in my work is my commitment to God. I totally believe that God does not answer prayer other than through other people. And I don't believe that he answers them just through the minister or the priest. I believe he answers them through everybody. Some that he answers them through don't even know that God exists. So my commitment is to follow the Scriptures and live it. Many times I have to use that seventy times seventy. There's a message in the New Testament that will let anyone become the light of the world—anyone. The message is, "As you think, that's what you'll be." I believe that you *must*, you *must* watch what you think. You *must* not allow that [anger, bad feelings] to stay in your consciousness.

The amazing extent of Mother Waddles's forgiveness and ability to set aside painful events is most evident when she talks about one of her sons, who had died just six months before the interview. This young man had served in Vietnam and had come back with terrible nightmares, flashbacks, and a drinking problem. In order to deal with these problems, he had volunteered to be "a guinea pig," trying out an experimental medicine that was expected to help with post-traumatic stress. But the medication seemed to make things worse and he asked to be hospitalized, fearing a complete breakdown. When he was denied access to hospitalization, the flashbacks recurred even more violently and he responded by taking an overdose of the medication. He went into convulsions, lost consciousness, and died three weeks later.

When asked how she responded to her son's death, Mother Waddles responded with this disturbing story:

> Well, I did pretty good. I did pretty good until about two weeks ago. Tom Brokaw did a special on Vietnam vets and I looked up and there was my son sitting up there crying and then another showing him laying there with this needle in his arm. And of all people in the world, there's my son laying there. And the commentator was saying that this drug would keep him from having all of this trouble, but that just two or three weeks after that, he died of a drug overdose. So I went to see a lawyer later, 'cause I really don't like the way they ended it. Because if anybody heard it they would think he was a drug addict. And he was not a drug addict. He just couldn't stand it any more. I think they should tell it like it was, the hospital refused to take him.

When Mrs. Waddles contacted the television network, they told her that she would have to send $150 to obtain a copy of the tape. Since an extra $150 is not easy to squeeze out of her budget, she has not yet been able to order the tape.

Although Mother Waddles expresses sadness and frustration over her son's death and its subsequent misrepresentation, she is not consumed by these feelings. She would like to have the television network offer a program on the lack of care some Vietnam vets are confronting, but she does not speak with anger about the war, the lack of follow-up treatment, or the news coverage. She is well aware of the injustice they represent, but her life is so consumed with positive feelings and a sense of purpose that she is able to act on and then set aside this kind of pain.

Just as Charleszetta Waddles's life illustrates vividly the positive approach to life we saw in our exemplars, it also illustrates an unwavering certainty of conviction and purpose. When asked about conflicts or uncertainty in relation to her work, Mother Waddles responds in terms of the sometimes hard choices of means to her ends rather than questioning in any way the ends themselves. She follows exacting ethical standards in missionary work and often encounters challenges to those standards. For example, it is not unusual for people to ask her for help in getting them out of trouble. Even though it is difficult to say no to someone who needs help, Mother Waddles will not lend her name to anything she considers ethically questionable. "When people want you to write letters [to the court] or they want you to get involved in something that you definitely don't know anything about, it's hard to turn them down, because they think you can do it. But you know you can't do this, because you can't back it up. And if something should come along and there come a time for you to back it up, you're lost. So I have to say no. [Interviewer: And that's hard to do?] Yes. But now, I've got a reputation, people know, 'Now Mother ain't gonna allow for it' [she laughs].

Although Mother Waddles does not think that maintaining her commitment to help others, to share what little she has, requires courage, she does feel the temptation at times to compromise in order to obtain more resources for the mission. Resisting this temptation does require courage. This most often arises in regard to funding. At a time of particularly great financial pressure, the mission was offered $250,000 to set up an abortion clinic. Mother Waddles is personally opposed to abortion on religious grounds and turned down the offer despite the mission's great financial need. Another group offered a $225,000 refrigerated kitchen for her restaurant but required that the mission take on a potentially restrictive governing board. In turning down the offer, Mrs. Waddles knew that she was not only losing the $225,000, but that this group would pass the word that she was turning down money and must not need donations. Another case involved a government grant for money to buy food. In order to be eligible for the grant, you had to promise to buy all the food at a government source. Mrs. Waddles was unwilling to do this, feeling that she must patronize the food companies that had stood by her during the long periods of time when she had no money to pay. She applied for the grant anyway, attaching a letter of explanation. In that case, she did get the grant without having to agree to the restrictions. "So I had the courage, and I said, 'If they don't do it, help me God another way.' So we must have that. There must be a line of demarcation, some things you wouldn't do for love or money. Sometimes you feel tempted. But when you pray about it and meditate and think on it and you realize it makes you feel uncomfortable, don't do it. Just don't do it."

Just as we saw with Suzie Valadez and Virginia Durr, the one area of real conflict for Charleszetta Waddles was her children. When she started her missionary work, the oldest children were teenagers and were able to take care of the house and the younger children, the baby being just three at that time. Although they helped out at the mission in many different roles, they were ambivalent about their mother's total devotion to the mission. "Mother didn't know anything about anything but the mission." They were proud of their mother's work, but they were also jealous of the attention she paid to others. "'Mama,' they ask, 'how come you couldn't have been a cabdriver or something?' [laughter]." Mother Waddles recognized the irreconcilable conflict between the demands of her work and her family, but made a clear choice in favor of her work:

INTERVIEWER: Did you feel any conflict between the demands of a public and a private life, and how did you resolve these conflicts or prevent them from arising?

MRS. WADDLES: Well, you can't hardly prevent them and you can't hardly resolve them. Really, I had to let loose the idea of being able to take your loved ones with you, so to speak; have them feel the same things that you feel, the same compassions. I found out that this is something that they have to choose for themselves. And coming to that decision has been about the hardest thing that I've had to do. Because there's a tendency always to want the best for [your] loved one, you know. And you think the best for other folks is what's best for you, which isn't always so. So I finally reached the conclusion not to stop hoping but to stop pulling.

INTERVIEWER: And have you felt pulled two ways, pulled by your work and the things you want to do in the community, and things that you think you want to do at home?

MRS. WADDLES: No. I just had to give up what I had to do [at home], for God. I gave up to that, because I don't think you can half-step with God. And to me, serving God takes on a different meaning. I just don't think you serve God by going to church. I think you worship God by going to church. But I think that service comes later. And I think some people are born to do one thing, and some born to do the other. I think I was born with a goodly share of endurance, and I don't think it was just for me. I feel, if I were to let that loose [give it up], what else would I do? And I surely am not the one to set out and loll in the sun. And I'm not the one to say, "Well, God, you have to forgive me, but I'm going to do [something else] instead."[14]

In the end, Mother Waddles is left without guilt in relation to her children, like Suzie Valadez but unlike Virginia Durr. It is unclear what it is that makes the difference in the three women's long-term responses to the conflict. It does not appear to be a reality-based difference in how well the children have done in life. Some of Mother Waddles's ten children have thrived but others have not. The question of why she does not blame herself whereas Virginia Durr does cannot be answered here. No doubt a complex set of factors is involved, including cultural and social class differences in expectations, religious orientation, and personality factors. The difference in style between people who directly serve others through charity and people who work for changes at the societal level may also be a part of the explanation. In any case, for some reason, Mother Waddles has come to see the mission as primarily a force for good in the children's lives, no matter if it did take their mother away from them. "I guess with their lives, being indoctrinated into the mission was one of the best things that could have happened to them. Because it gave them a basic sense that sort of kept them out of real trouble."

Clearly, the driving force behind Mother Waddles's dedicated service is her Christian faith, as it is for Suzie Valadez. But whereas Mrs. Valadez feels she has witnessed miracles and heard the word of God directly telling her to serve, Mrs. Waddles is more influenced by the biblical teachings of Christ.

I'm an advocate that you read the red letters because to be a Christian is to follow the teachings of Christ. The teachings of

Christ offer a challenge. He said that "I'm the light of the world, but after I'm gone you're the lights of the world. These things I do, ye should do and even greater things." He tells you to forgive seventy times seventy, He tells you to feed the hungry, clothe the naked, take the poor people in, and inasmuch as you do for the least of people, you've done unto Him. To me that offers a real challenge, that if Christianity is to be a viable, active, demonstrative thing, then we must do these things. That's what I believe. Everybody has their own belief, but I just don't think that sermons are enough. I think that we should be doers of the Word as well as hearers.[15]

This belief that she must live according to the Scriptures colors every aspect of Charleszetta's approach to life. Having been very hurt by the cruelty of members of her family's church when her father's business failed, she is acutely sensitive to the hypocrisy of people who adopt a Christian ideology but do not live accordingly. As she has grappled with the issue of hypocrisy, she has taken on a leadership role in the Pentecostal church and as an ordained minister preaches her message that one can and should live according to Christ's teachings. Her interpretation of the meaning of those teachings is mediated by her participation in African-American Pentecostalism.

Although Charleszetta Waddles is an unusual person within her own or any community, she does not stand outside that community. The context within which she lives and works helps to support many of the habits that have served her well in sustaining her commitment to her missionary work. For example, the religious commitment of Pentecostals is expected to be high, with many church members having a habit of reading the Bible frequently and holding independent study groups of the sort that Charleszetta and her friends organized in her early years in Detroit. Pentecostal preachers generally know the Bible thoroughly and forge many connections between the Scriptures and the everyday lives of their congregations, as Mrs. Waddles does so often.

The central themes of Charleszetta Waddles's life reflect the preoccupations of her religious denomination. Pentecostalism stresses love, fellowship, and charity. All people, rich, poor, black, and white are seen as brothers and sisters in Christ. There is a strong antimaterialistic ideology, with greed considered to be the root of great evil. God is seen as a personal deity who will take care of His people, and there is little need to fight competitively with others to protect oneself from insecurity.

Mrs. Waddles's positive attitude is also consistent with the general orientation of her chosen religious community. The emphasis of black Pentecostalism is on the positive side of the joy of salvation rather than the fear of damnation that may characterize some fundamentalist denominations. In Pentecostal churches there is often a jubilant atmosphere, and after the service it is common for the congregation to hug, kiss, laugh, and talk before leaving the church.

At least in the Northern states, black Pentecostalism focuses on saving the individual rather than changing the world. As Arthur Paris describes it, the church "calls" individuals to salvation out of the wicked world. This salvation is a personal one to be worked out inside the church itself. The world is taken as a given and is sinful; thus, the call is directed not to the community or society to work out a communal salvation but to individuals to work out their personal salvation.[16] Paris goes on to say that most Northern black Pentecostal churches "do not see themselves as institutions engaged in struggle on a secular front for social, political, and economic goods for an oppressed community. Insofar as the 'struggle' is perceived, individuals respond on a personal level, whereas the church's response is to 'call all men [sic] to Christ.' "[17]

This apolitical orientation characterizes Charleszetta Waddles's missionary work rather well. Although Mother Waddles is well aware of racial discrimination, greatly admires Martin Luther King and other activists, and works cooperatively with more politically oriented organizations such as the Urban League and the Southern Christian Leadership Conference, the Perpetual Mission for Saving Souls of All Nations does not itself engage in political organizing or work directly for social change on the societal level. Instead, Mother Waddles feels that her special niche is to provide "the basics." During the civil rights movement of the 1950s and 1960s, for example, the mission provided food, furniture, and other necessities to people who had been displaced from their homes during the struggle. As Mother Waddles says, "And I think when I watch the programs going—and there were educational programs and political programs and all kinds—I would always know that there would be a need for just the basics. Whenever there's a need for basic help, my name appears on that list. And that, to me, is an accomplishment."

Like Cabell Brand, but unlike Allison McCrea, Mother Waddles is attempting to help people live better within the existing system. Unlike Cabell Brand, Mrs. Waddles has not evaluated the existing political and economic system and judged it to be "the least worst

system there is.'' In fact, if asked, she will tell you that she considers
the system to be unjust in many ways. The reason for the apolitical
nature of her work is instead that she is operating within a religious
framework that, according to Paris, does not provide a way in which
to understand either the phenomena of secular politics or [one's] own
political action in a religiously meaningful manner.''[18]

Within the black communities of both the North and South, as
within the white communities, Christianity has been losing ground
to secularism since the mid-nineteenth century.[19] One of Charleszetta
Waddles's primary goals is to bring people back to what she believes
are the truest and best values and practices, those expressed in the
Bible's ''red letter words,'' the words of Jesus Christ. This is why
she has established a mission rather than a secular social service organization. In her view, to provide food and clothing alone will not have
any lasting effect on people. Instead, one must offer sustenance for a
change in their values and stance toward life. We referred earlier to
Mrs. Waddles's desire to remind young people of the importance of
''remembering the basics.'' What she means by this is that even as
they work hard in school to get ahead, to prepare themselves for
careers, and so on, they must also remember the most important aspects of life, as embodied in Christ's teachings.

INTERVIEWER: What are you really trying to do with the mission?

MRS. WADDLES: Hopefully, create an awareness among the people that
when they go there, they're going for not just food, but they want to
stay around and see what's this thing about the mind—the food for the
mind. What is it that makes that person that come out of prison eighteen
or twenty years ago, now able to have a fabulous program for ex-
offenders? What about the young man who has the church who came
through there who was twenty-two years at it and now he has a home
for the homeless? This is what I hope to see. And I hope they realize
that we're talking about both spiritual and physical foods. If we feed the
physical body, that won't do anything for the spiritual unless you reach
for it and you don't get what you don't reach for.

Mother Waddles's life exemplifies a message that we also heard
from Jack Coleman and several others. It is the message that people
must take responsibility for their lives, must learn to feel effective and
in control of the choices they make. Charleszetta Waddles wants
people to learn from her life story that ''there is a way that poor

people can be involved and make a difference. I was a single mother with ten children and I was able to do this. People really need to know this. So many people believe that they're caught, that circumstances can hold them down, when really they can't."

Charleszetta Waddles urges everyone, even the very poor, to believe in their own capacity to take control of their lives. Many people who work with the poor believe this. Cabell Brand stresses that low-income people need a "hand up, not a hand out." Among the exemplars we studied, those who came from a poverty background themselves are especially assertive in this belief. They express the exhortation more forcefully and with fewer qualifications than do those who came from more affluent backgrounds and are somewhat hesitant to make prescriptions for those facing more difficult circumstances than their own.

Mother Waddles is frequently invited to speak to organizations interested in poverty, social conditions for minorities, and social welfare. On these occasions, she urges African-Americans to be active in attempting to reduce discrimination, following the example of Martin Luther King, Jr., but she also speaks out about her perception that the messages of some black activists have undermined the work ethic and thus the upward mobility of their own people. Mrs. Waddles agrees with the activists she criticizes that African-Americans should aspire to the highest levels of education and leadership. But she also points out that for those who do not finish school, as she did not, there are still important ways to contribute and to live with dignity and self-sufficiency. Whereas she understands well the need for dignity among people with little education or money, she believes that such dignity is possible within a broad range of occupations:

MRS. WADDLES: I think they lost sight of a lot of things. I've seen people tell folk that service jobs was beneath the black man. Okay, so now we've got black people walking the streets, and the service jobs are being done by all the other ethnic groups. We've been told that you don't go to the white woman's kitchen. But now, if you're uneducated you cannot be the dean of a college, you cannot be an architect, so you have to work in a capacity that you are able to handle. And that's why my highest capacity is in the serving of people through basics. That's the only thing that I could do and be outstanding in. I'm capable of loving, I'm capable of taking what I can get and giving it to someone else. I'm not capable of being a dean of a college, I'm not capable of being a historian, a researcher. But I'm capable of being a missionary. . . . Because underlying all these things that I've done, uppermost in my mind has been to show that we as black people can have charitable organizations, and they're not confined to who has a degree to operate it, and who has the money to make it go, but who has the desire to do it, and that there is a way to do it, you know.

INTERVIEWER: So you don't feel that race has been a limiting factor?

MRS. WADDLES: Oh, sure it's been limiting. Yeah, it's been a limiting factor because were I a white person, I would have had more funds for this project. But it's been a challenging factor that I've enjoyed every minute of it.[20]

The second of Mother Waddles's central messages is related to the first: each person must take responsibility to do something about the problems they encounter. "And there's a little song that I sing, a little Christian song that I remind our congregation, 'Right in the corner where you are.' Right where you are, there's someone that's poor."

For Charleszetta Waddles it is not a struggle to live according to these lessons. They are completely interwoven through the fabric of her being. She does not have a desire to keep her small widow's pension for herself, overriding this desire through a belief that the moral thing to do is to give to others. Instead, what she most *wants* to do is help others. When she is concerned with keeping her ego in check, it is again not a conflict between personal and moral goals. Rather, she is concerned that she will overreach herself because it is hard to tolerate the limits on her ability to help. She sees her identity as a giving person as one of the most stable aspects of her life and interprets it as God working through her. She loves what she is doing, never plans to stop, and, asked what she would most like to do if she had unlimited time and money, she answers, "More of the same."

CHAPTER 9

Cabell Brand

Entrepreneur in Service to the Poor

C abell Brand's Southern charm barely masks his steely determination when he fixes upon a person or an idea. In the midst of the most casual conversation, what strikes you about him is his concentration, the way he holds onto you with his eyes, the way he pursues a question or a problem until it is resolved. He is gracious, forthright, and intense—an unusual combination whose effect is heightened by his towering, distinguished good looks. He has the appearance of a man who can get something done, and in Brand's case, appearances are not deceiving.

Cabell Brand is an entrepreneur, an ambitious businessman who built a small family company into a multimillion dollar corporation. At the same time, he has been for more than twenty-five years the volunteer president and chairman of the board of a social action program in the Roanoke Valley called Total Action Against Poverty (TAP). Through this program, he has dedicated himself to giving a "hand up" to Americans living in poverty.

> The weakness in the free enterprise system in the United States, in our capitalistic democratic system—the least worst system in the world—the weakness is the number of people who don't participate in what's going on. And that's measured by a poverty index which currently is 14 percent. There's another 14 percent or so that are the working poor, that struggle to get along, but they don't really have it either. They don't have health insurance, quality education, and these things we were talking about. So about 25 percent of the American population really needs a hand up so that they can participate in the system. . . . I guess my basic belief is that people can really do what they want to do if given the opportunity. I've tried hard to help put in motion processes that ensure that everybody has a chance of doing their own thing. That doesn't mean that everybody will win the race, but everybody will have a chance to try. And I really believe that. And I believe that if we start off with children early and they have proper health care and if the family is in a positive mode and they have a chance for a job and they are trying to improve themselves and the children are caught up in that kind thing, that the family will develop, the children will develop and they'll be participants, they'll live a happy life. The goal is to lead a happy life.

Cabell Brand in many ways is the quintessential American entrepreneur. He is a businessman. He believes in the American system. His goal is not to change the system in some fundamental way but rather to make it work as it should, to offer real equality of opportunity, to include a greater proportion of the people in the system so that they can enjoy its benefits. Cabell Brand values hard work, but he understands that without a "hand up" many hardworking people will continue to be poor because of unfair lack of opportunity for the good education, health care, housing, and other privileges that middle-class Americans take for granted.

Total Action Against Poverty has grown steadily since its establishment in 1965. It began with one of the country's first Head Start programs and went on to add programs for school dropouts, the elderly, ex-offenders, drug addicts, and the homeless, as well as a food bank, a program to bring running water to rural people, home weatherization programs, economic development programs for urban renewal areas, community cultural centers, and many other services, with a total of thirty-one programs currently in operation. Brand has thrown himself into making this happen with as much energy and creativity as he has brought to his business pursuits. Ted Edlich, the executive director of TAP, describes Brand as "a walking brainstorm. He never stops thinking; he never stops generating ideas. He's got more energy than any human being I've every known." Since its establishment, Cabell Brand has maintained a continuous active involvement with the TAP program, putting in as much as twenty-five hours a week on top of his full-time job in business.

In addition to his locally based antipoverty work, Brand is acutely aware of the broader international and environmental context within which the local economic issues are embedded. "My goal is to take whatever we have learned here in the last twenty-five years dealing with disadvantaged people and see whether there is a way that these lessons can be applied in the rest of the world. Because as I look at it, there's only one problem in the world and that problem is how can 10 billion people live a peaceful, reasonable life on a finite planet. I say 10 billion because that's what we'll have in forty-five years."

Cabell Brand was born in Salem, Virginia, in 1923. His grandfather had owned a small shoe business that he passed on to Cabell's father, who worked in the company until the day he died at age eighty-two. The business was only modestly profitable, and the family was middle class but not particularly affluent. Cabell's father and grandfather were both Republicans, opposed to government programs, and segregationist in their racial views. Even in childhood, Cabell differed from his father on these two key issues. Franklin Delano Roosevelt was elected in 1932, when Cabell was nine years old.

"I was always an admirer of Franklin Roosevelt and I was a little boy growing up. I liked what he was doing, and I remember putting an NRA sticker on my window and my father came up and tore it up. I didn't understand it. I thought that was good. I mean, people were poor and they were hungry and they were out of work and here the president of the United States was trying to do something, and I didn't understand why my father would be opposed to that."

This incident shows an independence of mind that seems to have characterized Brand from an early age. Another incident that occurred around age five also reveals the young Cabell as a boy who thought for himself. Roanoke had recently put in a bus line, and one day Cabell's baby-sitter took him for a ride on the bus to entertain him. You could ride the whole route for a nickel each, and Cabell looked forward eagerly to the adventure. However, he was a small child and disappointed to find that he could not see out the window. He soon discovered that the seats in the back of the bus were higher and afforded him an excellent view. Since buses were racially segregated in those days with blacks required to sit at the back of the bus, Cabell was told by the driver and his baby-sitter that he must stay in the front. He refused to cooperate, returning three times to the back. When the sitter reported Cabell's behavior to his father, Gerald Brand "raised Cain." As Cabell remembers the incident, he did not understand or acquiesce to his father's mandate that "you just cannot go back and sit with the niggers." Ted Edlich interprets this event, which is one of Cabell's favorite stories about his childhood, as revealing a quality that is still evident in the sixty-seven-year-old Cabell Brand—his unwillingness to let anyone push him around and a sense of fairness that led him to extend this same autonomy to others.

Cabell loved sports but was not big enough to play basketball or football. Still, when his goals were unattainable, as they often were, he dealt with the disappointments pragmatically. "If I can't do that, I'll do something else. If one thing doesn't work, you do something else." So when he was unable to become an all-American football player, he went into debating and public speaking and became the editor of the school newspaper. These activities reinforced his liberal views as he read and wrote about social issues. Cabell was proud of the newspaper and would bring it home and show it to his parents. His father was perplexed by his son's social and political views and, according to Cabell, never understood or appreciated his son's work on the paper. But Cabell was doing well in school and was seen by his parents as a good boy, so his relationship with his parents was harmonious despite their differences of opinion. Cabell did not take seriously his father's views, which he saw as indicative of his generation and lack of experience in the broader world.

Although Cabell Brand feels he has little in common with his family ideologically, he traces some of his values to the examples set by his parents. He describes both his mother and father as very honest, honorable, hardworking, and industrious—qualities that are very evident in Brand himself. Cabell is the middle of five children, with an older brother and sister and a younger brother and sister. All of his siblings have followed their parents politically and share few of Cabell's values and beliefs.

Brand attended Virginia Military Institute (VMI), as had his father and brother, and did well academically. In 1942 his class was called out to fight in World War II. He fought in the 70th Infantry Division in Europe as an officer, returning to VMI for one year after the war to complete his degree in electrical engineering. While in Europe during the war, he met a young woman from Estonia, Mariel Pichen, and returned after he finished college to resume the relationship.

In order to spend time in Europe, Brand took a job with the State Department, in the economics section of the military government in Berlin, and was there during the Soviet blockade. The Soviets had wanted to make West Berlin's "isle of freedom" within their East German territory untenable, so they attempted to stop all supplies from entering the city. Since all roads and rail lines were blocked, the United States responded by air lifting supplies directly into the city. Brand's job during the blockade was to figure out a way to bring in enough raw materials by the airlift to keep employment up in West Berlin, an exciting job for an inexperienced twenty-five-year-old. In his role as a member of the military government of Berlin, he briefed high-level members of the U.S. military and sat in on their meetings with the creators of the Common Market in Europe. "So it gave me an opportunity to listen to these great, great men talk about their vision for a united Europe and long-range planning, and it had a big influence on my life." This international political experience in Brand's early adulthood contributed to his global perspective on social issues and gave him a great deal of confidence in his beliefs and values, especially in relation to those of his parents, which now seemed more provincial than ever.

Brand had married Mariel Pichen soon after he returned to Europe in 1947, and over the next fifteen years they had four children. The fourth child suffocated in its crib at the age of about three weeks, and

both Cabell and Mariel were devastated by the loss. Not long afterward, Mariel broke both legs in a bad skiing accident and was an
invalid for many months. In response to these difficulties, she developed a drinking problem that contributed to the breakup of the marriage in 1962. Several years later, Brand began to date Shirley Hurt,
with whom he had been acquainted for many years. Shirley was also
divorced with three children. They married and had two more children together. Brand describes their efforts to "bring three families
together" (his children, her children, and their children) as one of the
most important goals of his life.

In spite of the excitement of his postwar foreign service work,
when the blockade was over Brand decided against a government career. He saw himself as a "marketing-salesman type" and felt that
he was better suited to a career in business than in the government
bureaucracy. With this in mind, he returned to Virginia to take over
his father's shoe company. In 1949, Gerald Brand had begun to liqui-
date the business. The profits were low, and it did not seem as if any
of his children (i.e., sons) wanted to come into the business with him.
Brand decided to take it on and try to build the business into a profitable company. "So I made an arrangement with my father, I had four
brothers and sisters and I didn't want any family problems, so we
struck an arm's-length agreement that he gave me 40 percent of the
business and I had a right to buy the other 60 percent at the value of
the total business. And I went around to my brothers and sisters and
got them to agree that that was a good idea and so started out in 1949
taking this economic base of a small business and building it up. And
I traveled a lot around the country and recruited more salesmen and
expanded a catalog and one thing led to another and twenty-one years
later took the company public as Stuart McGuire, Inc. We were doing
about $25 million worth of business."

This was not the happy ending to the story of Brand's business,
however. Several years after the company went public, some serious
problems arose. The system for distribution of Stuart McGuire's products became obsolete, because a door-to-door sales force was no longer
economical. At that point, Brand switched the company to a mail-
order business and then expanded to include a variety of mail-order
catalogs. But the mail-order business did not grow as fast as the direct-
selling business was declining. At that point he expanded the business
further by distributing not only the merchandise of Stuart McGuire
but also other companies' merchandise. "So we went into the fulfillment business of other mail-order companies," such as Bloomingdale's

and Hammacher-Schlemmer. In 1986, Brand sold the business to the Home Shopping Network. The effort to build and redirect the business was deeply engrossing and consumed most of Brand's energy during the 1950s and early 1960s. By the mid-sixties, his business was stable and successful enough to allow him to begin turning some of his attention elsewhere.

At the age of forty-two, Cabell Brand's activities on behalf of the community suddenly and permanently intensified when he became intrigued in 1965 by the Economic Opportunity Act and its implications for the Roanoke Valley area. He recalls that time this way:

> Well, first of all I'll never forget, after we were first married, Shirley and I lived in an apartment and we always watched the "Today" show and the early morning news programs, and I remember very clearly an interview with Shriver—Kennedy had been killed and Johnson was president and Shriver had been appointed director of the War on Poverty. And I remember the interview, I can see his face on the screen right now. And I . . . what the hell is this, this War on Poverty? What is this all about? I'd never heard of Michael Harrington [socialist author of *The Other America*] in 1965. I had never read that book, hadn't been aware of those problems. I'd seen poor people in slums and all that but really had never been alert to the fact that it was a serious problem. . . . I'd been all through the states building up the business, getting salesmen, and so forth, but I was never really overwhelmed with the thing, it was a federal responsibility or that anything could be done about it except people just go to work and so forth. And then when I read this bill, the real thing that changed me on that was when I read the Economic Opportunity Act of 1965 and got so interested in it that then I wrote away and got the committee hearings and read the verbatim text of the committee hearings where person after person testified, including Michael Harrington, as to the problems of the poor . . . and that how separated they were and all of that, and I said good God, I didn't realize that all of this was going on, and then the punch line was that suddenly the federal government was going to make some money available to the Roanoke Valley to do something about it but the local people had to get organized and take advantage of it. And if you didn't get organized and do it and request it you weren't going to get the money and the money goes somewhere else.

After studying the legislation and the text of the committee hearings in support of the law, Brand decided to investigate directly the relevance of the legislation for the Roanoke Valley area. He was scheduled to make a major presentation before the prestigious Roanoke Valley Torch Club and decided to drop the topic he had planned to address and talk instead about the new poverty program. In order to prepare for this speech and in the process determine whether to apply for federal funds under the Economic Opportunity Act, he took three months off from his business to study the situation. Through his membership on the board of the Council of Community Services, Brand was able to get the names of welfare recipients in the area. Along with his wife, Shirley, Brand went to call on the people listed in order to find out what they felt they needed. He described one of these visits as follows:

> I knocked on the door of this little ramshackle house and from my door-to-door selling experience I learned that you knock on the door and then you stand back, and the door opened—the Fuller Brush technique—this man came to the door and I explained that I was here to talk with him, and he didn't want to say anything. I kept asking him some questions like "Do you work?" "No." And if not, why not, and so forth and it occurred to me after about five minutes that the man didn't have any teeth and he wouldn't open his mouth, and he was obviously very embarrassed about the fact that he didn't have any teeth. And so the next week I was over at the welfare department and I said, "If a man doesn't have teeth, isn't there a place that he can go and get teeth?" They said, "Oh yeah, he can go to the health department, they'll give him teeth." So I went back and picked up the man, we hadn't even started TAP, I went back and picked up the man. I said I want to take you someplace over at the health department, do you feel comfortable enough to ride with me? I took him over to the health department; they gave him teeth. Don't know exactly whether he went to work; I didn't really follow it up the way I should have. But I'll never forget the fact that—the point is that he didn't have teeth and that help was available to him all along but he didn't know about it; he was illiterate, the other side of town, he had no transportation, he didn't have the means to go and seek it. And so it occurred to me as I made this study that one of the functions of a community action organization was to help the low-income people access the system.

After having collected information about the local poverty situation, Brand went to Washington and talked to people there. He also met with business leaders and local government officials in the Roanoke area. Everyone he talked to was enthusiastic about the opportunity presented by the new federal program, and Brand concluded that the program would allow them to bring into the community resources that had not been available previously. In the long run the program should be a boost not only to the recipients of aid but also to the local economy. The Torch Club speech was regarded as a major factor in bringing the community action movement to the Roanoke Valley area. For Cabell Brand himself, it was a major turning point in his life. According to his wife, "What started out as just an information-gathering exercise for the purpose of this paper was such an awakening." Brand succeeded in convincing himself as he prepared to make the case to the Torch Club group, "The more research I did, the more I learned, the more I saw the opportunity."

This incident illustrates a very important aspect of Cabell Brand's approach to life: his willingness to take full advantage of the promising opportunities he encounters. "I just saw an unusual opportunity, the opportunity presented itself. I didn't have anything to do with passing the Economic Opportunity Act of 1964. It was passed. It was a law. It was an opportunity for the local area to bring in resources and set up educational opportunities that were not present. Somebody had to do it. And I just happened to be there at the time and so seized the opportunity. That has been the way I have operated all my life. When you have an opportunity, do what you can with it."

We can assume that Cabell Brand's goals evolved more or less continuously across the course of his life. Nevertheless, as we have described it above, this period in his life was a time in which his commitment to fighting poverty began to emerge as a central guiding force in his life. As we have noted, at the age of forty-two he was a responsible and successful businessman. His primary professional goals (all of which are interrelated) were to build and maintain a profitable business, to treat his employees well, and to contribute to the health of the local economy and the welfare of the community. When he heard about the new Office of Economic Opportunity (OEO) legislation, he felt that the legislation could contribute to the latter two goals—bolstering the local economy and enhancing the welfare of the community. His interest in the legislation was stimulated by its relevance to these preexisting goals and led him to study carefully the legislation, the hearings associated with it, and the implications for the Roanoke Valley area. As he read about poverty in the United States, and especially when he visited the poor people of his community and saw their living conditions himself, his concern for the local economy and the welfare of the community expanded to include a desire to use the opportunity of the OEO and federal funding to do something about poverty in the Roanoke Valley. Once he started TAP, his goals in relation to poverty proliferated, became more differentiated, and superceded some of his previous goals. Within the overarching goal of making TAP into an effective organization with which to fight poverty were organized the subsidiary goals of providing housing, water, jobs, education, health care, and the like.

As Brand became more aware of the reality of American poverty, he also became more sensitive to poverty abroad. He had enjoyed travel even before he joined the war on poverty. But after he established TAP, he traveled with eyes newly opened to the extent and nature of global poverty. Thus, his travel began to educate him further, enabling him to put the local conditions into a global perspective, to understand the relation between poverty and environmental issues, and to begin to act on the international as well as the local level. Thus, the changes in his goals changed his perception of the world, which in turn further broadened his understanding and ultimately changed his goals again.

As he began to develop a program that would take advantage of the new OEO legislation, it immediately became clear to him that there was an urgent need to do something for children. "Forty percent of the poor people in the United States are children, and half the children under six years of age are poor. It was clear that the way to start was to attack the problem of the children, the next generation, which was what we did." In Brand's opinion, the long-range solution to poverty is excellent education and the health care, family support, and other help to make it possible for children to benefit fully from that education. "The root cause of poverty—and this has stood the test of twenty years of study—is lack of education. You need to start with the poor children, the disadvantaged children, and get them into school. Then you try to get them through twelve years of public school and have a good percentage of them go to college. We developed a theme: a hand up, not a handout. Sixty percent of all the money we've spent has gone to education-related projects for children."

With this in mind, the first step for Total Action Against Poverty

was to apply for a grant to set up a Head Start program in the Roanoke Valley. Brand worked with David Herbert, the executive director of the Roanoke Valley Council of Community Services, to develop
a proposal. The proposal was funded, and in 1965 the first Head Start
programs were initiated. They were originally summer programs of
six weeks designed to give a "head start" to poor children who would
be entering school for the first time that September. "This was June
of 1965, and the federal fiscal year ended on June 30. And there was
all this federal money that had not been allocated. So I learned in
Washington that if we put in a grant proposal real quick, we could
get this year's money. We put in a grant for $180,000 to establish
three Head Start programs that summer, one in each county, and we
got the grant approved. So here it was, approved the last day of the
fiscal year, June 30. And school started in September. And we had this
money to have a Head Start program." Brand, who was elected president and chairman of the board of the new private nonprofit corporation (TAP), hired an executive director and two other staff members.
The four of them had just a few weeks to find teachers and classroom
space and to develop a program. The Roanoke Valley Head Start Programs opened the last week in July and have been operating ever since.

Soon after TAP was established, the board hired Bristow Hardin
as executive director, Osborne Payne as director of education, and
Sam Barone as personnel director. Bristow Hardin served as executive
director from 1965 until his sudden death from a heart attack at age
fifty-two ten years later. He was a bold, unconventional, and colorful
leader, looking "just like a young Burl Ives," according to Cabell
Brand. Hardin had been the principal of a public high school and while
in that position had taken some pains to educate himself in the issues
and problems of poverty. He was a maverick who was not constrained
by mainstream assumptions and values. Cabell Brand calls Bristow
Hardin "the most innovative person I have ever met in my life." In
the early days of TAP, many of the ideas came from Hardin, and Brand
helped to implement them by bridging the gap to the mainstream
society.

Brand talks often about the importance of Bristow Hardin in bolstering his stamina during the early years of the organization. "There
have been times that I have been discouraged. When Nixon came in
he tried to kill the program. . . . And I thought everything was going
to just fall down. I was ready to throw in the towel, and Bristow
Hardin wouldn't let me. I mean, he was an inspiration. He said,

'No, we'll beat this!' And he got the Southern Law Institute and organizations like that to fight the president of the United States. And it turned out that what Nixon did was illegal. And we won!''

It is important to bear in mind that Cabell Brand is the volunteer president and chairman of the board of an organization with a full-time paid staff, an organization with a momentum and life of its own. The relationship between the board chair, the board, and the staff is one of mutual influence. None would have been the same without the others. In the evolution of the organization, ideas are generated by Brand, the other members of the board of directors, the staff, and the constituents from the poor community of the Roanoke Valley. In the course of implementation, the ideas are modified and adapted, so that in the end each is shaped by the group. As they work together over the years, the participants exert various kinds of influence on one another—changing, reinforcing, and encouraging one another. We can see this in Brand's relationship with Bristow Hardin: The ten-year partnership of an establishment businessman with a maverick activist changed both men and kept both deeply engaged in the joint enterprise. When asked whether Hardin played a role in shaping his ideas about TAP in the early days, Brand responded, "Oh good God, I learned all kinds of things from him! Most of the ideas came from him. He had the ideas and he saw the need, and I bridged the gap to the mainstream society and could help implement them. Because I could go to the business community more effectively than he could. . . . We set up structured time together. He had a boat. We used to go out on his boat. We used to talk all the time."

After Hardin's death, Theodore Edlich III became executive director and has remained in that position for over fifteen years. Despite the fact that he came from a privileged background, Ted Edlich is no less committed to the poor than Hardin was. A Presbyterian minister in a small town in Virginia before coming to TAP, he served as director of the Head Start programs and then of human services training before succeeding Hardin as executive director. Less flamboyant than Hardin, Edlich is still an extremely competent manager and especially skilled at finding support for TAP's programs at a time when such support is less easily available than it was in the 1960s and early 1970s.

Cabell Brand's role in TAP has included generating ideas, putting together support and funding for the ideas, and guiding the board in its decision-making and oversight of the organization. As president and chairman of the board, he has had to be reelected every year by the board, which includes representatives from local government, community organizations, and the constituents being served by TAP. The president does not choose the board members, and his reelection is not pro forma. Brand is, in fact, the only person who has served as president of a community action program for so long, and his longevity indicates the respect that his competent leadership has earned.

One of Brand's most important contributions has been to garner corporate support for TAP, bringing influential leaders onto the board and obtaining funds and cooperation of other sorts from local businesses. According to Edlich, Brand especially likes to take on the really hard issues. For example, the people of one poor neighborhood said that more than anything else they would like to have a supermarket in their neighborhood. Brand was able to meet personally with the head of a major supermarket chain and convince him to open a market in that neighborhood. He has access to political leaders as well and never hesitates to use his connections for the benefit of TAP. As Edlich says, "Cabell can get a meeting with any legislator and can sell the problem, sell the solution. Cabell is a salesman par excellence."

TAP's staff and board together built the organization over the years by adding new programs where they saw a need and eliminating programs that did not prove to be effective or could be taken over by someone else. In order to do this, they must "leverage" the money that they have available. They have been very successful in doing this. With core funding of $300,000 to $400,000, for example, they are able to raise $3 million.

One of the ideas initiated by TAP, the Virginia Water Project, illustrates the process by which new programs are introduced and developed:

MR. BRAND: The water thing was an interesting thing. We found out that there were many people that didn't have water. And I didn't know there were people that didn't have water in this affluent society. We found out that there were thousands and thousands of families that didn't have water. I mean no water on their property at all. No wells, no nothing! Today in Virginia, there are 79,000 families that don't have water on their property. *Today!* And in the last fifteen to twenty years we've brought that number down by half. And we've got a plan in the next fifteen years; we're going to eliminate it. That's the program, so we figured that out and we figured out a system of bringing water and where we'd get a federal grant from the Farmers' Home Administration to pay for a pump and we'd get some pipe either given to us or we would buy it. We'd get eight, ten, fifteen, twenty, thirty families together and we would charge them a dollar, dollar and a half a month for the maintenance of the thing once we'd put in the system, and then we'd lobby the county government to take it over and maintain it. And once there was water in the area, then all kinds of things happened. Developers came in, roads were built, and there was economic development. If people went to work, the families were no longer isolated so they kept their kids in school and all kinds of good things happened just because you brought water to them. So I didn't understand that but the process of working on it enlarged my vision and my motivation to do more of that.

INTERVIEWER: Well, now how would something like that happen?

MR. BRAND: Someone in the outreach department would say, "You know, there are people out there who don't have any water. I wonder what we can do about that." Then you sit around and you develop a plan for doing something valid—let's just see if we can do one. You do one and you come up with a model and you do two and you figure the thing out. And then you develop a system. And then we set up a separate organization for doing it.

One of the important tenets of TAP is to stress local solutions to social problems, and Cabell Brand likes to quote the popular exhortation to "Think globally, and act locally." According to Brand, "I have learned that there are not very many federal government solutions to local problems that have worked well without the participation of the local community. If the government provides the seed of a program, it's best to have a local organization use and leverage that money, because it can see where the need is greatest. The TAP board is made up of one-third from local government, one-third from poor people, and one-third from community organizations like social agencies, neighborhood groups, and the League of Women Voters. The staff doesn't report to anybody except the board."

Through his work with the TAP board, Brand developed a new respect for the contribution of the board members drawn from the poor community. In the beginning he had thought that including poor people on the board was a ridiculous idea. "How in the world could you have a board of directors with ignorant people who can hardly read and write making decisions as to how to spend hundreds of thousands of dollars? I've learned to eat those words because the best concept of all was having these people help us evaluate the practicality of the programs we were proposing." Brand goes on to give an example. The middle-class members of the board thought the rea-

son that so few of the local black kids went to college was the lack
of tuition money. When the board began to discuss where to find
tuition money, a woman who was one of the members of the board
drawn from the poor community suggested that the problem was not
the lack of tuition money, but rather that few of the poor black children thought college was an option for them and thus did not take
the college preparatory courses they would need if they were to enter
college. "That's what started Project Discovery. We go into the public schools and meet with the sixth and seventh graders, meet with
the teachers, meet with the principals, meet with the guidance coun-
selors, and tell them that there's tuition money available out there for
those who can qualify. We guide the young people through a number
of seminars held on college campuses and expose them to a variety of
schools. We talk to the parents and take them to the campuses to get
their support." Project Discovery is a program of workshops in study
skills, financial aid, life planning, and choosing a college. Since its
establishment in 1979 the program has been expanded to other communities in Virginia and recently received a major grant for dissemina-
tion nationwide.

According to Ted Edlich, the central role of the low-income
people themselves is critical to the philosophy of TAP. "What are
TAP's priorities? The priority of TAP is to organize local low-income
people to define their needs and express their concerns and their wants
and to do something about their condition—that is, we did not have
an agenda for the low-income people. But if they had an agenda, we
stood by them."

Another central tenet of TAP is that it offers only cost-effective
programs, and this can be shown very clearly. For example, the Virginia Cares Program helps ex-offenders get back into society and significantly reduces the recidivism rate for its participants. Given the
high cost of building prisons and keeping people in prison, it is easy
to show that the relatively low expenditure per person of Virginia
Cares is repaid many fold by the decrease in offenders returning to
prison. Brand describes one of the program's success stories as follows:

> I know of one young man, a high school dropout, who broke
> the law and spent two years in reform school and then two years
> in an adult prison. The Virginia Cares staff put on a forty-hour
> prerelease seminar in prison, for him and others, and helped him
> set employment goals and write a résumé pointing toward cook-
> ing, which was what he was doing before his release. When he

came home, he was met by Virginia Cares staff people, who helped him find a place to live and a job and counseled him on domestic problems. A support mechanism helped him back into society and away from the street and crime.

Not all of the programs developed by TAP have been successful or cost-effective. For example, an attempt to start a credit union for poor people without bank accounts turned out to be impractical and was dropped. Over the twenty-five years of its existence, TAP has added and dropped many programs, often transferring some of the most effective ones to independent status or to the state.

The most ambitious new program that Brand has helped establish in recent years is CHIP, the Comprehensive Health Investment Program, which provides comprehensive health care for all low-income children up to 150 percent of the poverty line. As with many of TAP's programs, the focus is on prevention, and the backing comes from private, public, and business cooperation. The goal is to enroll all 4,800 eligible children from the Roanoke Valley within the next two or three years and eventually to expand the program statewide. Brand has been on the state board of health for five years and was the first businessman to be appointed to that board. At the time of the interview, he had just been elected chair of that board.

The area served by TAP includes 250,000 people, 14 percent of whom are black. Although two-thirds of the poor people in the region are white, 38 percent of the black population is poor. From the beginning, the TAP board, staff, and all of the programs were fully integrated, and some of the programs served primarily minority populations. When this became clear to the local community, TAP lost much of its public support and became the object of considerable hostility from the large numbers of people who wanted to resist integration.

So it suddenly became clear to the community that this federal program was going to integrate the schools. And so, suddenly, there was all kinds of opposition. And for ten years, we operated our community action agency as low key as possible to try to get things done without stirring up public resentment, because we still needed local support. So we kept a low profile. And during that period, we had all kinds of things happen. We had a cross thrown on our lawn and our children threatened. And when I made a presentation at Bedford City Council, I was told to leave, get out of there. They didn't want this federal program, the concept being that if you didn't have a federal program, you didn't have to obey federal laws. They refused to integrate the schools. So the race issue then became paramount and overwhelming in this community. And Prince Edward County, Virginia, actually closed the public schools for ten years, rather than integrate them.

Because of TAP's involvement with the black community and because a large proportion of its staff is black, the agency has been able to contribute significantly to improving race relations in the area. At the time that TAP was established, the local schools were not integrated although it was more than ten years after the Supreme Court's *Brown* vs. *the Board of Education* decision that ordered school desegregation. Bristow Hardin believed strongly in the use of human relations training and brought his experience in that area to bear during the desegregation of the schools. When the decision was made to integrate the Roanoke schools, Bristow Hardin met with the school superintendent to urge him to set up dialogue groups between black and white students, black students and white teachers, and eventually, when they were hired, between black teachers and white students. The programs were voluntary for students but mandatory for teachers, and TAP provided the training to the schools for free. TAP also organized black and white young people to challenge the segregation of public facilities such as swimming pools.

At the time of the riots in Watts, Hough, and Detroit during the summers of 1967 and 1968, Brand went to Los Angeles and to Hough (in Cleveland) and met with the community leaders, asking what had happened and why. He concluded that one important factor that contributed to the crises was the isolation of the black communities. It was with a sense of the importance of communication between the black and white communities that TAP organized a meeting on the night after Martin Luther King was murdered. "We called a meeting in a black community center and convinced the whole Roanoke City Council and city manager and police chief to come down there and give people a chance to confront them and have a dialogue and feel like they were part of the community instead of being separate and barricaded in." Bristow Hardin, executive director of TAP at the time, then organized an integrated march, convincing the participants that King would have wanted them to shed blood in a peaceful way on that night. They marched through town to a blood bank and donated blood.

Cabell Brand's life illustrates well the way personal characteristics that are relatively stable over much of an individual's life can be reinforced and channeled as the individual's goals evolve. We see this in Brand's energy, competitiveness, entrepreneurial spirit, and love of a challenge. By the time TAP was established in 1965, Brand had spent almost fifteen years building a small, marginally profitable company into a thriving business and responding to shifts in the business environment that required radical changes in the direction of the company. He brought to this work, and developed within it, a number of personal qualities that later characterized his contributions to TAP. "First of all, I saw the long-range benefit [of a community action program]. I had learned to think long range. I saw the long-range benefits for the area. Second, I was a businessman and that means you know how to get things done. And so, I was well organized and had a sense of urgency. And I brought that dimension to the thing—getting the [preschool program] started in thirty days, getting it implemented in sixty days, and then that coincided with the fact that the opportunity was there and I was elected president of this new, private, nonprofit corporation. I had the responsibility. So it's a combination of responsibility, opportunity, and the skills that I had—a sense of urgency and the ability to get things done and to get other people to help. And everybody I asked to help helped." Brand was used to accepting and dealing quickly and decisively with challenges. As a manager, he was used to mobilizing others to join his effort. Having dealt successfully with the vagaries of the business environment, he was used to creating ingenious solutions to the problems he encountered. He believed in himself and had a "can-do" attitude.

Brand's ingenuity, as applied to TAP, is illustrated in the organization's approach to literacy and vocational education for adults. In dealing with school dropouts, they found that many of these adults had not learned to read and write.

> So we set up a school which would take someone that's functionally illiterate and in fifteen weeks bring them up to a fifth-grade reading level. We found that we couldn't bring them up to a seventh-grade reading level, but we could bring them up to a fifth-grade level. Then we discovered that most of the adult education classes in the public schools were based on seventh-grade reading skills and there's a lot of difference between a fifth-grade reading level and a seventh-grade reading level. For example, you couldn't take an electrician's course in the public school adult education class unless you could read the blueprint. Well, you can't really read a blueprint with fifth-grade level. Our goal was

to train people to work so they could function in society and be self-supporting. So we had to develop new curriculum based on fifth-grade reading level. And we did. We developed an auto mechanics class. We developed a seamstresses class so they could read the job tickets. We developed a sheet-metal thing and we developed job-training skills based on a fifth-grade reading level. And then we set up a whole organization to do this and eventually, after about fifteen years, we were able to transfer all that to the public schools. So we went out of business and we transferred that system to the public schools.

Brand has brought to bear this same kind of energy, ingenuity, and confidence when TAP faced serious challenges such as loss of federal and public support during the Reagan era:

INTERVIEWER: And how do you deal with that? What keeps you going and keeps your energy up when you face such a disturbing situation?

MR. BRAND: Well, I don't know. I think I'm reasonably creative and energetic and you have a problem and the way I've dealt with a problem is to get the people together that have a common interest and brainstorm and figure out what to do about it and that's always . . . you see a way of doing something. And then you go try to do it. We saw ways to replace the federal resources through state and local monies and foundations, and we've done it! And so, seeing a way to accomplish what you thought was important has been the thing that's kept me going on it. I guess if I reach the point of seeing it's absolutely impossible, I might give up. But I haven't reached that point yet.

This orientation toward results is very characteristic of Cabell Brand's approach to his work. To him, everything is a problem that needs to be solved. In this, he endorses Bristow Hardin, who used to say that ''Work is not when you push against the wall. Work is when the wall moves.'' Brand like Hardin, is more interested in moving walls than he is in pushing.

From fairly early in his life, it appears that Cabell Brand enjoyed and responded effectively to challenges. No doubt this quality both contributed to his interest in taking over the flagging family business and developed further as he met the considerable challenges that resulted from that decision. It was in part the challenge that excited Brand when he first decided to take advantage of the new OEO legislation. As Shirley Brand puts it, ''I think it was a challenge. And then with each little success, you know, it became a little more encouraging and a little more challenging." Brand's love of a challenge combines with an enjoyment of people and a desire to influence them, leading to his ability as a salesman in both the business and social action domains. To quote from Ted Edlich: "Cabell is an extrovert. He loves public gatherings. He loves to meet people. He really does. He really enjoys making contact with people. And the more inaccessible, the better. There's just nobody Cabell can't get to. And he will go through the most intricate measures to get to them."

One can see in these descriptions of Brand the cumulative nature of many of his personal characteristics. As we have discussed in Chapter 7, people often involve themselves in activities that amplify the very qualities that led them to engage in those activities in the first place. Thus, a positive response to challenges leads to a greater sense of effectiveness and a greater tendency to respond positively to the next challenge. A desire to interact with people leads him to choose settings and activities that call for and reinforce exactly this gregarious response.

To point out these relatively enduring characteristics does not mean, however, that Cabell Brand's persistence comes entirely from within him. To a very great extent, his persistence has depended on the social relationships with which he was engaged. We have talked about the influence of Bristow Hardin and about the interplay and mutual influence between Brand, as a strong individual, and the organization and the people with whom he worked over a quarter of a century.

Cabell himself identifies his wife, Shirley, as his most important source of inspiration, support, and guidance. As in many traditional marriages, she believes in her husband, urges him on, relieves him of most domestic responsibility, and shares fully in his values and ambitions, often leading rather than following as these values developed. He describes Shirley as optimistic, practical, wise, strong, and enlightened. "I think that Shirley's roots in the pioneer stock of her mother's family shows throughout her character, because it's great—great values, great principles, and self-sufficiency, honesty, integrity, and hard work. During the trips that the Brands have taken to the jungles of Ecuador, the Australian outback, or the rural areas of Kenya, it has always been Shirley who has had an easier time coping with the discomforts and rustic conditions. In dealing with their children, Shirley is the parent who insists upon uncompromising standards, never wavering once she has taken a position that she believes is right for the child and the family.

Brand sees his wife as having been always a step ahead of him in his awakening to poverty and racial injustice. For example, when they investigated the local poverty situation prior to the establishment of TAP, Cabell was shocked and astonished by the conditions, whereas Shirley was moved but not surprised, having been more aware of the extent of disadvantage surrounding their protected affluent world. This may have resulted from her rural background, from her years working as a kindergarten teacher in the local public schools, or from her volunteer work. She took a strong interest in the work of TAP, becoming involved directly in a number of important projects. At least as important from Brand's point of view was the support she provided for his involvement. At difficult times in his work with TAP or with family or business issues, she sustained him with her belief in him, "She always challenged me, 'You can do it! What do you mean you can't do it? Sure you can!' I would have a bad problem. She would say, 'It's going to work out.' She always had the optimistic view. 'Just get in there and don't worry about it.'"

Like our other exemplars, Cabell Brand expresses great certainty about his moral beliefs and social/political goals. Any examples of uncertainty he could provide concerned pragmatic issues such as which direction to take in a business venture or how TAP should respond tactically to a roadblock such as declining federal support. With regard to moral issues, he experienced no such dilemmas.

INTERVIEWER: And did you ever feel that you didn't know what the right thing to do was, in terms of the morally right thing, or the socially right thing?

MR. BRAND: I've never had any problem with the morally right thing. To me, that has been a given. I mean, no big deal about it, I really wouldn't be a participant doing something I didn't feel was right. I don't mean I haven't made mistakes. I don't mean I haven't done some things that weren't right.

INTERVIEWER: But were you always sure you knew what *was* right?

MR. BRAND: Yes. I've always been sure that I knew what . . . I have not always been sure that I made the right decision, the pragmatic business decision and all that, but I have always been sure that what I attempted to do was morally right.

INTERVIEWER: You never had any uncertainty about that?

MR. BRAND: Moral right or wrong? I don't think so. I don't think so.
I have always trusted my instincts on that.

   In order to understand better what Brand means here, let us consider for a moment his general conception of morality. To Cabell
Brand, morality and long-term self-interest are one and the same. Beyond that, morality is a kind of minimal and assumed baseline for
behavior.

INTERVIEWER: You have talked about a whole range of goals. Would
you consider some or all of these goals to be essentially moral goals?

MR. BRAND: No, I don't think of them in that way. I think that they're
sort of a given. If you don't really try to do what's right, there's no
point in doing anything. When you go to bed at night if you don't feel
good about the day and you wake up in the morning and you don't like
what you see, that's sort of a given. Obeying laws, following rules,
doing what's right, that's a given. It's like, people have said, "Well,
why in the world do you get involved in the poverty thing?" I don't
really look at it that way. I do it because I feel good about it. I don't
mind admitting it's self-interest. I think people do what is in their own
self-interest. And I think that it is in their own self-interest to obey the
law and obey the rules of society and try to protect the world and then
the family and raise children properly and set an example and do all that
and I think that that's just sort of given. And I think the end result is,
at my age looking back, I'm pleased with what I've attempted. But I
don't think that moral issues have been the motivating factor. To me,
it's just, that's a given in these other goals. Without that, you don't
have anything.

   Ted Edlich describes Brand as someone who "will make a decision
even if it's wrong. Not to make a decision doesn't sit well with him.
He doesn't flounder much at all. He thinks all the time. And when
it comes to making decisions, he doesn't endlessly analyze the data to
see which way to go. He just makes the decision. He's a walking
brainstorm and a walking decision-making machine."
   Closely related to the feeling of certainty in his basic direction and
beliefs is the familiar impression that Brand's awareness of possible
risks and dangers did not cause him to waver in pursuit of his goals.
During the years of racial tension surrounding integration of the local

schools, TAP was unpopular because of its integrated programs and staff. During this ten-year period Brand experienced some fear for his family, especially for his children. As we have seen, this conflict was mentioned by several of our exemplars. Brand felt (as did the others) that his awareness of the conflict did not affect his choices:

MR. BRAND: I was afraid a little bit for my children. I was never really afraid personally. Maybe I should have been, but I wasn't. I was fearful for the family.

INTERVIEWER: And did that present a conflict for you then?

MR. BRAND: Well, I was never so afraid that I would hesitate to do what I thought I wanted to do, or what needed to be done, or what ought to be done. I don't think the fear got in the way of . . . it caused me to take certain precautions, but it didn't cause me to waiver in what I thought I ought to do.

Cabell Brand is very clear about what his goals are—in his business, in his social action work, and in his personal life. Of all the people we studied, he was the most inclined to talk about his life as oriented by goals and about his goals as changing over time. (This may be due to his extensive experience as the president of a major company. In business, top managers learn quickly the importance of clear and attainable goals.) In thinking about continuity and change within his life, he points to continuity in his values and expansion of his goals. According to Brand's philosophy of life (a philosophy that he experiences as having been stable since his childhood), one ought to take full advantage of opportunities that may arise in life. It is because of the opportunities he has taken up that his goals have changed.

INTERVIEWER: When you were elected president of TAP, what effect do you think that had on you?

MR. BRAND: Well, it gave me a responsibility. When you're elected to something, you're always asked, "Will you do it?" and I said yes I'd do it. And so that gave me a responsibility. So that required that I do the best I could. And that became a primary goal of my life and my priorities. It's related to having an opportunity to do it. I felt good about it. I saw the opportunity, I thought I could do it, and I did it. I did the best I could with it.

INTERVIEWER: When you took on that responsibility, do you think that changed you in any way or affected your values or beliefs or goals? Do you see any change in yourself over time?

MR. BRAND: It changed my goals. It didn't change my values.

INTERVIEWER: Could you talk about both of those?

MR. BRAND: Well, I don't think my values have changed from early on in life. I think I've always tried to do the best I could under the circumstances with whatever the job was. That's just a very simple sort of thing, that you do the best you can, in school, or whatever. And I don't really feel that I have changed in values. I've grown, I've learned more and more about what's important, and so with that experience and so forth, I guess it changes it somewhat, but just fundamentally, my philosophy and values have always been to try to just do the best I could. Now the goals have changed as the opportunities have changed. When you're elected or appointed to some kind of position, then it gives you new opportunities. So then you have to evaluate whether you want to take advantage of that. . . . And so I try to seize that moment, that opportunity, and maximize the potential of that opportunity. So that changed my priorities. It gave me new goals, I didn't have a goal five years ago of a child health-care program. That goal evolved because of the opportunity of being appointed to the board of health, seeing the need, having the authority, and then doing something. So it's the opportunity that created the new goal.

Although Brand's main overarching moral commitment, his fight against poverty, did not change over the years since he established TAP, he experiences his goals within that fight as having changed in important ways. What does he mean when he says that his values have remained the same and his goals have changed? As we have suggested in Chapter 7, the process here is a gradual articulation, expansion, and reorganization of strategies. This process yields a gradual and continuous transformation of subsidiary goals within the context of his stable commitment to the overarching goal. The goals he developed were governed largely by the existing commitment and a new and changing set of social influences. Through the extended period of collaboration with the TAP board, Bristow Hardin, Ted Edlich, and other key staff members, Brand turned his intentions into a very deep and solid expertise in the wide-ranging and complex set of issues with which he had to grapple.

The importance to Cabell Brand of the changes in his goals is thrown into relief by an understanding of the relationship between his goals and his sense of self. When asked how his goals and values relate to his sense of who he is as a person, Brand responds, "It's one and the same. Without goals I wouldn't be. I don't think there's any way for me to separate who I am from what I want to do and what I *am* doing." This experience of unity between oneself and one's most cherished goals is an important part of what makes the goals so powerfully motivating. It is also related to the sense of certainty we see in the exemplars. If one is not divided within oneself, if what one is, one's own identity, is defined by pursuing what one knows to be right, the result is a person who is passionately committed to his or her life path and pursuits.

Brand differs from others in our sample, however, in the extent to which he separates his community-oriented goals from his personal or family goals. Bringing "three families" together has been a central life goal for Cabell and Shirley Brand. In order to prevent this set of family priorities from becoming submerged in the urgency of TAP and Cabell's business activities, the Brands go away for a week every year with one thing on the agenda, and that is to make a plan outlining their goals for the next five years and to revise the plan every year. They formulate explicit goals in each area of their lives and plans for coordinating the goals across the various domains. Now that all of their children are grown, the plans include such activities as family reunions and visits with the grandchildren. The Brands' approach to coordinating family and work goals exemplifies Cabell's systematic, orderly approach to his life, an approach that is no doubt parallel to his operating style within his work as a businessman and community activist. The approach also depends upon the considerable financial resources available to the Brands. To visit grandchildren in Dallas and Richmond every three months or to bring the family together for two weeks at the beach is beyond the means of many of our exemplars.

One of the ways that the Brands accomplished their joint goal of bringing three families together was to take adventuresome, often exotic family trips. In Ecuador they visited the colonial culture of Quito, took a survival course in the jungle ("living out among the monkeys"), and spent time in the Indian villages in the north of the country. They spent one Christmas in Israel, went to church on Christmas Eve in Bethlehem, toured Jericho and Jerusalem with a Christian Arab, visited Masada with an Israeli archaeologist, stayed on a kibbutz, and lived for a while in an Arab community. They took three of the children on a tour of the Soviet Union and went as a family to Norway, visiting the Laplanders in the North Cape. They took several trips to Africa, on one of which they met Richard Leakey and went up to Koobi Forae to visit his research station.

Clearly, these trips show the extent to which the Brands have enjoyed spending the considerable wealth Cabell accumulated as a successful businessman. But they also illustrate the imagination and interest that he pours into every aspect of life. As Ted Edlich puts it, "Cabell *loves* life. He has a good time. I remember at a roast, somebody was talking about a scene with Edward G. Robinson in a bathtub with a cigar in his mouth and he was asked 'What do you want?' And Edward G. Robinson says, 'I want it all, I want it all.' Well, that's Cabell. He loves life, and he wants it all." Cabell Brand's exuberance is anything but ascetic, and yet it is expressed in a constant desire to expand his understanding of what is going on in the world and what needs to be done. "That's the goal for the children as well—to expose them to everything that you can that's going on in the world, then they make their own decisions about what they want to do."

Cabell Brand's optimism and positive attitude suffuse his entire approach both to his business and to his efforts to deal with poverty and the environment. He rises to a challenge, because he believes a solution can be found. He does not expect a short-range solution, but he has no doubt that in the long run even the most intractable problems can be solved if people just pitch in and work on them. He approaches life with tremendous energy and numerous enthusiasms and interests. There are so many exciting and important things to do, that it requires self-control not to try to do them all. "I'm interested in a lot of things and there are a lot of things to be done in the world, so I've tried very hard to focus, because you can't do everything."

In spite of this effort to focus, the breadth and richness of Brand's life are remarkable. Having sold his clothing and mail-order fulfillment business, he has started a new company, Recovery Systems, which involves environmental recovery of precious metals and is meant as a model for Third World economic development through the private sector. He is working to establish a project in Bangladesh to help the people use the resources they have, in this case leather, to provide jobs and additional resources needed for development. He collects African art and oil lamps from 3000 B.C. to the present. And he takes his family on vacations to exotic places all over the world. In addition to his local involvement with TAP, he has become a national spokesman for the community action movement. The excitement and energy he brings to these varied pursuits seems to go hand in hand with his optimistic approach to the poverty problem. The optimism, in turn, is empowering. What's the use of trying if the problems are too great to solve? A belief that we can find a solution lends energy to the search.

Brand is almost always enthusiastic and optimistic, but he is not a Pollyanna. He is a realist about the barriers to success in the fight against poverty and is frequently disappointed, although seldom discouraged. He was disappointed, for example, about the election of Ronald Reagan and the subsequent cutbacks in programs for low-income people. In spite of such disappointments and realistic appraisal of obstacles, Brand does not become discouraged easily. If one avenue to success is blocked, he tries another approach. As Edlich puts it, "Cabell doesn't brood. You don't see Cabell really depressed. Everything is a problem that needs a solution."

Brand's positive, energetic approach sets the tone for the organization as well. According to Edlich, "There's excitement here, because Cabell provides a 'can do,' a '*we* can do,' a 'we *will* do' attitude to the whole thing. If Cabell's given anything to this agency, it's the sense of aiming high. Both he and Bristow established the sense that just because we are dealing with poor people, we are not a second-class agency and they are not second-class people. There's a sense that you belong to a first-class organization. But Cabell's view of things, and his feelings about who he is, have made this agency feel that way. So when you go in the agency the place looks bright, people are friendly. You go in a lot of places and people, you know, there's kind of a beaten attitude. So you get discouraged when you can't get the resources; and it certainly is draining, but it's always exciting."

Through his work with TAP, Cabell Brand has become well aware of the immensity of the poverty problem in the United States and abroad, but he is not discouraged by it. "What discourages me is those people who don't try to do something about it. If everybody tried to do a little bit, then the problem wouldn't be so enormous. The problem is that not very many people are trying. And that bothers me, so I try to motivate more and more people to be concerned." He knows that he will not complete his work, but rather he sets as his goal "to start processes which will be in motion that will have some effect over the next or succeeding generations." He likens this approach to that of a cathedral builder—that is, he and his coworkers chip away at social problems the way stonemasons of the Middle Ages inched along in building cathedrals, knowing that the massive churches wouldn't be finished for three or four hundred years.

A guiding principle of Brand's life is his desire to leave behind a positive legacy.

> I guess a motivating force in setting my specific goals has been what I'd like to leave behind. . . . So I have always been conscious of the legacy, what am I going to leave as a legacy, what are the lessons, what are the building blocks. . . . I really think that life is one thing after another and you build on the past and you're still building toward the future and you never finish building because there's so much to do. . . . The bigger the problem, the bigger the challenge, and the more important it is to get started. The problem is that not very many people are trying. And that bothers me, so I try to influence everybody I can, which is why I have accepted all these speaking engagements, to try to motivate more and more people to be concerned about the things that I think are important.

In describing his approach to social action, Cabell Brand stresses the need to take a long-term perspective. He believes that social responsibility is in one's long-range self-interest and that companies or individuals who exploit other people or the environment are doing so for short-term gain. They are failing to see that from the long-term point of view the ethical, responsible thing to do and the self-interested thing to do are inseparable. In line with this view, Mr. Brand has put as a high priority at this time in his life the transfer of the work he has done to a new generation. He has established at Roanoke College the Cabell Brand Center for International Poverty and Resource Studies, the primary purpose of which is to interest young people in the pressing social problems of poverty and the environment and to encourage them to become actively involved in solving those problems. As the center's brochure states, "The center believes that in the continuation of efforts to diminish world poverty and to reverse the earth's physical decay, the academic and religious community and institutions play a major role in generating a vision of service to society, in developing creative leadership, and in providing the ethical discernment necessary for using the material and human resources of the world for the benefit of all."

The Cabell Brand Center sponsors an internship program through which students at nearby colleges and high schools can participate in whichever of the many TAP programs most closely matches their interests. The center also works to create interest in students who otherwise would be unlikely to get involved in social action. For example, the center recently sponsored a conference on world hunger that required each participant, at the end of the conference, to sign up for some volunteer work relating to the issue. The scope of the conference was broad, ranging from international agricultural issues, to national programs of nutritional assistance, to local food banks and food distribution centers, so students were able to choose areas in which to work that matched their particular interests or expertise.

Although Cabell Brand has devoted a tremendous amount of time and energy to the antipoverty campaign over the past twenty-five years, he has not himself led a life of privation. He drives a Jaguar, lives in a beautiful home filled with art treasures, dresses in expensive clothes, and travels widely. In this he contrasts with some of our other exemplars, especially those concerned with poverty. Allison McCrea, Suzie Valadez, and other committed antipoverty workers often live very simply. Brand enjoys a luxurious life-style in the face of the deprivation that he fights so energetically.

The contrast between Brand's affluence and the poverty that he combats is dramatic and informative of both his social philosophy and his orientation to life. He believes that an important purpose of life is enjoyment, and he works hard to bring the possibility of greater enjoyment to others. He does not believe that fighting poverty necessarily entails an austere life-style. Allison McCrea, for one, takes a very different point of view on this issue. She gave up a successful career in advertising to devote herself to the cause of the homeless. She lives near the poverty level herself, because she found the more materially affluent life-style she lived as an executive to be empty and unsatisfying. In moving away from the life of luxury, she feels a greater sense of personal integrity and solidarity with the poor. "We live in a consumer-oriented society that is forever on the hustle with you— telling you what you need and what you want and what you have and shouldn't have, and what the Dow Jones's are having and what not, and so life is very distracting and you can be easily seduced. . . . But I live a very good life. I mean, I'm basically a hedonist. I manage to get everything I want and need or whatever. It's just that I've learned that I want different things and I don't need what I'm told I need."

But far from feeling that his business success has impeded his work on behalf of the poor, Cabell Brand sees it as an important means toward that end. As a successful and well-known businessman, he has been able to mobilize the business community to collaborate with the public sector to create programs such as the Comprehensive Health Investment Program that provides health care to poor children. On a more personal level, his financial resources have allowed him to contribute materially as well. For example, he and his wife donated an extensive and valuable collection of African art to an African-American cultural center that TAP helped to establish. In contrast, Allison McCrea feels that she can be more effective in her work by avoiding the seductions of the material world and "standing with the oppressed and fighting by their sides."

Cabell Brand offers no apologies for his involvement in business and his financial success in that arena. All of his social action work is premised on the belief that the American free enterprise system can work very effectively and that people need to be helped to take advantage of the strengths of that system. The problem, from Brand's point of view, is that the best parts of the system have not been extended to all groups. He works to extend the logic of the system to other people, a logic he fully endorses. McCrea differs from Brand in that she feels that much in the American economic and political system is inherently exploitative. This means that her fight for social justice involves a fundamental questioning of the existing system rather than an extension of that system to those who have not fully enjoyed its benefits. Clearly, these differences in political philosophy imply different personal and political choices.

As a man who believes in the American free enterprise system, Cabell Brand is devoted to making that system work for as many people as possible. He values hard work and believes that people should be prepared to take advantage of the opportunities life offers them. But he is aware that the system is often unfair in the differential opportunities it offers. He believes that it is in everyone's long-range self-interest to bring the disadvantaged more fully into the system. With energy, enthusiasm, optimism, and the skills characteristic of the successful businessman that he is, Brand has become ever more deeply engaged over the past twenty-five years in the struggle to pull people out of poverty and into the "least worst system in the world."

CHAPTER 10

Positivity and Hopefulness

Moral commitment may be celebrated in the abstract by socially conscious persons and institutions, but society does not always reward those who actually dedicate themselves to moral causes. The efforts of our exemplars have often been greeted by indifference, disdain, even anger. Year after year, the work that moral exemplars do can include giving away what little money they have; immersing themselves in unbearably squalid conditions to feed and clothe the destitute; caring for the ill, for drug-addicted babies, for the wretched of the earth; raising disturbed and highly rebellious adolescents; and fighting against powerful, hostile forces of injustice. Often these acts of goodwill will reap for them nothing more than ingratitude or betrayal.

Kay Hardie is a journalist (formerly a teacher) who raised thirteen foster children from broken homes. Although ultimately successful, these efforts met appalling challenges along the way. The children came from poor families, were troubled, and had a history of maltreatment. Ms. Hardie's account of her experience with these children sounds like an ordeal that would try anyone's endurance:

> Most of them had been abused in one way or another. Some of them were suicidal. Some of them had long, long [police] records, obviously acting out all kinds of things. And when they walked into our house, they did not stop lying and stealing and all of that. They didn't stop that survival behavior because they walked into our house. It went on for a while. And we had as a family to deal with all that. And the drug thing and all this.

Some of the kids were very rebellious because of their experiences with parents who had abused them. But we always had a pretty light rein anyway on the kids, and so we trusted them until they knocked us down, so to speak. They didn't, of course, knock us down physically. But they, you know, I can remember standing in the office one day at the school where I taught because my husband had called me just to make absolutely sure, but what he had discovered was that one of our kids had taken checks from our checkbook and written a number of small checks at a little local store. And I can remember the tears just running down my face standing in the office at school, and so we had to start over with that kid. And one of the kids also stole from one of my dear, dear friends in the neighborhood. One of my kids stole their coin collection and spent it at the bowling alley. . . . One of the girls who became our daughter was . . . from a family that believed she was demon possessed and began to tell her when she was three years old that she was possessed of a demon and no one else in the family must speak to her. And she was very brave and very abused: physically, psychologically, and every other way. . . . She tried to kill herself twice in our house. And she meant it. You don't drink two glasses of paint thinner and not mean to kill yourself.

Apart from these hair-raising incidents, Kay spent years feeding, laundering, and generally mothering as many as seven difficult teenagers at a time. All the while, she worked full time as a high school teacher. She recalls:

Finally I said, "If anybody else comes, they've got to have different underwear. I can't keep all the underwear sorted." . . . We had two cars and five drivers [during] a couple of summers, and people sort of had to sign up for the cars. But we tried to lay on as few rules as we could and to make the rules very important and to make the rules stick. And one of them was, "There will be no drugs in this house." We didn't always have no drugs in the house, but we found out about it because our kids knew we had to know. I remember doing a lot of praying about those kids, about the foster children particularly who, believe me, needed a lot of prayer. And I did a lot of praying for patience. I did a lot of praying for strength because I was tired a lot. A lot of times when they wanted to talk it was about one o'clock in the morning. And I would get up and teach school the next morning.

How does Kay Hardie represent these ordeals to herself? For one thing, not at all as an ordeal. In fact, Kay considered herself privileged to have had such an opportunity—a sentiment expressed by almost all of our moral exemplars. In Ms. Hardie's recollection of the troubled children that she raised there is a tangible sense of gratitude for the experience and the chance to serve. She speaks of her time with them in this way: "These were the funniest, most heart-rending, most wrenching, most beautiful years we had. And as a family, all those words would apply to the experience. . . . We were grateful for all of [the children], the natural born and the ones who came to us like gifts. . . . We were just, we were pretty lucky.

Many of our exemplars grew up in poverty themselves and led lives marked by adversity, discrimination, frustration, injustice, untimely bereavement, and other misfortunes—much of it socially engendered. Most of these people have continued to live humbly through the present time. Their commitments led them into activities that not only proved grueling but also provided them with little financial reward or security. Yet almost without exception these people report that they have been wonderfully happy. They express gratitude for what they perceive as their fortunate lives, seemingly unfazed by the difficulties they forever need to overcome.

Irma Johnson, for example, was sixteen when her mother died, and she grew up with very little money or family support. As a black woman, she encountered racism early and often in her life. She married young, and she and her husband were determined to work hard to provide their children with the best education possible. But Irma's husband died of cancer, leaving her with two small children and no income. She began taking care of other people's children, many of them full-time boarders, to make enough money to feed and clothe her own. After several years of this demanding life, Irma took on an even greater challenge. She began to take in babies born to drug-addicted mothers, raising them until they could be reunited with their mothers, usually at age three or four. She established a nationally known center to care for these infants and has now raised over six hundred children there. When the infants arrive at the center, many of them are terribly ill from the effects of their mothers' drug abuse while pregnant. Irma Johnson has run her center for over twenty-five years now, putting in long hours, with uncertain funding and frequent confrontations with various big city bureaucracies. While comfortable, pleasant, and clean inside, the center is located in the midst of an urban neighborhood that in recent years has come to resemble the aftermath of a war.

Mother Johnson, as she is called, radiates serenity and goodwill. A pressing crisis (not at all unusual at her center) made her many hours late for our appointment with her, yet when she arrived, any impatience that we were feeling dissolved in the warmth of this tiny woman's smile. When asked how she has coped with the difficulties she has encountered in her life, Irma replied: "I really don't think life has been that hard. I have great faith in God, and I think that He helps you and gives you what you need to do the things that He wants you to do. I've always prayed and whatever I wanted I always received. . . . And I try to do the right thing and help everybody— anybody else that comes in and not only the children—but to try to help everybody and keep smiling.

We asked, "When you say you keep smiling, is that because you feel like smiling or because you feel like you *should* smile?"

I feel like smiling and I think I should smile. People have so much trouble and life is so hard. Now they don't want to meet somebody and your face is all frowned and you're always giving out bad vibes, you know. So you keep smiling and if you do that, then you bring them in and it's so nice. When people walk away or leave me, I want them to go away with a good feeling. "She was eighty-two years old and at least she wasn't an old crab," you know. Make them feel good. . . . And life has just been beautiful! People say, "Oh, life is so hard now!" There's mean people, but there's a lot of good people in this world. There's some very good people—white, black, and every color—and they take care of us, and I lead a good life. And the children lead a good life. . . . By seeing the children and knowing that they're happy, I'm really happy.

In just about all of our moral exemplars, we observed a strong, enduring, and general *positivity* toward their lives, toward their work, and toward other people. What do we mean by "positivity"? First, we are referring to an enjoyment of life, especially an enjoyment of the work that they are doing—whether it is fighting for racial justice, helping the poor, or working for peace. A well-known neurologist who works fifteen-hour days in an effort to reform the policies and practices of medical ethics and has given up having a family for his work says, "I just love what I am doing. I would do it for nothing." Patrick Donaldson, a Catholic bishop who has devoted his priesthood to skid-row alcoholics, troubled youth, and criminals, says, "I don't know any priest in this country, in this world—I'm saying this world and I'm including John Paul the pope—who's had a priesthood as interesting as mine. Adventure, what an adventure! I didn't know what I was getting into.'' We have already quoted one advocate for the poor and homeless who says frequently, "I love the work we do."

Positivity also connotes hopefulness and optimism. Emmylou Davis, whom we met in Chapter 4, established and runs a multifaceted social service organization in the Watts section of Los Angeles. "Sweet Emmylou," as she is called, speaks of the importance of hope in her efforts to reclaim the lost youth of her low-income community.

> The ultimate goal is to bring out the best in a young person, because everybody has a gift. God gave that to you. Whether you know it or not, it's a good gift down there. Our job is to bring that best out of them. It's just a matter of finding it. And you say to yourself, "Oh well, it's here. I'll find it after a while, but it's here. So you never give up. And that's because you have hope. Hope keeps it from being so difficult. Anything that's really difficult is because the hope is gone. But if you have hope of doing a thing, then it's not difficult, it might be hard, but not really difficult. [Interviewer: But do you ever have trouble maintaining your hope?] Never! [You never do?] Never! [You never get discouraged?] Never! No! It's a challenge. And the harder the challenge is, the more you dig in.

Positivity, however, is not a naive optimism. It is not a denial of problems or an unrealistic, sentimental view of people. Cabell Brand is optimistic about poverty and believes that we could drastically reduce U.S. poverty within a generation if programs like TAP were put in place more widely. He recognizes fully the many barriers to this progress but treats them as problems to be solved rather than as causes for discouragement and despair. Although he loves life and approaches it with tremendous joy, he is also realistic. As TAP executive director Ted Edlich says,

> Well, I think Cabell's a realist. He's very much of a realist. But I don't think I've seen him so much discouraged as disappointed. Because Cabell doesn't discourage really easy. But I have seen him disappointed. And he was very disappointed with the [cutbacks] in programs for low-income people. And so with Reagan both tripling the debt and also cutting back 90 percent in the

housing area and really trying to eliminate the community action
programs and a host of other things, there's no question he's
experienced disappointment. But he's not. . . . Cabell's not one
to let one avenue being blocked leave him blocked. But he's been
disappointed, and Cabell's pretty open with his disappointment.
He's not a Pollyanna. You know, he's not "Mr. Happy" or
"Everything's going great." I mean, he's very real and because
of that, people are able to identify with him.

Another of our exemplars, David Linsky, has expressed the same
optimistic realism. When asked what keeps him going in the face of
the difficult challenges of international diplomacy, he says,

> Well, I guess I'm an optimist by nature. I guess by nature I tend
> to welcome the tough challenges. What keeps me going is, for
> one, a sense of optimism. Two, a sense of welcoming challenge
> and the harder the better. . . . And above all else that whatever
> it is, it's worth doing. That it is better to have tried and failed
> than not to have tried. That I feel better inside myself for having
> made an effort even though it doesn't succeed. . . . I don't know
> how I got to be this way. I think I have a profound faith in this
> country. My parents were Jewish immigrants. And what I've
> seen happen in my life not only supports my optimism but rein-
> forces my conviction that you can do well by doing right.

INTERVIEWER: What is it that allows you to be optimistic at this particular point?

MR. LINSKY: Well, to be an optimist is not to be foolish. I recognize
the problems and I recognize the reasons for concern and anxiety and
why one has to be troubled about some of the things that have happened.
And one has to be worried about what might happen. Having said all
that, I guess my optimism arises from the fact that we have shown great
capacity to weather very difficult problems and situations and emerge
steady on our feet. I think we're going to go through some more rough
periods again, perhaps some very rough periods. . . . But we muddle
through, we do get there, and we tend to be right, in my view, more
often than we are wrong. And we are strong enough, and decent enough
as a people, and bright enough deep down, to find our way. I feel, for
example, when you put side by side all the things that are happening that
are reasons for concern and you look at one thing side by side with them,
the development of arms control, we've made tremendous strides in the

right direction at long last in this one important, vital area. So for me, it's not scratching around and trying to find something good. It's realistically trying to enjoy all that's happened. . . .

Positivity may mean setting aside the bad events that occur, either by not focusing on them or by finding a way to construe them in a hopeful way; or it may mean finding a way to turn them to one's advantage; or it may mean accepting them as challenges that must be met. Our exemplars are brilliantly capable of making the best of a bad situation. As we saw in Chapter 8, Mother Waddles is highly conscious of her ability to do this. She describes, for example, how she turned the flooding of her offices into an important fund-raising opportunity. She tells how she has come to appreciate her experiences as a teen mother, welfare recipient, and widow for the deeper understanding they provided of others in these predicaments. She was also able to respond without despair to her son's suicide, an event that had occurred just six months before the interview; and her interview expresses a palpable sense of well-being in spite of her real sorrow and frustration about her son's death.

Emmylou Davis tells a story that demonstrates the positivity and resourcefulness that is so typical of our exemplars. Mrs. Davis and her Families in the Inner City program had worked for over two years with thirty-nine teenagers who had been sent to her because they were considered troublemakers and were not doing well in school. She and the program staff worked six days a week with these young people to get them back on the right track. They succeeded so well that they managed to have all thirty-nine accepted to a college in South Carolina, with full scholarship support. They lacked only the money to pay for transportation from California to South Carolina. Mrs. Davis describes the struggle to get the youngsters to their college destination:

> I would have loved for them to have went on a plane, because they had never gone out of the city, number one. And if you're going to build up a person's self-esteem, give them the best. But then we couldn't get a plane. I went to the mayor's office and the man there says, "Well, we're going to help you." And a week later, they come to me and says, "Well, you didn't start on time, so . . ." Now, this is in August and they were ready to go to school in September. He says, "So what you do is by June of next year, we would have had time to have all the trans-

portation and everything, and they can go in then.'' I said, ''No, you can't do that. I'll lose half of these kids between now and June of next year, they won't make it. They qualify now.'' So that's where they left me. . . .

We found a bus that would take them for $6,500. And I thought about well, you know, what could I mortgage, what could I give up, do something, they've got to go. Didn't have the money, so I called different agencies that I know. They said, ''Well, we already give our charity, you know. We've already gave our charity for this year. Catch us next year.'' Everything was told against next year. Now during these times, you can easily get upset. But you have to keep in mind, ''God didn't bring me this far with these kids to let them down. We just have to keep on, something will have to give.'' And so, finally, we have narrowed it down to five hours before it's time to go. Now, if they don't leave this particular day, they can't get there for school on Monday morning. Takes us three days to ride down there on the bus. We must leave Friday. Now, it got on to 5:00 in the afternoon, and everything get quiet. All the kids had moved in with their suitcases and everything. 'Cause I said, ''Yeah, we're going. Oh, we're going, come on.'' Finally, it's 5:00 in the afternoon, and everything get quiet. The parents are here, the suitcases are, and some moved in here the night before and slept here. Five o'clock in the afternoon and I called and the people says, ''Oh, we don't have any money . . .'' And finally I said, ''You know what? We got to do something. So one thing I know we can do. Surely, we can leave here walking. Now they tell me the way to go is south, so that's the way we going to head. So what we going to do, we going to leave here and walk to the freeway. And we going to hitchhike all the way. Because we got to get to college by Monday!''

In fact, the young people did make it to college, and without having to hitchhike. At the last minute, the bus company decided to give them a free ride. Mrs. Davis did not anticipate this but was not particularly surprised when it happened. One way or another, she was determined that her charges would reach college on time.

Only two of the exemplars in our study, Aline Burchell and Sharon Crandall, exhibited an approach to life that was significantly at odds with this picture of positivity, optimism, joy, and gratitude. Both are relatively (compared with others in our study) young women (one in her forties, the other in her fifties) who had spent many years devoted to social reform, one fighting for peace and nuclear disarmament, the other for civil liberties. Although each had contributed a great deal in her chosen sphere, neither seemed to take a great deal of satisfaction from what she had achieved. Both had been embattled, struggling not only against the forces of their oppositions but also against other members of their own movements. Both were fueled in their work by anger—anger at injustice, anger at those who abuse their power, anger at hypocrisy, and anger at men. Both felt that they had been double-crossed by men within their own ranks, and neither felt she could ever forgive the betrayal. Neither felt much satisfaction with her life overall, and both were given to spells of despair and depression. Although they had to maintain some belief in the possibility of change in order to go forward with their work, their vision of the world was much gloomier and less optimistic than we saw in the other exemplars.

The first of these two women, Aline Burchell, a peace activist, said that she considers the United States to be on the wrong course in many ways: "I fear that it's going to end up in total disaster for the world. And unless we take hold of ourselves and take some moral responsibility and have some compassion, and stop this addiction to greed and money, the earth is doomed."

The second, Sharon Crandall, is a lawyer who has devoted herself so completely to pressing for better protection of civil liberties that she has had time for little else in her life, including important personal relationships. She also expresses pessimism that the world's injustices can ever be set right. "That's exactly my reservation at this point in my life. Are there any political solutions? Are there any? It's no longer clear to me that there are. I wish I were more of a historian and knew more about the development of various movements and causes. Perhaps then I would take some hope, you know, from the long view. . . . Maybe if you can take the very long view, there is some reason to hope that there are political solutions. But looking just at my own experience, it's not clear to me that there are."

Along with this pessimism is a deep weariness, a lack of satisfaction with her life, and a sense of despair. "I used to have a kind of intensity. But boy that was so long ago, and it's hard to remember, and I'm all jaded and cynical now, and I was not then." In thinking back on her life over the past twenty years, she wonders whether she would make the same choices if she had it to do over again.

Well, I do think about whether I would do it all again. And the best answer I can give is there are days when I would and there are days when I would not, when I feel like I'm going to break under it. I tend to crash on weekends. My job keeps me up and moving during the week, then all of a sudden on the weekend I look down the years and look backwards and it seems very despairing to me. And on those days, let me tell you, I couldn't say that I'd go the same route again. On those days I'd be inclined to say, ''This is going to kill me'' and doing it over again I might make the compromises that I had to make to survive and be less alone. At this point, see, there's no turning back. You don't have the option, at a point, of undoing the way you've molded yourself. You can't go back and say, ''Oh, well, God,'' you know, ''this turned out to be a lot more expensive than I had anticipated, so I'm going to change myself so as to have the things I need.''

Aside from these two, negativity and doubt were uncommon experiences for our moral exemplars. What sustains their pervasive sense of hopefulness? How do they establish and maintain their positivity?

Many of our exemplars are sustained in their work by support from those close to them or by a strong sense of community with others who work with them. Virginia Durr mentions this as one of the most exciting things about the civil rights movement. Cabell Brand speaks of the critical role of his wife in inspiring and sustaining him in his work with TAP and of the importance of his collaboration with the TAP executive directors and staff. Luisa Coll has risked prison and even death for her work hiding and integrating into American life political refugees from Central America. She speaks of the importance to her of the support she receives from the refugees themselves and others in the sanctuary movement:

I guess you would call them [the refugees] prophets—those who really, truly give their lives on a daily basis to the little ones. And yes, I know many, many of them. And I think that is what sustains me—the fact that, spiritually, I feel this tremendous connection to this energy. . . . I don't feel alone. I don't feel isolated. Even the worst pain that I can go through, because working the way I work, I go through tremendous pain on a daily basis, but the pain becomes bearable when I know that there are others who are carrying the pain along with me. We are helping each other.

Most of our exemplars speak of the importance of solidarity with other people and a tremendous enjoyment of working with people as among the great joys and sustaining forces in their lives. We also saw a special skill or ability with people in almost all of our exemplars. Recall, for example, Ted Edlich's description of Cabell Brand as an extrovert who loves making contact with people and Suzie Valadez's or Mother Waddles's gregariousness and skill in garnering support for their missions.

When a sense of community is lacking, as it was for Sharon Crandall, its absence is a serious impediment to a lasting sense of inspiration and commitment.

> Perhaps the gravest disappointment I've experienced is that initially one of the things I longed for was a community. And I thought that this kind of work would put me in a community. And, you know, I would be aligned with and intimately connected to like-minded people. Well, I've found myself in conflict with them more often than I have felt intimate with them. And one of the things that I've learned about myself in the last couple of years, my life has been lived primarily by force of will. My willpower is very substantial, and I've gotten a long way on it. But it is giving out. One of the things that I'm learning is you can't just by forcing yourself, keep going indefinitely. Something's got to feed you at some point, or you're going to fall off the train. And I'm getting real marginal with that lack of community, that lack of intimacy with people that I had assumed when I went into the business, that was going to be provided. That's a real killer. That's a real killer.

We have seen in the cases described here both some exceptionally joyous people as well as two people who have experienced their share of anger, bitterness, and despair. These people represent ends of a continuum; it is clear that having a positive approach to life is not an all or nothing phenomenon. In our study, however, the sample was greatly skewed to the positive end. The great majority of our exemplars (seventeen out of twenty-three) showed an extremely positive approach to life, and only two showed real pessimism, anger, and bitterness. Of the remaining four cases, three were difficult to assess with regard to positivity. The interviews were either ambiguous or silent on this issue. The fourth "in-between" case was Virginia Durr. Mrs. Durr showed the same optimism, love of her work, and ability to make the best difficult circumstances that we saw in the others, but she also displayed a good deal of anger and regret. In this sense, she showed characteristics of both positivity and negativity, sometimes tilting one way, sometimes the other.

The exemplars' joyful absorption in their work is recognizable as the "flow" experience that we discussed in Chapter 4. Like Csikszentmihalyi's athletes, artists, and scientists, our exemplars report becoming so deeply immersed in their activities that they invest their sense of themselves in them. They gain a feeling of exhilaration, lose their concern over material and mundane considerations, ignore the press of time, overcome frustration, turn away discouragement, and come away with a profound sense of satisfaction.

Luisa Coll, for example, when asked what she considers to be her greatest successes, said, "Oh, goodness. I don't think in terms of successes at all. I think in terms of life. And living life to the fullest, I think, is enjoying every moment of what I am doing. And feeling the pain of every moment that I have to feel pain." She went on in response to a question about whether she felt she had been an influence on other people: "It's nothing that I feel because I am so involved in living my life and sharing my life with others that I don't stop to think of what I am doing. It's when other people bring it to my attention that I become aware of some of these things. But I'm not aware of them myself."

It is likely that many of the personal qualities that enable Csikszentmihalyi's creative people to experience flow are similar to those that enable our exemplars to carry out their commitments with a positive and hopeful attitude. The dedication, vigor, and openness to experience and new learning and the strong ties with friends, coworkers, and communities all characterize both our exemplars and Csikszentmihalyi's creative people. As we noted in Chapter 4, however, the "flow" arising from moral activities is unlike other types of flow. This is because the experience is centered around moral and spiritual values that transcend the self. As a consequence, the dynamics that establish and maintain the flow may be quite dissimilar to those that, for example, enable athletes to feel flow while striving to break a record. In many people who pursue their goals with undivided attention and thus experience flow, the external goals are intertwined with egoistic concerns for reputation, personal achievement, and the like. These more egoistic concerns cannot be discerned in our exemplars. For a moral exemplar, flowlike experiences derive from implementing their enduring commitments, and these commitments reflect a positive framework of values that anchor the exemplar's life. The exemplar's activities have neither worth nor meaning apart from these values.

In his book *Flow*,[1] Csikszentmihalyi offers suggestions designed to help the reader attain this state of mind. This may give the impression that people achieve flow by pursuing it directly, but it is unlikely that Csikszentmihalyi's creative people were seeking flow. Rather, they were seeking scientific truth, artistic expression, athletic excellence, or even recognition and power. Certainly our exemplars do not directly seek the experience of flow, although they may frequently attain it. Exemplars may control their inner experience so as to avoid fear and discouragement: This they often do in order to withstand pressures that could weaken their commitments. But we never observed an exemplar working to develop a happier attitude for its own sake. The moral values were primary, and if the pursuit of these values leads to misery and dejection rather than exhilaration, so be it. This orientation makes all the more remarkable the pervasive positivity that characterizes most of our exemplars. What makes it possible?

We know that all people face disappointments with their lives, with other people, and with themselves. All people encounter frustrations, large and small, barriers to achieving their most cherished goals, and setbacks even when things seem to be going well. We can find many occasions for cynicism about human societies and human nature; we can cite many reasons for disliking and mistrusting the people who get in our way. It is difficult to maintain a consistently positive approach to life in the face of all these opportunities for negativity and pessimism.

Yet positivity is clearly very desirable and adaptive. A positivity that includes optimism, love, and joy is also closely linked with morality, as we see in the lives of our exemplars. Some aspects of this kind of attitude, such as charity, have a moral quality themselves. Some support and make possible an enduring commitment to others or to social justice. Without a real love of the activity itself, energy will flag eventually. Without optimism, demoralization ensues. Without an ability to set aside or make the best of difficult circumstances, progress will soon be blocked.

The great majority of our exemplars approach life with stubborn positivity. How do they do it? They use a variety of psychological mechanisms and supports to maintain this attitude. Their positive approach to life is played out in a number of different ways that work together as a system to maintain the overall approach. Some of these are present in all of the cases, some are especially salient in particular people. All of the various manifestations can be seen as directly contributing to the exemplars' ability to maintain their hope, commitment, and dedication in the face of the many difficult challenges they faced. The exemplars are very aware of the importance of these patterns of behavior in helping them to sustain their commitment, sometimes making conscious decisions to react in a positive way rather than to give in to feelings of fear, anger, or discouragement. As we discussed in Chapter 4, Emmylou Davis speaks of the need to "give herself the positive answer" in order to avoid becoming discouraged. She avoids the word *can't* because she believes that she can do whatever she needs to do, and she reminds herself of the strength that comes from reliance on God.

An important component of positivity for many of our exemplars is a lively sense of humor, which helps them keep a sense of perspective on themselves, their work, and other people. This is often linked to humility, with not taking themselves and their mission too seriously. The ability to see oneself as contributing to an ongoing effort, not a savior who is out to change the world, is mentioned by many of the exemplars as a factor in their stamina and persistence. A willingness to poke fun at themselves can help to maintain their humility. We see this, for example, in Allison McCrea. Her awareness of the importance of not taking herself too seriously is evident in this description she gives of her role in the antipoverty movement:

> You could simply be one of the gang and just kind of join in the struggle, which is really the best lesson I ever learned in Roxbury. You didn't lead the struggle, you didn't follow it. It was there, and you were part of it. And that was a very good lesson to learn, because that was the reason I never burned out. A lot of white people, when they went to Roxbury, figured they were going to clean it up by Thursday. And I had the advantage of being taken into the hearts of the black people in the neighborhood. And their kindness to me, and their generosity and their humanity and their sense of humor collectively was my salvation. . . . Henry Nouwen, in *Calling in Rome,* talks about the acts of history like a circus. And there's the big center stage and there are the side ones. And I had wanted to look at myself as being center stage. And I realized that I was on one of the side ones, one of the clowns that would stumble and fall and get up and start again. But the interesting thing about the clowns was that they were always there. And they would never make the center stage, but they would always be there to remind people of the humanity, to remind you of what a fool you are, to remind you of how ridiculous we human beings are.

This humility and sense of perspective runs throughout the interview. And for her as well as many of our other exemplars, humor is a way to avoid the continuing bitterness and anger that we have seen in a small number of our people. She says: "I love the things we do. How effective are we? (Laughs.) What we do probably doesn't amount to very much of anything—in the long run. We haven't stopped homelessness, we haven't stopped hunger, we haven't stopped rotten things from happening. But that doesn't allow us the luxury of walking away from it. We are committed. Our destiny is a commitment to good and we may never achieve it. So, you know, you take your laughs where you can find them and you hang on to the rainbow when you see it."

Contrast McCrea's description of her role with that of Aline Burchell, mired in negativity and humorlessness. When asked about her goals, Ms. Burchell replies, "To save the world." In talking about her role in the movement, she says, "That's *my* organization. . . . I did the whole thing." Later she says, "I was too far out in front. . . . And when I had to leave for a while, someone said to me, 'Who's going to fill your shoes?' And I really couldn't think of anyone, and it absolutely devastated me."

For many of the exemplars, it is their sense of humor that helps them bounce back from disappointments, discouragement, and other setbacks. Recall the wry statement Mother Waddles made to the press just as her utilities were about to be shut off for lack of payment, "You send out hate, you get hate back. You send out love, you get love back. Course that doesn't do anything with the gas bill." Laughter also prevents these dedicated people from becoming depressed and dispirited by the grim conditions of poverty and injustice with which they deal day after day. As Mother Waddles has said, if you can't keep a sense of humor, antipoverty work can get "sad, hard, pitiful."

Of all the capacities that contribute to positivity in moral exemplars, the one most directly linked to their framework of values is the capacity to forgive. Forgiveness and mercy are widely recognized values in Western moral and religious traditions, and they were endorsed by practically all of our exemplars. Nevertheless, forgiveness and mercy are hard to sustain in the crucible of real life. Just like the rest of us, moral exemplars encounter persons who are difficult to forgive. In fact, because of the nature of their work, moral exemplars more than most are tested in their capacities for charitable responding—a special irony, since charity is often high in their priority of moral values.

Everyone, of course, encounters betrayal, ingratitude, or lack of cooperation at some point in life. But those working to make the world a better place are especially likely to face these painful realities. Perhaps they are ruffling feathers by challenging the status quo. Or they may be working for the sake of hostile people who have been abused in some way and therefore strike back, wholly inappropriately, at those who are trying to help them. Those who are trying to make the world a better place may need to ask others to join with them to help, and they are frequently denied that help and support. If they respond to these things with enduring anger, the accumulated bitterness can undermine their persistence, especially if the anger is directed toward the people they are trying to help or collaborate with. For this reason, many of our exemplars talk about forgiveness as a central personal goal.

According to Charleszetta Waddles, the biggest challenge that she has faced is to forgive time and time again the people who respond to her help with ingratitude, betrayal, or an unwillingness to help themselves. Suzie Valadez and Kay Hardie also talk of having to forgive those who do not immediately respond in a constructive way to their efforts to help. These and the others who are able to be especially forgiving do so by extending love and understanding to the offenders. As Kay Hardie puts it, "When they walked in our house, they did not stop lying, and stealing, and all of that. They didn't stop that survival behavior because they walked in our house. It went on for a while. And we as a family had to deal with all that."

Luisa Coll says the following about the ingratitude and lack of cooperation she encounters in some of the refugees she helps and her response to that ingratitude:

MRS. COLL: You know, I understand them. I understand why they act the way they act. They have lacked so much, and they have been victimized for so long, that they are not able to really, truly act upon their good nature. Consequently, they have been victims of what has been passed on to them in terms of patterns, mindsets, and behavior, that this is what they're doing. So I forgive them. I don't hold any grudges against them. . . . because I understand where they're coming from. And I understand that if I were to be in their position, I would be doing the same thing.

INTERVIEWER: And so it doesn't change your feelings toward them?

MRS. COLL: No, not at all. No, not at all. On the contrary, I want to give more to that person, if that person is willing to open up and to accept that there are some limitations. I am very willing to help that person. And there have been situations where . . . yes, there have been people who have become very aggressive toward me. I have been threatened with death several times by several of the people who have been here.

INTERVIEWER: By the people you've helped?

MRS. COLL: Yes, but, at the same time, I have never spoken against anybody in terms of punishment for their actions against me. Because I don't believe that that's the way it should be at all. And I really truly believe that we are products of our society, and if we are not able to really truly find the truth and the light, then we will continue to act out the roles and patterns society imposed on us. And a lot of people are victims of that. And I remember several incidents where one new man moved into this house two different times. And it was very difficult to try to help him overcome what was going on. But he was very very traumatized, and he was drinking very heavily. And he was not listening to reason. But we did as much as we could for him. And then, we just had to let go. Because we are all limited . . . but then, at the same time, in accepting these people and understanding that they really don't know what it is that they're doing.

Suzie Valadez shows the same kind of patience and acceptance toward the young people of the dump who continue to act up.

INTERVIEWER: When you're dealing with kids, no matter how much you try to give good values or the spiritual message, they're still going to go out and get in trouble anyway, regardless of all you do for them. How do you feel about that? Do you feel bitter or angry at them for not being grateful for what you do?

MRS. VALDEZ: No, no, I don't. I know they're more grateful than they're ungrateful. So you cannot be mad at them because of their . . . how they grew in the family. They didn't teach them anything, see. So you cannot be mad at the children.

INTERVIEWER: Doesn't it hurt you when they don't respond?

MRS. VALDEZ: No, no. I have learned to take everything normal because of the upbringing of the families. The families are not like ours over here. We teach them manners, we teach them how to behave, how to answer, you know. Over there sometimes they . . . you don't get a good morning. There's some, like maybe in lines, out of fifty you only get two thank-you's. And every time it's the same two.

INTERVIEWER: And that doesn't bother you?

MRS. VALDEZ: No, no. Because I mean I've dealt with them. Some of them they don't go to school, but there are two or three children who are very special because they always say "Mama Suzie, *muchas gracias.*"

The exemplars who seemed especially forgiving were women who were devoted Christians and who were helping low-income people directly rather than working at a societal level for institutional change. Their ability to forgive was linked in their minds to their religious faith—as was true for Luisa Coll:

And I can see Jesus on the cross saying "Forgive them, for they . know not what they do." Because we don't know. We really don't. We're so ignorant. So many many times, we just act things out because we have been programmed that way. But if they are given a chance—and I have learned to give second and third and fourth chances. And I have been rewarded in those instances by the people that I have been willing to give a second and a third and a fourth chance to. And they have proven that yes, once they are really able to tap into that goodness in themselves and to find that self-image based on the love that God has for us, and that he didn't create junk . . . that he created goodness in all of us. Those persons are doing perfectly well now. And they're raising their families and they're learning more and more of who they are and who God is in their lives.

Mother Waddles also describes her ability to forgive in religious terms.

INTERVIEWER: When you say you need to keep forgiving people, how is it that you're able to do that?

MRS. WADDLES: Because I want to. You can't do this if you don't want to do it. You can't do this if you feel it's against you. I say "Lordy, how many times must I do this?" (Laughs.) And then I think about the times I forgive my own children that came from my womb. So I say to myself, inside myself, "Do it for Him."

INTERVIEWER: It's not so easy, though, I guess for most people.

MRS. WADDLES: No.

INTERVIEWER: Maybe not so easy for you either.

MRS. WADDLES: Not always. (Laughs.) I'll practice a little more. I'll commit myself a little more. I'll pray to myself a little more to let me be. And let me see. You know, say, "Well, maybe you don't believe me—prove me." So as I go along, I prove you. I prove the work. I prove the answers, and the proof comes. It works.

In contrast, there were three women (Aline Burchell, Sharon Crandall, and Virginia Durr) for whom the inability to forgive those who had betrayed them was an important theme. As we have already seen, these three women experienced a good deal of anger. All three were fighting for justice at the societal level rather than extending charity or offering help on an individual level. It is probably not accidental that the three people who show anger and bitterness even to the point of not forgiving were fighters for justice. Such people may need to use righteous anger as a tool in their fight. They must perceive the conflict between people that constitutes the injustice, they must take sides in the conflicts, and they must tolerate the anger and outrage that they arouse as they challenge the status quo.

Personality theorist Rae Carlson distinguishes two kinds of altruists, which she calls reformers and helpers.[2] These two types exhibit distinctive personality styles and emotional reactions. The reformers are oriented to correcting social injustice. They tend to show a zest for combat and adventure and are much more likely to express anger or contempt. The helpers are motivated by a desire to alleviate suffering. They are more nurturant and tend to identify with the distress of the people they are helping. The helpers are less likely to exhibit anger than the reformers. Clearly, Dr. Burchell, Ms. Crandall, and Mrs. Durr match Carlson's description of reformers, whereas Mrs. Waddles, Mrs. Valadez, and Ms. Hardie correspond to Carlson's helpers.

We noticed an interesting twist to the anger of the three women we are calling reformers. Not only did they express outrage against the people they identified as true enemies of justice, people who created the arms race, pursued repressive social policies, or fought to maintain racial divisions, they reserved their most unyielding bitterness for the people on their own side of the struggle whom they felt had let down the cause. For example, Virginia Durr's most fiery anger was directed at the liberal lawyers in 1930s Washington, D.C., who expressed revulsion for McCarthyism but turned their backs on those who were accused of having communist ties.

We think that this phenomenon is an indication of the high standards of personal integrity our exemplars held for both themselves and others. It is one thing to oppose a righteous cause out of ignorance, fear, or self-interest, but it is another thing entirely to endorse the cause knowing full well that it is just, and then to betray both the cause and those who give their lives to the cause by withdrawing when times get tough. Our reformers greeted such betrayal with their most refined contempt.

Since all of the women who were especially forgiving were strongly religious, and since all of these but one explicitly tied their capacity for forgiveness to their Christian faith, it is revealing that all three women who could not forgive their betrayers were nonreligious. Neither Aline Burchell nor Sharon Crandall draw on a religious perspective at all. Perhaps coincidentally, perhaps not, neither sees her continuing anger as a problem. Instead, they consider the anger to be fully justified and see no reason to set it aside.

As for Virginia Durr, approaching her ninetieth year, she feels bothered by her continuing bitterness and wishes often that she could overcome it. She sees religion as an important part of this effort. Her struggle to forgive those who betrayed her and her husband is closely linked with her struggle to renew her faith in a benevolent God. In her spiritual struggle, Virginia Durr refuses to take on an easy religious faith that would gloss over the ugly world realities that she has seen; yet she looks to faith as a means for finding the good in her enemies—and possibly even in these ugly world realities.

Many of our exemplars express their positivity as a deep gratitude for the satisfaction they get from their work. Reminiscent of this is a comment Bishop Desmond Tutu made to us at Brown University when we mentioned our study. Bishop Tutu spoke of the prevalence of this kind of grateful attitude in the exemplary people he has known. He attributes the attitude to a particular way of thinking about what you are doing, a way of thinking that he shares with the others he has observed. He said that, in his view, Mother Teresa does not look upon her own acts as favors for the people she is helping. She feels instead that these people are doing *her* a favor by offering the opportunity for such a satisfying spiritual experience. Accordingly, she does not expect the people she helps to be grateful. Nor is she offended if they are not grateful.

Bishop Tutu spoke of seeing Mother Teresa smiling lovingly at a dying baby she was holding. She told Bishop Tutu that she was grateful to the child for giving her such a feeling of love, happiness, and satisfaction. Bishop Tutu interprets the capacity to relate to people this way as springing from a spiritual perspective that allows people to find God in everybody, their enemies as well as those who have little value in the eyes of the world. This perspective springs directly from the Christian tradition, though it need not be Christian or even explicitly religious: In some people it might consist of an ability to treasure the spark of humanity in everyone. Because this perspective leads to a feeling of solidarity even with one's persecutors, it prevents bitterness from arising even after years of abuse. According to Bishop Tutu, it is this attitude that allowed Nelson Mandela to love his jailers and harbor no bitterness after over two decades in prison.

The theme of love for all people was an important part of a positive approach to life for many of our exemplars, especially for those who work directly with the poor or with children.[3] This love for all people was less evident, and perhaps less necessary, in those working for change at the societal and institutional level.

All those who spoke of the importance of love in their work were deeply religious. They saw their love for others not as a personal feeling but as a value to be promoted, one that derives from religious truth. In fact, consonant with Bishop Tutu's message, love for others is seen as playing a part in spiritual self-discovery. One finds God in oneself as one finds God in others. This provides the basis for the gratitude that many of our exemplars feel toward those whom they serve: Since service to others helps one find one's own inner spirituality, one is grateful to the other for the opportunity to serve.

With this logic, we may understand a most mysterious puzzle: How is it possible to continue loving and serving those who show nothing but ingratitude for the greatest sacrifices that one can make? The answer lies in the fundamental belief that such sacrifices serve one's own spiritual well-being as much as the other's. And the more wretched and ungrateful the case, the richer the benefit. A moral exemplar may cherish those whom others find most unappealing precisely because such people grant them the opportunity to perform a truly needed act of service, one that no one else could or would do. With such acts, exemplars confirm their deepest moral and religious values and discover their own spiritual potential.

Many exemplars in our group express gratitude for the satisfaction they have found in their work. It is this feeling that Bishop Donaldson expresses when he speaks of the privilege of having had such an exciting priesthood. Allison McCrea speaks of being privileged to be able to shift in her forties to such a satisfying career and of her deep gratitude to the people of Roxbury for what they taught and gave her as she worked with for them. Matthew Goldberg, the pediatrician, is thankful for the chance to work long hours for a low salary treating indigent children in inner-city Baltimore. And Jack Coleman is as grateful for the challenges that he faced as a voluntary homeless person, prisoner, and laborer as for the accolades that he received when a college and foundation president.

For some of our exemplars, the meaning of gratitude lies in a desire to share with others all the privileges and good fortune they themselves have received. Kay Hardie speaks of it this way:

> I am one of these people who have been loved every day of my life. I am a person who has been told by the words or actions of those people closest to me, "We just think you're great. You can just do anything. You can be anything." I remember thinking a long time ago that in this painful world, if you have been given the kind of things I've been given which is the gift of limitless expectations for your life, and security, and a nest to come from, one that was warm and safe. And you look around you and if you have any sensitivity at all, you know that's not the way most people got their start or live their lives. And for me I would think it would be the road to madness if you didn't try to give some of it away.

Anne Hayes, a Zen Buddhist and environmentalist, expresses essentially the same feelings. Hayes says of her life, "I have felt that I've had a very, very full and engaging life and I want to give it back somehow. I want just to give back a little bit of what I've gotten from this world to the world." This feeling of gratitude and a desire to give back to others contributes to the confidence we saw in so many of our exemplars that they will be provided for somehow, that what they need will come to them. This means that they do not need to expend a great deal of energy protecting themselves or storing up resources for a secure future. This attitude in turn makes it possible for them to give what they have to others, to leave secure jobs to pursue their moral goals, or to work comfortably in organizations that operate with too few resources for their ambitious mandates.

Along with optimism, gratitude, and humor, then, our exemplars' lives are imbued with a sense of purpose and meaning—which does not in and of itself always establish positivity. Some people have a strong sense of purpose that they carry out with bitterness and negativity: For these people, the sense of purpose can be provided by the pursuit of revenge or other negative ends. But when based upon moral or religious values, a sense of purpose and meaning can do a number of things to support a positive attitude toward life. In fact, without it, positivity is all but impossible. In this sense, we believe that purpose and meaning are necessary but not sufficient for maintaining positivity.

Purpose and meaning can take many forms in a moral exemplar's life. For many of our exemplars, it is religiously based. We have seen this very clearly in Suzie Valadez and Charleszetta Waddles. Luisa Coll expressed her overriding sense of religious purpose this way:

> To me, there's always connections. Nothing happens just for the sake of happening. Things always happen because God has foreseen a plan and God's plan has been carried out. And I was five years old when I dreamt this house . . . I remember, I dreamt a big house where people who were hungry and thirsty and who didn't have a place to go could come to and feel comfortable in. And that is what this house is. This house does not belong to me or my husband or my children. This house belongs to those people who don't have anything.

In addition to being guided by her understanding of God's plan, Luisa Coll is also guided by her own vision of a better world. For a number of our exemplars, both the religious and secular, the sense of meaning and direction in life is provided by such a vision.

MRS. COLL: After it has been because of the discrimination that I myself have suffered. . . . The fact that I am an immigrant to this country, the fact that my father was born here, raised elsewhere, and came back with his young family when I was only five years old. And then, working in the fields of America and understanding the whole immigration program back then when I was only twelve years old and seeing the injustices that were committed against my own people, and how they were treated . . . you know, I just couldn't sit back and fold my arms and be part of the upwardly mobile community. And I felt very committed, from a very early age, to do something to help my people.

INTERVIEWER: And so you don't see it as a self-sacrifice? You see it more as a self-fulfillment of something?

MRS. COLL: Exactly. Exactly. Because, first of all, I feel that the world belongs to all of us—not just to a chosen few. . . . And that is something that I also need to see reaffirmed in my own Catholic religion, knowing full and well that the Gospel calls us to "love thy neighbor as thyself." The only way we can do that is to want for our neighbor what we want for ourselves.

INTERVIEWER: So you're never tempted to try, for example, to leave your past and your people behind and, for yourself, try to live a better, richer life-style, or something like that?

MRS. COLL: No. No.

INTERVIEWER: That's never been a temptation for you?

MRS. COLL: No. I know that there was a time when both my husband and I—my husband started a business, but eventually I was able to convince him to leave it—that we had a mission call. And that mission call has been to serve our brothers and sisters who don't have what we have; and for us to share what we do have with them.

Cabell Brand is also guided by a vision of a better society, one in which all people are truly given access to the system and the support they need to take advantage of the opportunities they encounter and one in which the environment is protected. This is a secular vision, as is that of John Thomas, a neurologist who has devoted his life to pursuing a vision of a rational and fair system of medical ethics.

Other exemplars are driven less by a vision of what is possible than by a personal quest—a quest to live well in an ethical sense, to do what is right, to achieve a sense of internal harmony, to live out their most deeply held values. We have seen this in Jack Coleman, who speaks of "following the head and the heart." We see it in David Linsky, who says that his life shows that "you can do well by doing right, that you don't have to cut corners." We see it in Kay Hardie, who, when she was a teacher, told her classes on the first day of school that she expected from them kindness, courage, and honor. She also said that she was determined to live according to these values herself. Kay Hardie's and Anne Hayes's feelings that they want to give back to others some of what they are so grateful for having received is also a kind of personal quest, one that is echoed by others in our group.

For many of our exemplars, the sense of purpose and meaning in their lives comes from being a part of an ongoing movement for social change, as we saw in Allison McCrea. Virginia Durr's life can be seen this way, as she fought over the years for civil rights and justice.

Other exemplars have organized their lives around multiple sources of meaning. Their goals combine religious and social commitments, charitable works with efforts directed at institutional change, personal quests with a vision of a better world. In these cases, too, we see a sense of continuing purpose that gives meaning to all the exemplar's actions.

It is such a sense of purpose that leads exemplars to focus above all on their goals and commitments, on what they must do to pursue these goals and commitments, and ultimately on other people and their welfare rather than on themselves and their own successes and failures.

For exemplars whose purpose is defined as a personal quest, such as Jack Coleman, the central focus does include the self—since, as in Coleman's case, a primary goal is personal growth. But even here, the notion of personal excellence is so closely bound with societal contribution that the vision is anything but self-centered.

For most of the exemplars, self-improvement per se was not an important goal. Nor did they gauge their self-worth by their victories or defeats. They invested themselves in the effort, the pursuit of the cause, rather than the moment-by-moment results of their struggles. They understood that great moral causes are always formidable, perhaps endless, and perhaps not even finally winnable. Accordingly, they refused to take their own successes and failures as reflections upon themselves, just as they refused to take much personal credit for whatever progress they were able to make.

There were only two exceptions to this, and they were significant ones. The two exemplars who expressed overall negativity toward their lives also exhibited marked self-referential orientations. This was discernible in Sharon Crandall's case by a tendency to evaluate herself by the effects of her efforts and in Aline Burchell's case by a vocal desire for recognition. The seventeen exemplars with strong positive attitudes focused little or no attention either on evaluating themselves or on making sure that they got credit for their work.

An explanation for the relationship between a positive approach and an absence of focus on the self has been provided by Martin Seligman's theory of ''learned optimism,''[4] which offers a way to understand our exemplars' positive attitudes and some of the psychological mechanisms that contribute to generating and maintaining those attitudes. Seligman argues that the key to understanding optimism (and its reciprocal, pessimism) lies in people's habitual styles of explaining to themselves the causes of good and bad events. As Seligman puts it:

> The defining characteristic of pessimists is that they tend to believe bad events will last a long time, will undermine everything

they do, and are their own fault. The optimists, who are confronted with the same hard knocks of this world, think about
misfortune in the opposite way. They tend to believe defeat is
just a temporary setback, that its causes are confined to this one
case. The optimists believe defeat is not their fault. Circumstances, bad luck, or other people brought it about. Such people
are unfazed by defeat. Confronted by a bad situation, they perceive it as a challenge and try harder.[5]

To optimists, bad events seem to result from temporary factors,
from factors that are specific to the particular bad event or situation—
and, most importantly, from factors external to the self. Optimists are
not immobilized when something bad happens because they don't
generalize a problem in one area of life to other areas. They expect
things will go better in the future, because the causes of the bad event
are temporary; they are able to maintain high self-esteem despite defeats because they don't blame themselves (at least not in a permanent,
pervasive way) for failure.

In contrast, pessimists think of bad events as resulting from enduring or even permanent causes, from causes that generalize beyond the
specific bad event to include much of life, and from factors internal
to the self. So, for example, a man who is laid off from his job might
say to himself, "I am a loser. I'm incompetent. I'll never find another
job." Seligman calls this way of thinking about bad events "cata-
strophizing," because a pessimistic style of thinking can turn even a
relatively insignificant setback into a catastrophe.

The habit of finding permanent and generalized causes for misfortune leads to an attitude of despair. As Seligman puts it, "People who
make universal explanations for their failures give up on everything
when a failure strikes in one area. People who make specific explanations may become helpless in that one part of their lives yet march
stalwartly on in others." In order for people to be hopeful rather than
despairing, they must see the causes for misfortune as temporary and
specific. "Temporary causes limit helplessness in time, and specific
causes limit helplessness to the original situation."[6]

Optimists and pessimists differ in their explanations for positive
events as well. The optimistic style of explaining good events is the
reverse of the optimistic style of explaining bad events. Optimists
believe that good events have relatively permanent and general causes.
They also tend to attribute good events to something about themselves
rather than to external factors. In contrast, pessimists attribute good

events to temporary, specific, and external factors, thus gaining little satisfaction and hope even from good things that happen to them.

Although we have not formally evaluated the explanatory styles of our exemplars according to Seligman's categories (the interview data were not structured in a way that makes this uniformly possible for all twenty-three exemplars), many of our exemplars' statements seem consistent with Seligman's predictions about optimistic people. Cabell Brand, for example, interpreted the decline to his door-to-door sales business as due to external market conditions, specific to that particular type of business. He saw this as a temporary problem, in that he could respond to new market conditions by shifting to a catalog fulfillment business. A less optimistic and less resilient person might have said to himself, "My business is failing. I must not be good at this. I'll never succeed in my work," thereby creating a self-defeating explanation based upon causes deemed to be general, internal, and permanent.

Charleszetta Waddles provides other clear examples of an optimistic explanatory style for good events. She believes that good events are sent by God—a cause that is both permanent and pervasive. Suzie Valadez, in her deep belief that "God will provide, God will take care of me," offers exactly the kind of explanation for good fortune that constitutes hopefulness in Seligman's scheme. And although such statements may sound external, in fact both Charleszetta Waddles and Suzie Valadez have a clear sense of God working *through them.* They speak of having long-standing and generalized personal characteristics to which they also attribute positive events. As Mother Waddles says, "I was born with a giving spirit. I remember when I was very young, my mother used to say, 'I wish I had a heart like you.'"

One of the debilitating consequences of a negative explanatory style is that pessimists give up more easily, whereas optimists bounce back and treat defeat as a spur to further action. Seligman speaks of this defeatist tendency of pessimists as learned helplessness, "the quitting response that follows from the belief that whatever you do doesn't matter." Helplessness is learned when people (or animals, for that matter—Seligman did his original research with rats) are put in situations in which they have no control over what happens to them. An optimistic explanatory style modulates learned helplessness in that a hopeful orientation protects people from developing helpless beliefs even if the people have been victims of uncontrollable events. A pessimistic style, on the other hand, makes people especially vulnerable to learned helplessness. People's ways of explaining the uncontrollable events therefore determine how helpless or energized they become when they encounter either minor setbacks or major defeats.

Seligman has shown us that learned helplessness can be an important disrupter of personal effectiveness. If a person believes that he is helpless to make a difference in the world, he becomes unable to act; and he will in fact cede control of events to others. People are empowered by a sense of their own personal control and are disempowered by a sense that they lack control. The irony is that they do it to themselves, through the kinds of explanations they construct for good and bad events. A double irony is that such events may defy explanation and may, in fact, be uncontrollable.

Charleszetta Waddles has been the victim of uncontrollable and unfortunate events over and over in her lifetime. She suffered through her father's business failure and subsequent death in her early childhood, her mother's illness and death a bit later, a shattering betrayal by her first fiancé, and constant poverty. If she had had a pessimistic approach to life and had been vulnerable to learned helplessness, she would have been unable to maintain her sense of personal control in the face of these tragedies. Instead, Charleszetta responded to each of these events as a challenge to be overcome. She developed a strong sense of personal control, which she also tries to impart to others in situations similar to hers. As she says, "People really need to know that there is a way that poor people can be involved and make a difference. I was a mother with ten children and no money and I was able to do this. So many people believe that they're really caught, that circumstances can hold them down, when they really can't."

Mother Waddles is arguing here against people's perception that poverty is a permanent condition, disabling in all areas of one's life, completely out of one's control. She is saying that people have more control than they think they do, and that she has a sense of control over her life in spite of the barriers she has faced. Mrs. Waddles continues later with the same message that people, even the poorest, will not be helpless if they think about their situation in the right way. "If people can really believe that there's a message in the New Testament that will let *anyone* become the light of the world, *anyone*. . . . I believe that there was a message there that, as you think that's what you'll be. I believe that *you must*, you *must* watch what you think."

Seligman argues that when people are committed to something larger than themselves, when their lives have a sense of transcendent purpose and meaning, they are much more likely to be optimistic than pessimistic. "Extreme individualism tends to maximize pessimistic explanatory style, prompting people to explain commonplace failure with permanent, pervasive, and personal causes. Any failure must be my fault, because who else is there but me?'' Several social scientists have claimed recently that we have experienced in this country a growing individualism, a decline in people's commitment to common goals. Seligman argues that this leads to a condition in which failure is experienced as permanent and pervasive: ''To the extent that larger, benevolent institutions no longer matter, personal failures seem catastrophic. Because time in an individual society seems to end with our own death, individual failure seems permanent. There is no consolation for personal failure. It contaminates all of life. To the extent that larger institutions command belief, any personal failure seems less eternal and less pervasively undermining.''[7]

In contrast to narrow individualism, commitment to the common good maximizes the optimistic explanatory style. People who focus on something beyond themselves are not as likely to be pessimistic, in large part because they do not define as many things that happen to them as negative events. Such people think of their larger goals and of other people's welfare, and so they are less sensitive to their own discomforts, slights, or other setbacks than are more individualistically oriented people.

Moreover, such people are resilient. They frequently use their considerable resourcefulness to turn what others would consider negative events into positive ones—such as the flooded office that Mother Waddles turned into a fund-raising opportunity. Perhaps most importantly, such people they have a meaning system within which to understand bad events, so that they can set the bad events aside by interpreting them in a benign light. When Mother Waddles interprets the ingratitude of the people she helps as God's way of ''proving'' her, she is better able to rise to the challenge and forgive the offenders.

In addition, as we have said, people who are committed to the common good typically do not consider the causes of bad events to be permanent, because they have faith in the possibility of change. They would not, in fact, be devoting themselves to changing society unless they thought it was possible. People who believe in a purpose that transcends their own lives tend to consider the good to be more pervasive and permanent than the bad, because they believe in the ultimate goodness of humanity, that ''God is in everyone,'' and that truth and justice have an enduring value. They do not blame themselves for inevitable failures and setbacks, because they are not preoccupied with evaluating their own performances. And as we have shown, they tend to work with others in the pursuit of a common goal, thereby garnering crucial social support when things don't go well. As Seligman also acknowledges, this kind of support reduces catastrophic thinking in that it makes bad events seem more temporary and specific.

Seligman's description of committed persons pursuing lives of meaning and purpose accords with our exemplars, almost all of whom are highly optimistic and positive in their orientations to life. Likewise, we can see that the two women with less positive approaches may be vulnerable, despite their valuable and dedicated lives, for just the kinds of predictions that Seligman has made. A focus on one's own successes and failures makes one more likely to interpret negative events as significant and to attribute them to permanent and pervasive causes. So, too, does a belief in the fundamental wickedness of certain other people, as opposed to a more charitable belief in the potential salvation of everyone.

In making recommendations for increasing optimism and decreasing a sense of hopelessness, Seligman points to a paradox that is evident in many of our exemplars' works. Seemingly grim tasks such as working with AIDS patients or the homeless actually make some people more optimistic and less depressed:

> One might assume that visiting mortally ill AIDS patients once a week would be a surefire recipe for weekly depression. And there's no denying that for some people that might be the case. But I would suggest that exposure to human suffering, while saddening, is not depressing. What is authentically depressing is to imagine oneself trapped in a world full of monsters—the uncouth, unkempt poor, the emaciated sufferer from terminal AIDS, and so on. Experienced volunteers, however, report that a major surprise for them has been the lift they derive from their work. They discover, through contact, that the poor and the sick are not monsters but very human beings; that while what they see as volunteers may sadden them it does not depress them; and that quite often they are deeply moved. It is liberating to see firsthand that among the theoretically helpless there is frequently an amazing degree of mastery, spiritual and psychological.[8]

Certainly, in descriptions such as these, Seligman has identified processes that may help us understand how and why so many of our exemplars maintain a positive attitude in the face of their most difficult challenges. But Seligman's theory cannot provide a complete account of moral positivity. There are two respects in which moral exemplars go beyond the general pattern of psychological adaptation that Seligman describes. First, moral exemplars have self-imposed constraints upon how they externalize blame—they do not readily blame others for mishaps. Second, moral exemplars are rigorous in their regard for the truth—they resist illusory interpretations of events.

There is a benign deceit implicit in Seligman's model: It is the notion that, for the sake of one's psychological well-being, one should accept credit for successes but resist blame for failures. There are no two-edged swords here, or even single-edged ones. The first principle is to avoid edges altogether, and the second is to reap self-congratulations whenever possible. The rewards for this psychological manipulation are enhanced feelings of optimism and control, but there is also a cost. One must forever maintain an interpretational bias that places the true value of events second to their effect on one's psychological state.

Studies of personality development have shown that most adults do in fact learn to accomplish this psychological manipulation during the course of their lives. A number of studies have shown that people generally feel they had more personal control over outcomes that proved successful than over failures. Moreover, recent evidence suggests that this tendency may increase with age. In one study with people ranging from twenty to eight-five years of age, Jutta Heckhausen and Paul Baltes[9] found that middle-aged and older adults were more likely than young adults to believe that they had control over desirable changes in their functioning but not over undesirable ones. The authors conclude that "this might occur because, with accumulating experience in life, there is an increased recognition of the importance of an optimistic attributional pattern for emotional well-being and effective functioning." In other words, most laypersons gradually discover the psychological benefits of optimistic biases and learn to guide their interpretations accordingly.

Reading Seligman and the other recent psychological accounts, one comes away with the impression that a sense of control and a sense of optimism, gained at whatever cost to the truth, are in themselves sufficient remedy for many of life's mental hazards. The strategies that psychologists have identified as enabling people to gain control and optimism in their lives are instructive. We have already noted Seligman's formula for externalizing blame and internalizing credit. Heckhausen and Baltes note other "mechanisms for coping" that can result in feelings of personal efficacy and optimism: "lowering one's

aspirations . . . selecting age peers as a reference group for social comparison . . . [and] activation of multiple selves.'' Moreover, these authors also note that, since ''accurate self-perceptions seem to be corre-
lated with undesirable correlates such as heightened depression and
lowered feelings of self-worth . . . some degree of nonveridicality in
perceptions may be necessary to enhance, or at least to protect, one's
sense of self-esteem and optimism.'' Nonveridicality is the term used
in perception research to connote inaccuracy—or, in the present case,
untruthfulness.

We believe that these indeed are strategies that people commonly
use to maintain their composure through life's vicissitudes, and we
also believe that these strategies may be effective in averting depression
and in building self-esteem. But some of these are strategies that moral
exemplars would not feel comfortable with. Despite the unremitting
positivity that we observed in most of our group, we saw no signs of
them blaming others, or even impersonal forces, for failures in which
they had participated. The importance of taking full responsibility for
their actions was a theme that we heard from almost everyone. Nor
did the exemplars seem especially eager to take credit for things that
were going well. Quite the reverse, they were often humble to an
extreme and readily attributed success to their coworkers rather than
themselves. They did not seem to lower their aspirations to any noticeable degree, and in fact often took on ever more daunting challenges
with increasing age. They almost never compared themselves with
others, in their own age group or not, for the sake of making themselves feel better. As for the activation of multiple selves, their single-
mindedness of purpose as well as their abiding integrity all but barred
this as a coping strategy.

Their greatest obstacle against interpretational biases, of course,
was their high regard for the truth. Distortion, whatever benign inner
function it may serve, was not a mental process to which they would
readily bring themselves. It is not that they were above all forms of
psychological manipulation—as we have seen in Chapter 4, some of
our exemplars would adamantly control their thoughts in order to
steel themselves against danger without risking the debilitating effects
of fear and doubt. But it was done without compromising the principle of honesty in any way: It was simply a matter of refusing to dwell
on negative consequences rather than denying that they could ever
occur. They do not read events in a nonveridical way in order to create
a certain psychological effect for themselves.

Moral exemplars establish and maintain a positive attitude within the constraints of truth and within the framework of their moral goals and values. In a sense, they are a subset of the optimists whom Seligman describes and of the "flow" experiencers whom Csikszentmihalyi describes. They focus on things beyond themselves but not just any things. They are part of a support group but not just any group. And they manage to feel good about themselves without intending this as a special goal or priority. All this is accomplished through their steadfast commitment to purposes larger than themselves. It is these moral commitments, and the humbling recognition of their formidable scope, that drives the exemplars out of themselves and into courses of action that absorb their attention and energy.

The demands of their commitments require action rather than rumination, mobilization rather than depression, hope rather than despair. Impediments along the way may be inevitable in the face of such large-scale demands. It becomes natural, then, to view such impediments as challenges that stimulate further effort rather than as signals that all is lost.

Missteps along the way are also anticipated and readily acknowledged without criticism. Issues of blame, for either self or other, become moot. Human failings can be seen charitably; self-esteem need not hinge upon the absence of failure, nor on the prevalence of success.

Positivity in moral exemplars cannot rely on a distorted view of one's capacity to control life events any more than it can rely on just any form of exhilarating experience. Positivity in such people springs from a noble commitment, fully seized and long maintained. It relies on a creative immersion in action consonant with the commitment and on an honest and humble assessment of the contributions that one's actions can make. It relies on the support of a network of people who share the commitment and prod one toward ever more effective courses of action. It relies on an attitude of forgiveness toward oneself as well as toward those whom one has chosen to serve. And it relies, for many, on a spiritual belief in transcendent forces for the good. This is a positivity of an inspirational sort, and it indeed does galvanize those who come in contact with it.

CHAPTER 11

The Uniting of Self
and Morality

Our exploration of twenty-three highly moral lives—or "coinvestigation," as we have more accurately called it—turned up a number of discoveries. Some of these conformed to our initial expectations, imparting further definition and clarity to patterns that we had already dimly anticipated. Others surprised us, providing us with wholly new insights. Among the noteworthy patterns that we encountered are:

- the exemplars' disregard for risks and their disavowal of courage
- their certainty of response about matters of principle
- their unremitting faith and positivity in the face of the most dismal circumstances
- their capacity to take direction, as well as social support, from the "followers" whom they inspire
- the dynamic interplay between continuity and change in their personal life histories

These patterns belie certain misconceptions that pop up from time to time in stereotypic portrayals of moral leadership. As the above statements imply, we did *not* find that moral exemplars struggle with themselves, stoke up their courage, or weigh alternatives; that they always lead the way or do their work in isolation; that they have their values and goals fully formed from the start; that they led grim, joyless, dreary lives; or that they are harsh and unforgiving with themselves and their followers. Nor did we find them to be a qualitatively unique psychological type, wholly distinct from other well-meaning people. The differences were more of degree than of kind, the developmental processes more continuous than discontinuous from those that govern other people's life courses.

To help explain the surprises, we presented an inner view of how exemplars sustain their bravery, certainty, and positivity in the face of difficulty, hardship, and defeat. We also saw how exemplars are able to maintain their humility even while receiving acclaim and adulation. Many turn away the perils of fear, doubt, and pride through a religious or personal faith in transcendent goodness. Some consciously control their own mental processes in order to resist discouragement and temptation. All endorse their moral commitments so single-mindedly and wholeheartedly that they become convinced that they have no choice but to act accordingly.

Perhaps most revealing in a developmental sense, we observed how the exemplars keep open to personal growth throughout the entire courses of their lives while at the same time steadfastly preserving their moral commitments. The exemplars' lifelong growth was spurred, shaped, and sustained through an unwavering dedication to an enduring purpose. For the exemplars, change and stability were part of the same developmental story. This was the first of the two intriguing developmental paradoxes that we found. The other was the way the exemplars, at critical junctures in their development, were led by their followers.

The dynamic relation between growth and commitment that we observed is central to the life stories of all these extraordinary people. In order to understand lives that are wholly dedicated to moral commitments, it is essential to recognize the vital ways in which these commitments are preserved and nourished. The continuing dynamism of the exemplars' lives *both drew from and guarded* the stability of their commitments. These are the two sides of the first paradox. As we noted above and discussed more fully in Chapter 7, the key to this first paradox may be found in the nature of lifelong moral change. The operative developmental process that we have identified is a socially influenced, yet individually regulated, transformation of goals.

Through goal transformation, our exemplars periodically gave new life to their commitments. They constantly found new ways in which their commitments could apply to human affairs. They found new strategies by which to implement the commitments. In the crucible of their own personal development, the exemplars recapitulate the old truism that the only way to conserve something valuable is to move it forward rather than allowing it to stand in place.[1]

All of this was done in communication with intimate associates who challenged, prodded, supplied information, asked questions, gave feedback, and otherwise supported the exemplar's movement toward an expanded moral vision. In most respects, of course, these intimate associates looked to the exemplars for inspiration and direction, but at critical junctions, their support became necessary for the exemplar's forward progress. For some, the direction of major influence even reversed itself on occasion, with the followers temporarily becoming the leaders. Cabell Brand's reliance on Bristow Hardin's creative initiatives is a case in point, and there were many others.

We have emphasized throughout this book the important role that this kind of social influence plays in spurring the exemplar's moral development. We believe that this point needs emphasizing because of the common view that highly moral people are independent spirits who stand apart from, and indeed in front of, the rest of humankind. Such a view needs correcting on two counts. First, as social theorist Michael Walzer and others have pointed out, even acerbic social critics often operate from within, wholly immersed in the communities they seek to improve.[2] We presented Virginia Durr as an example of this, perhaps the most effective type of social critic.

Moreover, as contemporary developmental theory has convincingly established, social influence is a necessary ingredient in all psychological growth, *even the growth of those who venture into realms of the untried and the unknown.* All creative people—artists, scientists, charismatic moral leaders—put together collegial groups with which they exchange their most revolutionary ideas.

We recall Howard Gardner's description of Gandhi's network of supporters. Gardner's accounts of his other creative "makers of the modern world" is rich in examples of such collaboration.[3] Gardner's subjects (e.g., Freud, Martha Graham, Stravinsky, Einstein) seemed light years ahead of their contemporaries in their visionary work. Yet all had colleagues—Freud's Wilhelm Fliess, Picasso's Georges Braque—whose eyes, ears, and voices were critical in helping the creative leader formulate and consolidate the new approach. The genius of such creative leaders, it seems to us, lies as much in their ability to profit from their interchanges with such colleagues as in their capacity for generating ideas on their own. Innovation always has a collaborative component even though the collaboration may be distant in time or place from the actual innovative act.[4] So, too, in the moral domain.

Yet our emphasis on social influence and collaboration must not blind us to the ultimately individual nature of responsibilities that the exemplars assumed. In most cases, the original act of commitment was an intensely personal experience. Witness the "triggering event" that sent Suzie Valadez to South Texas in search of poor children to aid. Suzie had always had some guidance from parents, friends, and religious leaders, but her lasting commitment was initiated by her own vision. Such commitments are often lonely affairs at first. There is a feeling of breaking away, even from those to whom one usually looks for moral guidance. So Cabell Brand resisted his father's views on racial inequality, as did Virginia Durr with her entire family tradition. When Jack Coleman took on the challenge of proving himself, it was Coleman, as an individual, who self-consciously strove for personal excellence. He listened and learned from those around him, but the commitment was his, directed and assessed from the start by his own personal standards.

Their manner of withstanding the inevitable hardships and risk that "come with the territory" is also intensely personal. In order to sustain themselves through years of pressure, exemplars often employ mental manipulations of the sort described by Emmylou Davis and several others. They rule out fear, ignore material consequences, and single-mindedly focus on activities that will further their commitments.

In so doing, exemplars create for themselves a dramatic "Rubicon effect"—that is, they do not allow themselves to look back on their commitments with a shred of doubt. In part, as we have acknowledged, this single-mindedness can be accounted for by the exhilarating sense of "flow" that many exemplars experience while in the midst of their moral activities. But during less "flowing" periods, there is a need for rigorous mental discipline in order to get past the frustrations, threats, and other hazards of moral work. Our exemplars not only demonstrated the capacity for such discipline but also indicated that they were conscious of the internal mental manipulations that made it possible.

Spiritual faith, which lies at the bottom of many exemplars' abiding positivity, is also a deeply personal matter despite the communal forms of expression that nourish it. Many of our exemplars found in their faiths a seemingly boundless capacity for forgiveness and charity—a capacity that lay at the heart of their moral activities. In fact, it is hard to imagine how the exemplars could have overcome the dispiriting frustrations of their work, such as betrayal and ingratitude from those whom they served, without such a capacity. Exemplars who exhibited the capacity of forgiveness and charity avoided the bitterness and negativity of the few who did not. Most often, this capacity was firmly rooted in a spiritual faith, a belief in God, a transcendent force for the good. The transcendent belief took many forms among our diverse group of exemplars. Often it was idiosyncratic, beyond encapsulation in a formal religious category. Invariably it was personally fashioned in synchrony with the exemplar's individual moral commitment.

The notion of individual commitment, and more generally that of "individualism," has become suspect in the social sciences these days. In fact, one can almost say that the phrase "individual commitment" has begun to be perceived as a contradiction in terms. Those who have studied the cultural climate of contemporary American life have suggested that individualism and commitment now coexist in an uneasy state of tension. Robert Bellah and his colleagues, for example, note that, 150 years ago, Alexis de Tocqueville portrayed a national climate that fostered both individualism and moral commitment—the former through our vital frontier mentality, the latter through voluntary associations and communal ties that encouraged charitable participation.[5] In more recent times, the communal ties have weakened while the frontier mentality has persisted (although in less tangible forms, as the frontier has become more metaphoric than geographic). As a result, the once creative tension between individualism and commitment has drifted into a state of opposition, all too often with commitment on the losing end.

While acknowledging the validity of Bellah's research findings, we have a very different perspective on individualism and its meaning, both for the developing person and for contemporary American society. We start with the assumption that fully developed individualism includes a dedication to the common good. Moral development is a fundamental part of any person's development as an individual. Moreover, mature individualism implies fully articulated links with others and with society as a whole. Even as individuals seek their own unique destinies, they do so in the context of relations with family, friends, and others in their communities. Strong social relations, in fact, provide a setting in which the exploration of self flourishes. So, in the course of human development, socialization and individuation are really opposite sides of the same coin.[6]

This conception of individualism is deeply rooted in the American tradition. It found its purest original voice in the preachings and writ-

ings of Ralph Waldo Emerson. We believe that it is a mistake to set
individualism in opposition to community commitment. When fully
realized in an Emersonian sense, individual agency remains the community's best hope.

Moral exemplars are both highly individuated persons as well as
highly committed ones. They report no conflict between these two
states. To the contrary, the two have supported each other's growth
in the course of the exemplars' personal development. As the exemplars have developed a finer sense of their commitments and how to
achieve them, they have acquired a better sense of who they are and
what they want to become. Conversely, as they have come to know
themselves better, they have better understood the limits and poten-
tials of their moral contributions, thereby sharpening their effectiveness and increasing the durability of their commitments.

This is not to say that exemplars never feel conflict in their lives,
but rather, when they do, it is a conflict between commitments rather
than between their individual welfare and their societal contributions.
For example, the most frequent conflict reported by our exemplars
was their need to divide their efforts between their families and society
at large. Regretfully, several felt that, immersed as they were in great
social causes, they had not given as much attention to their children
as they would have liked. It was the one regret that we heard expressed among many in the group. But should we take this as an
individual concern that was set against the exemplars' moral commitments? Or should we interpret it as a conflict in commitments, a
common impasse between two moral alternatives? We prefer the latter interpretation, because it comes far closer to the way highly moral
people always have experienced such conflicts.

The tug between one's obligation to family and one's obligation
to society at large is one of the classic themes in moral history and
literature. There are many, many poignant stories of parents being
torn by the feeling that they are letting their children down while
their energies are absorbed by a great societal cause. Struggling for
social justice, fighting poverty, championing freedom are all deeply
engaging endeavors that consume time and resources. Inevitably there
will be less of these precious parental commodities to share with one's
children. The brutal fact is that moral heroes do not always make
ideal parents. We are again reminded of Gardner's account of Gandhi:
"Asked whether a genius might leave a legacy through his family,
Gandhi answered with perhaps unappreciated revealingness, 'Certainly
not. He will have more disciples than he will ever have children.'"

With all the honesty and self-awareness that was their custom, our exemplars fully recognized the familial sacrifices that they felt called upon to make. To the extent that they had any regrets about their lives, this was it.

Feelings of parental and other familial responsibility are not what we would call selfish or nonmoral concerns. They are important inter-personal sentiments every bit as moral as passions for justice and char-ity. As the greatest lure toward doubt and hesitation among our exem-plars, family ties represented not a set of narrowly construed interests, not a temptation to sink into personal gratification but rather another worthy claim on the exemplars' efforts. The exemplars were sensitive to this but instead often followed the call of their broader commit-ments. Who could be in a position to judge their choice?

For now, we simply note that the exemplars were struggling to reconcile different elements of their moral selves. They were not set-ting their moral interests in opposition to their personal ones. Nor were they setting their own interests against those of others. The exemplars were starting from the assumption that their own interests were synonymous with their moral goals. Their real dilemma was in deciding how to parcel out their limited time and energy to all the others whom they felt called upon to serve. It was a dilemma in hu-man limits not one in personal temptation.

In the United States, as in any society, there are those who set their own interests against others and those who define their own interests as inseparable from the welfare of others. Our exemplars were unquestionably of the latter sort, but we do not consider the former to be individualists and the latter to be nonindividualists. To the con-trary, we consider our exemplars, and others with strong moral links to their communities, to be highly developed individualists, again in the Emersonian sense.

As for historical transformations in the American epoch, we do not contest those who have identified a loosening of community links. Nor do we doubt the importance of such links. Societies provide the conditions whereby people may or may not develop a fully moral individualism; a society with strong community bonds in place will provide the most likely developmental context for most people. But we note that, even in the modern era, we uncovered a wealth of moral commitment alive in twenty-three individuals—men and women who grew up and worked in practically every sector, geographic and other-wise, of this diverse nation. We note, too, that countless names of other living moral exemplars were proposed to us at each phase of our study. In the cultural context of contemporary American society, all these men and women have vigorously pursued their individual and moral goals simultaneously, viewing them in fact as one and the same.

The exemplars have done so without devaluing their own personal goals. Nor do they disregard their own fulfillment or self development—nor, broadly construed, their own self-interests. They do not seek martyrdom. Rather than denying the self, they define it with a moral center. They seamlessly integrate their commitments with their personal concerns, so that the fulfillment of the one implies the fulfillment of the other.

Often in public discourse we confuse altruism with self-denial. We take personal suffering as the truest sign of moral commitment. We expect our moral heroes to figuratively (or even literally) punish the flesh, lead woeful lives, go about their grim business grimly. Perhaps we acquired such notions by observing the decidedly woeful consequences that have befallen the many moral leaders who have been crucified, shot, imprisoned, or consigned to lives of poverty and deprivation.

But these are merely the external misfortunes that too many people with enduring moral commitments have had to endure. Unhappy as these misfortunes are, they are still no more than external consequences. They do not speak to the inner experience that determines the true quality of life for such highly committed persons. The exemplars expressed to us the kind of inner harmony characteristic of those who dedicate themselves to purposes beyond themselves. As Seligman has pointed out, the persons at greatest risk for depression and other psychological disharmonies are those who do not have "lives of meaning"—often manifested, Seligman writes, in an overcommitment to self and an undercommitment to the common good.[7]

We did not find our moral exemplars to be a suffering, grim lot. With but few exceptions, they were positive, cheerful, and optimistic. (Gladly, none had had their lives destroyed by adversity, but many had had their lives marked by privation, frustration, danger, and personal tragedy). *None saw their moral choices as an exercise in self-sacrifice.* To the contrary, they see their moral goals as a means of attaining their personal ones, and vice versa. This can only be possible when moral goals and personal goals are closely in synchrony, perhaps even identical. Our exemplars have been invulnerable to the debilitating psychological effects of privation because all they have needed for personal success is the productive pursuit of their moral mission. Their hopes for themselves and their own destinies are largely defined by their moral goals. In the end, it is this unity between self and morality that makes them exceptional.

We believe that this exceptionality is one of degree rather than of kind. It is an extreme version of a developmental process that accounts for self-formation and moral growth in every normal individual. Moral commitment, fortunately, is not a bizarre or even unusual part of human life. Almost everyone takes on moral commitments of some sort. These commitments become defining components of self in almost every case. Extraordinary moral commitments of the sort that we have examined, no matter how profound their social importance, function developmentally in a parallel manner to more ordinary ones. In our exemplars, we have seen processes of integration between self and morality that have much in common with those that all of us experience. Moral exemplars do not form their self-identities in a wholly different manner from other people.

The unusual feature of our exemplars' personal development is the strength of this integration and the extensivity of the moral engagements. The result of this strength and extensivity is a true uniting of self and morality. The unity that the exemplars achieve goes far beyond what is familiar to those who try to live a typically moral life. It lies at the heart of the exemplars' inspirational effect on others. This is indeed unusual and admirable, but it still does not set moral exemplars wholly apart from other people.

Extraordinary moral commitment has long been the subject of myths and misconceptions. We have noted one above—the confusion of altruism with self-denial. Other misconceptions arise from the tendency to place highly dedicated people on a pedestal, above the squalor of normal human affairs. Once a person has demonstrated a firm commitment to a noble cause, inflated expectations about all aspects of the person's behavior begin to appear. The person's moral perspective becomes endowed with a life and a status of its own, viewed differently from other people's values and commitments. Much the same effect can be seen among those who have shown great talent in the arts and the sciences. The label "genius" transforms immediately how we assess and understand the person's creative efforts. Society, in fact, is quick to deify those who excel in any area.

In the moral area, as in any other, inflated expectations are bound to be disappointed before long. Even highly dedicated persons are not perfect in all aspects of their lives. Even those whom society has deified remain stubbornly human. Inflated expectations may appear harmless, but they have their costs. When imperfections are discovered, disenchantment and skepticism arise about all aspects of the person's good works. The sincerity and worth of even the most beneficent deeds may be challenged.[8] This can generalize to a cynicism about the existence of true moral excellence in anyone. Because we were convinced that genuine moral commitment not only exists but that it always plays a crucial role in human progress, we resisted using perfection as an identifying criterion for our moral exemplars.

There are other problems and confusions created by the deification of moral exemplars. One that concerns us here is the way in which such a view interferes with our understanding of moral commitment and how it develops. Placing a person beyond the realm of normal human discourse—even a highly talented, gifted, or dedicated person—robs us of the capacity to discover what has made the person so extraordinary. It diminishes our chance to learn lessons for our own lives, or for the lives of future generations. It also sets the stage for the common myths and misconceptions that distort the exemplar's personal qualities, life history, and experience.

In fact, moral exemplars, while exceptional, should not seem altogether foreign to us. As we noted early in this book, it is possible to find some in every community of this nation. Nor are the ideals they exemplify unknown to the rest of us. To a greater or lesser extent, moral commitment is present in practically all human lives.

Most incidents of moral commitment are so common that they go unremarked. They may even be hard to recognize as examples of morality at all. A mother vigilantly holds her child's hand while crossing the street, a teacher cuts short her lunch break to assist a struggling student, a person tells a painful truth to a friend—such examples are commonplace in everyday social behavior.[9] Although the ordinariness of such actions often makes us take them for granted, they nevertheless reveal a well of moral commitment available to most mature members of society.

Even acts of omission may reveal an undiscerned sense of moral commitment. A man walks past a blind beggar on the street, never harboring a thought of grabbing the blind man's coins despite how easy it would be to get away with.[10] Every indication we have is that most people do so reflexively, not even tempted by the prospect of easy gain.

These ordinary examples of moral commitment reveal something about the nature of morality as it is played out in everyday social life. Perhaps the most noteworthy thing about these behaviors is their very unnoteworthiness. They are performed habitually, as a matter of course. They do not come about through a logical application of a well-worked-out belief system. They are accomplished almost automatically. They are experienced with little doubt, hesitation, or inner struggle.

The parallels between these ordinary examples of morality and the extraordinary actions that we have studied in this book are striking. Time and again we found our moral exemplars acting spontaneously, out of great certainty, with little fear, doubt, or agonized reflection. They performed their moral actions spontaneously, as if they had no choice in the matter. In fact, the sense that they lacked a choice is precisely what many of the exemplars reported.

But the parallels are not complete. By pointing out commonalities between normal and extraordinary moral commitment, we do not wish to blur the special characteristics of our exemplars or their commitments. The great difference between moral exemplars and most people is that exemplars act without equivocation about matters that go well beyond the boundaries of everyday moral engagement. They drop everything not just to see their own children across the street but to feed the poor children of the world, to comfort the dying, to heal the ailing, or to campaign for human rights. It is not so much that the exemplars' orientation to moral concerns is unusual but that the range of their concerns and the extensiveness of their engagement is exceptionally broad.

We have described the developmental processes that help exemplars acquire an extraordinary sense of mission. We have insisted that these are not a wholly different species of process than those that shape the moral selves of most individuals. All people experience social influence, and to the extent that a person acquires moral commitment at all, it is brought about through some developmental transformation in that person's goals. It is not that the exemplars have undergone a qualitatively different process of change. Rather, they have experienced, deeply and intensively, many moral goal transformations over long stretches of their lives. In this regard they are unusual.

Here we would make the same point again but in a broader context. The exemplars' expansive moral concerns, and their steadfast moral commitments, are extensions in scope, intensity, and breadth of normal moral experiences. Their moral concerns and commitments are continuous with that of most people but are greater in degree. It is the remarkable extensiveness of their concerns and commitments that must be explained.

What, then, are the reasons behind the remarkable extensiveness?

We believe that a central reason lies in the close relation between self and morality that exemplars establish. Over the course of their lives, there is a progressive uniting of self and morality. Exemplars come to see morality and self as inextricably intertwined, so that concerns of the self become defined by their moral sensibilities. The exemplars' moral identities become tightly integrated, almost fused, with their self-identities. Cabell Brand expressed this sense of fusion during one of our interviews with him. When asked "When you think about these [moral] goals and values and so on, how do these relate to your sense of who you are as a person and your identity?" he responded: "Well, it's one and the same. Who I am is what I'm able to do and how I feel all the time—each day, each moment. . . . It's hard for me to separate who I am from what I want to do and what I am doing."

Self and moral goals can be coordinated in any number of ways in a person's life. Self goals can be segmented from moral ones, as when we apportion our paychecks into amounts dedicated to ourselves and amounts dedicated to charity. The two can stand in opposition to one another, as when someone jumps in front of a bus to save a child, or reciprocally, as when someone cheats someone else in order to improve one's own lot. Or they can be united. In this last case, there is the sense that one's most powerfully motivating goals derive directly from one's moral convictions. Consequently, in serving morality one serves oneself. In this manner, one identifies oneself largely as an agent of one's moral goals.

Most people connect self and moral goals to some degree—as when, for example, they act altruistically toward their children or other loved ones. But most people also experience some degree of conflict between what they most want to do and what they feel would be best to do from the moral point of view. Although they may want to do the right thing, they also want things that clash with their moral goals. Unity between self and morality is far from typical, although it can be approached. Moral exemplars do so, and this is the key to the extraordinary range and depth of their moral commitments.

The co-occurrence of unified goals, effective social action, and sense of certainty that we found in our moral exemplars was not coincidental. Rather, it follows from a more general principle in the relation between moral judgment and conduct: *Where there is perceived concordance between self and morality, there will follow direct and predictable links between judgment and conduct as well as great certainty in the action choices that result.* Goals are a central component of self. When moral and personal goals are united, moral goals become central to the self.

The general principle operates most clearly in the cases of highly moral individuals, but is also applies generally in the course of normal human behavior and development.

In a previous developmental analysis of self-understanding, we have described periods in childhood and adolescence when concepts of morality and self become joined.[11] Early in life, morality and self are separate conceptual systems with little integration between them. When children refer to who they are or what they are like, they typically make no reference to their moral goals or beliefs. Instead, they focus on the surface features of their physical, active, social, or psychological selves. Children often speak about what is fair and what they would (or even should) do as wholly separate affairs. They will strongly affirm their desire to be fair with their friends, but this desire bears little implication for their self-concept: They do not think of themselves as individuals who are fair or unfair (instead, they define themselves by their physical features, their likes and dislikes, their activities, their family identities, and so on). Their moral concerns do not translate into their concerns about who they are. This segregation is resolved toward the end of childhood when, in fact, children begin to think about themselves in terms of how kind, how just, and how responsible they are.

When children begin to define themselves even to some small degree by their moral inclinations, a closer link between their moral interests and their self-interest is created. This leads to a bit more predictability between children's moral judgment and their conduct. We have evidence for this both from our own studies of children's sharing behavior and from other research on moral development during childhood and adolescence.[12] In experimental studies, for example, children become more likely with age to do what they say they should do. They show greater consistency between their actions and beliefs, even when they are tempted to act selfishly, cheat, or otherwise violate their moral codes.

For most people, of course, moral and self-interests become linked, but only up to a point. There remain prominent schisms between morality and the self after childhood and, indeed, all through life. The resolution of the two at the end of childhood remains only partial: in our self-concept study, only two adolescents showed a tendency to define their identities *primarily* in terms of their moral beliefs.[13] The self-concept study went only through late adolescence, so a stronger developmental trend toward integration might have been discovered by an extension of the study into adulthood. But it is safe to conclude that a true uniting of morality and the self remains a rare event, confined to exemplary individuals such as those in our study. In most persons, the relationship between the two varies from relative separation to relative integration. Moreover, the extent of unity is an aspect of personality growth that derives more from a person's sense of self than from the nature of the person's moral beliefs.

We would argue, therefore, that morality and the self grow closer together during the course of normal development, but they still remain relatively uncoordinated for most (but not all) individuals. What is more, it is not possible to gauge the extent to which an individual has integrated the two simply by focusing on his or her moral judgment. This is because a person's moral judgment does not determine *the place that morality occupies in the person's life.* To know this latter key quality we must know not only how the person views morality but also how the person understands the self in relation to his or her moral beliefs.

People with substantially similar moral beliefs may differ in their personal identification with them. Those for whom morality is central to their personal identities may be powerfully motivated by their moral beliefs and goals. Others may have equally elevated notions of the good but may consider these notions to be peripheral to many of their own life engagements.

In several theoretical papers and reviews, psychologist Augusto Blasi has made this point in a compelling way.[14] Blasi argues that a person's sense of responsibility to act morally is a conceptual system that is distinct from that person's conception of what is the moral thing to do—the person's moral judgment as traditionally defined by Kohlberg and others. In most people, the sense of responsibility is more directly linked to self-identity than is the conception of the moral. The sense of responsibility is also the primary operative agent in determining the person's actual moral conduct.

This is not to claim that the nature of one's moral conceptions is unimportant for self-identity, one's sense of responsibility, or moral conduct. Certainly there are conceptual moral positions from which it becomes practically impossible to deny one's personal responsibility on critical occasions—for example, a sincere moral belief in the sanctity of life makes it very difficult for a person to ignore the pleas of a person whose life is being threatened. Many moral positions resist separation from a sense of responsibility: They can only be segregated from the self (or separated from their action implications) through rationalization and/or distortion of the facts in the case.

Nevertheless, even though the nature of one's moral beliefs may place limits on how one places morality within the frame of one's personal life, there is still considerable variation possible within these limits. In other words, moral beliefs in themselves may bear *some* implications for how they are to be used in one's personal life, but these cannot cover every circumstance, and at best they offer only partial solutions to real-life problems. At worst, they can be ignored or denied. This is as true at the most elevated reaches of moral judgment as at the less sophisticated levels. In the end, moral behavior depends on something beyond the moral beliefs in and of themselves. It depends on how and to what extent the moral concerns of individuals are important to their sense of themselves as people. For some strongly committed people, these concerns are of absolute and undeniable importance to their sense of who they are. But the reason for this lies less in the nature of their moral concerns than in the way they integrate these concerns with their sense of self.

If, as we believe, the extent of unity between morality and the self is not bestowed by a person's particular moral beliefs, then we should find such unity among persons with widely varying moral judgments. This, in fact, is exactly what we have found among our moral exemplars. Moreover, like Blasi, we have found evidence that such unity can create a firm bridge between moral judgment and action. This stands to reason because of the strong moral focus that such unity provides. People who define themselves in terms of their moral goals are likely to see moral problems in everyday events, and they are also likely to see themselves as necessarily implicated in these problems. From there it is a small step to taking responsibility for the solution.

Just as there is little separation between moral and personal goals among our moral exemplars, so, too, is there little divergence between judgment and conduct. The unity of goals provides a compelling call to engagement as well as a sense of certainty about one's course of action. Where one's personal choice seems predetermined by one's sense of self, there is little room for hesitation or doubt. Hence the "automatic pilot" quality of the exemplars' moral actions.

As we noted earlier in this chapter, most moral actions in everyday life are accomplished without much reflection or self-awareness. In this sense, exemplars' moral commitments are extensions in scope but not in kind from most people's typical moral engagements. Such extensions are made possible by a progressive uniting of self and moral goals during the course of development. This progressive uniting does not rest upon greater capacities for moral reflection, as some contemporary moral development theories have implied. Rather, it reflects an increasingly functional integration between one's sense of self, one's moral beliefs, and one's habits of social conduct.

In a theoretical paper examining the relations between morality and identity, psychologists Philip Davidson and James Youniss propose that moral growth is a matter of ever greater facility in making transitions between theoretical belief and direct action.[15] They distinguish between a person's theoretical beliefs, which are reflective and highly conscious, and his or her habitual mode of action, which is spontaneous and embedded in one's immediate experience. Both can be sources of moral action, although of very different kinds. Theoretical beliefs give rise to deliberative and highly rationalized moral choices of the sort measured by Kohlberg's famous story dilemmas. These sorts of deliberative choices can be crucial during certain turning points in life. As just one historical example, the tormented musings of Thomas More leading to his principled denial of Henry VIII's theological demands no doubt hinged upon such self-conscious moral reflection.

But action choices based upon self-conscious moral reflection are relatively rare in human affairs. Of course, such choices are likely to be noteworthy because they are disruptive of life's normal flow. Habitual responses, on the other hand, frequently generate moral actions, in ways so common they usually go unnoticed. All the acts of commission and omission noted earlier in this chapter—the mother watching over her child, the dedicated teacher helping her student, the man not thinking to steal from the blind beggar—represent moral acts commonly conducted through habitual processes.

We have made the case that moral exemplars generally carry out their commitments in a spontaneous and nonreflective manner, as if by force of habit. We noted the quality of "automatic pilot" that defines some of their most courageous acts. On a lesser scale, this orientation is in fact similar to the way most people operate when carrying out commonplace moral acts. *What is extraordinary about moral exemplars is that they apply this habitual moral mode to the farthest reaches of their social vision.* Their moral sensibilities are quickly engaged by any number of observations or incidents. When so engaged, their moral sensibilities wholly immerse the exemplar in the moral concern.

Such immersion is accompanied by feelings of great certainty and clarity of purpose. As we have noted, this psychological state is reminiscent of flow, which Csikszentmihalyi defines as "the holistic sensation that people feel when they act with total involvement." Davidson and Youniss make the point that flow is a primary product of strong habitual modes of moral responding.

We would add that direction of causality also goes the other way: Frequent states of flow can contribute to the articulation of social action systems that make up one's habitual moral conduct. The satisfaction that a person receives from optimal psychological experience no doubt encourages people to seek similar engagements in the future. The flow that Suzie Valadez receives from her trips into Juarez must make further charitable work all the more appealing to her. No doubt this was true from the time of her earliest missionary visits to the poor children of Texas and Mexico. In such a manner, habitual moral conduct both arises directly from social engagements and creates the conditions for its own further development. Over a period of time, supported by virtuous goals and optimal experiences of flow, a system of reliable—even noble—moral habit begins to take shape.

Examples of how such a process may stimulate moral growth can be found in Chapter 7, where we pointed to two long-term developmental processes, cumulative and interactional continuity, that work by creating conditions for the expansion of such personal characteristics as empathy, honesty, and decency. We noted how, from an early age, each of the five profiled exemplars demonstrated such characteristics. Throughout later life, their continued habitual modes of moral responding fed upon the information and experiences these characteristics generated. So, for example, Jack Coleman's early decency kept him in contact with others concerned about society's outcasts and exposed him to the prisons and streets where they dwell—all of which forced the continued growth of his sense of human decency.

Adding to this developmental pattern was Coleman's conscious sense of the kind of person he wished to become: his reflective self-identity. We conclude from this and other cases that *the optimal condition for moral development is when habitual morality is supported by one's reflective sense of self*—that is, when one's reflections about who one wants to be encourage rather than collide with one's gut reactions to moral events. The critical issue in moral development is whether one's overall personal goals—and ultimately one's sense of self—support an immersion in moral concerns and moral action. Personal reflection about one's self-identity cannot create moral habits, but in the long run it can either nurture or sap them, depending upon the nature of the personal reflections. As Davidson and Youniss write, "The principal developmental issue concerning the two identities (habitual and reflective) is their manner of intercoordination."[16] As the two become increasingly coordinated, ever greater support becomes possible.

The united self that we observed in our exemplars was a result of this integration process taken to its human extreme. By directing their personal goals entirely toward their moral commitments, and by defining themselves primarily through these commitments, the moral exemplars established a conceptual self system that supported their natural moral inclinations at every turn. This is why we never observed the hesitation, doubt, fear, or uncertainty that is typical of a divided self.

The integration of conscious moral reflection and habitual moral reaction, of primary and autonomous identities, makes possible the uniting of self and morality in two ways. First, the integration joins together the various intellectual and active ways that one can respond to a moral event. The self-reflective judgment lends support and perspective to the habit, and the habitual reaction lends substance and shape to the reflection. This makes a powerful combination, one that is both effective and inspiring.

Second, the integration facilitates the key developmental processes that we have discussed in this book: goal transformation, cumulative continuity, and interactional continuity. It facilitates these processes by creating coherent systems of action and reflection that *at the same time* bolster and challenge the exemplars' moral commitments. Neither action nor reflection alone could accomplish this. Habitual action by itself would lead to stagnation; reflection without ingrained habits would lead to ambivalence or passivity. When the two combine, the exemplars' moral commitments can be kept alive in the truest sense—that is, they not only endure but keep growing.

In the process, the exemplar's own continued moral growth is assured. We remarked on the striking propensities for our exemplars to retain their capacities for growth all through life. This capacity springs from the joining of self-reflection to moral action—from the coordination of psychological systems that have been called primary and autonomous moral identity. When these systems come together in the critical moments of development, the conditions are set for an eventual uniting of self and morality.

The exemplars' extraordinary degree of integration between reflection and action goes to the heart of their capacities to live out their moral commitments. A true integration of reflection and action rests on a unifying belief that must be represented in all the cognitive and behavior systems that direct a person's life choices. It must be represented at the level of habit, at the level of judgment, and at the level of reflective self-understanding. The belief must be so compelling that it both preserves the stable commitments and guides the dynamic transformations of each system.

Many of our exemplars drew upon religious faith for such a unifying belief. In fact, as we noted in the previous chapter, this was the case for a far larger proportion of our exemplars than we originally expected. But even those who had no formal religion often looked to a transcendent ideal of a personal sort: a faith in the forces of good, a sustaining hope in a power greater than oneself, a larger meaning for one's life than personal achievement or gain.

We believe it is accurate to say that, among the twenty-three exemplars, there was a common sense of faith in the human potential to realize its ideals. Although the substance of the faith and its ideals was too varied and too elusive to be captured in a final generalization, it can perhaps best be described as an intimation of transcendence: a faith in something above and beyond the self. The final paradox of our study is that the exemplars' unity of self was realized through their faith in a meaning greater than the self.

It is this faith, this hope, this meaning that provides the glue joining all the self's systems of action and reflection. This is what held the exemplars together during all the trials, the successes and failures, the "times at 2:30 in the morning" (to use Jack Coleman's phrase) that would test the strength and endurance of their commitments. This is what kept them moving toward the progressive fulfillment of their commitments without digressing, as others might, toward other, more personal desires—or away from other, more personal fears. It is what kept them on target through all the changes and challenges that distract most people. It is, in short, what made the center hold throughout all the decades of the exemplars' uniquely consequential lives.

The Nominating Study

With the support of a grant from the Social Science Research Council's Giftedness Committee, we conducted a two-year study designed to develop criteria and compile a list of potential participants for our study of the lives of moral exemplars. As indicated in Chapter 2, we interviewed twenty-two moral philosophers, theologians, ethicists, historians, and social scientists in the course of this nominating study. The nominators were deliberately selected to include both men and women and to be diverse in regard to race, religion, geographic location, and political ideology.

After recruiting the twenty-two nominators, we interviewed them for several hours each, guided by a list of open-ended questions. During these interviews, we presented a preliminary list of criteria that we believed offered a basis for identifying moral exemplars. We then asked each nominator to comment in detail on each of the preliminary criteria. The nominator was given an opportunity to modify our criteria, to add new ones, and delete those with which he or she disagreed. During the remainder of the interview, the nominator was asked to suggest and describe living people that fit the revised criteria and to comment on the appropriateness of exemplars suggested by other nominators. In each case, we thoroughly explored with the nominator the reasons behind his or her suggestions.

We began with six criteria for identifying moral exemplars, and one of our early nominators suggested a seventh. The seven criteria, as we formulated them early in the process, were:

1. a sustained commitment to definable moral principles
2. a consistent tendency to act in accordance with these principles

3. a willingness to affirm (rather than deny or misrepresent) one's acts, and to overtly express the principles that constitute one's moral rationale for such acts
4. a willingness to risk personal well-being for the sake of one's moral principles
5. a capacity for creating and projecting a moral vision, including particularly the ability to generate innovative solutions to moral problems
6. a talent for inspiring others to moral action
7. a dedicated responsiveness to the lives of others

In addition, of course, we had some selection criteria with practical rather than moral significance. The moral exemplars whom we wished to study needed to be living, English-speaking, and accessible for interviewing. We restricted our study to those who have done much of their moral work within the United States, since at this time we did not wish to take on the complexities of understanding the moral traditions of other societies. Of the twenty-three exemplars that we interviewed and discuss in this book, two were foreign-born. One of these (Jack Coleman) has lived in this country for most of his adult life, and the other (unnamed) has lived for much of her life in the United States and has focused much of her moral work here.

From their earliest rendition, our criteria embodied a conviction that moral excellence requires personal integrity—that is, not merely a belief in certain noble moral principles but also a pervasive consistency between those principles and one's conduct.

Consistency means a willingness to translate one's principles into effective action, whatever the personal cost. But it means something more than that as well. It means a concern not only with what one accomplishes but also with *how* one accomplishes it. We believed that a truly moral leader would not resort to deceit in order to pursue a goal, no matter how noble the goal. Rather, the moral leader would openly affirm the goal and build a social consensus in support of it. The leader's means of achieving the goal would reflect the same high standards of truth and decency as the noble goal itself.

As we became aware, there remained a number of problems in our early formulations that the original seven criteria did not resolve. For one thing, we had not specified what qualifies as a "moral principle." Nor had we distinguished between the pursuit of noble ends and the pursuit of ignoble ones. How would we respond to a Nazi who claimed Aryan superiority as a moral principle? Or to a Stalinist who would sacrifice human freedom and dignity to the needs of an impersonal state? More generally, how could we weed out fanatics, many of whom couch their missions (perhaps cynically, perhaps with genuine though misguided fervor) in righteous and idealistic terms?

We knew that most fanatics would fail either the consistency or the honest test—after all, Hitler and Stalin, like many other tyrants, relied heavily on the "big lie," but we were not at all certain that these criteria alone would reliably rule out all fanatics. We needed criteria that specified more directly the domain of morally valid commitments without at the same time arriving at too narrow a definition of what qualifies as a valid moral principle. The criterion must, we felt, remain open to moral principles beyond our own awareness or vision, yet it must not be so open as to allow the inclusion of impassioned pursuits of evil causes. Definitionally, this was a fine line to walk.

The nominating process was designed to help us with such problems. Our conversations with nominators probed extensively for each nominator's ideas about how to reformulate our selection criteria.

As it turned out, our preliminary list of criteria did serve its purpose of establishing a satisfactory initial framework for the nominators. All twenty-two endorsed at least some part of the preliminary list, and all were willing to suggest revisions or additions that would make the list acceptable to them. There was some variation in these suggestions but not as much as one might expect, especially considering the diverse backgrounds, disciplines, and ideologies they represented.

The final set of five criteria were presented in Chapter 2 and are repeated here:

1. a sustained commitment to moral ideals or principles that include a generalized respect for humanity, or a sustained evidence of moral virtue
2. a disposition to act in accord with one's moral ideals or principles, implying also a consistency between one's actions and intentions and between the means and ends of one's actions
3. a willingness to risk one's self-interest for the sake of one's moral values
4. a tendency to be inspiring to others and thereby to move them to moral action
5. a sense of realistic humility about one's own importance relative

to the world at large, implying a relative lack of concern for one's own ego

The first criterion, as revised, makes reference to virtues as well as moral principles. Several of our nominators commented that our original focus on "definable moral principles" loaded the criterion too heavily with cognitivist and rationalist connotations. One should not assume that moral exemplars always follow explicit, rulelike moral principles. As McIntyre and other contemporary philosophers have argued, moral commitment may be more realistically described as consistent virtue, at least in most cases.[1] Accordingly, virtue theory has provided a philosophical alternative to the Kantian tradition that frames morality in terms of universal principles such as justice. For our own purposes, we wished to preserve the legitimacy of both positions by recognizing either sustained commitment to principle or sustained evidence of virtue as meeting our first criterion. This solution was suggested by several of our nominators and endorsed by the others. As one of our nominators argued:

> Alasdair McIntyre's recent work and Elizabeth Anscombe's in the last decade or two suggests that one of the preoccupations of modern moral philosophy has been with principles. And that is, in their view, an unfortunate preoccupation. And that, again in their view, the richer ethical foundation concept is not principles but virtues. And they invite in their critics' eyes a nostalgic, but nevertheless real, return to the Greek and medieval conceptions of ethics which tend to emphasize habits of character rather than principles—principles in their view being a peculiar artifact of the scientific revolution and the model of knowledge as virtue that it brought with it. Whereas habit as virtue is less cognitive and less deductive in its metaphors.
>
> I think that one way to avoid the problem is to disjoin the word *virtues*—that is, "a sustained commitment to defined principles *or* sustained evidence of virtues." That way your net is [broadened] . . .

Along similar lines, we gave more substance to the previously abstract notion of principles by specifying that exemplars' principles reflect *a generalized respect for humanity rather than a discriminatory regard for particular groups at the expense of others.* In our revised version, not just any principle counts as a moral one: Principles that cause harm or injustice to some people are excluded. The new wording of the first criterion implies that moral principles must be compatible with concerns for people generally. Several of our nominators emphasized the importance of grounding the abstract notion of principles in this manner. A typical comment was: "That [the importance of someone's moral principles] might depend upon what the moral principles are. If the moral principles are too superficial or too narrow in some way, the fact that you have a sustained commitment to them wouldn't by itself necessarily be so impressive."

This nominator, like the others, urged us to specify that moral exemplars are dedicated to principles that reflect some sense of "the value of human beings and of human life, their worth." We note that this concern was shared by all our nominators. The nominators' terms of expressing it may have varied, but they all touched on it. The value of human beings stood out in our nominating interviews as the prime case of a substantive moral principle that all moral exemplars should hold.

Overall, these revisions in Criterion 1 allowed us to weed out fanatics who are passionately dedicated to immoral goals. The addition of virtues and the further definition that we gave principles enable us to specify that our exemplars would be individuals devoted to the human good generally.

The other criteria, in the form that they were adopted, are discussed in Chapter 2 and will not be repeated here.

In addition to helping us further define and revise the five criteria that we established as our final set, the nominating process also enabled us to eliminate some unnecessary features. First, we were able to eliminate the notion of always "openly affirming" one's moral positions. Several nominators pointed out that exemplary people must often survive in oppressive societies. Under such conditions it is unrealistic to expect forthrightness on every occasion. The general issue of integrity, it was felt, was better expressed by the "means/ends consistency" clause that we added to Criterion 2.

We also eliminated the criterion implying that exemplars always create new visions and innovative solutions. Several nominators insisted that moral exemplars need not be extraordinarily inventive people, as they often dedicate their lives to visions originally expressed by others. What was required, however, was an unusual commitment to commonly known values. It is the expression of these values throughout their lives that is exceptional, not the origination of a unique vision.

Finally, we dropped the last criterion on the original list. Whereas the nominators agreed that moral exemplars would be responsive to others, they believed the criterion was too vague to be useful. It left undefined the nature of the response as well as the object of the response. How exactly does a moral exemplar respond and to whom? Is the response directed at particular others, an entire social collective, humanity at large? Because we had no definitive answers to these questions beyond what the other criteria already specified, we decided to eliminate this statement.

After offering us their suggestions about the criteria, the nominators proposed the names of individuals who, in their opinion, were a good fit with the entire set. Almost all the nominators were able to identify some people they considered to be moral exemplars. Most selected three or four names, although some offered several more. In all, eighty-four people were nominated as living moral exemplars.

For all the compatibility in the nominators' comments about the criteria, there was little overlap in their actual nominations. Only eleven persons on the list were nominated more than once, and the greatest number of times any one person was nominated was five. No doubt this was because at least half of those nominated are known only locally and thus were not familiar to other nominators.

Methodological Concerns

It was clear from the start that all twenty-three of our moral exemplars were highly conscious of their moral ideals. This awareness was an inevitable by-product of their long-standing commitments. We were determined to fashion an investigatory method that enabled the exemplars to express their own interpretations of the meaning of their commitments and ideals. Accordingly, we used methods that took seriously our subjects' conscious articulations of their beliefs, values, and life histories. We were disinclined, with such a sample, to rely on projective tests, experimental manipulations, or instruments aimed at hidden psychodynamic processes. Apart from the practical question of whether our heavily occupied subjects would have the patience to sit through such manipulations, we were more interested in their own representations—the meaning that they themselves assigned to the events in their lives—than in their unconscious motives. In addition, we were interested in how they saw their moral goals, their moral values, their challenges, and their virtues (such as their courage and their endurance). Accordingly, we developed the following interview schedule:

Table B.1
Moral Exemplar Interview

INTRODUCTION

We are studying people who in their lives have made sustained commitments to moral values. You have been suggested to us as someone who has done so. We would like to ask you some questions about how you, in your own life, have thought about your values. We are also interested in how you have confronted moral issues in your life, especially in critical life decisions.

A. MORAL OBJECTIVES OR GOALS
1. What would you say at the moment you spend most of your energy on? What are your goals?
2. Which of these goals would you consider essentially moral goals? How would you characterize the other goals?
3. You've mentioned a number of goals, objectives, and values, do these (or some of these) contribute to your sense of who you are as a person? How?
4. What kinds of things make it difficult to reach these goals?

B. MORAL ACTION
5. What are you currently doing to try to achieve these objectives, and what have you done in the past?
6. Can you tell me about an incident in your life where you weren't sure about the right course of action? How did it become clear to you what to do?
7. Was there a time when the course of action was clear but for other reasons it was difficult for you to follow this course?
8. Why do you keep going in the face of difficulties?
9. What does the phrase moral courage mean to you? Would you say that when you faced the difficulties you described you demonstrated moral courage? Were there times when you think you were a coward?

C. DEVELOPMENTAL HISTORY AND INFLUENCES
10. Are there incidents that have changed your beliefs? Did this alter how you behave?
11. Can you tell me how you got involved in the things that currently preoccupy you? Would you say that your friends are preoccupied with the same things as you are? What about spouse, lover, etc.? Did you try to impart these values to your children? Have you encountered opposition from your friends, spouse, etc.?
12. Apart from particular people, were there other things that influenced you, e.g. books, films, particular experiences, etc.?
13. What do you think have been your greatest successes?
14. Have you felt that you have ever been an influence on others?

We gave this interview in a semi-structured, flexible manner. We covered all the points with each exemplar but varied the order and phrasing of the questions whenever this improved our ability to communicate our intent. When necessary, we added probe questions, countersuggestions, and other follow-up interrogatories.

In both the questioning and the analytic phase, we considered the exemplar a collaborator in the exploration. Although we did not end with the exemplar's own account (we had, after all, our own theoretical framework that we wished to elaborate through this study), we did wish to begin there. This meant taking seriously the exemplar's own interpretations. It also meant trying to capture the unique meaning that each exemplar had constructed for his or her individual life and all the events that constituted it.

Our determination to treat the exemplars as coinvestigators and as individuals led us to the traditions for investigating individual lives that have arisen from "idiographic" approaches to personality research. This approach has been widely used in case studies and also in studies of moral judgment, social cognition, and attitude formation.

The version of idiographic research that fit our purposes most closely is a recent incarnation called "assisted autobiography." In this approach, an investigator examines (or, more precisely, coexamines) a subject's life in collaboration with the subject as a fully sentient partner in the venture.[1] The collaboration extends from the exploration phase to the interpretive phase. The subject, of course, does not determine the investigator's interpretive framework. But the subject is aware of the framework and how it is being applied to his or her life. The subject is given a chance to respond to the interpretations, and the investigator's final determination is affected by this response. In this sense, subjects become coinvestigators in the exploration of their own lives.

It should be evident why one would choose such an approach when studying a distinguished group of moral exemplars. For one thing, there is a primary need to preserve the exemplars' own understandings and explanations. The "face value" of their beliefs are themselves of great interest. Moreover, their high level of self-awareness makes their own representations of events an invaluable resource for the exploration. Given the reasons for their nomination to the study sample, we may even conjecture that our subjects are likely to be more honest than the average person, both with themselves and with us.

In these regards, the exemplars were ideal collaborators in a "coexamination" based upon the principles embedded in an assisted autobiography approach. Indeed, such an approach seems so appropriate for truthful, self-aware people that one might expect that it was explicitly designed with such people in mind. In fact, however, the approach has been used more generally and with far less reputable populations.

Most notably, the assisted autobiographical approach has been used to study the lives of nine hundred Belgian murderers. Over the past thirty years, criminologist Jean-Pierre DeWaele has been commissioned by the Belgian government to assess the likelihood of convicted murderers repeating their homicidal behavior if they were released. DeWaele's assessment weighs heavily in determining whether or not to release prisoners after they have served the minimum portion of their sentences. In preparing his assessment, DeWaele relies on an intense idiographic procedure centered around a year-long assisted autobiography conducted with the prisoner. DeWaele's thirty-year record of recommendations is extremely good. It is especially noted for its avoidance of "false negatives"—that is, a prediction that a certain prisoner will never kill again when in fact he does so after release. For society, of course, this is the all-important mistake to avoid. Other psychiatric methods of assessment, in Belgium as well as in other countries, have yielded unacceptably high rates of false negatives. For this reason, the Belgian government has placed its confidence in DeWaele's approach despite its lengthiness and labor intensity.

The second author spent some time in Brussels with DeWaele and his staff learning about this approach. For our own purposes, we had neither the resources nor the availability of subject time to conduct similar studies with our exemplars. We were, however, able to borrow from the principles underlying the method as well as from some specific interview techniques. One of the ironies of the present study, then, is that its source of methodological inspiration lay in an approach developed with people who had committed a heinous moral breach rather than those who had sustained a noble moral commitment.

Throughout our study, as a rule, we aspired to combine standardized and more clinical or individualized procedures for examining the exemplars' lives. Our wish to do so reflects our belief in the usefulness of both nomothetic and idiographic approaches to broad questions of human development. From the beginning, we rejected the traditional split between these approaches that has long hindered American social science. The stage for this unfortunate split was set by Gordon Allport, who introduced the terms *idiographic* and *nomothetic* to American psychology. The terms were taken from Wilhelm Windelband, a turn-of-the-century German philosopher who was interested in the history of science. Allport's intention was to give the case study approach a positive introduction to the positivistic American social science community.[2] (See his 1942 SSRC report, *The Use of Personal Documents in Psychological Science.*) But in his manner of dichotomizing nomothetic versus idiographic inquiry, Allport set up an opposition that has distorted methodological debate in psychological inquiry ever since.

In Allport's vision, the nomothetic was to be the pursuit of general laws, while the idiographic was to be the description of individual variance. Depending upon the goals of the investigator, both could be legitimate. The nomothetic was for those who wish to do normative science, the idiographic for those who wished to fully understand individual cases. Although Allport emphasized that one could look for lawfulness within an individual life, he doubted whether such laws would have general applicability.

When phrased like this, the nomothetic/idiographic split posed no great dilemma for American social scientists. Needless to say, the great majority of them would choose the approach enabling them to discover and test general laws. There were some exceptions, like anthropologists espousing ethnographic perspectives or psychoanalysts continuing in the Freudian tradition. But the existence of these exceptions has tended to polarize the dichotomy even further. One side is accused of generating norms that trivialize human behavior while the other is accused of spending their time describing the infinite vagaries of snowflakes. In this atmosphere there is little exchange of insight.

But Windelband, unlike Allport, never intended a dichotomy in the first place. The point of Windelband's essay was that every predictive scientific enterprise (and Windelband had no doubts that prediction was the essence of scientific achievement) requires both nomothetic and idiographic inquiry. In this way one determines the general laws as well as their rules of application to individual cases. If one wishes to predict the speed of various falling bodies, one needs to know both the law of gravity and the specific properties of each body in which one is interested.

In psychological science, the work that has come closest to Windelband's ideal was the personological approach developed by Henry Murray and his colleagues at the Harvard Psychological Clinic.[3] Murray's group assembled a series of case studies by using a number of standard and newly developed testing procedures. (The TAT is perhaps the most enduring of the new procedures developed in Murray's lab.) Murray was concerned about verification in a traditional scientific sense. His means of establishing validity was to generate diverse measures of the same personality construct. Each member of his team was responsible for a particular measure. A subject was given the various tests. If there was agreement in the results, fine; if not, the team would adjudicate between the discrepant findings through discussion, debate, and, if necessary, further testing. In *Explorations in Personality,* Murray's best-known work, it is clear that he sought through such procedures the existence of general principles.

DeWaele and Harre's "assisted autobiography" approach represents another advance in idiographic methodology that captures the spirit of Windelband's vision. More than any previous idiographic method, this approach fully employs the subject's own understanding by placing the subject's interpretation of life events at the center of the investigation. The subject's reconstructions become the foci of the case study, the starting-point that then may be enhanced, corrected, and renegotiated if necessary. It is because of its respect for the subject's perspective that we were inspired by the methods of Harre and DeWaele for the present study.

Individual case studies such as those we conducted for this study have always been seen as excellent ways to gain insight and generate hypotheses about little-understood phenomena. They have not generally been seen as good sources of data for testing these hypotheses. We accept this common usage and do not contest its implications: We did not aspire in our study to produce final evidence for new psychological laws. Our purposes, rather, were to provide rich descriptions of some remarkable life stories, to point to some apparent commonalities among them, to link the commonalities with the capacity to maintain an exceptional moral commitment, and to suggest some developmental principles that, we believe, account for how some people manage to form such a commitment in the course of their transactions with the social world. In the language of science, ours was intended as a hypothesis-generating study rather than as a hypothesis-testing one.

We do not claim to have definitively proven or confirmed by rigorous scientific standards the ideas presented in this book. We endorse such standards and would be pleased to see our ideas subjected to scrutiny in future research. In order for this to occur, a number of control conditions would need to be arranged. The most important of these would be matched comparison groups for our sample of moral exemplars. Such groups would be given the same interview schedules as the moral exemplars in order to determine precisely where the exemplars differ from all the others. The challenge would be to establish the entire range of groups necessary for systematic comparisons. Certainly one would want to assess the responses of "ordinary" citizens (although defining this group would require some thought), criminals, fanatics, dedicated high-achievers in fields that are not morally oriented, and so on, across a host of other issues and concerns. This would be an instructive project but one that was not possible within the resources available to us.

Not only did our empirical focus rest on individual case material as well as group comparisons across our twenty-three interviews, but the case material itself was largely retrospective in nature. With the exception of some supporting documents used for the five in-depth treatments, our data were largely restricted to the prompted recollections of the study's participants. Retrospective accounts can be problematic data sources for a number of reasons, the most important of which is veridicality. In our case, although we had reason to be confident about the exemplars' truthfulness, we could not attest to the accuracy of their memories. Many of the exemplars in our study were elderly. For many, the key choices and events in their lives occurred long ago. It is well known that the emotional tone of difficult events fades over time; an emotional tone of pain or fear may be glossed over by more positive feelings as the years pass. This is an inevitable hazard of retrospective data, and it might well have distorted the views that we had of our exemplars' inner lives.

Within the limits of our data sources, we did what we could to verify the accuracy of the exemplars' recollections. Our only alternative, a literally impossible one, would have been to conduct a prospective study—that is, to follow thousands of persons from birth to maturity, record their thoughts, emotions, and behaviors as they occurred, mark which of these people spontaneously became moral exemplars, and draw our conclusions accordingly. Since the records of many moral exemplars are built over decades rather than years, there is a real question about whether investigators who initiated such a study would live to see it completed.[4]

Action, Commitment, and Moral Judgment

The Kohlberg Measure

In addition to the personal interview schedule that we prepared for this study, we also gave each exemplar two standard dilemmas to assess Kohlberg's stages of moral judgment: the Heinz dilemma, which asks a subject to decide whether or not a man should steal an expensive drug that he cannot afford in order to save his wife's life, and its follow-up dilemma, which asks whether (and how) the man should be punished if he does steal the drug. These are the most widely used portions of the Kohlberg moral judgment interview. The measure provides an assessment of the maturity or sophistication of an individual's theoretical moral reasoning.

We knew that we had in our twenty-three moral exemplars a group of people who had demonstrated high levels of moral commitment in their everyday behavior. We were curious to see whether this commitment would be reflected in high scores on the Kohlberg measure. Many populations of adults have been assessed with the Kohlberg interview; our intention was to compare the twenty-three exemplars with a more ordinary group of people. In this way, we hoped to learn something about our moral exemplars as well as about the strengths and limitations of the Kohlberg measure.

The moral judgment interviews (MJI) were scored blind to the nature of the study, sex, education, age, the other rater's scores, and other information about the respondent, by two highly experienced raters using the Standard Issue Scoring System. One interview was judged to be unscorable. The two raters agreed completely on the scores for 77 percent of the cases. They assigned scores within one-half stage of each other on the remaining cases.

The scores assigned ranged from Stage 3 to Stage 5 (see Table C.1). As indicated in the table, half the group scored at Kohlberg's conventional level (Stages 3, 3/4, and 4), and the other half scored at the postconventional level (Stages 4/5 and 5). The most obvious factor that appeared to be related to these scores was the subject's education. All but one of those with advanced degrees scored at the postconventional level, as did the majority of those with college degrees. The remaining college graduates scored at Stage 4. In contrast, no one without a college education scored above Stage 3/4. (Due to the small size of the sample, statistical analyses were not carried out.)

Among those who had attained college or graduate degrees, there were no sex differences in moral judgment scores. Men and women were equally likely to be Stage 4 or postconventional. Since there were no men in the sample with less than a college degree, we could not compare men and women at the less-educated level.

In surveying published literature reporting scores on the moral judgment measure, we were not able to identify a comparison group matched for education with our sample (due to the dearth of studies of adults with less than a college or high school education). For this reason, it is not possible to say whether our moral exemplars show higher scores on the MJI relative to their education than other groups.

We do know that the exemplars' scores are not dramatically higher than those of nonexemplars. It is also clear, of course, that one need not score at Kohlberg's highest stages in order to exhibit high degrees of moral commitment and exemplary behavior. This is not

Table C.1

Kohlberg Stage	Number of Exemplars
3	2
3/4	3
4	6
4/5	7
5	4

especially surprising, since sophistication in reasoning about complex moral issues does not seem to be required in order to carry out many of the altruistic activities in which our exemplars engaged. This contrasts with the requirements for certain other kinds of roles, for example, a Supreme Court Justice, where careful justifications of moral decisions are needed.

NOTES

Preface

1. Address at Brown University, November 1990. When referring to his own struggles against the seemingly insoluble problem of South African apartheid, Bishop Tutu quoted a favorite riddle: "How do you eat an elephant? One bite at a time!" Among our twenty-three exemplars, we found many like strategies for resisting discouragement in the face of overwhelming odds. As we discuss, this is an important indication of how lifelong moral commitment may be sustained, even when there is little foreseeable hope of success.

Chapter 1: Mysteries of Moral Commitment

1. See L. Kohlberg (1969), "Stage and Sequence: The Cognitive Developmental Approach to Socialization," in D. A. Goslin, ed., *Handbook of socialization theory and research* (Chicago: Rand McNally).

2. M. Hoffman (1981), "Is Altruism Part of Human Nature?" *Journal of Personality and Social Psychology,* vol. 40, pp. 121–37; N. Eisenberg (1989), "Empathy and sympathy," in W. Damon, ed., *Child Development Today and Tomorrow* (San Francisco: Jossey-Bass); and J. Kagan (1984), *The Nature of the Child* (New York: Basic Books).

3. See R. Shweder, M. Mahapatra, and J. Miller (1987), "Culture and Moral Development," in J. Kagan and S. Lamb, eds., *The Emergence of Morality in Young Children* (Chicago: University of Chicago Press); and R. LeVine, and M. White (1986), *Human Conditions: The Cultural Basis of Educational Developments* (London: Routledge and Kegan Paul).

4. R. Emde, and H. Buchsbaum (1990), "'Didn't You Hear My Mommy?': Autonomy with Connectedness in Moral Self-emergence," in D. Cicchetti and M. Beeghly, eds., *The Self in Transition: Infancy to Adulthood,* pp. 35–60. (Chicago: University of Chicago Press).

5. E. O. Wilson (1978), *On Human Nature* (Cambridge: Harvard University Press).

6. J. Rest (1985), "The Major Components of Morality," in W. Kurtines and J. Gewirtz, eds., *Morality, Moral Behavior, and Moral Development*, pp. 24–41. (New York: Wiley).

7. See A. Blasi (1980), "Bridging Moral Cognition and Moral Action: A Critical Review of the Literature," *Psychological Bulletin*, vol. 88, pp. 593–637; A. Blasi (1983), "Moral Cognition and Moral Action: A Theoretical Perspective," *Developmental Review*, vol. 3, pp. 178–210; and A. Blasi (1984), "Moral Identity: Its Role in Moral Functioning," in W. Kurtines and J. Gewirtz, eds., *Morality, Moral Behavior, and Moral Development*, pp. 128–140. (New York: Wiley).

8. We do not, however, subscribe to the antiexperimental view that laboratories always constitute invalid settings for research because they provoke only strange and decontextualized behavior. As social psychologist George Homans once wrote, people do not remove their personalities like a coat and hat prior to stepping into a laboratory. Indeed, laboratories themselves constitute a social context, although a particular sort of one. Human behavior within them can be informative to social scientists for many reasons.

Still, we doubt that the whole extended range of principles, feelings, habits, and awareness that constitute moral commitment could be recreated through a laboratory experience. Most experimental manipulations in the moral area seem as silly and ungenuine as dropping paper clips. Even the more realistic ones (the Milgram experiment, for example, where subjects were convinced by professional acting that someone actually was in distress) provide only one-shot glimpses into the subject's moral responsiveness. This may be one index of moral commitment, but it is a shallow one. Moral commitment is actively played out over years of social engagement and pervades every corner of a person's life. It is far more than a single response, however intense or sincere. For this reason alone, it is hard to imagine any experimental manipulation that could provide a reliable measure of it.

9. There are conceptual and theoretical problems as well. For decades, the definitive word on altruism from the field of social psychology has been Edwin Hollander's "theory of idiosyncratic credit." In this treatment, the distinguishing mark of an extremely altruistic person is "marginality"—that is, altruists simply don't fit in. They stand on the outside of social life looking in. From this marginal vantage point, the altruist sees other's needs with objectivity and sympathy. The marginality of the altruist's position in relation to others frees the altruist from the bounds of conventionality and makes possible the extreme kinds of action that make a difference.

Apart from its implausibility, such a view does little to explain how altruists develop their social sensitivities and what sustains them. Nor are we granted insight into the altruist's own goals, how altruists represent their own life missions to themselves, or how they manage to translate their goals into effective social action. We are given no more than an external description, possibly distorted, and certainly disembodied from the altruist's own sense of commitment.

10. S. Oliner, and P. Oliner. (1988), *The Altruistic Personality* (New York: The Free Press).

11. Ibid.

12. W. Damon, and A. Colby (1987), "Social Influence and Moral Change," in W. Kurtines and J. Gewirtz, eds., *Moral Development through Social Interaction* (New York: Wiley).

13. H. Gardner, *Creators of the Modern Era* (manuscript in preparation).

14. B. Gifford, *Chronicle of Higher Education*, November 1991.

15. E. Erikson (1968), *Young Man Luther*, (New York: Norton).

16. J. P. DeWaele, and R. Harre (1979), "Autobiography as a Psychological Method," in R. Ginsburg, ed., *Emerging Methods of Research in the Social Sciences* (New York: Wiley).

17. C. Lasch (1982), *The Culture of Narcissism* (New York: Basic Books).

18. B. Berkowitz (1987), *Local Heroes: The Rebirth of Heroism in America* (Lexington, Mass.: Lexington Books).

19. Ibid.

20. Ibid.

21. S. Moscovici (1976), *Social Influence and Social Change* (London: Academic Press).

Chapter 2: Identifying Moral Exemplars and Studying Their Lives

1. See M. Krausz, and J. Meiland (1982), *Relativism: Cognitive and Moral* (Notre Dame, Ind.: University of Notre Dame Press), for various statements of the relativistic position, all of which we by and large reject.

2. J. Rawls (1972), *A Theory of Justice* (Cambridge: Harvard University Press).

3. A. McIntyre (1980), *After Virtue* (Notre Dame, Ind.: University of Notre Dame Press).

4. Most of those who declined to participate wrote to say that they would like to take part but could not find the time. For example, we wrote to Jaime Escalante, a dedicated mathematics teacher about whom a popular film, *Stand and Deliver*, had recently been released. He wrote to say that he would like to be included in the study but that he was receiving so many speaking, consulting, and other invitations as a result of the film that if he accepted even a small fraction of them, the work he was doing (which, after all, was the reason for all the attention) would be sabotaged.

5. Among the study's twenty-three participants, there were some who gave us full permission to quote from their interviews and reveal their identities (the five profiled in depth were of course in this group), some

who wished parts of their stories to be obscured, and some who wished us to cloak their identities entirely. In order to best protect all desires for complete and partial anonymity, and to establish a uniform reporting procedure, we have changed the names of all but the five exemplars whom we studied intensively.

In retaining other potentially identifying material (such as geographical location), we have disguised some facts more heavily than others. For exemplars who indicated no concern for anonymity, we have changed their names and little else. For those who requested greater disguise, we have changed some potentially revealing facts; although, in the course of doing so, we have tried not to distort any of the information crucial to our analyses.

Chapter 3: Suzie Valadez, "Queen of the Dump"

1. H. Akiskal, and W. McKinney (1975), "Overview of Recent Research in Depression: Integration of Ten Conceptual Models into a Comprehensive Clinical Frame," *Archives of General Psychiatry*, vol. 32, pp. 285–305.
2. H. Haste, and D. Locke (1983), *Morality in the Making: Action and the Social Context* (New York: Wiley).
3. E. Villafane (1989), "Toward an Hispanic-American Pentacostal Social Ethic with Special Reference to North Eastern United States." Unpublished doctoral dissertation, Boston University, p. 263.
4. G. L. McClung, Jr., ed. (1986), *Azusa Street and Beyond: Pentecostal Missions and Church Growth in the Twentieth Century* (South Plainfield, N.J.: Bridge Publishing, Inc.), pp. 74–75.
5. Villafane, p. 242.
6. L. P. Gerlach and V. H. Hine (1970), *People, Power, Change: Movements of Social Transformation* (Indianapolis: Bobbs-Merrill). Cited by Villafane, p. 269.
7. Villafane, p. 270.
8. Gerlach and Hine, p. 161.
9. Villafane, p. 273.
10. Ibid., p. 274.
11. Ibid., p. 276.

Chapter 4: Courage and Certainty Amid Risk

1. J. Rest (1985), "The Major Components of Morality," in W. Kurtines and J. Gewirtz, eds., *Morality, Moral Behavior, and Moral Development*, pp. 24–41 (New York: Wiley).
2. See J. Rest (1983), "Morality," in P. H. Mussen, ed., *Handbook of Child Development*, 4th ed., pp. 556–629 (New York: Wiley).
3. Even the two exceptions to this revealing commonality "proved the

rule'' because, as they saw it, they needed courage not simply to bear a risk to themselves (or even to their families) but to withstand the frightening possibility that their work would not succeed in helping others. One of these two exemplars saw her work with drug-abusing teenagers as morally courageous because she was forced to watch so many of them return to their old ways and then perish. The other spoke of her moral courage in starting a home for abandoned children because she was not sure at the beginning whether she would be able to sustain the institution long enough to rescue the endangered children that she had seen.

4. Courage in these two cases was conceived as the strength to carry on in the face of possible failure—with failure defined by the inability to save another person. Courage was not seen in its more usual guise as a brave attempt to overcome one's fears about one's own fate.

5. V. Hugo (1862), *Les Miserables.*

6. H. Haste, and D. Locke (1983), *Morality in the Making: Action and the Social Context* (New York: Wiley).

7. M. Csikszentmihalyi (1990), *Flow: The Psychology of Optimal Experience* (New York: Harper & Row, Publishers).

8. Ibid., p. 4.

9. Ibid., p. 218.

10. Ibid., p. 10.

11. Although we have only seen glimpses of Csikszentmihalyi's data, it would appear from his descriptions of the people that he has studied who best exemplify the flow phenomenon that they are like our exemplars in that the goals that they are pursuing are external to themselves. They are immersed in solving scientific problems, creating artistic works, or pushing the limits of athletic skill. They are not seeking the flow experience but rather they achieve it as a by-product of their search for truth and beauty. Given this, we wonder whether Csikszentmihalyi's implicit suggestion that flow is a legitimate goal in itself is well placed.

12. H. Heckhausen (1991), *Motivation and Action* (New York: Springer).

13. Ibid.

14. Note the similarity to Bishop Tutu's elephant story, quoted in our Preface.

Chapter 5: Virginia Durr, Champion of Justice

1. V. F. Durr (1985), *Outside the Magic Circle* (New York: Simon & Schuster), p. 9.

2. Ibid., p. 5.

3. Ibid., p. 3.

4. Ibid., p. 17.

5. Ibid., p. 20.

6. Ibid., pp. 62–63.

7. Ibid., p. 58.

8. Ibid., p. 63.
9. Ibid.
10. The fable of the grasshopper and the ant is a story in which the ant diligently stores up food for the winter while the grasshopper leads a happy-go-lucky existence and suffers later for his lack of industry.
11. Durr, p. 44.
12. Mrs. Durr went to the Supreme Court and the congressional hearings with Stella Landis, the wife of Jim Landis, a lawyer and member of the Securities and Exchange Commission. Mr. Landis had clerked with Justice Brandeis.
13. Durr, p. 108.
14. Ibid., p. 103.
15. Ibid., p. 103.
16. Ibid., pp. 101–102.
17. Ibid., p. 120.
18. Ibid., p. 127.
19. Ibid., p. 124.
20. Ibid., p. 107.
21. Ibid., p. 104.
22. Ibid., p. 105.
23. Ibid., pp. 153–54.
24. J. A. Salmond (1990), *Conscience of a Lawyer: Clifford J. Durr and American Civil Liberties, 1899–1975* (Tuscaloosa: University of Alabama Press).
25. Durr, p. 224.
26. Salmond, p. 144.
27. Durr, p. 235. At the time of this incident, there were only three children at home, as the Durr's oldest daughter, Ann, was twenty-three years old and had already graduated from college.
28. Ibid., p. 251.
29. Ibid., p. 244.
30. Ibid., p. 245.
31. Ibid.
32. Ibid., p. 266.
33. Ibid., pp. 271–72.
34. Ibid., p. 272.
35. Ibid., pp. 269–70.
36. Ibid., p. 333.
37. Ibid., p. 218.
38. Ibid., p. 337.
39. Ibid., p. 93.

Chapter 6: Jack Coleman, Seeker of Personal Excellence

1. *Faith and Practice: A Book of Christian Discipline.* Philadelphia Yearly Meeting of the Religious Society of Friends, p. 20.

Chapter 7: How Moral Commitment Develops Throughout Life

1. The model has multiple sources, owing debts especially to Piaget's writings on equilibration, Vygotsky's on communication, Moscovici's on social influence, and the American work in the attribution and socialization traditions. For a further discussion of these theoretical roots, see W. Damon and A. Colby (1987), "Social Influence and Moral Change," in W. Kurtines and J. Gewirtz, eds., *Moral Development Through Social Interaction* (New York: Wiley).

2. H. Werner (1948), *Comparative Psychology of Mental Development* (New York: Science Editions).

3. We do not believe that this is the primary condition for all types of psychological growth, or even for all types of moral growth, at all ages. In the early years of life, for example, natural emotional responses such as empathy do not require goal transformation for their elaboration (see W. Damon, [1988], *The Moral Child* [New York: The Free Press]. Goal transformation becomes a key process when a person communicates regularly with others about moral values. For those who continually immerse themselves in moral concerns, and in social networks absorbed by such concerns, goal transformation remains the central architect of progressive change throughout life.

4. See R. Brown (1986), *Social Psychology: The Second Edition* (New York: The Free Press).

5. J. Wertsch (1985), *Vygotsky and the Social Formation of Mind* (New York: Cambridge University Press).

6. See R. Archambault, ed. (1964), *The writings of John Dewey* (New York: Vintage).

7. D. J. Wood (1980), "Teaching the Young Child: Some Relationships Between Social Interaction, Language, and Thought," in D. R. Olson, ed., *The Social Foundations of Language and Thought* (New York: Norton).

8. Even in the case of adult-child relations, some theorists have questions about whether the scaffolding metaphor is wholly accurate or sufficient. These questions center around the child's role in the process and whether the notion of scaffolding portrays it in too passive and restricted a manner. Some developmentalists who are generally sympathetic to this theoretical approach have worried that it may miss some of the individual's own creative contributions to the adoption of another's goals. Peg Griffin and Michael Cole have written: "The scaffold metaphor leaves open questions of the child's creativity. If the adult support bears an inverse relation to the child's competence, then there is a strong sense of teleology—children's development is circumscribed by the adults' achieved wisdom" (P. Griffin, and M. Cole, [1984], "Current Activity for the Future: The Zo-Ped," in B. Rogoff and J. Wertsch, eds., *Children's Learning in the Zone of Proximal Development* [San Francisco: Jossey-Bass], p. 47).

The same authors are also concerned with the model's seeming implication that the adult's guidance occurs mechanically, programmed to
match the sequence in which the behavior is modeled. They argue that
social influence is a more irregular, almost organic, process. It takes place
on many psychological levels at once and remains closely in tune with
the child's own agenda:

> (S)caffolding—bolted together tiers of boards upon which humans
> stand to construct a building—admits far more easily of variation in
> amount than in kind. Yet the changes in adult support ordinarily re-
> ported in scaffolding research point to qualitatively distinct kinds of
> support.
>
> Sometimes the adult directs attention. At other times, the adult
> holds important information in memory. At still other times, the adult
> offers simple encouragement. The metaphor becomes more problematic
> when we focus not on the execution of a specific task but on the
> changes in the child. A central notion shared by Vygotsky, Dewey,
> and theorists who use the scaffolding notion is that the discovery of
> new goals is central to the process of development. To capture the
> important way in which adult understanding of goals structures the
> sequence of activities, we would need to add architects and foremen to
> the building process that scaffolding indexes. Building would have to
> begin with all the scaffolding in place, and it would have to admit to
> work starting with the uppermost reaches of the roof as well as the
> basement.

It is not difficult to see why much of the empirical evidence behind
the scaffolding notion derives from experiments in which adults teach
children how to model their behavior (or literally build a model). In
fact, the notion seems best suited for explaining those instances of social
influence in which a skill or belief is directly copied.

9. J. Heckhausen, R. Dixon, and P. Baltes (1989), "Gains and Losses
in Development Throughout Adulthood as Perceived by Different Adult
Age Groups," *Developmental Psychology,* vol. 25, pp. 109–21.
10. J. Heckhausen, and J. Krueger (in press), "Similarities and Differences in Developmental Expectations for the Self and Most Other People:
Age-grading in Three Functions of Social Comparison," *Developmental
psychology.*
11. Heckhausen, Dixon, and Baltes, p. 109.
12. A. Caspi, and D. Bem (1990), "Personality Continuity and Change
Across the Life Course," in L. A. Pervin (ed.), *Handbook of Personality:
Theory and Research,* pp. 549–75, (New York: The Guilford Press).
13. Ibid.
14. P. B. Baltes (1990), "Entwicklungspsychology der Lebensspanne:
Theoretisches Leitsaetze," *Psychologische Rundschau,* vol. 41, 1–24.
15. Ibid.

16. P. B. Baltes (1987), "Theoretical Propositions of Life-span, Developmental Psychology: On the Dynamics Between Growth and Decline," *Developmental Psychology,* vol. 23, pp. 611–626.
17. Heckhausen, Dixon, and Baltes (1989).
18. A. Caspi, D. Bem, and G. Elder (1989), "Continuities and Consequences of Interactional Styles Across the Life Course," *Journal of Personality,* vol. 57, pp. 376–406.
19. Ibid.
20. Ibid.
21. L. A. Stroufe, B. Egeland, and T. Kreutzer (1990), "The Fate of Early Experience Following Developmental Change: Longitudinal Approaches to Individual Adaptation in Childhood, *Child Development,* vol. 61, pp. 1363–73.
22. K. Dodge (1986), "A Social Information Processing Model of Social Competence in Children," in M. Perlmutter (ed.), *Cognitive Perspectives on Children's Social and Behavioral Development: Minnesota Symposia on Child Development,* vol. 18, pp. 77–126 (Hillsdale, NJ: Erlbaum).
23. W. Damon (1988), *The Moral Child.* New York: The Free Press.

Chapter 8: Charleszetta Waddles, Matriarch of Faith

1. Charleszetta Waddles interview from the Schlesinger Library, Radcliffe College, *Black Women Oral History Project,* pp. 9–10.
2. Ibid., p. 23.
3. Ibid., p. 70.
4. Ibid., p. 20.
5. Ibid., p. 23.
6. Ibid., p. 32.
7. Ibid., p. 36.
8. Ibid., p. 37.
9. Ibid., p. 20.
10. Ibid., p. 3.
11. Ibid., p. 45.
12. Ibid., p. 46.
13. Mrs. Waddles is referring to the fact that in some editions of the Bible, the words of Jesus Christ appear in red type in order to highlight them.
14. Ibid., p. 45–64.
15. BWOH, p. 2.
16. A. Paris (1982), *Black Pentecostalism (Southern Religion in an Urban World* (Amherst: University of Massachusetts Press), p. 97.
17. Ibid., p. 129.
18. Ibid., p. 136.
19. Ibid., p. 19.
20. BWOH, pp. 59–60.

Chapter 10: Positivity and Hopefulness

1. M. Csikszentmihalyi (1990), *Flow: The Psychology of Optimal Experience* (New York: Harper & Row, Publishers).
2. R. Carlson (1982), "Studies in Script Theory: II. Altruistic Nuclear Scripts," *Perceptual and Motor Skills,* vol. 55, pp. 595–610.
3. The exceptionally creative people described by Howard Gardner in his forthcoming book *Creators of the Modern Era* exhibited many of the characteristics we identified in our moral exemplars, such as certainty and single-mindedness. Notably lacking in his exemplars of creativity, however, was the love for other people that we saw in so many of our moral exemplars. This is one critical difference between people who excel in the moral area and people who excel in such domains as science, art, and literature.
4. M. Seligman (1991), *Learned Optimism* (New York: Alfred Knopf).
5. Ibid., p. 5.
6. Ibid., p. 48.
7. Ibid., p. 286.
8. Ibid., p. 290.
9. J. Heckhausen and P. Baltes (in press), "Perceived Controllability of Expected Psychological Change Across Adulthood and Old Age," *Journal of Gerontology: Psychological Sciences.*

Chapter 11: The Uniting of Self and Morality

1. In a seminar that he gave toward the end of his life, Jean Piaget once commented that "Swimming is a more viable means of staying afloat than treading water." He was trying to get across to his students the concept of dynamic equilibrium, an exasperatingly difficult notion that lay at the heart of Piaget's final position on human development. The notion came from biology, where it has long been established that only through constant change can organisms achieve true homeostatic adaptation. Piaget's attempt to explain psychological functioning and growth through this lexicon never found a significant audience, perhaps because the terminology becomes too complex and elusive when applied to human thinking. But the central idea of a dynamic, expanding equilibration, we believe, remains sound, at least as a metaphor for the formation and transformation of mental states such as long-standing moral commitments.
2. M. Walzer (1988), *The Company of Critics* (Cambridge: Harvard University Press).
3. H. Gardner (in preparation), *Creators of the Modern Era.*
4. In some creative work, an important part of the collaboration may be at a distance, or with those who have come before, as in the phrase of the scientist who once said, "If I have seen further, it is because I have stood on the shoulders of giants."

5. R. Bellah, R. Madsen, A. Swidler, and S. Tipton (1985), *Habits of the Heart* (Berkeley: University of California Press).
6. For a fuller exposition of this position, see W. Damon (in press), *Social and Personality Development,* 2nd ed. (New York: Norton).
7. M. Seligman (1991), *Learned Optimism* (New York: Alfred Knopf).
8. As occurred recently after revelations concerning the personal lives of Gandhi and King.
9. They are not, of course, universal: People also can neglect children, tell lies, and steal from blind beggars. Just as acts reflecting moral commitment are commonplace, so, too, unfortunately, are acts reflecting moral nonresponsiveness.
10. We draw this example from P. Davidson and J. Youniss, in press.
11. W. Damon and D. Hart (1988), *Self-understanding in Childhood and Adolescence* (New York: Cambridge University Press).
12. For an account of these data, see W. Damon (1988), *The Moral Child* (New York: The Free Press).
13. See Damon and Hart.
14. See especially A. Blasi (1984), "Moral Identity: Its Role in Moral Functioning," in W. Kurtines and J. Gewirtz, eds., *Morality, Moral Behavior, and Moral Development* (New York: Wiley).
15. P. Davidson and J. Youniss (1991), "Which Comes First, Morality or Identity?" in W. Kurtines and J. L. Gewirtz, eds., *Handbook of Moral Development and Behavior,* vol. 1. (Hillsdale, N.J.: Erlbaum), pp. 105–121.
16. Ibid.

Appendix A: The Nominating Study

1. A. McIntyre (1980), *After Virtue* (Notre Dame, Ind.: University of Notre Dame Press).

Appendix B: Methodological Concerns

1. J. P. DeWaele and R. Harre (1979), "Autobiography as a Psychological Method," in R. Ginsburg, ed., *Emerging Methods of Research in the Social Sciences* (New York: Wiley).
2. G. Allport (1942), "The Use of Personal Documents in Psychological Science." Report to the Social Science Research Council.
3. H. A. Murray (1938), *Explorations in Personality* (New York: Oxford University Press).
4. Of course, datasets can be handed down to new generations. Or secondary analyses can be conducted on existing longitudinal datasets as in the Fels, Oakland Growth, and Terman studies.

ACKNOWLEDGMENTS

Our first debt is to the Social Science Research Council committee on the Development of Giftedness and Talent, chaired by David Feldman and staffed by Lonnie Sherrod. The committee supported the project during its earliest phase, with sage advice as well as financial assistance for our meetings with nominators. Members of the committee, especially David Feldman, Howard Gardner, Howard Gruber, and Helen Haste, continued to counsel us on subsequent phases of the project. We also owe notes of thanks to Professor Feldman for helping us secure additional financial support beyond the nominating phase; and to Howard Gardner for his valuable comments on our manuscript, and also for sharing with us an early version of his soon-to-be seminal study *Creators of the Modern World.*

During the project's nominating phase, we benefited from the counsel of twenty-two distinguished theologians, philosophers, and moral scholars with a wide range of ideological persuasions. Because we promised anonymity to the group, these persons must remain nameless here. We thank all our nominators for the richness of their advice and the excellence of their nominations. Our project could not have taken shape without the initial lead they gave us.

The study itself was supported largely by a grant from the Altruistic Spirit program of the Institute of Noetic Sciences. We are grateful to Tom Hurley, our program officer, not only for facilitating the financial support but also for many insightful questions and suggestions over the years. The Institute also sponsored meetings that brought together the grantees of its Altruistic Spirit program. We found those meetings to be good occasions for sharing methods and findings with other researchers working on similar issues.

Because we did the interviewing ourselves, and because the interview material was personal and often highly sensitive, we had fewer than the usual number of research assistants working with us. But the ones that we had were exceptionally able and trustworthy, and we owe them an unusual degree of gratitude. At Radcliffe, Martha Morelock, Mary Lou Arnold, and Casandra McIntyre helped us work with the transcripts; at Brown, Laura Grasecchi coded the protocols in order to check our hypotheses. Also at Radcliffe, Evelyn Liberatore provided her usual stellar support services for all phases of the project, and Janet Gibeau helped with valuable library work.

We thank Bill Puka and Eliot Turiel for much good advice throughout the project, although we hasten to relieve them of responsibility for choices that, perhaps foolishly, departed from the directions they suggested. We benefited from the constructive and creative editorial work of Susan Arellano, who helped us shape the book even before she participated in it formally at The Free Press.

Martin Marty, Karl Peters, and others provided help in identifying sources of information on African-American and Hispanic Pentecostalism. We are grateful for their help.

Our families supported our work in crucial ways. We especially thank Emily Jane Colby and Norbert Bidwell for rescuing us from our child-care duties in the hectic last days of preparing the final manuscript.

INDEX

Printed in the United States
737000003B